ROYAL CAPITALISM

New Perspectives

in Southeast Asian Studies

Series Editors

Alfred W. McCoy
Ian G. Baird
Katherine A. Bowie
Anne Ruth Hansen

Associate Editors

Warwick H. Anderson
Ian Coxhead
Michael Cullinane
Paul D. Hutchcroft
Kris Olds

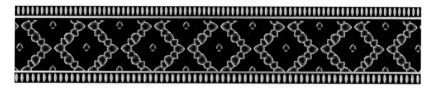

ROYAL

WEALTH, CLASS, AND MONARCHY IN THAILAND

CAPITALISM

PUANGCHON UNCHANAM

THE UNIVERSITY OF WISCONSIN PRESS

The University of Wisconsin Press
728 State Street, Suite 443
Madison, Wisconsin 53706
uwpress.wisc.edu

Gray's Inn House, 127 Clerkenwell Road
London EC1R 5DB, United Kingdom
eurospanbookstore.com

Printed in the United States of America

This book may be available in a digital edition.

Library of Congress Cataloging-in-Publication Data

Names: Unchanam, Puangchon, author.
Title: Royal capitalism: wealth, class, and monarchy in Thailand / Puangchon Unchanam.
Other titles: New perspectives in Southeast Asian studies.
Description: Madison, Wisconsin: The University of Wisconsin Press, [2019]
| Series: New perspectives in Southeast Asian studies | Includes bibliographical references and index.
Identifiers: LCCN 2019008293 | ISBN 9780299326005 (cloth)
Subjects: LCSH: Bhumibol Adulyadej, King of Thailand, 1927-2016.
| Monarchy—Thailand. | Capitalism—Thailand.
Classification: LCC DS586 .U425 2019 | DDC 959.304/4092—dc23
LC record available at https://lccn.loc.gov/2019008293

Contents

ILLUSTRATIONS

FIGURES

TABLES

Acknowledgments

A number of people have played a crucial part in producing this book. My greatest intellectual debt is to my teacher, Corey Robin. It has been my privilege to receive helpful comments and intellectual support from Susan Buck-Morss, Susan Woodward, Timothy Pachirat, Tyrell Haberkorn, and Vincent Boudreau. I greatly benefited from the comments on the draft at different stages from Alan Koenig, Allen Hicken, Amy Schiller, Charles Keyes, Christine Gray, Duncan McCargo, Jim Glassman, Joanna Tice-Jen, Joshua Sperber, Kevin Hewison, Matt Reeder, and Patrick Jory. Special thanks are due to the University of Wisconsin Press for publishing a book that focuses on controversial and forbidden topics in Thailand. At the UW Press, I would like to thank the series editors of New Perspectives in Southeast Asian Studies and the editorial staff, Gwen Walker and Sheila McMahon, for their confidence in the book and support of its publication. I also appreciate the invaluable comments and advice of the anonymous reviewers of the book manuscript. Grateful acknowledgment is given to all members of the Faiyen band for permission to use their lyrics in this book. Above all, in the course of writing the book, there have been many victims of political violence, economic inequality, and social injustice in Thailand. Their tragedies gave me the will to finish the book. I dedicate it to them.

Abbreviations

AIS	Advance Info Service
BOT	Bank of Thailand
CEO	chief executive officer
CIA	Central Intelligence Agency
CP	Charoen Pokphand Group
CPB	Crown Property Bureau
CPT	Communist Party of Thailand
EOI	export-oriented industrialization
FDI	foreign direct investment
FIDH	International Federation of Human Rights
GDP	gross domestic product
IMF	International Monetary Fund
ISI	import-substitution industrialization
MPI	Material Power Index
NESDB	National Economic and Social Development Board
NGO	nongovernmental organization
OHM	Office of His Majesty's Principal Private Secretary
ORDPB	Office of the Royal Development Project Board
PAD	People's Alliance for Democracy
PDRC	People's Democratic Reform Committee

PPB	Privy Purse Bureau
PPP	People's Power Party
PTP	Pheu Thai Party
SCB	Siam Commercial Bank
SCC	Siam Cement Company
SCG	Siam Cement Group
SEP	sufficiency economy philosophy
SME	small- or medium-sized enterprise
TNSO	National Statistical Office of Thailand
TRT	Thai Rak Thai Party
UDD	United Front for Democracy against Dictatorship
UNESCO	United Nations Educational, Scientific and Cultural Organization

A Note on Translation and Transliteration

Unless stated otherwise, all translations in this book are mine. For the transliteration of Thai words, I follow the Royal Institute of Thailand's "Principles of Romanization for Thai Script by Transcription Method." Exceptions are those names adopted by individuals themselves (e.g., Bhumibol, Vajiralongkorn, Sirindhorn). Furthermore, while westerners are referred to by their surnames, Thai people are normally referred to by their first names. Therefore, I use first and last names when I mention an individual Thai for the first time in the text, and I subsequently refer to Thais by their first names. Likewise, in the bibliography, I list Thai authors alphabetically by first names. I also provide both the original Thai and English translations of the bibliographic information for Thai-language materials to aid readers in locating my sources.

ROYAL CAPITALISM

INTRODUCTION

The King Is (Not) Dead, Long Live Capitalism!

In the age of global capitalism, monarchy has been treated as if it were dead, theoretically and literally. In philosophy, political theory, and political economy, monarchy is no longer a central topic of debate. For contemporary theorists, once capitalism becomes the dominant mode of production in a state, a monarchy is supposed to be either abolished by the bourgeoisie or transformed into a constitutional monarchy, a symbolic institution that plays no significant role in the economic and political realms that are ruled by the bourgeoisie. Rather than discussing how a king should rule his kingdom, theorists today tend to focus on how the bourgeoisie accumulates capital in the market and runs a state or how other social classes should organize to resist bourgeois domination. The fate of monarchies in history is no better than their fate in theory, as the majority of monarchies around the world were abolished in the twentieth century in the face of the social classes that capitalism begot. Even though a handful of monarchies still survives today, most of them are deprived of control over the state and the market and merely serve as ceremonial institutions representing a kingdom's historical continuity and cultural roots. The glorious days when kings, queens, and emperors were the most powerful and wealthiest people and shared every corner of the globe among themselves have been considered gone forever.

Current thinking about a monarchy in the age of capitalism tends to conceptualize it as one or the other side of two dichotomies. First, there are binary oppositions between a royal institution and the economic forces or social classes that capitalism begets. These include the monarchy versus the market, the crown versus capital, a monarch versus merchants, a high-born king versus bourgeois commoners, and conservative royalty versus bourgeois revolutionaries. The second dichotomy is the contrast between ethical values that monarchy traditionally embodies and bourgeois ideology: glory versus greed, prodigality versus prudence, extravagance versus economy, idleness versus industry, sovereignty versus self-control, highness versus humility, and holiness versus humanity. In these binary oppositions, what is associated with monarchy is conventionally deemed a remnant of the past while its opposite is thought to be a relevant issue of our time. In other words, a traditional proclamation that signifies the continuity of monarchies for centuries—"The King is dead, long live the King!"—seems to be obsolete in the twenty-first century. Today it would be up-to-date to proclaim instead the demise of monarchy and the triumph of the capitalist mode of production around the globe, "The King is dead, long live Capitalism!"

This book sets out to challenge the conventional wisdom that monarchy must eventually give way to capitalism. It argues that it is precisely under the conditions of capitalist development and expansion that a monarchy finds a way to not only survive but also thrive. The most emblematic embodiment of this novel form of monarchy is the monarchy of Thailand. What makes the Thai crown an exemplar of the resilience of the monarchy in the face of capitalism is a remarkable turn of its fate—from standing on the brink of extinction in the early twentieth century to becoming the dominant institution in national politics, the popular and beloved institution of the masses, and, most important, the wealthiest monarchy on earth in the twenty-first century. How was the Thai monarchy able to rebound, redefine its role in the kingdom, and stand tall in the face of multinational corporations, economic crises, and technological advances in the age of global capitalism? This book tells a story about the comeback crown in Thailand.

To understand those remarkable features of the Thai monarchy, this book brings the reign of King Bhumibol Adulyadej (1946–2016) into focus. Named King Rama IX in accordance with his rank as the ninth monarch from the Chakri dynasty, Bhumibol ascended the throne on June 9, 1946, and at the time of his death on October 13, 2016, he was the world's longest-serving head of state and the longest-reigning monarch in Thai history. In total the eighty-eight-year-old king reigned for 70 years and 126 days.[1] Under this historic reign, the transformation of the Thai monarchy took place in concert with Thailand's transition to industrial capitalism. That is, during this great transformation of the kingdom's political economy, the crown was transformed into what I call a "bourgeois monarchy"—a monarchy that is composed of three bodies, each of which embodies new features that make the Thai monarchy today distinctive from a traditional form of monarchy and emblematic of a new form of monarchy in the age of capitalism.[2]

The first body is grounded in the natural bodies of the Thai monarch and the royal family. Rather than representing only royal and religious values from the past, Thai royalty now embrace and embody the bourgeois ethic of hard work, frugality, and self-sufficiency. The second body is the political body of the Thai monarchy. Rather than relying merely on the extraeconomic coercion of the state apparatus, the crown also seeks and secures political legitimacy from bourgeois democracy and mass politics. The last body is the capitalist body of the Thai monarchy. Rather than simply obtaining wealth as a rentier, the crown also accumulates capital in the market economy as the biggest conglomerate in the domestic market, as a broker who connects business elites and patronizes their industries, and as a business partner of giant corporations both inside and outside the kingdom. In response to these measures, the bourgeoisie in Thailand—its industrialists, bankers, stockholders, entrepreneurs, bureaucrats, and other white-collar workers—has never restrained the monarchy. On the contrary, it joins with the monarchy, forming a dynamic symbiotic relationship that has left the lower classes to struggle with both powerful forces. Thanks to the distinctive features that it has recently embodied, the Thai crown enjoys hegemonic status in the capitalist state, preeminent status in the market, and popular support from the urban bourgeoisie. It shows the world that kings, queens, and royalty are not necessarily humbled by capitalism; they still live long and large in cooperation with the bourgeoisie's politics, interests, and ideology. It is an epitome of what a monarchy can become under capitalism in the twenty-first century.

Although this book is a study about the monarchy and capitalism in Thailand, it is not a work for Thais alone. Instead this investigation of the symbiosis between the crown and capital in the Thai case sets forth alternative notions for rethinking how the sovereign, social class, and capital are all connected but in tension with one another in a capitalist state. First, there has been an underestimation of the ability of a monarchy to adapt itself to capitalism. Instead of an outmoded, static, and conservative institution, a monarchy can be the first institution that embraces socioeconomic change and transforms its mode of political control, surplus extraction, and class alliance in concert with a kingdom's transition to a capitalist state. There has also been an overestimation of the power of the bourgeoisie and an insufficient examination of the ideology of this capitalist class. Instead of a full-time progressive and revolutionary class, the bourgeoisie frequently turns out to be a reactionary class that seeks political, economic, and ideological sponsorships, all of which a new form of monarchy is able to supply. Moreover, if a monarchy is not necessarily the first victim of the so-called bourgeois revolution, as is so often assumed, it is necessary to rethink a theory of class struggle in some capitalist states where monarchies still reign, if not rule. Instead of resisting the bourgeoisie alone, the lower classes in those states have to struggle with two types of capitalists: first, the bourgeoisie proper; and, second, a bourgeois monarchy that has congealed into a capitalist state, the market economy, and bourgeois ideology. In this two-front struggle that the lower classes have to face, their road to unchaining themselves from the fetters of capitalism appears to be as hard as, if not harder than, social emancipation in a capitalist republic. Finally, a monarch who lives like a bourgeois billionaire in a capitalist kingdom is not a mad monarch but a man who mirrors the sovereign in a capitalist republic. In the land where the sovereign has never been crowned, a bourgeois billionaire can become a president, administer a country like a company, and live extravagantly like no one else but a king. They are the Siamese twins who loom large in our capitalist world today—a world in which a monarch and a mogul are virtually indistinguishable.

ONCE a KING, NO LONGER a KING?

Monarchy—by definition, a form of government in which one man rules—used to be the leading topic in philosophy and political theory.[3] How should a monarch rule his kingdom? What justifies his right to rule? What constitutes a kingdom where justice, order, and peace prevail? These are major questions that run throughout classic works. The crown jewels among them—Plato's *Republic*, Niccolò Machiavelli's *The Prince*, and Thomas Hobbes's *Leviathan*—are no exception. Plato discussed the best form of government, which can only be found in a polity where a "philosopher king" rules, a kingdom where either a philosopher is crowned a king or a king himself learns to philosophize.[4] Machiavelli wrote a political treatise about the ways in which a new king can constitute a unified, secure, and long-lasting kingdom by pursuing the art of government and warfare instead of otherworldly morality.[5] Monarchy is also a central theme for Hobbes. He not only argued that the best form of government is monarchy but also justified absolutist rule on the condition that an absolute sovereign keeps his subjects safe from the state of war and anarchy.[6]

Kings and kingdoms also used to be omnipresent in history. Throughout recorded history, monarchy has been one of the most familiar and predominant forms of government.[7] People around the globe may have given a person who presided at the pinnacle of their political communities different names—king, queen, emperor, empress, raja, pharaoh, sultan, shah, emir, khan, tsar, caesar, or kaiser—but there were common features that made him (or sometimes her) a monarch. His post as the head of a polity usually derived from birthright and lasted until his death or abdication. He claimed to hold sovereign power over his subjects. His court was publicly recognized as a center for the distribution of power, wealth, and social status; the control of manpower; the appropriation of surplus; and the socialization of the highborn and blue-blooded. At one time, all roads in any kingdom metaphorically, if not literally, led to the court.

The archaic world in which a handful of royalty could rule the rest of the kingdom would be turned upside down once capitalism, which took shape in the sixteenth and seventeenth centuries, began to make its presence felt globally in the eighteenth and nineteenth centuries. In political economy, Adam Smith was among the earliest to recognize that a new age was coming. Instead of monarchy, royalty, and the crown's monopoly over trade, Smith believed that the world would soon be driven by the forces of the market, merchants, and free commerce. In his projection of the four stages of social development—hunting, pasturage, agriculture, and commerce—monarchy has a central role only in the first three. In the last stage, which he called a "commercial society," it is the market economy instead of the crown that has the power to improve the standard of living among commoners in a kingdom. It is the mundane ethic of hard work, frugality, and self-interest instead of royal heroism or charity that creates universal opulence. Most important, it is the "invisible hand" of the market, not the royal touch of a king, that begets the wealth of nations.[8] Similarly, G. W. F. Hegel realized that the market economy, which he called "civil society," would become the central and most distinctive feature of the modern world. In Hegel's version of the four historical stages—Oriental, Greek, Roman, and Germanic—monarchy gradually loses its prominent role in each stage and it is eventually transformed in the last one into a constitutional institution that symbolically reigns over a "Germanic state" but no longer rules the bourgeoisie in civil society.[9] This theoretical trend was reaffirmed by Karl Marx. In his theory of four modes of production in history—primitive, slave, feudal, and capitalist—monarchy is central only in the first three precapitalist modes. In capitalist society, Marx predicted, a monarchy would be subjugated by a bourgeois revolution that would end monarchical control of wealth and power in the state and the market. The main purpose of government in the capitalist state, therefore, is not administering the royal affairs of kings and queens but "managing the common affairs of the whole bourgeoisie."[10]

Three historical events influenced Marx's confidence about the demise of monarchy in the age of capitalism: the English Civil War (1642–51), the American War of Independence (1775–83), and the French Revolution (1789–99). What these three classic bourgeois revolutions had in common was that they exemplified both the progressive tendency and the destructive force of the bourgeoisie when this class rose up against the arbitrary rule of a monarchy and emancipated themselves, their commercial prospects, and their private property from the crown's control and exploitation. Another legacy of these historic revolutions was that they paved the way for commoners in other kingdoms to consider how to settle the question of a monarchy. Either the crown was abolished once and for all or it was constrained under a bourgeois constitution.

In nineteenth-century Europe, as merchant and agricultural capitalism began to be replaced by industrial capitalism, most European kings and queens gave way to the rising bourgeoisie in their kingdoms. They were placed under constitutional constraints and left with limited powers. The emancipation of the bourgeoisie from the monarchical yoke reached its apex in the twentieth century. As industrial capitalism spread its wings globally, the majority of the world's monarchies were abolished. Today, among 193 sovereign states, only 43 have monarchs as the head of state.[11] Among those 43 surviving kingdoms, 16 are under the Commonwealth of Nations, which recognizes the British monarch as the ceremonial sovereign.[12] Twenty-two are under monarchies whose powers are restrained by a constitution.[13] Only 5 are still officially ruled by absolute monarchs.[14] In this regard, the history of the relationship between a monarchy and capitalism seems to confirm what those classical theorists predicted: a monarchy is an archaic institution of the feudal past that must eventually give way to capitalism.

Thanks to this trajectory of the decline and demise of monarchies around the world in the last two centuries, some thinkers expressed concern about the traditional values, authority, and leadership that were once embodied in monarchies. These had recently vanished when the royals, courtiers, and aristocrats were subjugated, if not driven to extinction, under bourgeois domination. In the late nineteenth century, Friedrich Nietzsche lamented the loss of noble values such as glory in war, the courage of the "conqueror" and "military genius," and heroism in a capitalist society where the bourgeois multitudes were obsessed with only the "dignity of work" and their own enrichment.[15] Likewise, in the mid-twentieth century Joseph Schumpeter and Karl Polanyi worried about the liberation of the market economy from noneconomic institutions such as kinship, kingship, and religion. If capitalism was no longer embedded in but set free from those precapitalist institutions, these thinkers believed, the impact of capitalism on society would be disastrous.[16]

Their warnings of the threat of unchained capitalism apparently fell on deaf ears. In the last two centuries, except the monarchies of Spain and Cambodia, hundreds of monarchies and royal dynasties around the world were abolished completely; and even in those two cases where monarchies were restored, the crown was brought back to life merely to serve as a constitutional monarchy. In this sense, the bourgeois emancipation from monarchical fetters looks like a one-way ticket. Once the bourgeoisie takes over the state and the market from a monarchy, the crown will be declawed by the bourgeoisie, and it will not be allowed to regain its political and economic strength. Instead, if it is allowed to exist, the crown will merely serve the bourgeoisie as a figurehead of a capitalist state.

As monarchies become a rare species in the world today and those that still survive are mostly under bourgeois domination, any reference to monarchy in capitalist society seems to be merely a reminiscence of the old days when kings and queens still ruled. Clark Gable might be crowned the "King of Hollywood," Elvis Presley the "King of Rock and Roll," Michael Jackson the "King of Pop," LeBron James "King James" of the basketball court, and Donald Trump's lofty and luxury penthouse "Versailles in the Sky." These nicknames, however, simply connote an individual's success, the fame and wealth that he accumulates from his career and business, not his birthright as royalty. Likewise, an automobile corporation may advertise its luxury car as "Fit for a King"; a five-star resort may promise its customers the fantasy that they will be "treated like a King"; and an investment bank may persuade their clients that they can found their own "dynasty" or "empire." However, these are marketing strategies that simply send an appealing message to the nouveau riche that, despite being low born, they, too, can live, consume, and spend money as royalty did in the past.

Moreover, this ideological motivation among the bourgeoisie today lacks the ultimate goal of climbing the social ladder in order to literally be a member of a royal family or court society. Instead, the apex of the social ladder that this class wants to reach turns out to be the highest stratum and most exclusive club in capitalist society, the so-called 1 percent of the population. Just a few centuries earlier, references to the top 1 percent—the wealthiest men who had a disproportionate share of the wealth, power, and means of production—would have led to the assumption that the 1 percent comprised a king, a royal family, courtiers, and aristocrats in a kingdom. In the twenty-first century, by contrast, talk about the 1 percent leads to consideration of the bourgeois elite, which is composed of successful entrepreneurs, corporate executives, industrialists, investment bankers, and stock traders. They have offices in commercial districts and corporate buildings, not in a court. They possess cash and capital, not a crown. Their merit tends to be verified by a bank statement, not a bloodline and birthright. They do not decorate themselves with a divine sword and scepter but a dapper suit and suspenders. Most important, their authority can be seen through their command of an army of laborers who work on farms and in factories, not the command of an army of warriors to fight on battlefields.

Given these distinctive and dominant features of the bourgeoisie in our world today—the world where eight non-royal billionaires reportedly own the same amount of wealth as the world's 3.6 billion poorest people—a discussion about monarchy in the age of global capitalism seems to be out of place or even ignorant.[17] Discussing the ruling class that controls wealth and power in a capitalist state, regardless of its form of government, monarchy or republic, leads all eyes to the bourgeois class, not an endangered species of blue bloods. In short, the ones who run a capitalist state and the market economy in the twenty-first century are the wealthy and powerful members of the bourgeoisie. Despite never having been officially crowned, they are kings of capitalism.

CAPITAL SAVE THE KING

The decline and demise of monarchies around the world in the last two centuries, however, do not tell the whole story about the history of monarchies in the era of capitalism. Challenging the reductionism of the conventional theory, historical studies have shown that the history of monarchies does not always fit the theoretical projection. The complications in the history of monarchies that these studies reveal can be categorized in three themes. The first casts doubt on what classical theorists take for granted: the antagonistic relationship between a monarchy and the bourgeoisie. The second rejects the theoretical notion of the fall of a monarchy in the face of capitalism and emphasizes several roles that a monarchy can perform in a capitalist state. The third highlights the survival of some absolute monarchies despite the socioeconomic changes that accompany a transition to capitalism. This last theme challenges the notion that a monarchy must be either abolished or transformed into a constitutional monarchy.

How Revolutionary and Antiroyalist Is the Bourgeoisie?

The conventional narrative that outlines the grim fate of a monarchy in the age of capitalism is based on a subplot, the theory of the bourgeois revolution. The bourgeoisie, this theory argues, is a revolutionary class that seeks to destroy any political fetters that hinder the full development of capitalism. Since the last fetter, the last remnant of the feudal era, is a monarchy, the bourgeoisie would certainly turn, at last, into an antiroyalist class that puts a final end to the monarchical regime. This theory of the bourgeois revolution has been challenged by historical studies. Two of the most popular cases that are used to show how this theory fails to reflect the complexities of history are the English and French revolutions.

The English Revolution of the mid-seventeenth century is normally accepted as the critical juncture during which capitalism in England finally liberated itself from the old regime whose apex was the English monarchy. At first some historians, such as Christopher Hill, followed the conventional theory by interpreting this revolution as the first bourgeois revolution in Europe. They argued that the English Revolution was carried out by the urban bourgeoisie, the revolutionary class that struggled against the absolute monarch, whom it perceived as a political tyrant and an economic parasite who produced nothing for the national economy but relentlessly taxed bourgeois enterprises and monopolized the national market.[18] This interpretation, however, is decried by contemporary scholars such as Perry Anderson, Tom Nairn, Ellen Wood, and Vivek Chibber. Their arguments can be summed up as follows.

First, the urban bourgeoisie did not actually play a heroic role in the English Revolution. In fact the revolution was led and dominated by aristocratic landlords in the countryside and later supported by the masses of the urban bourgeoisie, yeomen, and artisans.[19] Furthermore, as it was carried out by aristocrats who were in the process of successfully transforming themselves into capitalist landlords, the revolution was not led against the aristocratic order, the pinnacle of which was the English monarchy. Rather than destroying that order, English capitalism continually developed in the shadow of antiquated institutions like the monarchy and aristocracy.[20] Last, unlike the monarchies on the European continent, the English monarchy never really had the absolute power required to monopolize wealth and power because political and economic powers in England had always been shared among its aristocratic elites. The English Revolution, therefore, did not end an absolute regime of the monarchy that was hindering capitalist development in England since there was no such regime in the first place.[21]

The deviance of the English Revolution from the bourgeois revolution theory should lead to the consideration of the French Revolution at the end of the eighteenth century as a better case with which to illustrate the theory. However, the history of the French Revolution seems too complex to be placed in the narrow frame of the conventional theory for several reasons. Even though the French Revolution was indeed carried out by the bourgeoisie, it was not led by capitalists, the bourgeoisie in the strict sense, as in the late eighteenth century the seeds of capitalism had just been planted in France. Instead the revolution was led by other groups in the fledgling bourgeoisie in France: state officers, professionals, clerks, and intellectuals.[22] Moreover, the French bourgeoisie was not fundamentally revolutionary and antiroyalist. Since its primary goal was to restrain the monarchy under constitutional limits, it was only when this class was pushed by the lower classes during the revolution that the French bourgeoisie dared to abolish the monarchy.[23] Most important, even though the bourgeoisie in the French Revolution had enough nerve to cut off the head of the king and inaugurate a republican regime, this class did not initially sweep away the political and economic structures that were established by the French monarchs of the previous regime; instead, they strengthened them. Thanks in part to this fortification of the existing structures of the political economy, the French monarchy was not completely destroyed. Instead it was later restored in the first half of the nineteenth century, and France had to wait until the latter half of that turbulent century for a wave of revolutions to finally sweep away the monarchy for good and pave the way for capitalism to develop freely.[24]

The theory of the bourgeois revolution has not only been challenged by the history of those two well-known revolutions. In fact this theory is also disputed by scholars, such as Benedict Anderson, who maintain that it cannot explain the history of the abolition or transformation of monarchies around the world. Two major arguments can be drawn from their challenge to the reductionism of the bourgeois revolution theory. First, although the fall of monarchies in many countries is the consequence of revolutions, these revolutions are usually led not by the bourgeoisie but by either communist vanguards or military leaders. The downfall of monarchies in Russia, China, and Vietnam, for instance, exemplify the former pattern, while those in Brazil, Egypt, and Ethiopia follow the latter.[25] Second, the fate of monarchies does not depend on domestic factors such as the rise of the bourgeoisie. It is often based on two international factors: wars among states that undermine monarchical power in the national territory and the role of western imperialism in their colonies.[26] While the two world wars that damaged the power of monarchies in Europe represent the former external factor, the role of the British and French empires in abolishing, preserving, or reinstalling indigenous monarchies in Africa, the Middle East, and Southeast Asia indicate the influence of the latter.[27]

Is Monarchy Really Irrelevant to Capitalism?

In addition to the bourgeois revolution theory, there is another subplot in the conventional narrative of the fate of a monarchy in the age of capitalism: the idea that once an absolute monarchy is transformed into a constitutional form it is just a ceremonial institution that is irrelevant to the capitalist state, a domain that is politically and economically dominated by the bourgeoisie. This subplot, likewise, is challenged by historical studies of constitutional monarchies. In spite of such constraints, many constitutional monarchies around the world are not considered irrelevant to capitalism because they play many significant roles in the capitalist state.

First, a constitutional monarchy offers and maintains ideologies that lessen class tensions in a capitalist state. As one of the oldest monarchies that still survives in the world today and the first to be restrained under a constitutional order, the British monarchy is frequently used as a case study to reveal how the crown can tame the crowd. With majestic dignity and a glamorous "royal class," which distinguishes itself from other political institutions, the British crown is considered by Walter Bagehot and Nairn to be an ideological tool adapted by bourgeois elites to distract the multitudes, especially members the working class, from government affairs in order to keep the hierarchical and social structure intact.[28]

Moreover, thanks to the uneven development of capitalism on a global scale, the monarchies in those countries that need to catch up to the advanced capitalist states economically can be called on to play a historical role as the leaders of development. Despite the fact that the real power of the state was in the hands of military officers and bureaucrats, the monarchies in Imperial Germany and Japan, for example, were an integral part of the state-building project and state intervention in the national economy, as they were used as national symbols of progress, modernity, and imperialism.[29] Armed with these royal symbols, the military officers and bureaucrats acquired the political legitimacy to make, as Barrington Moore put it, the "revolution from above" that propelled Germany and Japan into the exclusive ranks of the capitalist states at the beginning of the twentieth century.[30]

A constitutional monarchy also promotes consumerism and tourism in the age of global capitalism. The British monarchy is the most popular case; it is used to show how the crown can become what might be called a brand that promotes consumerism and tourism in a capitalist state.

The power of the branded British crown is supported by the fact that royal residences such as palaces and castles are among the most popular destinations for tourists in the United Kingdom, and the capitalist corporations that use images of the royal family in their merchandising and advertising are continually profitable.[31] The monarchies in Japan, the Low Countries, and Scandinavia, in contrast, do not attract as many tourists as Britain does. The modern bourgeois lifestyle of the royal families of these countries, however, also promotes consumerism by showing the masses how to live comfortably and consume trendy commodities in a capitalist society.[32]

How Universal and Destructive Is the Impact of Capitalism on Monarchies?

The case of absolute monarchies that still survive in the world today, like that of constitutional monarchies, casts doubt on the validity of the conventional theory about monarchies when it is put to the empirical test. The most popular cases used to demonstrate how absolute monarchies can survive the challenge of capitalism are the Arab monarchies. Socioeconomic changes during the twentieth century led to a popular theory that the Arab monarchies, mostly invented and installed by the European powers in the colonial era to serve their own interests, would quickly collapse due to the "king's dilemma." According to Samuel Huntington, socioeconomic changes are supposed to push the Arab monarchies to reform their political institutions, develop basic infrastructure, liberalize their national markets, and provide social welfare for their citizens. Nonetheless, those monarchies are still concerned that reform and development would beget and empower the new social classes and lead to demands for the end of the royal monopoly on wealth and power. Thanks to this dilemma, the Arab monarchies, as the theory goes, would end up doing nothing and their refusal to change would eventually trigger other political actors in the state, especially the rising bourgeoisie, to topple this idle and obsolete institution.[33] The downfall of monarchies in Egypt, Tunisia, Iraq, and Libya in the second half of the twentieth century made this theory even more convincing.

The remaining absolute monarchies in Arab countries, nevertheless, have proven to be more resilient to capitalism than the theory predicts. In the age of global capitalism, the monarchies of Saudi Arabia, Qatar, and Oman not only have kept their absolute power and excessive wealth intact, but they are also embracing the foreign investment of multinational corporations in their oil-rich kingdoms. Although the monarchies of Bahrain, Jordan, Kuwait, Morocco, and the United Arab Emirates no longer officially hold absolute power, as they allow their parliaments to possess the legislative power, they still retain the executive power, their rule is still unchecked by the parliament, and the wealth they derive from business partnerships with multinational corporations remains intact. The resilience of these wealthy and powerful monarchies has long been a puzzle in Middle Eastern studies. The results of the Arab Spring uprisings during 2010–12, which seriously damaged the authoritarian regimes in the republics of Tunisia, Egypt, Libya, Yemen, and Syria while leaving monarchies in other Arab states unscathed, make the resilience of these monarchies even more puzzling.[34] Several factors are invoked to explain why the Arab monarchies have been able to withstand socioeconomic changes in the age of global capitalism.

First, most Arab monarchies are supported by the revenues of their rentier states. Deriving national revenues from the sale of rich natural resources in their countries to external clients, these monarchies use those revenues to tame social grievances by appeasing their people with the provision of expansive budgets and generous welfare.[35] As a result, when the mass protests began in the region during the Arab Spring, for example, the Arab monarchies were able to prevent a domino effect in the region by spending a tremendous amount of oil revenue on job creation, salary increases, and development projects.[36]

Furthermore, the Arab monarchies have long been backed up by external patrons. On the one hand, as clients of rentier states, multinational corporations and their home governments continue to protect the monarchical regimes in this region by supplying military and financial support as long as those regimes guarantee political stability and economic partnership. On the other hand, to prevent the collapse of any monarchy that may trigger a chain reaction in the region, the wealthiest Arab kingdoms—Saudi Arabia, Kuwait, Qatar, and the United Arab Emirates—offer generous economic assistance to poorer monarchies whose lack of oil-derived income or the burden of foreign debt hinder any effort to lessen social grievances in their nations.[37]

Finally, in order to develop their nation-states in the postcolonial era and catch up with advanced capitalist states, the Arab monarchies are called upon to play a leadership role that is not so different from that which communist leaders or nationalist bureaucrats have played in other late-developing countries: the role of national founders and developers. Their vital role in nation-state building and development projects in turn gives the Arab monarchies sufficient political legitimacy to rule and maintain their sovereign power despite socioeconomic changes in the era of global capitalism.[38]

As the history of monarchies around the world reveals, there are general historical trajectories that diverge from the conventional theory of monarchy in the age of capitalism: the bourgeoisie is not necessarily antagonistic to a monarchy because this class does not play a decisive role in the overthrow of the monarchical order, a constitutional monarchy is not irrelevant to capitalism because it can tame class tensions while endorsing consumerism and tourism in a capitalist state, and some absolute monarchies do not have to be abolished or restrained under a constitution since they are well suited to the political and economic structures of rentier capitalism. Thanks to these historical critiques, the conventional wisdom that classical theorists held stands on shaky ground. Rubbing salt in the wound, the history of the Thai monarchy is the strongest case that turns the conventional theory about the relationship between the crown and capital upside down.

THE JEWEL IN THE CROWN

There was a time when the monarchy of Thailand virtually followed the theoretical and historical path of monarchies in the age of capitalism. In the early twentieth century, the Thai crown was on the brink of extinction. Unable to deal with the economic crisis and incorporate new social classes into the state structure, the absolute monarchy in Thailand was overthrown by the so-called Siamese Revolution of 1932 led by the People's Party. Thanks to this revolution, the Thai monarchy—an ancient institution, the roots of which reach back to the thirteenth century—was first restrained under a national constitution. Deprived of most of its wealth and power, the monarchy became dependent on the government budget and was constrained to serve merely as the ceremonial figurehead of postrevolutionary Thailand. The end of the monopoly of wealth and power invested in the throne, in turn, marked a new era for the kingdom's national economy and politics. Domestic entrepreneurs could finally do business with foreign corporations without royal licenses, and those with nonroyal backgrounds could enter into and advance in legislative, executive, juridical, and bureaucratic offices. Despite a counterrevolution orchestrated by royalist nobles in 1933, their defeat at the hands of the People's Party cemented the legacy of the revolution. Absolutism in Thailand was forever gone. Since the

1932 revolution, even though there have been twenty constitutions, twenty-nine prime ministers, sixty-two cabinets, and twelve coups d'état, the monarchy of Thailand has remained de jure a constitutional monarchy.

In addition to the downfall of the absolute monarchy in the first half of the twentieth century, another significant condition seems to suggest that the case of the Thai monarchy closely converges with the conventional theory. Although economic growth in Thailand from the 1950s to the 1970s was noteworthy, the economic boom from the mid-1980s to the mid-1990s was nothing short of spectacular. This boom not only transformed the Thai economy from an agrarian to an industrial one, but it also heralded the rise of a new social class, the Thai bourgeoisie, which is apparently more coherent, numerous, and powerful than other bourgeoisies in Southeast Asia.[39] The rise of the nouveau riche, in turn, has had a tremendous impact in Thailand, as it played a crucial role in the historic events of the 1990s: the popular uprising that ended the military dictatorship, the national pursuit of "Fifth Asian Tiger" status following in the footsteps four other newly industrialized countries in Asia, and the rise of Thai pop culture.[40] Thanks to its political, economic, and cultural influences, it looked as if capitalism in Thailand would be steered from then on by this rising class, the Thai bourgeoisie.

The official status of the Thai monarchy as a constitutional monarchy and the rise of the bourgeoisie in contemporary Thailand, however, can be misleading and results in the belief that the monarchy in this country has given way to capitalism. Under the façade of the "constitutional monarchy," the Thai crown since the late twentieth century has de facto played a hegemonic role in the economic, political, and cultural realms of the Thai state that might be supposed to be occupied by the bourgeoisie. In the national economy, the monarchy is simply the biggest capitalist enterprise in Thailand.[41] King Rama IX was ranked in 2008 the richest royal in the world thanks to his estimated fortune of US$30 billion.[42] Ascending the throne in 1946, during a nadir in the fortunes of the Thai monarchy, Rama IX and his royal family were able to regain their wealth a few decades later due to the business success of the Crown Property Bureau (CPB). As the largest corporate group not only in Thailand but in all of Southeast Asia, the CPB not only owns the largest and most valuable collection of commercial land in Thailand, but it is also the biggest stockholder in the Siam Commercial Bank (SCB) and the Siam Cement Group (SCG), respectively one of the country's four largest banks and its largest industrial conglomerate.[43]

The wealth of the king is even more astonishing compared to that of the richest members of the bourgeois class in Thailand, Charoen Sirivadhanabhakdi and Dhanin Chearavanont. Although these two moguls are the richest businessmen in Thailand and Southeast Asia thanks to fortunes of US$3.9 billion and US$2 billion, respectively (an estimate made in 2008), their wealth is still only a fraction of that of the monarch and his enterprises.[44] In 2018 Charoen and Dhanin were finally ranked among the world's hundred richest billionaires as their wealth had ballooned to US$17.9 billion and US$14.9 billion, respectively.[45] Their business empires, however, were dwarfed by what the crown had accumulated. When Rama IX breathed his last, he reportedly left both his role as monarch and the wealth of his throne, which according to different analysts varied between US$30 billion and US$60 billion, to his heir apparent.[46] With this fortune, the new monarch of Thailand could be numbered among the world's richest capitalists along with Warren Buffet, Bill Gates, and Mark Zuckerberg.

Meanwhile, in national politics, the Thai monarchy has played more than the ceremonial role that is enshrined in the constitution. During the Cold War, the palace backed the military regimes and state oppression of leftist movements and the communist insurgencies around the country. Although the royal interventions in 1973 and 1992 delegitimized particular military governments and supported the popular uprisings that toppled the authoritarian regimes at those times, royal involvement in the massacre of student activists in 1976 and coups in 1957, 2006, and 2014 seriously hindered any national progress in the establishment of a parliamentary democracy. Moreover, the monarchy during Rama IX's reign was influential in the making of policies and their implementation regardless of whether the government was military or civilian. The king's vision of national development, the so-called sufficiency economy philosophy (SEP), was integrated into the 2007 and the 2017 constitutions, as well as in the National Economic and Social Development Board (NESDB) plans of 2003, 2007, 2011, and 2017. In spite of the royal influence on Thai politics, there has been no attempt on the part of the bourgeoisie to restrain the power of the monarchy. Ironically, it is this class that keeps asking the palace to intervene in political conflicts and to topple elected governments, which it perceives as the root of corruption, capitalist crises, and antiroyalist sentiments in the Thai state.

In addition to the political and economic realms, the monarchy has also dominated the cultural arena of the Thai state. Royal ceremonies were reinstalled by the military junta in the late 1950s and have been officially promoted in public since then. However, state authorities are not the only ones who have revived the royal prestige and ideology in public. The bourgeoisie has played a vital role in popularizing the monarchy in the era of mass media and pop culture since the turn of the twenty-first century. The popularity of the monarchy in the cultural realm manifests itself most noticeably through the bourgeoisie's obsession with Rama IX. After the economic crisis hit Thailand in 1997, the king's supposed lifestyle of frugality, industry, and self-control was praised by the bourgeoisie as the proper ethical mode of life in the age of global capitalism. That proclaimed royal ethic was widely promoted and reproduced ubiquitously in award-winning television dramas, movies, commercials, novels, magazines, pop songs, theatrical plays, art exhibitions, and websites. The collective body of Rama IX's biographies, speeches, and celebratory print commemorations of his reign has become the best-selling genre in Thailand's print industry. As one popular song among the Thai millennials rejoices, "There is always one picture that every home has, whether it be a rich, poor, remote, or urban home"—the picture of Rama IX, with beads of sweat covering his face, overseeing one of his development projects in a rural province of Thailand.[47]

Given those features, the Thai monarchy is the jewel in the crown compared to its peers around the world. Not only does it embody some features that diverge from the conventional theory, but it also represents a hybrid form of monarchy that combines the strongest components of the other two extreme types: constitutional monarchies in Europe and absolute monarchies in the Middle East. The Thai monarchy has the best of both worlds in the areas of financial resources, extra-economic powers, class relations, external factors, and the transition to capitalism.

Financial support for the Thai monarchy is not based mainly on government funds but on the palace's own capital accumulation in the market. Like the constitutional monarchies in Europe, the Thai crown receives government support for the financial expenses of state ceremonies in which the royal family participates. However, government support is the main financial resource for the European monarchies, and the income these monarchies accrue from other sources is accountable to the public and checked by the parliament, while the excessive wealth of the Thai monarchy is based mainly on the profits it gains from the business investments of the CPB in the market.[48] There is also no official public accounting or parliamentary inspection of royal wealth in Thailand. In this regard, the Thai monarchy's unrestrained accumulation of capital bears some similarities to the Arab monarchies. Yet the Thai crown possesses an advanced means of accumulating capital. While the wealth of the Arab monarchies is primarily based on the revenue that these monarchies obtain by allowing foreign investors to exploit the oil resources of the region, the Thai monarchy does not act as what Mao Zedong called the local "comprador" seeking revenue from foreign investment.[49] In fact the Thai crown has built its own financial and industrial enterprises to both cooperate and compete with multinational corporations in the country, as well as to expand its capitalist ventures beyond the national borders.

Moreover, the Thai monarch reigns neither coercively nor merely ceremonially. Although the Thai monarchy is officially deprived of extraeconomic powers of surplus extraction, it still wields them informally. Unlike the absolute monarchies in the Middle East, the Thai monarchy no longer holds a monopoly on wealth and power. In the Thai kingdom, capitalist enterprises can freely do their business without royal licenses. Extraeconomic powers—military force, political rule, and juridical authority—are extensively distributed among nonroyal actors such as state officials, the army, politicians, corporations, and ordinary citizens. In this regard, like the constitutional monarchs of Europe, the Thai monarch no longer rules the state absolutely. He does not, however, merely reign, as the European monarchs do. Rather than standing above all political conflicts as a neutral institution, the Thai monarchy is one of the most crucial political actors in Thai politics, as the royal family and the Privy Council have influence over juridical reviews, military coups, and state policies. The Thai monarchy does not have coercive forces in its hands, but it has the ideological power to create consent among nonroyal actors and to co-opt them in following royal leadership.

The hybridity of the Thai monarchy can also be seen in its relationship with the bourgeois class. That is, the Thai crown is no longer the dominant economic patron of the bourgeoisie, yet it resists giving way to this class totally. Unlike the Arab monarchies, the Thai monarchy no longer feeds the fledgling bourgeoisie by providing government jobs, welfare payouts, and state contracts. Since the role of economic patron was taken from the monarch in the 1932 revolution, the bourgeoisie has mostly had to accumulate capital by itself ever since. The emergence of a large bourgeois class and the transformation of the state into the constitutional monarchy, meanwhile, makes the Thai case closer to the European ones. However, the Thai monarchy differs from those in Europe because it has not been subjugated by the bourgeoisie. While it is often argued that the European monarchies are passive actors that are used by the bourgeoisie as a political facade to distract the lower classes, lessen class tensions, and promote consumerism, it is still unclear who is using and taming whom in the Thai kingdom.[50] Rather than taking a backseat to or being a junior partner in the bourgeois order, the Thai monarchy has domesticated the bourgeoisie and taken the leadership role in the national economy, politics, and culture.

Furthermore, external factors are no longer the most decisive influences in the fate of the Thai monarchy. During the Cold War, the United States was the country's external patron, promoting the Thai monarchy as a symbolic institution in the fight against communism, which was becoming increasingly appealing in Thailand and Southeast Asia generally. China, on the contrary, was the primary external threat to the Thai throne due to the military support it provided to the Communist Party of Thailand (CPT). It is arguable that in this era there was a parallel between the Thai monarchy and the Arab monarchies since their survival was similarly determined by external patronage and threats. The events at the end of the Cold War, however, set the former apart from the latter. Thanks to the withdrawal of the American military from Thailand, the renewal of diplomatic relationships between Thailand and China, the breakup of the CPT, and the decline of other communist parties in Southeast Asia, the external factors that either supported or threatened the Thai monarchy began to diminish in the late 1980s. They are now less decisive than domestic factors such as military and popular support for the monarchy. The survival of the Arab kingdoms, on the contrary, is still significantly determined by external patronage and threats over the economic and political interests in the region.

Finally, the Thai monarchy still holds on to political and economic power in spite of the fact that Thailand is a newly industrialized country. It is conceivable that one of the reasons why the Thai monarchy is still wealthy and powerful is that it plays a role similar to that of the Arab monarchies, the role of leadership in several projects that are integral to the transition to capitalism such as nation building and economic development. It is doubtful, however, that this proposition still holds, as those projects are more prevalent in Thailand than in the Arab kingdoms. Similarly, the history of European kingdoms reveals that royal leadership was crucial to the transition from agrarian to industrialized economies. Once the transition was over in Europe, however, it is clear that the monarchies simply became supporting actors playing a subordinate role in the political domination and economic production of a bourgeois state. As Thailand finally joined the exclusive club of newly industrialized countries in the late twentieth century, the resilience of royal hegemony in the economy, politics, and culture of the country makes the case that the Thai monarchy has deviated from its European counterparts.

THE KEYS TO THE KINGDOM

Given its resilience in the face of capitalist expansion and its hybridity embodying the strongest components of surviving monarchies, the Thai crown is worthy of critical and comprehensive study. In past decades this kind of study, however, was hardly touched on by scholars specializing in the political economy of Thailand for several reasons. On the one hand, some scholars passed over the Thai monarchy and focused instead on other political institutions, such as the army, bureaucracy, and business corporations, as the locus of Thai politics.[51] Following the conventional theory, they tended to consider the monarchy as either politically neutral or occasionally political but still subordinate to other institutions. On the other hand, although some scholars acknowledged that the Thai monarchy needs to be seriously examined as one of the most important political actors in the Thai state, they tended to avoid discussing this issue due to the harsh punishments incorporated in and the arbitrary implementation of the lèse-majesté law in the kingdom.[52]

Only a handful of scholars in Thai studies took the post-1932 monarchy seriously and put it at the center of their studies of Thailand.[53] Thanks to their contributions, the monarchy's hegemonic status in the political, economic, and cultural realms has recently been exposed. Nonetheless, the existing studies of the Thai monarchy still have some limitations that need to be overcome, and some of these can be highlighted here. To begin, the role of the monarchy in the political, economic, and cultural realms of the Thai state has often been studied separately. For example, a study of the monarchy's intervention in national politics leaves its dominant role in the market and the mass media unexplored, while an investigation into how the monarchy accumulates capital through business investments overlooks the ways in which royal wealth depends on and benefits from political and cultural powers that the crown also recently regained.[54] As a result, in Thai studies the question of how royal intervention in national politics, royal wealth in the market, and royal popularity in the mass media are interconnected and interdependent has not yet been comprehensively examined and analyzed. To overcome this shortcoming, a new study of the Thai monarchy should pay attention to the construction and maintenance of this tripartite symbiosis of royal powers in Thailand's politics, economy, and culture.

Moreover, inquiries into the hegemonic status of the monarchy in Thailand normally focus on the historical continuity of the crown. For instance, most scholars pay attention to how the historical symbiosis between Thai kingship and ancient beliefs in Buddhism, Hinduism, and animism in Thai society keeps the monarchy relevant despite the kingdom's transition to industrial capitalism.[55] As a result, what has been left understudied is how the Thai monarchy—an ancient institution dating from the feudal era—broke with the past, that is, how it transformed itself in the age of capitalism, reinventing its old traditions to serve its new interests, and adapting itself to new social classes that emerged without precedent as Thailand underwent its transition to becoming a newly industrialized country.[56] The great transformation of the monarchy, instead of its continuity, should be a crucial theme in any new study.

Most important, studies of the Thai monarchy have mostly focused on the relationship between the crown and the nation's elites or political institutions. The political alliance between the crown and the judicial, military, bureaucratic, the intellectual elites has been a common topic in studies of the Thai monarchy.[57] Although it is hard to deny that the Thai monarchy has long been dependent on the political support of the elites and state authorities, these actors alone are not responsible for the revival of the crown. Especially after Thailand was transformed into a capitalist state, new social classes such as the urban middle class, the growing number of industrial workers, and capitalist peasants have become crucial actors sharing the national stage of Thai politics. In this new era of mass politics, the legitimacy of the monarchy in Thailand, therefore, cannot be based merely on the endorsement of the military and bureaucratic institutions; it also requires the wide support of these social classes. Rather than merely focusing on political institutions, factions, and elites, a new study of the Thai monarchy must take the social classes of newly industrialized Thailand and their relationships with the throne into consideration.

This book makes a start on that kind of study. To overcome all these shortcomings, it relies on three theoretical concepts to study the Thai

monarchy: the division of the monarchical bodies, the invention of tradition, and social class. Studying European monarchies in the Middle
Ages, Ernst Kantorowicz argued that a king has two bodies, a natural
body and a political one. While the first body of the king is mortal, since
its organic components must grow, decay, and die, the second body is
immortal because the crown as a political institution transcends the
death of an individual king and continues to hold sovereign power in
the kingdom.[58] What still needs to be explored in Kantorowicz's seminal
theory is whether and how those monarchical bodies evolved centuries
after medieval-feudal kingdoms developed into modern capitalist
states. By bringing the case of the monarchy and capitalism in Thailand
to light, this book picks up where Kantorowicz left off. In the age of
capitalism, the Thai king not only embodies two traditional bodies but
also develops a third body, one that guarantees financial security to the
crown—a capitalist body. Although the roots of this invented body
reach back into previous reigns of Thai kings, it was only after the successful revival of the first two bodies during Rama IX's reign that the
third body became a money-making machine for the crown and made
the Thai monarch the richest royal on earth in the twenty-first century.

   Borrowing the concept of the "invention of tradition" from Eric
Hobsbawm, this book challenges the overestimation of the historical continuity of the Thai monarchy and focuses instead on how royal rituals,
images, and ideologies were revived, reinvented, and institutionalized
during the reign of Rama IX.[59] The main reason for the crown's popularity among many Thais, especially those in the urban bourgeoisie, is
that this institution successfully rebranded itself by embracing ideological values and images that are well suited to the kingdom's transition
to capitalism. What makes the bourgeoisie obsessed with the monarchy, therefore, is not simply the ancient beliefs of Buddhism, Hinduism, and animism, which present a monarch as a divine Hindu king, a
virtuous Buddhist king, and an ancient warrior-king. In fact in the early
twenty first century the nouveau riche perceived Rama IX less as a divine and religious figure than as a beloved and ordinary father figure
who embraced the bourgeois ethic of hard work, frugality, prudence,
and self-reliance—the new ideology that this rising class was also promoting just as global capitalism was finally making a deep impact on
Thailand.

   Social class and class conflict are also crucial themes in this book.
Since the book focuses on the Thai monarchy in the age of capitalism, the
main social class that will be discussed is, to follow Marx, the possessors

and bearers of capital itself—the bourgeoisie or capitalists.[60] As Hal Draper pointed out, Marx did not provide a definite distinction between the capitalist class and the bourgeoisie; instead he used those two terms interchangeably. Therefore, to make it clear what the term *bourgeoisie* means in this book, I borrow Draper's clarification of this term.[61] Members of the Thai bourgeoisie are first and foremost capitalists proper: industrialists, bankers, stockholders, merchants, and entrepreneurs. Yet the term is also used in a broader sense to include various social groups orbiting the core of capitalists and functioning as servitors and beneficiaries of capital without owning capital themselves. In this regard, an army of corporate managers, bureaucrats, professionals, intellectuals, and white-collar workers—the "middle class" as we know it—is also viewed as a crucial part of the Thai bourgeoisie. It is the dynamic and symbiotic relationship between the Thai bourgeoisie and the crown in national politics, the market, and the mass media that is the key to understanding the hegemony, wealth, and status of the Thai monarchy in the twentieth-first century.

MAPPING THE CAPITALIST KINGDOM

This book is divided into five chapters. Chapter 1 focuses on the historical background of the Thai monarchy before the reign of Rama IX. The history of the monarchy from the feudal era to the early stage of capitalism in Thailand reveals that there was a time when the crown virtually followed the conventional projection of monarchy in the age of capitalism. The crown was almost abolished in the early twentieth century by the new social classes that capitalism begot in Thai society. The nadir of the Thai monarchy was a result of the crown's inability to handle critical challenges during the transition from feudalism to agricultural and mercantile capitalism in Thailand. Powerless in the face of economic crises and penniless as a result of royalty's bad investments and personal prodigality, the crown was eventually constrained under a national constitution and deprived of royal wealth and power just a few years before Rama IX took the throne.

Chapter 2 examines the reversal of royal fortunes and the great transformation of the monarchical role during Rama IX's seven decades on the throne. In the early phase of the king's reign, the crown was closely and actively associated with extraeconomic forces, its revival of wealth and power was based on military intervention, and the main social class that supported the crown was the rural peasantry. Despite this revival of power and wealth in Rama IX's early reign, the crown's reliance on military force created a backlash among some progressive and leftist sectors of the bourgeois class. Only in the later phase of the king's reign did the monarchy finally make a great comeback in national politics and the economy, thanks to the renovation of the crown in several respects. The monarchy distanced itself from the military and embraced society's demands for demilitarization and democratization. Instead of contentious politics, the crown engaged more with economic policies of industrialization, development, and urbanization. Critically, instead of the rural peasantry, the crown sought and secured the active consent of the urban bourgeoisie—the social class that concurrently rose to prominence in Thailand's political economy during the late reign of the king.

Chapter 3 focuses on the monarchy's reinvention of its public images and the interpretation of those images by the urban bourgeoisie. In the early reign of Rama IX, although the palace tried to promote the king in public using three major themes—the religious king, the cosmopolitan king, and the warrior-king—these themes failed to resonate with the daily life of the urban bourgeoisie. Only in the later phase of Rama IX's reign did the monarchy become widely popular and celebrated among the nouveau riche, thanks to the rebranded look of the crown based on a set of new themes: the developer king, the economist king, and the jubilant king. The bourgeoisie's interpretation of royal images also has its own history. Barely seeing how the monarchy and its images were relevant to its commercial activities in the early reign of the king, it ultimately changed its perception of the crown. Members of the nouveau riche began to appreciate the crown's new look; they selectively idolized and glorified those royal images that were compatible with their class ideology. Further, they created and popularized their own version of royal discourse in the mass media, which can be divided into four themes: the hardworking king, the frugal king, the father king, and the cosmopolitan king. Thanks to this symbiosis between the rebranded images of the palace and bourgeois ideology, the crown has reigned supreme in Thailand's culture industry.

Chapter 4 examines the political, economic, and cultural consequences of the triumph of the bourgeois monarchy in Thailand. Despite all its successes during Thailand's transition to industrial capitalism, the bourgeois crown embodied intrinsic problems that later developed into critical challenges for the monarchy in the last few years of Rama IX's time on the throne. The crown's success in accumulating capital and establishing monarchy-led capitalism in Thailand came at a price. It fostered socioeconomic inequality, uneven development, and capital concentration, which created a wide gap between the rich and the poor and the city and the countryside. While the monarchy successfully developed an ideological, political, and economic partnership with the urban bourgeoisie, this symbiosis alienated the majority of the Thai population: the rural peasantry and urban working class. Although the crown had recently secured its hegemonic status in the government, the market, and the mass media, it still relied on extraeconomic coercion as a last resort in restoring political order when royal ideology failed to maintain public consent. Above all, the popular king who embraced bourgeois ethics and images was anything but immortal, and it was uncertain whether the unpopular prince who stood first in line of succession by the virtue of his birth—instead of through the bourgeois ethic of hard work, frugality, and merit—would be able to follow in his father's footsteps. Unable to handle these major challenges, the bourgeois monarchy of Rama IX did not end on a high note. Instead, it turned reactionary and violent in the face of political instability, class conflicts, and anxiety about the royal succession.

The last chapter discusses the legacy of Rama IX, the prospects of the Thai kingdom under the new monarch, and the lessons that can be drawn from the Thai case. During Rama IX's historic reign, the Thai monarchy was transformed into a bourgeois monarchy—a novel form of monarchy that is deeply embedded in a capitalist state, the market economy, and bourgeois ideology. Against all odds, the crown has weathered political instability, survived the demise of a popular monarch, and maintained its wealth and power under the newly crowned King Rama X. Showing how a monarchy can survive and thrive in the age of capitalism, the Thai case pushes us to rethink the relationship between the crown and capital in the twenty-first century, its role in a capitalist kingdom, its relationship with various social classes, and even its image mirrored in a capitalist republic.

THE GENESIS
OF THE BOURGEOIS MONARCHY

The rise of the Thai crown at the turn of the twenty-first century as the richest monarchy on earth and the hegemonic institution of the Thai state was a spectacular phenomenon, especially considering the conventional wisdom that monarchy must give way to capitalism instead of adapting and thriving through it. To really appreciate how spectacular this phenomenon has been, however, we have to compare the current status of the Thai monarchy with the lowest point of the crown before King Rama IX ascended the throne in the mid-twentieth century. At that time, the monarchy was virtually on the brink of extinction, as it had been humbled by the forces of capitalism, the forces that the crown itself had played a vital role in setting in motion a century before.

A history of the Thai monarchy before the reign of Rama IX, a chronicle spanning from the early thirteenth to the mid-twentieth century, comprised these major features. First, the Thai economy's mode of production before Rama IX's reign was predominantly precapitalist, and the monarchy during this period appropriated economic surplus from producers through extraeconomic coercion comprised of political rule, military conquest, and juridical power. This historical process of primitive accumulation allowed the crown to accumulate wealth and become a pioneer in the kingdom's earliest stage of capitalist development. Second, despite a slow move toward capitalism, ancient monarchs still justified their monopoly of power and wealth with feudal ideologies that depicted the king as a godlike, prodigal, and extravagant figure. Third, the boundary between the two bodies of the monarchy in the precapitalist era, the natural and the political, was still ambiguous. Although the monarchy attempted to establish a third body of the monarchy via the Privy Purse's investment in the expanding market, the indistinct boundaries between the king, the crown, and royal enterprises hindered the professional management of the Privy Purse and led to its failure. Finally, the monarchy's accumulation of capital and monopoly over state power did not last long once the new social classes that developed during Thailand's transition to capitalism began to flex their muscles. Railing against the burden of royal extraction and disenchanted with royal ideology, the bureaucratic bourgeoisie overthrew the absolute monarchy, deprived it of most of its wealth and prerogatives, and pushed the institution to the brink of extinction in the first half of the twentieth century, the dark days for the crown before Rama IX became king.

THE ANCIENT MONARCHY AND THAI FEUDALISM

Before encountering the global economy for the first time in the mid-nineteenth century, the Thai monarchy had been able to maintain its wealth and power in the kingdom through its rent-seeking activities, ideological justification, and patronage of social classes. In the long history of Thai feudalism, the monarchy's means of accumulating wealth were rooted in different kinds of rent-seeking activities: the corvée, taxes, and trade monopolies. In this period of primitive accumulation, however, royal wealth was still spent unproductively as it was wasted on armories, religious ceremonies, and luxury goods. To justify the right of a monarch to rule and accumulate wealth, the crown depended on various types of a royal ideology: the virtual god, the virtuous ruler, the great warrior, and the merchant-king. This kind of ideology worked its magic on the majority of the kingdom's population in the precapitalist era, when most Thais were still rural peasants. The ancient monarchy in the age of feudalism, despite this, still faced a challenge when it came to two social classes: Thai nobles and Chinese merchants. Even though these two classes were instrumental in monarchical rule, their increasing wealth and power occasionally undermined the crown's political legitimacy and economic primacy in the feudal kingdom.

ROYAL EXPLOITATION IN THE FEUDAL MODE OF PRODUCTION

Before the expansion of the market economy in the second half of the nineteenth century, agriculture was the principal economic activity of the mass of the Thai population, and the Thai economy was primarily dominated by the production of use value: agrarian products necessary for the subsistence and reproduction of society.[1] In this precapitalist era in the Thai kingdom, the dominant mode of production was a local form of feudalism (*sakdina*), which was first codified by King Trailok (r. 1448–88) in 1454.[2] What apparently distinguished Thai feudalism from the classic form of feudalism in Western Europe were its three major characteristics: the emphasis on labor control, the absence of the notion of private property, and the lack of landlordism.

While land control was a key component of European feudalism, the heart and soul of Thai feudalism was the control and allocation of labor.[3] Occupying the apex of the *sakdina* system, a monarch gave different ranks (*sakdi*) to different princes and nobles. Even though those ranks formally signified the right of each person to possess a specific area of paddy fields (*na*), they actually indicated the number of commoners or serfs that a monarch assigned to the lords individually to be ruled at their command. As a result, in spite of its connotation of "ranks or power over paddy fields," *sakdina* was the practice of labor control that the monarch employed to manage manpower in his kingdom.[4] Moreover, unlike European feudalism, a concept of private property and its legal application did not exist in *sakdina*. Traditionally revered by his subjects as the "Lord of the Land" (*phrachao phaendin*), a monarch in Thai feudalism was officially the sole owner of all the land in the kingdom.[5] Allowing princes, nobles, and commoners to possess the king's land temporarily in order to produce agricultural goods, a monarch had the legal right to take it back anytime he found that the land had been left unoccupied or used unproductively.[6] In this respect, despite their possession of land, no Thais, with the exception of the monarch, had a right of ownership over landed estates in this precapitalist era. Finally, due to the absence of a legal right to private property, feudal nobles, unlike those in Europe, were not "little monarchs" or "fragmented and parcelized sovereigns" who monopolized wealth in and power over their own estates.[7] Residing mostly in the capital city, Thai nobles did not own vast landed estates or plantations, and thus landlordism was virtually absent in *sakdina*.[8] In a kingdom where land was abundant and producers were desperately needed, manpower rather than land was the most valuable means of production that the royalty and nobility sought to control.

In spite of these differences, Thai feudalism did share one crucial component with the classic form of feudalism in Western Europe: surplus extraction via extraeconomic force.[9] Allowed by a monarch to temporarily occupy land and cultivate agrarian products on it, male commoners had to repay him and the royal family, which, as a Thai Marxist sarcastically remarked, "sacrificed their precious time to rule subjects and provided them land for cultivating, rivers for drinking, and air for breathing."[10] To be precise, "to return the royal favor" commoners needed to provide three to six months of labor to the palace per year.[11] By royal command, commoners were forced to perform several unproductive activities. They variously staffed royal administrative positions; fought in royal battles between dynasties and kingdoms; built new palaces, temples, and fortresses; and did odd jobs such as feeding the royal elephants and simply standing by to accompany their royal masters.[12] In addition to forced and unpaid labor, the crown appropriated surplus from commoners through various types of taxation. A farm tax (*akon kha na*), for example, obliged peasants to pay a specific rate of tax in kind to the crown: 10 percent of the crops cultivated in their fields.[13]

Thanks to this heavy burden, some commoners deserted the cities along the Chao Phraya Delta and migrated to the rural hinterland, forests, and mountains while some others were forced to sell themselves to nobles and become slaves in their households.[14] As the lowest social class, perceived by royalty as "subhuman" and mere "speakable tools" meant to serve the nobility, slaves were exempted from the corvée and taxation.[15] To prevent the desertion of forced laborers and the lack of an adequate labor supply, the palace's punishment for any disloyalty on the part of commoners was harsh. Those who refused to labor in the corvée system were "bound in shackles and 'squeezed to death,' or sometimes left in the sun to die," and those who settled and cultivated the hinterland without the king's permission would also suffer capital punishment.[16] Meanwhile, those who lived in forests and mountains were frequently kidnapped and dragooned into forced labor.[17] In addition to the corvée and taxation, the monarchy also used force to accumulate and maintain manpower by making war on neighboring kingdoms. When a Thai monarch prevailed in war, he did not merely force the monarchs who were defeated to pay tribute to him in kind. He also took away the masses of the population, relocating them in his underpopulated kingdom and incorporating them into the existing system of forced labor.[18]

Since the production of use value was the dominant mode of production under Thai feudalism, agrarian goods were primarily produced not for trade but for the subsistence of commoners and the consumption of the privileged classes that did not produce, that is, royalty, the nobility, and an army of courtiers and slaves in the royal and noble households.[19] Surplus that the monarchy extracted from commoners, however, occasionally exceeded royal consumption and became surplus that the crown could appropriate for its overseas trade. This surplus did not result from the frugality or diligence of Thai royalty but from its extraeconomic extraction. Living far away from the palace, some commoners fulfilled their labor obligations by paying the crown in kind.[20] As a result, forest goods such as elephant tusks, spices, herbs, animal essences, and gems were collected and transferred to the king's warehouses.[21] In addition to these forest goods, the warehouses were stocked with two types of products: agrarian goods, especially rice, that commoners had paid as taxes in kind; and luxury items, such as miniature trees of gold and silver, that some neighboring kingdoms were obliged to send to the Thai throne as tribute.[22] Furnished with these goods, the crown exported them to the biggest market for Thai exports before the nineteenth century, the Chinese empire.[23] This overseas trade was monopolized by the monarchy, and it became one of the crown's most valuable means of accumulating wealth. Royal wealth that came from trade monopolies, however, was not invested in production but wasted on consumption. That is, a Thai monarch usually used revenues from overseas trade to purchase military weapons, to buy luxury goods that promoted royalty's splendor and prestige, and to fund religious ceremonies.[24]

Besides unproductive expenditures, a Thai feudal monarch had another problem when it came to the accumulation of wealth, the confusion between the kingdom's treasury and the king's personal purse.

In theory, as the Lord of the Land, a monarch had a right to all land in his kingdom. Revenues from taxes and tolls that came from the land were also royal revenues, and thus a monarch could spend them as he pleased.[25] In practice a monarch usually extracted a certain amount of gold, silver, or money from the kingdom's treasury, put it in his purse, and kept it beside his throne or bed. Traditionally known as the "Red Purse" (*ngoen thung daeng*) or "the store beside the king's bed" (*phrakh-lang khang thi*), the Privy Purse was supposed to be a fiscal account of a monarch's personal savings and expenditures.[26] Under Thai feudalism, however, it was difficult to draw a line between the treasury and the Privy Purse. That is, when the kingdom faced a fiscal problem, a monarch sometimes used money from the Privy Purse to alleviate it, and there was no attempt on the part of the nobility to check or control the specific amount of money the Privy Purse extracted from the treasury.[27] In other words, there was then only "one body" of the king in Thai feudalism; the king's corporeal body and personal wealth were not clearly distinguishable from the political body and state treasury.

The Justification of the Divine Right of the King

Even though extraeconomic force was used by the monarchy to control manpower, levy taxes, make war, and monopolize overseas trade, force alone was not a sufficient way to extract surplus, accumulate wealth, and maintain monarchical rule. Indeed, ideology was instrumental in maintaining the legitimacy of the monarchy under Thai feudalism. Before the kingdom encountered western imperialism in the mid-nineteenth century, four types of ideology were the means by which the crown justified its right to rule and extract surplus. As noted above, these were the virtual god, the virtuous ruler, the great warrior, and the merchant-king.

The first ideology was the notion that a Thai monarch was a virtual god or a god-king (*devaraja*). At the beginning of the Ayutthaya King-dom in the mid-fourteenth century, the Thai monarchy imported the Hindu belief in a *devaraja* from the Khmer empire to justify its divine right to rule.[28] According to this ancient belief, a monarch was a reincar-nation of the Hindu god Vishnu; he embodied a duality of divine and secular power in one person. As the "Lord of the Universe," he pos-sessed absolute power over his kingdom, and his palace was the cen-ter of the "galactic polity" around which princes and nobles orbited.[29] To dramatize and enhance the divinity incorporated in the *devaraja*, the Thai monarchy also imported Brahmins to perform rituals in the palace.[30] Thanks to these rituals, the monarch was portrayed to the public not only as an absolute and divine figure but also as a ruler who was mystical, formidable, and detached from all vulgar subjects. As a result, Thai monarchs before the mid-nineteenth century barely showed themselves in public; their corporeal bodies were deemed untouchable, and it was a taboo for commoners to gaze at their god-king.[31]

Merely making commoners fear and submit to the divine power of the Hindu god, however, was not the most effective ideological justification for Thai kingship. Even though Hinduism and the practices of the *devaraja* cult were influential in the Thai court, Buddhism was a popular religion among commoners, and hence the Buddhist notion of the virtuous ruler (*dharmaraja*) was crucial for the public perception of the king's legitimacy.[32] According to a Buddhist belief, a monarch was a reincarnation of the Buddha or a bodhisattva (Buddha-to-be).[33] The verification of whether he would be the next Buddha, nevertheless, was not based on his birthright but on the merit of his actions in his present life. To be precise, justification for the rule of a Buddhist monarch was based on the public's evaluation of whether he practiced the ten kingly virtues (*thotsaphit ratchatham*): munificence, moral living, generosity, justice, compassion, absence of bad ambition, suppression of anger, nonoppressiveness, humility, and upholding of dharma.[34] If a monarch did not practice these ten virtues, his subjects had a right to find a new ruler, one they perceived to be a more virtuous monarch. Thanks to this Buddhist notion of the virtuous ruler, royalist historians usually claimed that there had long been a social contract between the monarch and his subjects in the Thai kingdom, a concept they expressed long before the days of Thomas Hobbes and John Locke.[35]

Buddhism also embodied two ideological themes that were instrumental in legitimizing Thai kingship in the feudal era. The first was that a monarch was the greatest warrior of the kingdom.[36] According to Stanley Tambiah, in theory a Buddhist monarch always faced a dual challenge. On the one hand, as the Buddha-to-be, he had to perform numerous religious duties: practicing the ten kingly virtues; patronizing the community of monks, nuns, novices, and laity; and preserving monasteries. On the other hand, a monarch was revered as the "universal emperor" or the "wheel-rolling monarch" (*cakkavatin*) who made war in order to establish a political order and stability, sought glory for the kingdom, and rolled the wheel of dharma to conquer all subjects of and territory in his galactic polity.[37] Facing this dual challenge, a Buddhist monarch, as Tambiah put it, was socially expected to be both the "world renouncer" and the "world conqueror," and sometimes "kings must be good killers before they can turn to piety and good works."[38] This theme of the bloody warrior-king was widely reproduced in Thai literature in the age of the Ayutthaya kingdom. *The Tale of Prince Sammuttha-khote*, for example, emphasizes the ideal of a Thai monarch; he must have "martial prowess and his ability to discern skilled warriors, build camaraderie, and inspire their loyalty."[39] With this ideology, Thai historiography has dramatically glorified the legacy of two monarchs, King Naresuan (r. 1590–1605) and King Taksin (r. 1767–82). Having liberated the Thai kingdom from Burmese domination, they have been praised not as *devaraja* or *dharmaraja* but as the greatest warrior-kings in Thai history.

The last ideological theme was the wealthy monarch. As Christine Gray pointed out, since the notions of wealth, fortune, and prosperity in Buddhism were closely associated with virtue, merit, and power, a Buddhist monarch—who was supposed to be a virtuous, meritorious, and powerful ruler—was traditionally accepted by his subjects as the wealthiest man in the kingdom. According to Gray, a Buddhist monarch's wealth was believed to "flow" naturally to him in response to his great virtue. His fortune was not explicitly connected or articulated in terms of hard work but appeared naturally or effortlessly in response to his superior merit. Furthermore, his kingdom was supposed to have plentiful rainfall, thriving rice crops, and social harmony as a result of his virtuous actions.[40] This social acceptance of the wealthy monarch, however, came at a price: he was expected by his subjects to donate money and property to alleviate poverty, financially support Buddhist monks and monasteries, and keep the kingdom prosperous. The first three monarchs of Thailand's current dynasty, the Chakri dynasty, exemplified the application of this royal ideology. Although King Yodfa (Rama I, r. 1782–1809), King Loetla (Rama II, r. 1809–24), and King Nangklao (Rama III, r. 1824–51) were called "the merchant-kings," as they became wealthy by means of royal overseas trade with China, they were also revered by their subjects as great Buddhist kings thanks to the large amounts of money they spent on the construction of new Buddhist temples in the capital city.[41]

THE CROWN, NOBLES, AND MERCHANTS

The prior discussion of the monarchy's surplus extraction and ideological justification might lead to the assumption that the Thai monarchy in the feudal era had a firm economic, political, and ideological basis on which to claim and secure its absolute power over the kingdom. That assumption does not hold up, however, if we further examine the history of the relationship between the monarchy and two social classes that were influential under Thai feudalism, the nobles and the merchants. Although these two classes shared an interest in the process of extracting, redistributing, and consuming the surplus that commoners produced, they occasionally challenged the royal right to control labor, land, taxes, and trade. In other words, they could be both allies of and threats to the throne.

In theory, under Thai feudalism the monarchy and the nobility enjoyed mutual interests in various ways. While nobles were granted ranks from a monarch and these ranks guaranteed their right to control a specific number of commoners, a monarch in turn received support from the nobles, who sent the men under their command to labor on the public projects the crown initiated.[42] Due to the lack of reliable tax collectors who could levy various types of taxes, a monarch also depended on nobles to perform this task. In turn, the latter were allowed to keep a part of those revenues for themselves before remitting the rest to royal warehouses. Moreover, despite the royal monopoly on overseas trade, a monarch not only spared space in his trading ships for nobles to fill with their trade goods, but he also employed them in the port authority, a valuable office where they could extract a portion of import duties before remitting the rest to the crown.[43] Critically, while the monarchy provided political protection to nobles in its royal domain, the latter had an obligation to send the commoners under their command to fight in royal battles with neighboring kingdoms.[44]

The relationship between the monarchy and the nobility, in reality, was not always mutually advantageous. It was often contentious, violent, and bloody. In terms of labor control, nobles frequently kept many commoners with them instead of commanding them to labor on royal projects. Unable to bear the burden of laboring on royal projects, most commoners preferred to work in noble households, and, as mentioned earlier, some even entered slavery in order to live under noble protection.[45] Similarly, in terms of taxation, nobles usually hoarded revenues beyond what they were allowed or they delayed their remittances to the crown. Thanks to this practice of labor control and taxation, the nobility became the crucial player in the "game of thrones" in the Thai kingdom. On the one hand, since the law of royal succession did not exist in Thailand until the early twentieth century, nobles had long been the king makers in Thai history. They were influential in the process of selecting one prince over another as the next monarch. Moreover, whenever nobles realized that the current reign did not benefit them, they could stage a coup and dethrone the reigning monarch.[46] As the history of the Ayutthaya kingdom reveals, the bloody end of one dynasty and the founding of another usually derived from the machinations of the nobility. On the other hand, nobles could put monarchical rule in jeopardy when there was a war between the Thai kingdom and its neighbors. The fall of Ayutthaya in 1767, for example, was in part a result of the monarchy's failure to secure the nobility's loyalty. When the Burmese army invaded the Thai kingdom, several nobles failed to put up any resistance but concentrated all the manpower under their command awaiting the fall of the monarch in the capital city.[47]

As it was with the nobility, the monarchy's relationship with the class of merchants was anything but secure. In the long history of Thai feudalism, this class was predominantly composed of one ethnic group, the Chinese. Even though the monarchy welcomed merchants of diverse ethnicity—Arab, British, Dutch, French, Japanese, Persian, and Portuguese—to participate in the royal trade when Ayutthaya was one of the world's biggest entrepôts in the seventeenth century, the crown privileged the Chinese in numerous ways. It exempted the Chinese from the labor obligation and taxed them more lightly than local Thais. It preferred to employ Chinese workers in royal ships engaged in overseas trade with China and European colonies in Southeast Asia.[48] It staffed state offices with Chinese literati and gave them ranks and honors. It permitted intermarriage between Thai royalty and Chinese merchants.[49] Most important, during the first half of the nineteenth century, Chinese merchants became a wealthy class in the kingdom thanks to the system of tax farming that thrived during the reigns of Rama II and Rama III.[50] Under this system a monarch sold tax farmers (nai-akon) a license to tax a specific market item in a specific area, and the holders of these licenses were remunerated by collecting taxes beyond what the crown required.[51] Since most tax farmers were Chinese merchants and the most valuable tax farms were those associated with Chinese communities in Thailand—liquor, gambling, opium, prostitution, markets, and commercial buildings—the Chinese who worked for the crown not only accumulated massive wealth but also utilized state offices to support their personal enterprises.[52]

One reason that the monarchy traditionally trusted the Chinese is that they not only had trade networks with overseas Chinese communities but were also locally perceived as mere sojourners or aliens whose presence was temporary. Thus, it was believed that they would not engage in the local politics of their host country.[53] The economic activities of the Chinese, however, could not be separated from politics in the Thai kingdom. Like Thai nobles, Chinese tax farmers frequently hoarded royal revenues or delayed their remittance to the crown. This subsequently caused a financial shortfall in the royal treasury.[54] Moreover, while many Chinese merchants enjoyed royal patronage, some also sought political protection from the great nobles. Crucially, Chinese immigrants began to flood into the Thai kingdom with the establishment of Bangkok as the new capital city in the late eighteenth century.[55] While the Chinese were obviously an ethnic minority in the kingdom, they were overrepresented in Bangkok. According to G. William Skinner, most nineteenth-century travelers generally recognized that "the Chinese outnumbered the Thai in the Thai capital city."[56] Looking at their increasing wealth, uncertain allegiance, and crowded population in the capital city, the monarchy began to have doubts about the Chinese in the Thai kingdom.

THE MONARCHY AND THE FORMATION OF CAPITALISM IN THAILAND

The signing of the Bowring Treaty in 1855 between the British and Thai monarchies is normally considered by historians of both the Right and the Left as one of the most critical junctures in Thai history. It marked the beginning of a new era. For the first time the Thai kingdom was incorporated into the global economy that was dominated by Western powers. Even though the treaty did not end Thai feudalism once and for all or suddenly beget capitalism in the kingdom, it did set in motion economic and political forces that had been stagnant during the feudal era. As a result, the Thai monarchy during the second half of the nineteenth century had to adapt itself to the forces of the world economy and Western imperialism in numerous ways. To begin, the monarchy had to improve its mode of surplus extraction by launching fiscal and bureaucratic reforms. The monarchy also needed a new kind of ideological justification for its new type of government. It accomplished this goal by rebranding itself as the bearer of bourgeois culture and the embodiment of the nation-state. On top of that, the monarchy had to deal not only with the old contentious classes of nobles and merchants but also the newcomers: bureaucrats, wage laborers, and free peasants. All of them were affected by the formation of capitalism in the Thai kingdom.

THE ENCOUNTER OF THE THAI KINGDOM
WITH THE GLOBAL ECONOMY

Even before the signing of the Bowring Treaty, Thai feudalism had already shown signs of its structural decay. During the eighteenth century, the monarchy's feudal mode of surplus extraction had gradually deteriorated in response to the growing demand for Thai rice exported to China and Western colonies in Southeast Asia. As rice cultivation in the kingdom began to shift its mode from a production of use value to that of exchange value, the self-subsistence economy that had been dominant in Thailand for centuries gradually shifted to a market economy.[57] This change had an impact on the monarchy in several respects. The corvée became a less effective means for the crown to control and extract labor. Thanks to the growth of the market economy, most commoners decided to labor in paddy fields all year long and began to fulfill their labor obligation to the crown in kind and in cash.[58] The crown, therefore, lacked forced labor to work in public projects and mobilize for royal battles, and it had to import Chinese workers to do the former job while hiring Western mercenaries for the latter.[59] Furthermore, the monarchy lost its power to control land in the kingdom. As rice was in high demand in the market, commoners no longer conformed to the legal prohibitions imposed by their Lord of the Land. Instead, they pioneered in the hinterland in order to find unoccupied areas for farming.[60] The monarchy also faced the fiscal problem of unpredictable royal revenues. The rise of the market economy provided economic opportunities for Thai nobles and Chinese tax farmers not only to hoard more tax revenue but also to use that accumulated wealth for their investments in trading enterprises. While the former approach reduced total revenues in the royal treasury, the latter challenged royal trade monopolies.[61]

As if the situation of the monarchy could not get any worse, Sir John Bowring, an envoy of the British Empire, arrived in Bangkok on April 18, 1855, and demanded that King Mongkut (Rama IV, r. 1851–68) end the two means of surplus extraction that the crown had long enjoyed: overseas trade monopolies and heavy taxes on foreign businesses in the kingdom. The Bowring Treaty set the British free from royal fetters in several ways. Economically, they were given the right to trade freely in all Thai seaports without a royal restriction except for fixed duties on imports and exports. Legally, they were granted extraterritoriality and placed under British consular jurisdiction. Geographically, they were free not only to buy and rent land but also to travel into the hinterland to buy and sell commodities directly with individual Thais in lieu of having to deal with the crown's middlemen.[62] After the British successfully challenged royal prerogatives, other western powers rushed into the Thai kingdom to sign similar treaties: the United States (1856), France (1856), Denmark (1858), Portugal (1859), the Netherlands (1860), Germany (1862), Sweden (1868), Norway (1868), Belgium (1868), Italy (1868), Austria-Hungary (1869), Spain (1870), and Russia (1899).[63]

Consequently, during the second half of the nineteenth century, the Thai kingdom was abruptly opened to the West and brought into the international division of labor. Domestic producers were now driven by economic instead of political forces to produce not only rice but also teak, tin, and sugar in order to supply a market demand from European colonies in the region.[64] At the same time, western trading, banking, and manufacturing enterprises began operating in the kingdom. As Marxist scholars of Thai history have asserted, the Bowring Treaty marked both the end of classic Thai feudalism and the beginning of a new era for the Thai economy, which extended from the late nineteenth to the mid-twentieth century. While some called this era "semicolonial, semifeudal," others described it as "underdeveloped capitalism" or "peripheral capitalism."[65] Even though the appropriate term with which to describe this transitional period is still debated by Thai scholars, there is no debate about the fate of the monarchy.[66] To withstand the sociopolitical changes triggered by the force of the global economy and to survive western imperialism, the monarchy needed to reform itself, politically and economically.

On losing its right to monopolize overseas trade, the monarchy turned to the domestic market to compensate for the loss of royal revenues. Rather than returning to the old mode of surplus extraction, King Chulalongkorn (Rama V, r. 1868–1910), launched several groundbreaking policies that eventually increased the monarchy's wealth and power. Recognizing that the system of labor control had already decayed, the monarch set all forced laborers in the kingdom free by officially abolishing the corvée and slavery. Thanks to this royal decree, the monarch killed two birds with one stone. On the one hand, the abolition of the corvée and slavery at the beginning of the twentieth century inevitably ended the subjugation of commoners and slaves by the nobility. From then on, nobles were no longer a serious threat to the throne as they did not possess an army of commoners in their households; all Thai subjects finally became the "king's men." Further, the entire population was obliged to pay poll taxes, which the crown had just introduced.[67]

On the other hand, because the forced laborers and slaves had been emancipated, they could spend their time producing agrarian goods rather than wasting their labor on performing unproductive services for the royalty and nobility. The more those emancipated commoners used their labor to produce goods, the more the crown could tax their products and fill the royal treasury. Unchained from the fetters of a feudal mode of labor control, all Thais under the king's guidance were now free to participate in the growing market economy.

Rama V also launched a crucial policy that, for the first time in Thai history, eventually created the absolutist state: the installation of a modern bureaucracy. In place of a few nobles who formerly had hoarded a portion of tax revenues beyond those they were allowed to collect with the crown's permission, the newly installed bureaucracy was staffed by an army of salaried officials who came from a wider range of backgrounds: royalty, nobility, and commoners. Under this new system, tax revenues that were locally collected would be directly transferred to the capital city without the nobility's interference. Tax farms, which were once a valuable source of capital accumulation among the Chinese, were gradually reduced by the crown and eventually replaced with a new system of taxation. Instead of indirectly taxing market items via tax farmers, the crown sent bureaucrats to tax those items directly.[68] Moreover, a modern judicial system was introduced in the kingdom. The legal right of landownership, which had been introduced by Rama IV, was strengthened and secured under Rama V.[69] In addition to private property at the microlevel, the boundaries of the kingdom were also officially drawn at the macrolevel. Pushed by the British and the French empires, which had colonized all of Thailand's neighboring kingdoms, Rama V, as Benedict Anderson put it, internally and indirectly colonized the hinterland and tributary states by coercively incorporating them into the newly drawn territory of the invented nation-state.[70] This was an innovative policy in a kingdom where royal authority had been based on control of the population instead of territory. Besides sending bureaucrats from Bangkok to staff provincial offices that used to be occupied by local princes and nobles, the monarch made sure that his project of centralizing state power would prevail over any resistance by creating the Royal Military Academy in 1887 and introducing national conscription in 1905.[71] Financed by the crown instead of noble patronage, the modern army was designed to serve only the monarchy, and hence the notion of the "soldiers of the king" was introduced. Unprecedentedly armed with centralized state power, professional civil servants, efficient taxation, a modern judiciary, and a national army, the absolute monarchy was born in the Thai kingdom.

Under the reign of Rama V, there was an attempt to officially separate the fiscal body of the kingdom from that of the king. In 1890 Rama V founded the Privy Purse Bureau (PPB). Designed as an institution that managed the income and expenditures of the monarch, the royal family, and the royal household, the PPB received a fixed rate of the state budget annually, 15 percent of government revenues.[72] The forces that drove the monarch to institute the PPB were the burden of royal expenditures and the growth of the market economy.[73] To feed a large number of queens, princes, princesses, royal consorts, and courtiers, Rama V needed an institution such as the PPB, which could provide not only financial security to the throne but also professional management of royal wealth.[74] Acknowledging economic opportunities in the expansion of trading, banking, and manufacturing in the kingdom, the monarch also established the PPB to serve as a royal enterprise that would productively invest the crown's capital in the rising economy. The PPB did not let the king down. Thanks to the reformed taxation and centralized bureaucracy under Rama V's leadership, the overall revenues of the government increased considerably, and so did the PPB's budget.[75] By the early twentieth century, this budget had increased to such an extent that the PPB not only had sufficient funds to cover all the personal expenses of royalty and the royal household but had also accumulated a large surplus, which was invested in the market.

The PPB invested capital in three major economic activities: land rental, banking, and manufacturing. After the introduction of a legal right of landownership in the second half of the nineteenth century, even though the Lord of the Land could no longer claim a right to all the land in the kingdom, he was still the biggest landowner and possessed both the economic and extraeconomic means with which to acquire more landed estates. These economic means were based on the ability of the PPB to use its capital to either purchase occupied land or make loans to peasants and entrepreneurs, whose property would be seized by the crown if they failed to repay.[76] The extraeconomic means resided in the power of the PPB, on behalf of the absolute monarch, simply to claim its right over unoccupied land or evict peasants from their property.[77] With these two means of leverage, the PPB became the owner of the most valuable land in the kingdom and hence prosperously accumulated capital from land leasing.[78] The PPB also constructed commercial buildings and markets on its most valuable land in Bangkok

and major provinces and leased them to entrepreneurs.[79] At the same
time, the PPB involved itself in banking and manufacturing through
substantial stock holdings in the SCB, which was established in 1907,
and the Siam Cement Company (SCC), created in 1913.[80] As a junior
partner, the PPB also invested in numerous joint ventures associated
with rice milling, tramways, electricity generation, canal construction,
and shipping.[81] As Chollada Wattanasiri noted, a lot of foreign companies voluntarily offered stocks and positions on their boards of directors to the PPB. From the point of view of these foreign investors, given
the fact that the PPB was the king's enterprise, having it as a joint investor "raised the company's credibility and prestige in the Thai market
and in the public eye."[82] In this regard, from the beginning the monarchy, via the PPB's ventures, was the first and most dominant investor in
Thailand's capitalist development.

The Justification of the Absolute Monarchy

To establish the absolutist state, the crown also introduced and propagated a new type of ideology to justify its regime: nationalism and
bourgeois culture. That is, the formation of Thai absolutism—the centralization of state power, the installation of a modern state apparatus,
the concentration of state revenues, and the subjugation of local provinces and tribunal states under royal authority—was rationalized by
the crown as a countermeasure against western imperialism. Without a
unified nation-state and what it called a civilized culture, the Thai kingdom, according to the crown, would be judged by western powers as
barbarian, and it would inevitably be colonized by them.[83] To create a
unified nation-state, the monarchy introduced the notions of "Thai
identity" and the "Thai nation" into the kingdom, which had long been
composed of diverse ethnicities and cultures other than Thai. These included the Lao, Khmer, Mon, Shan, Vietnamese, Malay, Indian, and
Chinese.[84] Rama IV wrote a book that claimed a linear history of the
kingdom and its dynasties beginning with the founding of Ayutthaya
in the fourteenth century.[85] Responding to a border dispute with the
British Empire in the late nineteenth century, Rama V asserted, "The
Thai, the Lao, the Shan all consider themselves peoples of the same
race. They all respect me as their supreme sovereign, the protector of
their well-being."[86] King Vajiravudh (Rama VI, r. 1910–25), reproduced
this theme by promoting the monarchy as both the embodiment and
the protector of the Thai nation. "Being loyal to the king," he claimed,

"is the same as loving oneself because the king has the duty of protecting the nation."[87] The nation, the king added, is "analogous to the ship, the king to the captain, and the people to those in the ship," and thus "people in the ship must always obey the captain's orders. If they do not, the ship might be wrecked and the people in the ship in danger of losing their lives."[88] In this sense, an "imagined community" in the Thai version, as Thongchai Winichakul contends, has long been influenced by the imagination of the monarch, not by that of the ordinary people.[89]

Nationalism also served as an ideological justification for royal involvement in the expanding market economy. To be precise, the PPB's investments in three economic activities were rationalized as investments made in the national interest. First, the PPB's investments in land rentals and property development could hardly be separated from the government's projects of developing infrastructure such as roads, canals, and railways. Once those projects received the green light from the monarch, the PPB had the privilege of occupying valuable land alongside the construction sites, constructing commercial buildings and markets on its estates, and then leasing them to entrepreneurs. Second, funded by the PPB, the SCB had a nationalist origin. Prince Mahisara, a brother of Rama V, wished to see the first Thai bank competing with the western banks, which "did not care about Thai customers," and the Chinese banks, which "welcomed only those who could speak Chinese or English."[90] When the SCB faced a financial crisis, the crown asked not only the PPB but also the state treasury to bail the bank out since the SCB was perceived by the monarch as a national bank, which could not be liquidated. Finally, the idea of founding the SCC as the first cement plant in the kingdom was supported by Rama V, who believed that this enterprise would serve the interests of the nation.[91] The nationalist idea of creating a "Thai capital for Thais" was also promoted by Rama VI. The PPB's investments in the founding of the Siam Steamship Company and the Siam Mining Industry were rationalized by the monarch through the notion that the Thai nation should have its own shipping and mining enterprises.[92]

In addition to nationalism, the discourse of civilization (*khwam si-wilai*) was employed by the monarchy to justify its new regime. To survive western imperialism, Thailand, according to the royal ideology, needed to be transformed from a barbaric to a civilized nation, and the bearer of this transformation was none other than the king. The irony of this royal ideology, however, was that what was called Thai civilization was anything but Thai. Instead it was influenced by a particular culture that had been dominant in Europe since the eighteenth century, that of the bourgeoisie. In other words, unlike their forefathers prior to the mid-nineteenth century, the self-proclaimed civilized monarchs in the Thai kingdom presented themselves in public less like an Indian god-king, a Buddha-to-be, or a wealthy Chinese merchant and more like a bourgeois westerner. However, it is worth asking how "civilized" or bourgeois the Thai monarchs had become, as the crown no longer pursued Indianization and Sinicization but had turned instead toward the West.

According to an observation by John Bowring, which he made after visiting Rama IV's European-style apartments, the monarch had "all the instruments and appliances which might be found in the study or library of an opulent philosopher in Europe."[93] Noticing pendulums, watches, barometers, thermometers, and microscopes in the royal residence, the Englishman concluded that "almost everything seemed English."[94] Florence Caddy, an Englishwoman who was a guest of Rama V, described a banquet hosted by the Thai king in the following way: "Dinner was served in European style, the glass and porcelain, all from Europe, were engraved and painted with the royal arms and King Chulalongkorn's long name."[95] Noticing that "the king and princes all drank European wines," she remarked that there was only one thing that looked local on the dinner table: "The dessert was the only thing presenting any great novelty to us."[96] Following the king, male royals and courtiers began to copy the western fashions of longer hair, mustaches, shoes, trousers, tailored suits, hats, and dress uniforms.[97] Besides his preference for European fashions and commodities, Rama V highly valued western technology, knowledge, and education. He unprecedentedly sent hundreds of Thai students, including a large contingent of his own children, to study in Britain, France, Germany, Austria, Hungary, Denmark, Russia, and the United States.[98] The best and brightest among these students seemed to be his son Vajiravudh. Having studied law, history, and public administration at Oxford and written a dissertation titled "The War of the Polish Succession," Rama VI was a man of letters indeed.[99] Introducing a western style of writing novels, newspaper articles, poems, and plays to Thai literary circles, he was the first writer to translate any of Shakespeare's plays into Thai: *The Merchant of Venice*, *Romeo and Juliet*, and *As You Like It*.[100]

This newly invented image of Thai royalty as the bearers of bourgeois western culture was supported by a new medium that shaped the mass perception of the monarchy, photography. Before the nineteenth century, images of monarchs and royal families were virtually absent from Thai society. Depictions of Thai royalty were banned by the palace because they were deemed to be a threat to the royals' life spirits and could also expose the physical vulnerability of the monarch, who was socially worshipped as an immortal and transcendent god-king. Consequently, the monarchy had long prohibited the gaze of commoners on royal bodies, and a monarch normally hid himself from the public in order to maintain his mystique, sanctity, and purity.[101] This tradition was seriously undermined by the introduction of photography in Thailand during the second half of the nineteenth century.

As a monarch who was enthusiastic about western technology, Rama IV broke the royal taboo by allowing a Scottish photographer to take pictures of him dressed not only in full Thai regalia but also in French and Russian military uniforms and to bring those photos back to the British court in 1865.[102] Seeing the Thai monarchy as not inferior but equal to its counterparts in Europe and usually calling Queen Victoria his "distinguished Friend" and "very affectionate Sister," Rama IV wanted the West to get a glimpse of what Thai royalty really looked like via the medium of photography.[103] According to Rosalind Morris, this was a crucial moment because it launched the era of photography in the kingdom, which in turn marked not only the end of the king's absolute withdrawal from public space but also his increasing emergence into the public sphere.[104] Photography flourished in Thailand even more during the reign of Rama V. Frequently expressing enthusiasm about cameras, photographs, and stereoscopic images, the king supported the circulation of his photographic portraits throughout the kingdom.[105] Photography became the most popular medium for depicting images of the monarchy under the reigns of Rama VI and King Prajadhipok (Rama VII, r. 1925–35). In this period it was normal for ordinary Thais to see photographs of their monarchs in daily newspapers and magazines.[106] Instead of passive subjects under the absolute gaze of the monarch, Thai commoners were now able to gaze back at the royal bodies. With photography a cat may look at a king after all.

THE MONARCHY, BUREAUCRATS, AND THE "CHINESE PROBLEM"

The formation of the absolutist regime in the Thai kingdom during the late nineteenth century had an impact on class composition and alliance. To end its long struggle with the nobility and claim its absolute power in the kingdom, the Thai monarchy followed the path of absolute monarchies in Europe: absorbing the nobility into newly installed bureaucratic offices. Instead of competing with the crown over surplus extraction, nobles were transformed into civil servants and were compensated not only with fixed salaries but also with high ranks in the bureaucratic hierarchy. The modern Thai bureaucracy, however, absorbed into state offices not only the nobility but also numerous members of the class the crown had recently emancipated, the free commoners.

While the royals and nobles occupied the upper echelons of the state apparatus, the middle and lower ranks of the bureaucracy were staffed with an army of commoners.[107] Instead of birthright or royal patronage, members of this new bureaucratic bourgeoisie climbed the political ladder via their own merit, education, and skill.[108] Self-driven and more talented than many royals, some bureaucrats from humble backgrounds won the king's scholarships to study in Europe.[109] On returning to the kingdom to teach and train a new generation of civil servants, the young bureaucrats brought back the bourgeois ethic of self-motivation, hard work, productivity, and meritocracy. As one of them remarked, "The national income was used to feed many people who actually did not work. In addition, the national decay and the inefficiency in the administration was due to the fact that there were many incompetent men in high positions. Hence, the absolute monarchy was the cause of this injustice."[110] Although they were frustrated by the monarchy's favoritism, which promoted only the highborn to high ranks, these young, ambitious bureaucrats were not able to challenge the absolutist regime, as their resentment toward the crown had not yet found popular resonance among the masses of other Thais.

Once the beneficiaries of a feudal mode of surplus extraction, Chinese merchants had to adapt themselves to the absolutist regime and the penetration of western capital into the Thai economy. The crown's centralization of state revenues and introduction of modern taxation hit the Chinese hard as these policies put an end to tax farming, their most valuable means of accruing wealth. Furthermore, the western ultimatum of free trade for Thailand ended the trading privileges that the crown had once provided the Chinese.[111] As the monarchy began acting more like a bourgeois enterprise via the PPB's investments, it was no longer a protector but a competitor of Chinese merchants. Although the crown compensated Chinese tax farmers for their loss by giving them loans to invest in the expanding market economy, they could not compete with western entrepreneurs, who were armed with large amounts of capital and advanced technology. Given the latter's economic and technological advantages, the monarchy even preferred to invest in joint ventures with western firms instead of its old Chinese partners.[112] Worse than that, unable to repay the royal loans, many Chinese estates, factories, and commercial buildings were seized by the crown. Once a privileged class that was known as the "royalist Chinese," these merchants drastically declined in terms of influence in the nineteenth century due to business failures and bankruptcies.[113] In Skinner's words, under the royal hand "the practice of ennobling wealthy Chinese was allowed to die."[114]

Nevertheless, the relationship between the Thai monarchy and the Chinese minority did not end with the extinction of that generation of Chinese tax farmers. Thanks to the abolition of the corvée and slavery, the monarchy needed a new source of manpower to labor on royal projects. Since Thai commoners preferred to either labor in paddy fields or enter the bureaucratic system, the monarchy turned to Chinese labor for a solution. During the second half of the nineteenth century, thousands of Chinese immigrated to Thailand annually and sold their labor to the crown.[115] Penniless in China, most of them initially participated in the labor sector. Once they could stand on their own feet, they entered into other economic activities in the kingdom such as commerce, manufacturing, finance, and mining.[116] Some thrived and became wealthy traders and entrepreneurs in one generation. Unlike the former generation, the new wave of Chinese immigrants was more self-reliant, as they lacked the political protection and patronage of the crown.[117]

Chinese immigrants brought not only their corporeal bodies but also their ethical values to the host kingdom. According to Skinner, nineteenth-century travelers commonly recognized some prominent characteristics among the Chinese minority in Thailand: "extreme industriousness, willingness to labor long and hard, steadiness of purpose, ambition, desire for wealth and economic advancement, innovativeness, venturesomeness, and independence."[118] Local Thais, in contrast, were described as "indolent, unwilling to labor for more than immediate needs, contented with their lot, uninterested in money or economic advancement, conservative, and satisfied with a dependent status."[119] These fundamental perceived differences between the two ethnic groups were explained by Skinner in terms of nurture, not nature. Not only growing up in overpopulated, unfertile, and socially competitive regions of China but also coming to Thailand in order to work and send money back to families in their homeland, the Chinese immigrants had been socially and mentally trained to be industrious, frugal, and abstemious. Thai commoners, on the contrary, tended to enjoy life and lived in the present thanks to both their underpopulated and fertile motherland and their Buddhist culture, which discouraged economic advancement, social mobility, and anxiety about the fortune and social status of one's family.[120] These differences between the Thai majority and the Chinese minority, however, did not create ethnic tensions between them. For most of Thai history before the early twentieth century, the Chinese were not the victims of ethnic discrimination by the locals. In fact, unlike other Southeast Asian natives, Thais seemed to welcome the Chinese and held them in high regard because of their work ethic, their entrepreneurial skills, and even their fair complexions.[121]

The comfortable relationship between these two ethnic groups was turned upside down by royal intervention. Promoting the idea of nationalism to justify its project of nation building, the monarchy in the early twentieth century raised the mass consciousness of "Thainess" by contrasting it with Chinese otherness. Royal prejudice against the Chinese was exemplified by Rama VI's most notorious written work, *The Jews of the Orient*. Influenced by the discourses of racism, xenophobia, and anti-Semitism to which he had been exposed in fin de siècle Europe, the king asserted in this 1917 publication that the Thai people "are no more like the Chinese than any of the European races are like the Jews."[122] Chinese immigrants and their descendants in the Thai kingdom, Rama VI elaborated further, were "no more Buddhists than the Jews Christians" and were "every bit as unscrupulous and as unconscionable as the Jews," as they were "utterly without morals, without conscience, without mercy, without pity . . . where money is concerned." He continued, claiming that they were "like so many vampires who steadily suck dry an unfortunate victim's life-blood" and were not only born "aliens by birth, by nature, by sympathy, by language, and finally by choice" but ultimately "bound one day to come into bloody conflict with the inhabitants."[123] Once an ethnic group that had long obtained royal privileges and patronage, the Chinese now were alienated from the monarch and stigmatized as the "Chinese problem" in the kingdom of Thais.[124]

THE CONTRADICTION AND CRISIS OF THAI ABSOLUTISM

Unlike European monarchies, the Thai monarchy could enjoy and maintain its absolute power for only a short period of time. The absolutist regime that Rama V installed in the late nineteenth century began to show its structural problems in the early twentieth century during the reign of Rama VI. Drastically declining under the reign of Rama VII, the absolute monarchy was overthrown in 1932 by a small group of middle-ranking bureaucrats organized under the banner of the People's Party. The end of the absolute monarchy in Thailand was mainly a consequence of the following causes. First, the monarchy failed not only to make itself sufficiently bourgeois in the market but also to administer the national economy, which was deeply incorporated into the global market. While the former failure led to royal debts and bankruptcies, the latter intensified an economic downturn and public resentment toward the crown. Moreover, the royal attempt to re-create itself as bourgeois in the ideological sphere undermined rather than sustained the justification for the absolutist regime. Instead of admiration and appreciation, the masses resented, criticized, and even mocked the bourgeois lifestyle and conspicuous consumption of royalty. Worst of all, the middle-ranking bureaucrats were no longer the only group that recognized the incompatibility between the absolute monarchy and the nation's transition to capitalism. With strong support from a new class of "vulgar bourgeoisie"—entrepreneurs, professionals, and intellectuals— the People's Party did not face social grievances or political resistance when it deprived the crown of its power and wealth and consequently ended absolutism in Thailand.

THE MONARCHY AND THE MODERN ECONOMY

The economy was the Achilles heel of the absolute monarchy in Thailand. Incorporated into global capitalism since the mid-nineteenth century, the kingdom had to respond not only to a high demand for agricultural goods, especially rice, but also to the insecurity and vulnerability of the global economy and foreign affairs. The monarchy in the early twentieth century failed to handle these critical challenges. Rama V failed to undertake the construction of a large-scale irrigation facility that would have effected a major increase in rice production and alleviated the agricultural recession and poverty among the peasantry.[125] Rama VI struggled to reverse the economic downturn during World War I. Rama VII was powerless in the face of the economic crisis triggered by the Great Depression. Having graduated from a British military academy, Rama VII often confessed his lack of knowledge about the national economy. "I'm only a soldier. How can I understand such things as the gold standard?" he once said.[126] "The financial war is a very hard one indeed. Even experts contradict one another until they become hoarse. Each offers a different suggestion. I myself do not profess to know much about the matter and all I can do is listen to the opinions of others and choose the best. I have never experienced such a hardship," he said on another occasion. He went even further, saying, "If I have made a mistake [on economic policies], I really deserve to be excused by the officials and people of Siam."[127] In this critical moment when the monarchy was humbled by a series of economic problems, the absolute monarch himself, as Handley put it, "conceded that the king wore no clothes."[128]

The only way a monarchy can survive the force of capitalism, according to Max Weber, is to step back and let state affairs be managed by bureaucrats. In other words, the administration of the national economy and politics in a capitalist state is not the political vocation of a monarch who lacks modern knowledge of the market and the state. Instead, it should be done by bureaucratic experts.[129] The Thai monarchy, however, did not follow the Weberian path. Despite its inability to solve the economic crisis, the crown refused to decentralize state power and distribute government responsibilities to bureaucrats thanks to a simple rationale among the king's advisers, who feared that it would make the absolute monarch look "weak" and "unable to rule" in the public eye.[130] To make the situation worse, the palace banned modern instruction in politics and economics in the schools. Rama VI allowed only princes and high nobles to study political theory, economics, law, philosophy, and public administration.[131] Worried that modern knowledge of the state and the market would promote class consciousness among his subjects, Rama VII made the study of political economy a criminal offense.[132] Even among princes and nobles who had permission to study this "forbidden discipline," whenever some of them dared to analyze the problems of the kingdom through the lens of political economy, they tended to be neglected by the monarch, and their careers simply came to an end.[133]

In addition to its struggle with the crisis of the national economy, the monarchy had to deal with the financial problems of the crown itself. Even though the establishment of the PPB was supposed to guarantee financial security to the monarchy, the bureau during the reigns of Rama VI and Rama VII could not find enough revenue to balance royal expenditures for several reasons: the failure of the PPB's investments, the nature of royal spending, and the lack of royal leadership. With the exception of royal investments in the cement industry, the PPB's ventures in other economic sectors were in the red. Lacking accountability in banking, the SCB almost went bankrupt during its early days in the 1910s and needed to be bailed out by the government.[134] The Siam Steamship Company and the Siam Mining Industry, unfortunately, were shut down only a few years after their founding due to a lack of the advanced technology and overseas networks necessary to compete with western and Chinese enterprises.[135] The monarchs, in addition, did not make the fiscal situation of the PPB better, thanks to the way they managed its revenues. Rather than reinvesting royal capital in the market, the kings drew large amounts of the PPB's revenues and squandered them in unproductive activities: purchasing landed estates and constructing new royal residences; granting monthly allowances to princes, princesses, queens, royal consorts, and courtiers; and buying luxury items from Europe. Granted capital by the monarchs, an army of royalty, meanwhile, did not engage in business. While male royals chose to serve the king by working in state offices, female royals were prohibited by the palace from work of any kind because it would "tarnish the royal prestige."[136] The few royals who did engage in business invested their capital in land rentals instead of industrial production, commerce, or banking.[137] The nature of royal spending meant that investment of royal capital was barely set in motion and did not create a new means of reproduction and reinvestment. Instead, it was constantly taken from the market, hoarded, and unproductively consumed.

Under Rama V's leadership, despite the high and unproductive expenses of royalty, the PPB had thrived. The king balanced the PPB's accounts and paid close attention to its investments and expenditures on the royal household.[138] Rama VI, by contrast, abused the institution that his father had prudently founded. Besides the regular expenses of the crown, the monarch added a financial burden to the PPB with several costly projects, including a dramatic funeral for his father; an extravagant coronation for himself; the purchase of jewels for his male escorts; the establishment of his personal guards, the Wild Tiger Corps (*suea pa*); and the construction of playhouses, movie theaters, the Dusit Thani miniature city, and seaside palaces.[139] Consequently, the prodigal monarch overspent the annual budget that the treasury provided to the PPB tenfold and used up almost 8 percent of the government's annual revenues. The king's reckless expenditures, as Benjamin Batson put it, were also "tucked away" in the state budget or disguised as "loans" and "advances" from the treasury.[140] Eventually, Rama VI had to seek foreign loans to cover his personal debts. Once he passed away, Rama VII inherited a throne that was heavily burdened by royal debts, and the PPB's business under his reign was contracting.[141] What Rama V envisioned—a separation between the purse of the monarchy and the treasury of the kingdom and the professional management of royal businesses that would provide financial security to the crown—virtually crumbled in the hands of his two sons.

THE MONARCHY AND THE LEGITIMACY CRISIS

Instead of supporting the monarchy, the bourgeois image that absolute monarchs tried to embody and present to the public undermined their legitimacy to rule over the Thai kingdom. Even though the bourgeois lifestyle was popular in the Thai court during the age of absolutism, this new culture imported from the West alienated the majority of the population from the monarch. According to Maurizio Peleggi, there was a huge difference in the early twentieth century between the bourgeoisification of the royals in Europe and that same process in Thailand. In Europe royalty had no choice but to blend themselves into bourgeois culture as they could not resist the bourgeois class, which held political and economic power in the new capitalist state. In fin-de-siècle Thailand the majority of the population still lived in poverty, and formation of the Thai bourgeoisie was still in its nascent stage. As a result, Thai royalty's emulation of the European bourgeoisie was simply a narcissistic attempt to bolster their self-esteem instead of creating a social bond with the mass of local Thais.[142] Thak Chaloemtiarana shared the same idea about the bourgeoisification of Thai royalty. As he remarked, while the royal elites in the reign of Rama V drove their luxury cars imported from Europe on Ratchadamnoen Avenue, a grand boulevard newly constructed simply to connect the old palace with a new one, "most of the Thai people still commuted with their own bare feet or bullock carts powered by horses or water buffaloes."[143]

Like his father, Rama VI enjoyed an excessive bourgeois lifestyle at the court. What differentiated them, however, seemed to be their will to rule and sexual orientation. While Rama V was publicly praised as a monarch who relentlessly put his efforts into state administration in order to modernize the kingdom, Rama VI was deemed an idle king who enjoyed writing novels and performing plays at court. Moreover, while the former filled the court with queens, princesses, consorts, and female servants, the latter did so with a troop of young male pages at a time when homosexuality was frowned on in Thai society. As Chanan Yodhong revealed, the daily routine of Rama VI, who was normally escorted by as many as seventy pages, was as follows. The king woke up at 1:00 p.m. and drank cocktails while signing state papers until 3:00. After having a Thai lunch, he played tennis or cricket and then had a western dinner and cocktails at 9:00. At night he played bridge, performed dramas, watched Japanese movies in the royal theater, and told ghost stories with the pages. After having dessert at 3:00 a.m., the king finally went to bed at 5:00.[144] Living extravagantly while the masses still lived in destitution, Rama VI ironically stated, "I am able to attest that no other country has fewer poor or needy people than Siam."[145] The king's lavish lifestyle and sexual orientation did not go unnoticed by young bureaucrats, especially those in the army. In 1912 a group of military officials—who not only had lost patience with the idle and spendthrift monarch who favored his pages with high official ranks and supplied them with luxury items but also worried that the monarch's personal troops would soon replace the army—plotted a rebellion against the monarchy.[146] Even though their plot was leaked and hence preemptively aborted by the crown, the army did send a clear message to the public: the legitimacy of the absolute monarchy was in decline.

The public did respond. Thanks to the popular circulation of royal images via photography, a new class of journalists, columnists, and intellectuals had a chance not only to get a glimpse of royalty's conspicuous consumption but also to mock the royal bodies and manners that were exposed in public. In the late 1920s and early 1930s, political cartoons and caricatures that criticized and satirized the monarchy were published in newspapers, magazines, and journals. In publishing a portrait of Rama VI in honor of his birthday, *Bangkok Kanmuang*, for example, juxtaposed that portrait with an essay titled "The Suffering of the Rich," which begins with a passage that seems to refer to the penniless monarch: "Who would have thought that the rich could suffer? Since they usually obtain everything they desire, what could possibly upset them?"[147] On another occasion, the same newspaper published a caricature that criticized Rama VI's leadership by depicting a rickshaw driver named "morality" struggling to pull "a paunchy king" up a steep incline.[148] Political satire that undermined royal legitimacy was also popular during the reign of Rama VII. *Kro Lek*, for instance, mocked royal favoritism in the absolutist regime with a drawing titled "Let's Not Have It Be Like This, Beloved Comrades!" In this caricature, the king was depicted as cradling his relatives and sycophants while giving his boot to the nation's "honest, hard-working, straight-talking officials."[149] In light of these political criticisms and satires, it was clear that the days of the absolute monarchy were numbered.

THE END OF THE ABSOLUTE MONARCHY

On the morning of June 24, 1932, while Rama VII was playing golf with the queen at his seaside palace, a group of military and civilian officials known as the People's Party seized control of the government and brought to an end the absolute monarchy in Thailand. Read in front of the palace and circulated in the capital city, *The Declaration of the People's Party* vividly illustrated critical problems of the absolute monarchy that the young bureaucrats had long recognized. To start with, the absolute monarchy did not promote meritocracy but royal favoritism and sycophantism. Coming from the humble background of commoners, the young officials were frustrated by the fact that the top echelons of the bureaucratic hierarchy were reserved exclusively for the royals and nobles, whose justification for their ranks was based merely on blood and birthright instead of merit and a work ethic. Worse than that, when the royal government faced a financial crisis in the early 1930s, Rama VII cut the national budget of the bureaucracy, increased taxes on civil servants, and sacked a huge number of officials in the middle and low ranks of the bureaucracy to save on government expenditures while leaving the royals and nobles in high positions in place.[150] Given this resentment toward royal favoritism, the young bureaucrats asserted in the *Declaration* that Rama VII "appointed his relatives and incompetent favorites to important positions without listening to the voice of the people." It further stated that he "allowed [them] to abuse their power, such as by receiving bribes in government building projects and buying supplies, seeking profits in the exchange of government money, and spending public money extravagantly" and "elevated the royal class and gave them many privileges so as to allow them to oppress the common people."[151]

Furthermore, the absolute monarchy lacked sufficient modern knowledge of political economy to administer the state and the country's finances. Educated in Europe, the leaders of the People's Party had the privilege of studying political theory, philosophy, law, public administration, and economics, subjects reserved only for royalty and nobility in their home country. On returning to Thailand, they challenged the traditional principle of royal service (*lak ratchakan*)—that of civil servants serving only at the pleasure of the king—by introducing new administrative principles based on academic knowledge, law, rationality, and professionalism (*lak wicha*).[152] They were also frustrated by the monarchy's failure to renegotiate the trade treaties between western powers and the Thai kingdom that had long benefited the former at the expense of the latter. Despite presenting itself as the protector of the national interest, the crown was perceived by the People's Party as a supporter of the penetration of western capital into the kingdom.[153] Written at a critical moment when Thailand was struggling with an economic crisis, the *Declaration* stated that the royal government "has made the people believe it would promote their economic well-being. But the people have waited in vain."[154] Putting the spotlight on Rama VII, the *Declaration* asserted that the monarch had failed to lead the nation: "[The King] rules without any guiding principle. As a result, the destiny of the nation was left at random, as evidenced by economic depression and the misery and hardship of the people, which is generally known." The absolute monarch, the *Declaration* announced, "was unable to remedy these wrongs."[155]

Finally, the absolute monarchy was an institution that did not represent or protect the country but appropriated surplus from the producers of the national economy, the ordinary people. Echoing the popular discourse in the early 1930s that the crown was an economic parasite that had harshly exploited poor peasants by "farming on their backs," the People's Party criticized the way royalty accumulated wealth and enjoyed their extravagant lifestyle at the expense of taxpayers.[156] "Where does the money come from that royalty uses?," the *Declaration* asked, and then gave a simple answer: "It comes from the people." Despite this fact, as the *Declaration* stated further, the royal government "regards the people as servants, as slaves, and even as animals." It went on to state that "the taxes collected are used personally by the king" and "royalty sleeps, eats, and is happy. No other country gives its royal class so much." In contrast were the ordinary people: "For them to earn even a little money requires them to sweat blood" and "if the people cannot pay taxes, their property is seized or they are forced to labor without pay." In light of this, the People's Party unprecedentedly declared a radical principle for the administration of the national economy: "Our country belongs to all citizens, not the king as it has been propagated," and "money collected by taxation should be used on behalf of the nation and not for the enrichment of royalty."[157]

In the *Declaration* it was implicit that "the people" on whose backs royalty "had farmed" and whom the People's Party claimed to represent were the majority of the national population at that time, Thai peasants. The overthrow of the absolute monarchy in 1932, however, did not alienate but rather garnered popular support from the Chinese.

Like Thai bureaucrats, Chinese businessmen did not believe that the monarchy was the right institution to administer the economic and political affairs of the new nation-state. Even though they had long pleaded with the monarchy to set high tariffs in order to protect the country's nascent industries from foreign competition, the crown disappointed them by welcoming a flood of western capital into the kingdom and favoring business partnerships with western companies. Domestic enterprises, therefore, were left by the crown to stand on their own.[158] As a result, unlike their forefathers, new Chinese entrepreneurs were independent of the palace and relied on their business connections both inside Chinese communities in the kingdom and overseas. As one royal recounted, "In the old days, the Chinese . . . always visited princes and nobles, or high officials, and were very close to the Thais." She felt bitter about the new wave of Chinese in the twentieth century. "Now they are different," she averred; "they see no need to visit or please anyone," and "[they] do not even want to be ennobled." She further maintained that they "come in to pursue large businesses, investing in rice mills and trading firms with thousands or millions of baht, without having to have connections with anyone."[159] Detached from royal patronage and frustrated with the royal government, Chinese businessmen did not lament but welcomed the end of the old regime. For the Chinese, the new order that was steered by the People's Party was supposed not only to purge all royal fetters from the national economy but also to end the royal prejudice they had endured. They hoped that the prejudice about them as the "Jews of the Orient" or "vampires of the national economy" would disappear with the demise of the absolute monarchy.

THE NEW ORDER AND RELICS OF THE ROYAL PAST

The legacy of the absolute monarchy did not go simply but lingered after the 1932 revolution. Even before the revolution, Rama VII had warned that Chinese domination of the national economy would become a big problem for Thai politics should a parliamentary system be introduced into the kingdom. As the last absolute monarch predicted, "The Parliament would be entirely dominated by the Chinese Party. One could exclude all Chinese from every political right; yet they will dominate the situation all the same, since they hold the *hard cash*. Any party that does not depend on the Chinese funds cannot succeed, so that politics in Siam will be dominated and dictated by the Chinese merchants."[160] A royal ideology associated with nationalism and ethnic prejudice against a Chinese minority remained alive in the postrevolutionary government led by the People's Party. Like the king, the young bureaucrats were deeply concerned about the "Chinese problem." According to Skinner, by the 1930s the Chinese "were estimated to constitute 85 percent of the 'commercial class' and to hold in their hands 90 percent of the country's commerce and trade."[161] Thanks to this background, the People's Party not only perceived Chinese merchants as a self-interested group seeking their own economic gain instead of promoting the national interest, but they also worried that Chinese domination of the Thai economy would eventually empower this ethnic minority to play a political role on the national stage.[162]

The Chinese problem became a bigger concern of the government when the military prevailed over civilian officers in a struggle for power inside the People's Party. Driven by protofascist and nationalist ideologies, Field Marshal Plaek Phibunsongkhram launched several policies in the early 1940s that glorified the ethnocentrism of "Thainess" while discriminating against the Chinese business class. The government promulgated a new slogan, "Thais produce, Thais consume, and Thais prosper." Several occupations such as driving taxis, slaughtering pigs, fishing, and planting rubber were legally reserved for Thais alone. The official name of the country was changed from Siam to Thailand. Every non-Thai citizen was required to adopt a Thai name, and Thai became a compulsory language in school. Chinese schools were forced to close permanently, and Thais were to hold at least half the jobs in any firm with more than ten employees. In addition, Chinese enterprises in the rice, fishing, rubber, tobacco, and petroleum industries were seized by the state.[163] To survive the government's militant nationalism, wealthy Chinese businessmen had no choice but to seek political protection from bureaucrats, especially the military. To be precise, they asked some high-ranking generals to take positions on the boards of directors of their enterprises and then compensated those generals with stock and salaries. As Skinner remarked, "In one of the most intriguing paradoxes of Thai history, militant economic nationalism has resulted not in the defeat of the enemy but in cooperation between the antagonists." On the one hand, "The Thai ruling group found in the new Sino-Thai alliance a satisfactory and legitimate source of wealth and economic power." On the other hand, "Chinese merchants profited from the political protection and special privileges the alliance afforded."[164] This mutual relationship between Thai bureaucrats and Chinese businessmen marked a new era in the Thai economy in the mid-twentieth century that later became known as "bureaucratic capitalism."[165]

In addition to the Chinese, the post-1932 government attempted to control the crown under the newly installed regime, a constitutional monarchy. Seeing the British monarchy as a model, the People's Party ended royal prerogatives in national politics and reduced the monarch to serving merely as a figurehead of the state. The revolutionary party also attempted to effect ambitious changes in royal wealth by distinguishing the property of the monarch, the monarchy, and the kingdom from one another and by taxing the first like the property of commoners while making the latter two national treasures and sources of government revenues. Facing the elimination of royal wealth and power, the crown did not give up without a fight. One year after the 1932 revolution a group of princes and high nobles staged a counterrevolutionary movement, the Boworadet rebellion. Rama VII, meanwhile, continued to do what he had secretly done even before the end of absolutism: transfer money from the PPB to his bank accounts in Singapore, London, and New York.[166] As a justification for his action, the monarch declared, "When I was the king in the absolutist regime, everything in the country was mine. [Though] now we have a constitution, I must still have a right to use the property of the crown. No one could argue that I am cheating and exploiting the national treasury."[167]

The revolutionaries, nevertheless, gained the upper hand over the reactionaries. Seeing that the government had defeated the royalist rebellion, imprisoned some of his relatives or forced them to live in exile, and continued to promulgate new acts that limited royal wealth and power, Rama VII lost his will to fight for royal dignity. He abdicated just three years after the end of the absolute monarchy in Siam and decided to live in Britain for the rest of his life. His nine-year-old nephew, Ananda, ascended the throne in 1935 as King Rama VIII (r. 1935–46) but spent most of his reign in Switzerland instead of his home kingdom. With the absence of a reigning monarch and the decline of royal power, the government had a great opportunity to pursue several projects that had a critical impact on the status of the monarchy.

In 1939 the government filed a lawsuit against Rama VII, accusing him of an illegal transfer of PPB money. At the end of a notorious trial in 1945, the former monarch lost, his personal properties in Thailand were seized as government compensation, and the government even tried to sell those properties by advertising them in newspapers.[168] Most important, as the king's bank accounts and estates both inside and outside the kingdom were revealed in the trial, for the first time ordinary Thais had a chance to comprehend not only how wealthy the monarch had been but also how enormous was the gap between the wealth of the king and that of commoners.

The government also drastically cut financial support for the monarchy. During the reigns of Rama V and Rama VI the crown on average accounted for 20 percent of government expenditures per year. This percentage is remarkable if it is compared to the absolutist government's average expenditures for public education per year, 2 percent. Facing criticism for royal profligacy, Rama VII reduced the crown's expenses to 8 percent of government expenditures. The government of the People's Party nonetheless took the reduction of the government's budget for the monarchy to the next level, an annual average of 0.9 percent of the government expenditures during 1935–50. With this drastic reduction, the postabsolutist government could spend its budget on more fruitful national projects. Government spending on public education, for example, rose to 9 percent of national expenditures during the same period.[169]

On top of that, the government passed the Crown Property Act in 1936 in order to clarify and manage three types of property associated with the monarchy. The first type was defined as the king's private property. Composed of property that belonged to the king before he ascended the throne, property conferred on the king by the state, and property acquired by the king by any means and at any time other than property acquired on account of kingship, including any fruit accrued therefrom, the private property of the king was subject to taxation. The second type was public property, which the act defined as property of the king used exclusively for the benefit of the state, such as palaces. Identified as a national treasure, this property belonged to the state, and thus it was tax free. Also exempted from taxation, the last type comprised the remaining property outside the first two categories.[170] This last category included landed properties and investments in the SCB, SCC, and other companies that had formerly belonged to the PPB. All these properties were placed under the control of a new institution, the CPB.[171] In this critical moment it looked as if for the first time the bodies of the king in the Thai kingdom had been clearly distinguished in three categories: the corporeal body as a symbolic sovereign, the political body as a national institution, and the fiscal body as a state enterprise.

Once the royal arm of investment in the market, the CPB—the third body of the king—came under the control of the Ministry of Finance under the new constitutional monarchy, and it became a financial source of government funds. During the 1940s, the government asked the CPB to fund several state enterprises that were newly established in order to compete with the Chinese and western companies that had dominated the national economy. At the same time, generals and politicians who had positions in the government occasionally withdrew money from the CPB and used it illegally for personal investments.[172] While this phenomenon illustrated corruption and cronyism among bureaucrats and politicians, which would be a symptomatic feature of Thai politics in the decades to come, it also revealed the lowest point of the monarchy. The crown now completely lacked the power to stop the exploitation of royal wealth by government officials. The golden age of the Thai monarchy seemed to be forever gone. Instead of relying on the highborn, such as royalty and nobility, the national economy and politics were dominated by the class of ordinary Thai bureaucrats and Chinese businessmen. As if the fate of the monarchy could not get any worse, during a short trip in Thailand in the summer of 1946, Rama VIII was found in his palace bed, dead from a single bullet in his head.[173] Thanks to the mysterious death of his brother, Bhumibol, then eighteen years old, ascended the throne precipitously as King Rama IX and faced a task that seemed impossible to accomplish, taking the monarchy back from the brink of extinction.

CONCLUSION

Before Rama IX ascended the throne in 1946, the Thai monarchy was destined to meet its doom. The decline of the crown was due to its unsuccessful attempt to embed itself into the kingdom's transformation in its mode of production, from late feudalism to the early stage of capitalism. In the feudal era, the ancient monarchy enjoyed its accumulation of wealth through forced levies, compulsory labor services, and trade monopolies. At that time the crown ruled through religious and feudal beliefs that were still effective in taming the mass of producers, most of whom were rural peasants. A critical juncture for the crown, however, came in the second half of the nineteenth century. While the monarchy in this period was forced by western imperialism to end royal trade monopolies and embrace the new economic order of so-called free trade, the crown effectively monopolized political power in the kingdom. In the era of absolutism, the monarchy freed all producers from feudal fetters. It justified its rule as the bearer of bourgeois culture, appropriated surpluses via a new tax system, and acted like a bourgeois enterprise by investing its capital in banking, manufacturing, and land development. This brief royal experiment in "bourgeoisification" ended in disaster. As a political institution, the crown was unable to lead the country out of economic crises. The natural bodies of royalty added insult to injury. Living extravagant and lavish lives, wasting state budgets on new palaces and luxury goods, and lacking professional management of royal investments, the king and the royal family were not only burdened with royal debts but also publicly stigmatized as national parasites. These royal failures cleared the way for the 1932 revolution, which ended the absolute monarchy in Thailand. Under the new order, the crown was constrained by the national constitution. The new era in the kingdom seemed to belong to a new class of bureaucratic and commercial bourgeois who had the power, wealth, and knowledge to deal with the formation of a capitalist market and a bourgeois state.

At that moment, it looked as if the story of the Thai monarchy would follow the path that classical theorists in political economy predicted. The monarchy then seemed like a remnant of the feudal past that would not play a dominant role in the political and economic realms of the bourgeois state. Consequently, the odds were stacked against Rama IX when he ascended the throne in 1946. Under his reign, how could the monarchy revive its power in a kingdom that had developed as a bourgeois state dominated by bureaucrats and businessmen? How could the crown regain its wealth within a Thai economy transformed by capitalism? How could the palace restore the tarnished public image of royalty? This would have been an uphill task for any monarch, let alone the young, shy, and quiet king of Thailand, who had spent most of his childhood and adolescence in western countries, spoke European languages more fluently than his first, and barely knew his home kingdom or its local populaces.

THE RISE AND TRIUMPH
OF THE BOURGEOIS CROWN

The revival of the Thai monarchy—from the brink of extinction in the mid-twentieth century to one of the most influential and wealthy institutions of the kingdom in the twenty-first—was nothing short of spectacular. How did the monarchy turn things around? What was the historical background behind the success of the crown? What were the secrets of the monarchy under King Rama IX that helped that institution not only survive but thrive under capitalism? Besides its pure will to survive, the monarchy's rise from the ashes stemmed from major historical shifts during the Thai economy's transition to industrial capitalism in the late twentieth century. That is, the historical context of Thailand's late capitalism made the comeback of the crown possible in the first place.

The political context during the second half of the twentieth century provided an opportunity for the monarchy to revive its role in national politics. During the Cold War, as the monarchy still lacked political strength and agency, it was the military that brought wealth, power, and prestige back to the crown on the condition that the king would serve as an anticommunist figurehead and legitimize the dictatorial military regime. With the end of the Cold War and the beginning of demilitarization and democratization in Thailand, the monarchy in the late twentieth century began to distance itself from the military and fully show its strength and independence as a political agent in Thai politics. The crown acted as an umpire in political conflicts between the military and civilians, as a symbolic figure of national reconciliation between the Left and the Right, and as a last resort for the fledgling parliamentary democracy in the kingdom. Furthermore, the monarchy adapted itself to Thailand's transition to industrial capitalism remarkably well by applying a Janus-faced approach to this historical juncture. In public the monarchy promoted itself as an antidote to critical problems of uneven development, economic inequality, and social uncertainty unleashed by rapid industrialization. As a result, instead of being seen as the nation's rentiers, the monarch and the royal family were perceived by their subjects more as philanthropists, as well as developers and saviors of the poor. At the same time, the monarchy enjoyed its own accumulation of wealth during the economic transition and became the biggest capitalist conglomerate in the nation. The palace also acted as a broker for elite businessmen in the expanding market. Most important, the monarchy was quick-witted when it came to class alliances, as it successfully secured popular support from different classes in different eras. In Rama IX's early reign, the rural peasantry was the main client of royal patronage, as agriculture was still dominant in the national economy. When capitalism flexed its muscles later in the reign of the king, Thai royalty turned their attention to the emerging bourgeoisie and developed a strong partnership with an army of industrialists, bankers, and members of the urban middle class. This approach to political change, economic transformation, and class alliances accounted for the rise of a novel form of monarchy in Thailand in the early twenty-first century. The monarchy was not only actively engaged in bourgeois activities in the market, but it also drew political legitimacy and popular support rather than resentment and revolution from the bourgeoisie itself. The term *bourgeois monarchy* fits these new features of the Thai crown.

THE RETURN OF THE KING

In the early phase of Rama IX's reign, from the mid-1940s to the late 1970s, extraeconomic forces played a significant role in bringing power back to the throne. These were the political, judicial, and military interventions carried out by three political actors: the military, royalist movements, and the United States. The monarchy, in turn, served these actors as a symbolic institution legitimizing their political causes. The revival of monarchical power in the Thai state helped the crown to reenter the national market. After Thailand launched its national project of industrialization, royal enterprises relentlessly accumulated capital and thrived in the expanding market. Besides its political and economic activities, the monarchy attempted to revive its public image in Thai society and improve its relationship with different social classes. Even though Rama IX had begun to develop a connection with the nascent bourgeoisie in the early years of his reign, the crown's main priority was seeking mass support from the rural peasantry—the majority of the kingdom's population at that time.

Bringing the Monarchy Back into Thai Politics

Rama IX ascended the throne in 1946. It was the time when the Thai monarchy had hit its lowest point due to a series of tragic events the crown had faced just a few years earlier. These included the overthrow of the absolute monarchy, the abdication of the last absolute monarch, the dispossession of royalty's wealth and power by the revolutionary government, and the mysterious death of the teenage monarch under the newly installed constitutional regime. Once the most powerful and the wealthiest person in the kingdom, the Thai monarch in the mid-1940s was constrained by bureaucrats and politicians who controlled the state apparatus and by businessmen who ruled the market. Rama IX himself recalled the time when the palace was no longer the center of power and wealth in the Thai kingdom: "When I was young, we had nothing. The carpets and upholstery in the palace were full of holes. The floor creaked. Everything was so old. Yes, we had a piano. . . . But it was out of tune. . . . The whole palace almost crumbled. No one cared about it whatsoever."[1]

The nadir of the crown, however, did not last long. Thanks to the changing contexts of both domestic and international politics, the monarchy was revived by extraeconomic forces from the late 1940s to late 1970s. Domestically, a series of critical events unfolded in favor of the crown. In 1947, just one year after Rama IX ascended the throne, the military staged a coup d'état that toppled the civilian government. Tarnished by its cooperation with the Imperial Japanese Army during World War II, the military lacked the political legitimacy to rule and allied itself with its former political foes, who had been suppressed for a decade, the royalist nobles and politicians. Under the military-royalist partnership, the new government overruled many legal programs that the People's Party established after the overthrow of the absolute monarchy. The monarch now had royal prerogatives to both appoint and discharge the prime minister, the cabinet, and senators. The Privy Council was reestablished. A revised lèse-majesté law was promulgated, and the maximum punishment was set at seven years in prison. Further, royal ceremonies such as Brahman fertility rites associated with the royal plowing ritual (*raek na khwan*) and the celebration of the king's birthday were revived in public.[2] Most important, in 1948, under the administration of Prime Minister Khuang Aphaiwong—the founder and leader of a conservative and royalist party, the Democrat Party— the CPB was transferred from governmental authority to the monarchy's control. As the Crown Property Act of 1948 stated, the CPB's income could be "expended in any way at the king's pleasure," and its expenditures could be approved only by His Majesty.[3] The separation of the corporeal body of the king from his politico-economic bodies— the revolutionary project of the People's Party—was now reversed.

The restoration of the monarchy was taken to the next level when a new generation of military officers staged double coups in 1957 and 1958. Led by Field Marshal Sarit Thanarat, these coups ended the revolutionary era of the People's Party by expelling its key members from Thailand once and for all. They also marked the beginning of a brutal era of military despotism that lasted for fifteen years. Abrogating the constitution, dissolving the parliament, banning political parties, and suppressing all political opposition, Sarit sought a ceremonial symbol that could legitimize his dictatorial regime, and he found it in the king and the royal family. While Rama IX actively endorsed the coups and supported military rule, Sarit returned the favor by launching several campaigns that significantly restored the status of the monarchy. Royal trips to the rural hinterland and foreign countries were arranged and financed by the government in order to promote the monarchy's popularity. Royal ceremonies such as the king's presentation of degrees to university graduates (*phraratchathan parinyabat*) and his donations of new robes to Buddhist monks (*kathin phraratchathan*) were revived in public. In addition, royal projects and charities were financially supported by the government. Rama IX was granted honorary positions in the army, and several military units were transferred to serve as royal guards. The period also saw the reintroduction of the court language (*rachasap*), which emphasized the social distinction between royalty and commoners.[4] Most symbolically significant, Thailand's National Day was changed. Once having celebrated the day on which the People's Party overthrew the absolute monarchy and installed a constitutional regime, National Day was changed from June 24 to December 5, Rama IX's birthday.[5]

After Sarit's death in 1963, the monarchy seemed to be more confident that it could spread its wings in national politics without military backup. While the army still held on to despotic rule into the early 1970s, in spite of increasing frustration among civilians, the king jumped on the civilian bandwagon and started to criticize the military regime. Outraged by the army's indifference to popular democratic demands, an uprising finally broke out on October 14, 1973. Even though Rama IX had enjoyed a long and fruitful relationship with the military despots, the uprising provided an opportunity for the king to test the waters. After it was clear that the military regime was about to collapse, the king made a political move, intervening by appearing on television and announcing the formation of a new civilian government led by Sanya Dharmasakti, the first prime minister handpicked by Rama IX.[6] The withdrawal of the military from politics and public excitement over the unprecedented liberalization during 1973–76, however, seriously backfired on the monarchy. Without state censorship, intellectuals, journalists, and university students rediscovered, circulated, and discussed leftist writings that had been banned by the military regime. The most popular among them was Chit Phumisak's *The Real Face of Thai Feudalism*, the iconoclastic book that historically exposed the parasitic nature of the monarchy in Thailand's political economy.[7] This sudden resurgence of Thai radicals—plus the growing influence of the CPT among students, peasants, and workers and the triumph of the Communists in Vietnam, Laos, and Cambodia—became an imminent menace to the monarchy. Consequently, the palace needed to use violent force to protect the throne. This was the last time in Rama IX's early reign that this became necessary; nonetheless, it was the bloodiest.

Outraged by a rumor that some radical students had mocked Prince Vajiralongkorn, the king's only son, at a political gathering at Thammasat University, royalist elements launched a campaign known as "Right Kill Left." They committed one of the most violent crimes in Thai history, the massacre of university students on October 6, 1976.[8] In this bloody and gruesome event, as Katherine Bowie put it, "Some students were shot, others garroted, and yet others doused with gasoline and set ablaze."[9] The Far Right forces that participated in this brutal crackdown came from both the civil and state sectors. The civil mobilization was driven by royalist vigilante organizations: ex-convicts, former soldiers, hooligans known as the Red Gaurs (*krathing daeng*), and the paramilitary rural organization called the Village Scouts (*luksuea chaoban*).[10] The state mobilization, meanwhile, was organized by members of the Border Patrol Police and Metropolitan Police. After the crackdown, the government reported that 46 people had been killed, 180 injured, and 3,059 arrested, even though the unofficial estimates were higher.[11] Thanks to this bloody massacre, the civilian government's inability to control the political chaos and royalist hysteria among members of the Far Right, the military eventually found a way to return to national politics. Legitimizing its political intervention with the claim of restoring political order and protecting the throne, the 1976 coup makers formed a far right government led by Thanin Kraivichien, an ultraroyalist premier whom the king personally endorsed.[12] Under the new military-royalist rule, radical books were banned and burned, journals closed, and political movements outlawed.[13] Crucially, the government increased the maximum sentence for contravening lèse-majesté to fifteen years and unprecedentedly set the minimum sentence at three years.[14] Consequently, Thailand, as David Streckfuss pointed out, "is the only 'constitutional monarchy' to have increased punishment for *lèse-majesté* in the last century."[15] Barely used after the end of the absolute monarchy, the lèse-majesté law from this point on became a popular and violent means by which the military and royalists could suppress anyone they deemed a threat to the throne.

In addition to domestic politics, the reversal of royal fortunes was also shaped by global politics. In the early years of Rama IX's reign, Thailand was drawn deeply into the Cold War as the kingdom was a major ally of the United States in Southeast Asia. In the face of the penetration of communism into the region, the United States began providing economic and military aid to Thailand in the 1950s. The escalation of the Vietnam War from 1960 to 1970 made the American presence on Thai soil even more overt, since the kingdom was at the center of U.S. military operations. During the war, the United States poured US$3 billion in military and economic assistance into Thailand and sent fifty thousand servicemen there. Eighty percent of all the American air strikes over North Vietnam originated at Thai air bases. Bangkok, Pattaya, and cities near air bases were packed with bars, nightclubs, and so-called massage parlors newly created for the US soldiers' rest and relaxation tours.[16] In this period of Thai history, which Anderson called the "American Era," both the military and the monarchy appeared to be runaway beneficiaries.[17] Preferring the right-wing military rule in Thailand over left-leaning or democratic parliamentary regimes, the United States not only left the military dictatorship intact but also promoted Rama IX as a symbolic figure embodying the fight against the communist insurgency in Southeast Asia. In Thailand, the US Information Service and US Agency for International Development supported the distribution of pictures, posters, radio and television programs, and calendars that featured the king and the royal family. This promotion of royal images particularly targeted poor households in the rural provinces where communism had started to gain local support.[18] Beyond the kingdom, the United States also promoted Thai royalty's trips to several countries in what was known as the Free World. Spending the longest time in the United States and invited by his hosts to give a speech in Congress in 1960, Rama IX showed his appreciation of American patronage by stating, "We are grateful for American aid."[19] Additionally, the king called for a further collaboration between the United States and Thailand in the Cold War: "In view of the present world tension and the feeling of uncertainty apparent everywhere, it is my sincere feeling that the time is ripe for an even closer cooperation."[20]

During Rama IX's early reign, two major aspects of the relationship between the monarchy and extraeconomic coercion were notable. First, rather than staying above contentious politics as a constitutional monarchy, the monarch and the royal family actively participated in the violent acts that brought them back to power. Similarly enhancing royal prerogatives in national politics, the 1947, 1957, and 1976 coups were publicly approved and praised by the palace. The king and queen paid a personal visit to the despotic leader Sarit when he was on his deathbed.[21] After Sarit died, Rama IX not only declared an unprecedented twenty-one days of mourning in the palace but also presided at Sarit's cremation.[22] During the government campaign to fight communism, the king, queen, and crown prince donned military uniforms and frequently visited military camps in order to show their political solidarity.[23]

Likewise, after the 1976 massacre, the palace seemed to be unapologetic about the tragedy as the royal family publicly saluted right-wing forces such as the Village Scouts and the police officers who participated in the violent crackdown on students.[24] In this respect, a boundary had not yet been clearly drawn between the monarchy and violent oppression. Second, the monarchy in this period tended to passively follow the political leadership of the military and royalist movements. In other words, the monarchy was still a political puppet or at best a junior partner of the Thai ruling class during the Cold War. The crown's political agency and hegemonic status over other political actors were still works in progress in the first phase of the king's reign.

THE MONARCHY AND ECONOMIC CHANGES

When Rama IX ascended the throne, the Thai economy was hardly built on industrial capitalism. Indeed, it was anything but. In the late 1940s, agrarian goods still constituted a vital component of domestic capital; 60 percent of the kingdom's gross domestic product (GDP) came from agriculture, whereas manufacturing represented 10 percent. Among the working population, 85 percent were peasants, 2 percent were urban workers, and only 0.04, 0.06, and 0.01 percent of the whole population had private telephones, personal automobiles, and university degrees respectively.[25] Despite the founding of Thai capitalism in the mid-nineteenth century, the national economy was still underdeveloped. According to James Ingram, "There were virtually no liquid funds for capital investment, no banking system to provide such funds or to facilitate the transfer of money within the country, and little or no entrepreneurship except that supplied by foreigners and the government."[26] In short, Ingram noted, there was "not much 'progress' in the sense of an increase in the per capita income, and not much 'development' in the sense of the utilization of more capital, relative to labor, and of new techniques."[27]

Thailand's long-awaited progress and development finally came into view in the 1960s. As if Thai history was repeating itself, the Promethean force that set the national economy in motion in the second half of the twentieth century came from outside the kingdom. While it was the British Empire in the mid-nineteenth century that incorporated Siam into the global market, the external force that kicked off Thailand's industrialization in the mid-twentieth century was the global power of the United States. In addition to serving as a base for US military operations during the Vietnam War, Thailand was seen by the American government as a potential model of capitalist development for Southeast Asian countries.[28] According to U. Alexis Johnson, the American ambassador from 1958 to 1961, Thailand could serve as "a showcase in which US firms would demonstrate the benefits for economic development of openness to foreign capital."[29]

Under American patronage, the Thai economy was rapidly transformed in numerous respects. Import-substitution industrialization (ISI) was promoted by the military government with the idea that the local production of industrialized goods would become a major component of domestic capital, taking the place of agrarian goods.[30] The industrial orientation of the military regime in the American era diverged from the former major policy of promoting agrarian production and the peasantry's well-being under the leadership of the People's Party. Instead of state-led industrialization, the government took a backseat to the private sector and let it play an autonomous role in the market. In contrast to what the People's Party did, the junta promoted economic growth by supporting private sectors while minimizing the economic scale and activities of state enterprises.[31] The government also promoted foreign investment and partnerships with domestic enterprises during Thailand's nascent development of industrial capital. Attracted by Thailand's cheap labor and harsh repression of labor unions under military rule, American capitalists and their global partners, Japanese capitalists, quickly entered the Thai market.[32] Further, the government facilitated the expanding market by developing national infrastructure. With economic aid from the United States, the government constructed new highways, connected electricity, supplied tap water, and expanded landline networks in order to support American access to Thailand's provincial air bases.[33] These development programs, in turn, facilitated the extraction of national resources, brought labor from rural provinces to industrializing Bangkok, and fostered the penetration of capitalism into the hinterland.

Thailand's orientation toward industrial capitalism from the 1960s on provided an opportunity for the monarchy to play an active role in the national economy, a role that had been taken from the palace with the end of the absolute monarchy. Against the background of economic change and uncertainty, the monarch and the royal family promoted themselves as both the catalysts of national development and the saviors of those who had missed the rapid train of industrialization. Rama IX initiated several projects that focused on rural development in order to alleviate poverty among the peasantry, the class that still constituted the majority of the national population during his early reign. Inside his main residence, the Chitralada Royal Villa, the king ran experiments and conducted research on agriculture, forestry, irrigation, small-scale manufacturing, rice milling, fisheries, dairy farming, and livestock husbandry.[34] During his trips to the rural provinces where communism and poverty were prominent, he attempted to adapt his development projects to local villages. Observing a rapid shift in the national economy, the monarch expressed his concern in 1974: "If we want to only pursue progress and economic growth, without any plan that is related to the conditions of the nation and the people, there would be an imbalance in many ways. It would create problems and failures, like what happens to many civilized countries that are facing the economic crisis right now."[35] Like her husband, Queen Sirikit initiated various projects in the rural provinces. Most of them aimed to preserve ancient crafts and cultural artifacts, the precapitalist products that had drastically declined after the introduction of mass commodities from Bangkok and beyond into the countryside. The local production of handicrafts, textiles, clothing, weaving, pottery, ceramics, glass, and leather were all patronized by the queen's charitable organizations.[36] "People in rural Thailand," the queen remarked, "say they are neglected and [the king and queen] try to fill that gap by staying with them in remote areas."[37] Thanks to this symbolic role of royalty and their projects, the monarchy during Rama IX's early reign not only acted as the institution that checked the national pursuit of industrial capitalism but also partially fulfilled what the government failed to provide to the poor: social welfare and moral support. In this respect, Thai royalty seemed to embrace the role of a "welfare monarchy," a term Frank Prochaska used to describe the British monarchy and its provision of welfare to the underprivileged in industrialized Britain.[38]

This public image of royalty, nevertheless, might mislead an observer into believing that the Thai monarchy was essentially in the vanguard of anticapitalism. The crown, in reality, not only played a crucial part in but also massively benefited from Thailand's industrial development. Returned to palace control by the royalist government in 1948, the CPB was driven by the accumulation of capital and maximization of profit in the market. As Porphant Ouyyanont noted, the CPB under the management of the People's Party was run as a state enterprise, and the creation of social well-being was its primary goal. Once it was returned to crown control, however, the CPB became a corporate body.

Unrestricted by government management and unchecked by parliamentary scrutiny, it chiefly pursued the maximization of royal profits in the market.[39]

During the American era, the CPB revived the royal fortunes via its three major investment divisions: The SCG, SCB, and real estate.[40] As the virtually monopolistic producer of cement in Thailand, the SCG reaped enormous profits from the flourishing construction of national infrastructure, and its total assets escalated from 124 million baht (US$5.8 million) in the early 1950s to almost 10 billion baht (US$480 million) at the end of the 1970s.[41] As banking and finance were integral to Thailand's rapid industrialization, the SCB also thrived. Its deposits grew impressively from 557 million baht (US$26.2 million) in the early 1960s to 16.7 billion baht (US$816.5 million) in the early 1980s.[42] In the real estate market, the CPB, as the biggest landlord in the kingdom, leased its valuable plots, especially those in the commercial districts of Bangkok, to investment and financial firms, shopping malls, entertainment complexes, and luxury hotels. Besides these major investments, the CPB welcomed and prospered from its joint ventures with foreign capitalists. The most prominent among the latter were the Japanese, who had surpassed the Americans as the biggest foreign investors in Thailand by the end of the 1970s.[43] Prospering from economic growth and rapid industrialization, the monarchy embraced and facilitated instead of rejecting and hindering the penetration of global capitalism into the kingdom.

THE YOUNG KING AND SOCIAL CLASSES

In the early stage of Rama IX's reign, the palace aimed to secure support from the peasantry, the social class that constituted the majority of the population. From the 1950s through the 1970s, in spite of Thailand's orientation toward industrial development, the peasantry's proportion of the population only shrank from 82 to 70 percent of the working population.[44] In addition to its size, the peasantry also drew royal attention because of its susceptibility to communist ideology. Having seen the monarchies of Vietnam, Laos, and Cambodia crumble in the face of communist guerrillas who drew popular support from poor peasants, Thai royalty during the Cold War could not afford to neglect the peasant question.[45] The extent of the royal concern about the rural peasantry could be seen in the thousands of rural development projects Rama IX initiated from 1960 to 1980.[46] Indeed, it could also be measured by the amount of time the king spent in the countryside. That is, Rama IX visited the kingdom's rural provinces for only 5 days in 1950 and 2 in 1960. By contrast, once the threat of communism escalated in the kingdom, the king's trips to the countryside comprised 114 days in 1970 and 165 in 1980.[47] By spending four to six months a year in rural provinces during the peak of the Cold War, the monarch apparently achieved his goal since his industrious efforts were appreciated by the local populations. According to Charles Keyes, most peasants in the northeastern provinces, the poorest region of Thailand, generally held a positive attitude toward the monarchy in the Cold War era. Although these poor peasants were frustrated by local bureaucrats and politicians who exercised power without moral constraints, they revered Rama IX as the moral figure of the nation and "viewed the king as embodying benevolence, manifested in his highly publicized visits to rural areas."[48]

In spite of its primary focus on the peasant question, the monarchy did not overlook another crucial class in the kingdom, the bourgeoisie. In fact, three major components of this class—bureaucrats, businessmen, and ordinary members of the middle class—were also persuaded by the palace to create a political alliance. In his early reign, Rama IX was only able to establish a partnership with the bourgeoisie rather than leading it. Despite having restored the power and wealth of the monarchy, the military faction of the Thai bureaucracy tended to exploit royalty for its political causes, and it was not afraid to clash with the palace when the royal-military partnership did not go well. The 1948 and 1977 coups, for example, toppled the royalist governments that similarly came to power through military intervention, but they each eventually alienated high-ranking generals and contravened their interests.[49] Likewise, civilian bureaucrats apparently had not yet accepted royal leadership. According to Handley, Rama IX in his early reign remained disappointed that bureaucrats and development specialists ignored the projects he initiated and lacked any motivation to apply them on a national scale.[50]

A class of Sino-Thai businessmen, on the contrary, tended to have a healthier relationship with the palace than the bureaucrats did. From the late 1950s on, the monarchy attempted to draw wealthy businessmen into the royal network via their private donations to royal charities and development projects. In this partnership, the business elites—who had long faced an identity crisis as they were the second or third generations descended from Chinese immigrants—donated money to royal projects in order to obtain symbolic recognition and decorations from

Thai royalty. The monarch and the royal family, in turn, were able to tap private funds for use in their projects outside the constraints of state finances.[51] In addition to court society in Bangkok, the partnership between business sectors and the palace made its presence felt in the countryside. Studying the Thai ritual of the royal presentation of new robes to Buddhist monks in rural provinces, Gray argued that in the 1970s this popular ritual allowed royalty to help Sino-Thai businessmen from Bangkok who were expanding their capital investments in the hinterland. By donating money to the royal rite, these bankers and industrialists could introduce themselves and their enterprises to rural Thais and make the point that they were not immoral capitalists but sponsors of the benevolent Buddhist king. From Gray's perspective, the business elites merely took advantage of the monarchy, using it as a puppet to disguise their capitalist investments and activities. Once the class of Sino-Thai capitalists had become stronger and bigger in the 1980s, it no longer needed royal patronage and fully took over the capitalist state of Thailand.[52] In this regard, the monarchy, to Gray, was useful to the business sectors as an ideological facade only in the early stage of capitalist development, but it would become an irrelevant institution once capitalism was fully advanced in Thailand. Yet, as the later stage of Rama IX's reign unfolded, this presumption did not stand the test of time. It underestimated the ability of the crown to adapt itself to advanced capitalism.

The last group of the Thai bourgeoisie was the middle class. Thanks to a variety of socioeconomic changes that began in the 1960s—industrial development, the increase of foreign investment in the domestic market, the expansion of higher education, and the growth of service and tourist industries triggered by the American presence in Thailand—a middle class had formed and finally made its presence felt in the 1970s. Encompassing white-collar workers and salespeople, engineers and artists, and intellectuals and hotel managers, among others, the middle class might have posed a political challenge to the monarchy. While the middle class was virtually absent in former reigns, Rama IX had to deal with this prospering and well-educated group, which constituted around 10 percent of the working population in the 1970s.[53] In the early reign of the king, the crown's attempt to ally itself with this growing class had mixed results.

As the tragic 1976 massacre revealed, the middle class was not homogeneous but deeply divided into two camps: royalist and radical. According to Anderson, the withdrawal of the American military from

Thai soil, economic uncertainties, and the communist threat in Southeast Asia drove the insecure members of Thailand's middle class to rally around and protect what they perceived as the last bulwark of the nation's historical continuity and spiritual pinnacle, the monarchy.[54] Others in the middle class, in contrast, were the victims of royalist repression: radical students, journalists, and artists. Witnessing how brutal royalty and royalists could be to their disloyal compatriots, the radicals eventually turned to the political force that the palace had long battled during the Cold War, the communist guerrillas. After the massacre, the CPT was suddenly empowered by the flight of thousands of liberal and leftist youngsters into the deep forest, where the party initially welcomed and protected them.[55] The leftist mobilization and antiroyalist resentment among the young radicals would never be higher than it was in the late 1970s. In this regard, although the monarchy virtually secured the popular support of the rural peasantry, it failed to achieve the same goal when it came to those students turned guerrillas who still licked their wounds in the jungle.

ROYAL HEGEMONY IN THE AGE OF CAPITALISM

The great transformation of the monarchy began in the 1980s, and it dramatically changed the way the palace engaged with politics, the economy, and the different social classes. Contentious politics during Rama IX's early reign gradually evolved in favor of the crown once the second phase of the reign began. Communism in Thailand drastically declined in the early 1980s and was virtually extinct once the decade came to an end. In addition, the military gradually withdrew from politics as the popular demand for bourgeois democracy escalated in the early 1990s. In the face of the political winds of change, the monarchy adapted by less directly engaging in national politics. Instead of bloody violence, the crown established its hegemonic status via public discourses and put military backup aside. Thailand's economic boom from 1986 to 1996 and the economic crisis of 1997–98 also set the stage for the new role of the monarchy in the economy. The royal focus now shifted from the rural and agrarian question to the urban and industrial challenge. Royal enterprises reached new heights during the boom, and they impressively survived after the bust. Socioeconomic changes from the 1980s onward also shook the relationship between the monarchy and the different social classes. In place of the rural peasantry, popular support for the monarchy shifted its base to the urban bourgeoisie.

Establishing its hegemonic status in bourgeois democracy, prospering from bourgeois activities in the market, and widely supported by an army of bourgeois urbanites, the crown during the later phase of Rama IX's reign was transformed into a bourgeois monarchy—a novel form of monarchy that is deeply embedded in the capitalist mode of production and is able to tame the latter's prime mover, the bourgeoisie.

THE MONARCHY "ABOVE" POLITICS

At the end of Rama IX's early reign, political contexts inside and outside Thailand made the prospects of the monarchy look bleak. In 1975 communism in mainland Southeast Asia was at its peak. Saigon had fallen. The Khmer Rouge captured Phnom Penh. In Laos the six-hundred-year-old monarchy was abolished by the Pathet Lao, the crown prince was sent to and died in a so-called reeducation camp, and the king's youngest son had to escape his motherland by swimming across the Mekong River to Thailand.[56] As if it could not get any worse, the United States withdrew its military presence from Thai soil in the late 1970s due to the American defeat in Vietnam, the normalization of relations between the United States and China, and popular resentment toward the American presence in Thailand. Without American patronage, the monarchy and military had to fight the communist forces on their own. The exodus of radical youngsters into the guerrilla strongholds rubbed salt into the royal wound. Broadcasting its manifesto from the deep jungle, the CPT called the royalist-military government a regime of "fascist reactionaries" that submissively served "American imperialism, great landlords, and big capitalists." What had to be done, the CPT declared, was "eradicate the influence of imperialism and purge all remnants of feudalism" from Thailand. In 1977 the communists strongly believed that they had history on their side and thus confidently announced, "No enemies can prevail over the people's power" and "New Thailand, which belongs to the people and ensures liberty, democracy, and prosperity, will come."[57] Concurring with this projection, the US Central Intelligence Agency (CIA) station chief in Bangkok bleakly predicted that the Thai kingdom would be the next domino to fall to communism.[58]

Thai history in the last two decades of the twentieth century, however, was on the royal side. Even before the 1980s, the CPT was struggling with internal and external conflicts. Inside the party, a rift had opened between the senior vanguard and the newcomers. The former were older, Maoist, pragmatic, and tended to be more Chinese in terms of both ethnicity and cultural preference. The latter, in contrast, were younger, embracing "Thainess" despite their Chinese lineage; former university students from Thailand's best schools; and readers of Antonio Gramsci, Louis Althusser, and the Frankfurt school.[59] In addition to their different backgrounds, the two camps could not find common ground on which to confront the important questions that ultimately undermined their political cause and actions. They could not agree on exactly what Thailand's mode of production was, feudal or capitalist, and what role the monarchy played in it.[60] Political situations outside the party fanned the flames further. China, the major sponsor of the CPT, normalized its relations not only with the United States but also with Thailand. "The Machiavelli of Beijing," as Anderson put it, arranged an alliance with Thai military leaders against Vietnam—the Soviet Union's follower and China's foe—in exchange for an end to Chinese aid to the CPT.[61] Thanks to this political shift, the Thai government finally put the last nail in the CPT's coffin. During 1980–82, the government issued a series of decrees that gave amnesty to all communist insurgents who surrendered and joined in national reconciliation.

Unable to deal with both its internal and external problems, the CPT quickly declined and broke up. A mass of defectors, mostly university students who had joined the party in the late 1970s, gave up their arms and returned to Bangkok. In 1982 the *Bangkok Post* ran a big headline declaring the downfall of the communist insurgency in Thailand: "Communist Defections Gather Pace: Rebels Weakened as Amnesty Offer and Counter-insurgency Takes Its Toll on CPT."[62] Just one year later the newspaper printed a much smaller headline with a satirical tone: "From Communist Sanctuary to Hilltop Tourist Retreat."[63] Once a threat to the Thai state, the CPT now became a farce for the bourgeoisie, as the communist camps in the jungle were transformed into museums and opened to the public as tourist attractions beginning in the mid-1980s. "The End of History" and "Post-Communism," Anderson noted, seemed to happen in the Thai kingdom even before the fall of the Berlin Wall in 1989.[64]

Without the threatening presence of a communist insurgency, the right-wing forces gradually loosened their violent rule. Studying the rise and decline of the Village Scouts, Bowie revealed that this paramilitary-royalist association reached its apex in terms of membership and mobilization in the second half of the 1970s. In 1976, the same year in which the massacre of leftist students occurred, the Scouts welcomed 1,897,540 initiates and organized 2,387 mobilization sessions. During the early 1980s, however, this association became less active and drastically declined. In 1985 the number of initiates dropped to 37,820 and mobilization sessions numbered a mere 200.[65] Likewise, military oppression was on the wane in the 1980s. Besides offering amnesty to the communist defectors, the military ushered Thailand into the age of "semidemocracy." In this new order, democratic institutions—political parties, elections, and a parliamentary assembly—would be allowed to exist and develop on one condition: the premiership had to be occupied by the military. The government under the leadership of General Prem Tinsulanonda epitomized this era since he was chosen by the elected parliament to repeatedly serve as prime minister from 1980 to 1988. Late in Prem's premiership, however, political demands for full democracy grew among the bourgeoisie, and he was pressured to step down in order to give an elected civilian an opportunity to lead the country.

The military withdrawal from national politics that progressively took place in the 1980s was shortly interrupted by the 1991 coup. Toppling the first full-fledged civilian government in fifteen years, the junta was reluctant to renounce its role in politics. Its attempt to hold state power ended with a political disaster. In May 1992, a popular uprising broke out in Bangkok. With popular support and the active participation of businessmen and the middle class, the uprising was dubbed the "mobile-phone mob."[66] Faced with strong objections by the urban bourgeoisie, the military had to leave the government's building and grudgingly go back to its barracks. As Somsak Jeamteerasakul noted, the 1992 uprising marked a new phase in Thai politics. From that point on, the locus of political power was the parliament. "Whoever controls the parliament," Somsak remarked, "surely controls the state apparatus."[67] Thanks to this critical phase in the transition to parliamentary democracy in the 1990s, Thailand was widely praised as a shining "beacon of democracy" in Southeast Asia.[68]

Political changes in the last two decades of the twentieth century provided an opportunity for the monarchy to wash itself clean of bloody violence and dirty politics. Thanks to the fall of communism, the political threat to the throne was gone, and thus it was no longer compulsory for the monarch and the royal family to actively engage with right-wing mobilization. The pictures of the king and the queen donning military and Village Scout uniforms gradually disappeared from public view. As a royalist, Prem smoothed the path for the royal withdrawal from contentious politics. Under his premiership, the royal activities of a "welfare monarchy" were promoted by the government and bureaucracy. In 1981 the Office of the Royal Development Project Board (ORDPB) was founded to serve as an institution for centralized management and financial support of thousands of royal projects that had been left disorganized and overlooked by former administrations. With a strong endorsement from the government, the monarchy shifted its priority from national security to economic development, social welfare, and philanthropy. As Handley noted, government aid made Rama IX "essentially the bureaucracy's new chief of development, with the entire resources of the government to undertake operations that he alone would enjoy credit for."[69] Despite the general trend of a royal retreat from national politics, Rama IX still chose to openly intervene in two political conflicts.

The first royal intervention came in 1981 when a coup d'état was attempted by a military faction, the so-called Young Turks, who wanted to oust Prem from power. As Bangkok was quickly seized by the coup plotters, the royal family decided to stand with its loyal strongman by fleeing the capital city for a military base in a northeastern province, where Prem regrouped his forces. Lacking royal support, the Young Turks eventually failed, and their coup attempt was mocked as the "April Fools' Day Coup."[70] The failed coup may have been laughable in the public eye, but the political message that the palace sent to the young soldiers was serious. The monarchy now had its own political agency; it could act jointly with or independent of the army; and, most important, from this point on any coup would need a green light from the crown.

Another royal intervention occurred during the 1992 uprising. At the height of the violent clash between the junta and urban protesters, Rama IX appeared on television, summoned the leaders from each camp, and asked for a peaceful solution. Even though the king was skeptical of parliamentary democracy and anything but critical of the ruling junta, his intervention was interpreted by the bourgeois protesters as the king's restoration of democracy and condemnation of military violence involving civilians.[71] This event had a lasting impact on the monarchy-military partnership in the kingdom. From then on, the monarchy was no longer a political puppet of the military. Tarnished by its violent crackdown on the protesters, the military was kicked off the political stage and ostracized by the urban bourgeoisie as the last hindrance to democratization in Thailand. Instead of patronizing the palace, as it did in the Cold War era, the army now was subordinate to royal leadership. Successfully jumping on the bandwagon of the transition to bourgeois democracy, Rama IX, in contrast, was widely praised by the urban bourgeoisie as the "democratic king"—a monarch who stood above contentious politics and only undertook exceptional interventions to end a threat to parliamentary democracy.[72]

Distancing itself from the military and right-wing forces, the monarchy at the end of the twentieth century applied two informal approaches to its participation in national politics. The first was the king's speech. Instead of physical action, Rama IX now employed a "speech act," a verbal request to his primary audiences—the prime minister, the cabinet, members of the parliament, bureaucrats, and elite businessmen—to solve what he considered the critical problems of the nation, ranging from political and civil conflicts to economic and environmental crises. Rama IX's most important speech of the year was normally delivered on December 4, one day before his birthday. On this occasion, the king would review the annual performance of the government and provide both advice and criticism to audiences at the royal hall. What is remarkable about the king's birthday speech is that it was an invented tradition of Thai kingship. Only in the late reign of Rama IX did his verbal expression draw national attention.

Before the 1980s, only a few groups of Thais attended the king's birthday address, and the press barely paid attention to it. In 1972, for example, there were 909 people from 30 associations who stood before the king as he gave his birthday speech. From the 1980s on, in contrast, crowds of Thais squeezed themselves into the royal hall to listen to the king on December 4, even though his speech was broadcast nationwide on radio and television and topped the front-page headlines the next morning. To be precise, the number of audience members who attended the king's annual address massively increased from 7,028 in 1985 to 13,095 in 1995 and 21,859 in 2005. Likewise, the number of government and civil associations attending the event grew. There were 261 in 1985, 415 in 1995, and 633 in 2005.[73] While European and Japanese monarchs are constrained by their constitutions to speak to the public only with the permission of the government, Rama IX had been able not only to speak to the public as he pleased but also to use his words to influence the government. Public addresses by other members of the royal family were also widely publicized. None of them, however, drew as much national attention as the king's words.[74]

Another royal means of participating in politics was the monarchy's political proxies and networks. According to Duncan McCargo, the style of royal intervention in Thai politics was significantly transformed

after the 1992 uprising. As Rama IX grew older, he "appeared less inclined to make direct personal interventions."[75] Instead he worked
through his proxies such as the Privy Council, retired generals, senior
bureaucrats, social activists, and prominent intellectuals. McCargo
called this new royal feature a "network monarchy." Stepping down
from his premiership in 1988 and instantly appointed by Rama IX as a
privy counselor, Prem was the key broker of this political network.
During constitutional deadlocks and political crises in the late 1990s
and early 2000s, it was Prem who acted on behalf of the monarchy to
maintain political equilibrium. Lobbying behind the scenes, Prem also
played a vital role in the arrangement of the coalition government, the
promotion of generals and civilian officials, and implementation of
the king's development projects.[76]

Given that the king's proxies and networks tended to work behind the
scenes, it is possible to be skeptical of the existence of a "network monarchy" in Thailand and whether it has been as influential as McCargo
described. That skepticism, however, appeared to carry no weight after
diplomatic cables of the American ambassadors to Thailand were
leaked to the public in 2010. Thanks to WikiLeaks, it has become clear
that Thailand has its own version of a "shadow government" or a "deep
state."[77] As the cables reveal, "whispers," "calls," or "signals" from the
palace that were carried out by the king's proxies could either strengthen
or undermine the political leadership of prime ministers.[78] In this regard, at the turn of the twenty-first century, Rama IX apparently decided to stay "above" contentious politics, although all the "king's men"
still tacitly intervened in national politics in the interests of His Majesty.
Virtually gone were the dark days when the monarch and the royal
family directly and personally engaged in bloody violence.

The Monarchy and the Newly Industrialized Kingdom

After Thailand launched its industrialization program in the 1960s, the
kingdom saw an impressive rate of economic development. Its GDP
growth was at least 7 percent a year. Furthermore, during the mid-1980s
and mid-1990s, the Thai economy experienced an unprecedented boom.
Its performance was nothing short of spectacular. Its GDP growth rate
reached double digits in the late 1980s, and the World Bank reported
that between 1984 and 1994 Thailand had registered the most rapid economic expansion in the world.[79] In the mid-1980s, manufacturing eventually replaced agriculture as the major contributor to the kingdom's

GDP. In place of rice, tin, teak, and rubber, the most valuable commodities for export were industrial products such as electronics, automobiles, and mechanical appliances—all of which were virtually absent from national exports before the 1980s.[80] Following the "Four Asian Tigers"— Hong Kong, Singapore, South Korea, and Taiwan—Thailand was rapidly transformed into a newly industrialized country and dubbed the "Fifth Tiger."[81] Several factors account for this great transformation in the Thai economy.

In the early 1980s, the Thai government replaced the ISI model with labor-intensive, export-oriented industrialization (EOI).[82] This historic shift was due to the growing strength of domestic capital after two decades of industrial development. Facing the challenges of overproduction and overcapacity in the domestic domain, large Thai corporations successfully pushed the government to support their expansion into the global market. In just one decade exports of manufactured goods multiplied twelve times.[83] Beginning in the mid-1980s, as Thai capital went global, foreign direct investment (FDI) flowed massively into the domestic market. With conditions that constituted a virtual sweatshop—cheap labor, few restrictions on FDI, oppressive measures against labor movements, and weak labor unions—Thailand became a destination for multinational corporations wishing to invest their over-accumulated capital offshore. Leading the relocation of global capital were the Japanese conglomerates, which had long developed joint investments with local entrepreneurs and familiarity with the Thai bureaucracy. After Japan, the United States and the Four Tigers also played a role in the influx of FDI into the kingdom.[84] Furthermore, following the advice of the International Monetary Fund (IMF) and the World Bank advice to make the Thai economy more efficient and accessible to foreign capital, Thailand liberalized its financial system in the early 1990s. After decades under the control of oligarchic Sino-Thai bankers, the kingdom's financial market was opened to the world. Western banks and brokers set up offices in Bangkok, provided loans to local entrepreneurs, and built their presence in the rising stock market. As hot money freely and massively flowed into the financial market, technocrats and pundits confidently predicted that Bangkok would become the financial hub of Southeast Asia.[85]

Thailand's rags-to-riches story was shockingly interrupted, however, by the economic crisis of 1997. Several factors—the lack of economic transparency, the unproductive investment of foreign loans in property development and the stock market, the decline of exports, financial speculation, and the government's misstep in stubbornly protecting the currency—came together to play a role in the economic bust that triggered financial crises across the Asia-Pacific region. Pasuk Phongpaichit and Chris Baker captured the impact of the 1997 crisis in Thailand, writing, "Firms that had taken foreign loans were rendered illiquid as well as technically bankrupt. Banks that had intermediated the loans were wrecked. Creditors stopped paying their bankers. Consumers stopped spending. Over 2 million people lost their jobs."[86] To solve the crisis, the Thai government asked the IMF for help. The US$20.9 billion bailout came with a price: an austerity program, the closure of weak financial institutions, restructuring of the Thai economy, and facilitation of foreign access to it.[87] In the early 2000s, despite the fact that the Thai economy had successfully recovered and revived, the 1997 crisis had made several lasting marks on the kingdom.

First, the crisis led to a further influx of global capital into Thailand. Thanks to the weakness of Thai capital after the economic crisis, foreign corporations were able to take over or pursue mergers with local companies. The majority of manufacturing businesses were transferred to foreign ownership, and only a handful of domestic firms remained serious participants.[88] Moreover, foreign corporations industrialized the kingdom even further by promoting technology-based industries while sectors in which domestic capital still had a significant role—agriculture, resource-based industries, and labor-intensive industries—declined sharply.[89] The crisis also emasculated the two giant sectors of Thai capitalism: banking and manufacturing. After the crisis, Thai elite business groups became associated with postindustrial and service industries: information and communications technology, entertainment, retailing, and tourism.[90] Finally, the local survivors of the crisis tended to be only major capitalists while many smaller entrepreneurs had to withdraw from the national market. Within the top 150 Thai business groups in 2000, assets were heavily concentrated among only the leading 25.[91] A tendency for capital to be concentrated in the hands of the richest capitalists, as Marx predicted, clearly made its presence felt in Thailand after the economic crisis.[92]

Standing head and shoulders above national capitalists during the boom, the bust, and the recovery of the Thai economy was the monarchy. That is, royal enterprises had developed in parallel with Thailand's economic changes. During the great boom, the CPB thrived thanks to its investments in manufacturing, banking, and real estate. After decades of success under the ISI policy, the SCG diversified its enterprises by investing in various ventures—petrochemicals, paper, construction materials, steel, and electronics—and stood out as the frontrunner among Thai conglomerates that went global under the EOI policy. In addition to Southeast Asian countries, the SCG rapidly expanded its capital investments to include the United States, Mexico, and Europe. In the late 1980s, the SCG was clearly the largest industrial conglomerate not only in Thailand but also in Southeast Asia.[93] Likewise, the SCB expanded its capital reach during the boom. In the early 1990s it was one of the four largest banks in the kingdom and stood shoulder to shoulder with the elite banks of the Sino-Thai moguls. It also transformed itself from a bank into a conglomerate, as it owned subsidiary companies in asset management, real estate, warehousing, insurance, sugar, mining, construction, entertainment, and vehicle production.[94] The dividends of the SCG and SCB accounted for 60 percent of the CPB's total income, while land rentals and other subsidiary investments made up the rest. Prior to the crisis, the CPB's income was around a billion baht (US$40 million) a year, and this capitalist body of the monarchy easily overtook the Bangkok Bank as the largest conglomerate in the Thai economy.[95]

Like other Thai business groups, the CPB was severely hit by the 1997 economic crisis. Suddenly it lost 75 percent of its income. Overwhelmed by bad debts and foreign loans, the SCG and SCB paid no dividends to stockholders for five and three years respectively. Undermining the financial security of the crown, the crisis forced the CPB to borrow US$200 million and mortgage some of its estates to cover royal household expenses.[96] The royal conglomerates, in spite of this, were among a handful of survivors after the crisis. The crown's successful recovery from the economic slump, according to Porphant, was a result of two strategies.

First, unlike most Thai companies, the royal enterprises quickly responded to the crisis and adapted themselves to global capitalism. Both the SCG and SCB downsized their business empires by selling their stock in subsidiary companies and focusing instead on their major ventures. While many Sino-Thai conglomerates struggled with global capitalism because they could not abandon their traditional management style, which was based on family connections and the monopolistic control of the patriarch, the CPB was the model for modern Thai companies. It not only recruited top talent and professionals for its conglomerates, but it also separated the managing boards of directors from the owners of the enterprises.[97]

Another secret of the royal success was the special relationship between the CPB and the government. During the crisis, the government launched several programs intended to relieve the financial burdens of many Thai conglomerates, and the CPB was the top beneficiary of those programs. The SCG benefited from the government's promotion of construction and property development. The SCB enjoyed the government's provision of additional funds to recapitalize elite Thai banks. The CPB was unprecedentedly allowed to buy its own stock, which was formerly sold to the government, by using its estates as payment.[98] In this regard, it was clear that the capitalist body of the monarchy, from the government's perspective, was vital to the national economy and that the bankruptcy of royal enterprises would be disastrous for the greater economic system. In other words, the crown's business empire was too big to fail and needed special treatment by the government.

After the economic crisis, the CPB not only survived but also thrived in both domestic and international markets. In 2001 the SCG expanded its ventures into East Asia, South Asia, the Middle East, and South Africa.[99] In 2002 the CPB leased one of its best commercial estates to the Central Group for a rent of 200 million baht (US$4.5 million) annually for thirty years. The latter, in turn, used the land for the construction of CentralWorld, the nation's biggest shopping mall and one of the world's ten largest.[100] In 2004 the SCB was Thailand's most profitable commercial bank.[101] Given its outstanding performance in the industrial, banking, and real estate sectors, the crown's business empire unquestionably made a great comeback after its critical crisis.

Like the capitalist body of the crown, the corporeal body of the king adapted itself remarkably to both the economic boom and bust. Thailand's economic boom brought not only the growth of GDP but also the expansion of urban areas, a large migration of labor to industrial cities, and an increase in the urban population. In response to these socioeconomic changes, Rama IX in the late 1980s began to pay attention to the problems of rapid industrialization and unplanned urbanization. Instead of rural development and national security, the king's speeches and development projects became more associated with urgent solutions to traffic congestion, flooding and drainage, air and water pollution, and inadequate urban infrastructure.[102] Moreover, while the royal conglomerates reaped an immense fortune during the economic boom, Rama IX ironically presented himself as a moral economist in the face of a national transition to what was styled immoral capitalism. In 1991 the king addressed his concern about Thailand's relentless pursuit of capitalism. "We have enough, enough to live. We don't want to be a very advanced country," said the monarch. The economic principle of profit maximization, Rama IX clarified, should not be prioritized in Thai society. Instead, the king believed that the government should not worry about the budget deficit if it resulted in the improvement of people's well-being. "Our loss is our gain," the king reminded his subjects when the kingdom reached the peak of its economic miracle in the early 1990s.[103]

Based on this, the assumption that Rama IX was essentially anticapitalist, envisaging a welfare state for all Thais, might not be unreasonable. However, in the same speech the monarch unveiled another side of his moral economy when he touched on the problems of the welfare system in industrialized countries. "In some countries," he said, "in a large city like New York in the United States of America, public welfare money for those who are jobless amounts to millions of baht. These people don't want to work because if they do, they will not receive welfare money." On the contrary, "those who work," the king asserted, "will have their welfare money cut, even though the remuneration they got from their work could perhaps be less than what they would receive from welfare." Therefore, Rama IX concluded that Thailand should not imitate a welfare system like those that existed elsewhere: "If we follow this system, we would suffer. We would be squandering our national budget by distributing the money earned by hardworking people from whom taxes are levied, to lazybones who make it a point not to work." In place of social welfare, the monarch seemed to endorse the bourgeois ethic of hard work, ascetic sacrifice, and self-reliance. Thailand, Rama IX stressed, was different from the United States because in his kingdom "everybody works, some more some less, but everybody works."[104] In this respect, the king's speech strongly echoed what neoliberals have long advocated, the idea that "human well-being can be best advanced by liberating individual entrepreneurial freedoms and skills within an institutional framework characterized by strong private property rights, free markets, and free trade," while state intervention in markets "must be kept to a bare minimum."[105]

Rama IX's ambivalence toward capitalism was unveiled yet again when the economic crisis hit the kingdom. In 1997 the king used his birthday speech to show that his skepticism toward unbridled capitalism and consumerism had been vindicated. In the landmark address that kicked off Rama IX's widely promoted discourse, the "sufficiency economy philosophy" (SEP), the monarch reviewed the rapid transformation of the national economy during the previous decade: "Recently, so many projects have been implemented. So many factories have been built that it was thought Thailand would become a little tiger [economy], and then a big tiger. People were crazy about becoming a tiger." Having seen the economic bubble suddenly burst, he reminded his audiences, "To be a tiger is not important. The important thing for us is to have a self-supporting economy. A self-supporting economy means to have enough to survive. . . . Each village or each district must have relative self-sufficiency. Things that are produced in surplus can be sold, but should be sold in the same region."[106] In contrast to the capitalist economy that integrated Thailand into the global market, SEP promotes self-sufficient production for a local market and a moral constraint on consumerism and materialism.

Acknowledging that his economic vision might sound outdated, Rama IX admitted, "Those who like modern economics would perhaps not appreciate this [philosophy]." However, the king made it clear that "[a] careful step backwards must be taken; a return to less sophisticated methods must be made with less advanced instruments." Believing that his economic model could lead the kingdom out of the crisis, the king confidently remarked, "Thailand is a country that is blessed with self-sufficient productivity. . . . Wherever the Self-Sufficient Economy can be practiced, we can survive. We don't suffer."[107] The king's speech, as Handley noted, hit the bull's-eye in terms of the common mood among many businessmen, office employees, middle-sized entrepreneurs, and workers—all the "losers" who were fired, went bankrupt, struggled with heavy debts, and sought a solution to the crisis. Leading by example, Rama IX claimed that, unlike other monarchs, he did not lead an extravagant but rather a self-sufficient life as he normally ate, as the poorest Thai peasant did, coarse unmilled rice (*khao klong*). "I eat *khao klong* every day because it is healthy," spoke the king. "Some say it is the poor man's rice. [But] I am also a poor man."[108]

Despite his anticapitalist tone, Rama IX on several occasions clarified that his economic vision did not include promoting a return to a precapitalist economy. In the same 1997 speech, the king stated, "I have often said that a self-sufficient economy does not mean that each family must produce its own food, weave and sew its own clothes. This is going too far."[109] A year later, he defended SEP against criticism that it was backward, saying, "Perhaps I did not speak clearly enough. . . . I meant that the application of the sufficiency economy does not necessarily mean full sufficiency, and I may add that full sufficiency is impossible. If a family or even a village wants to employ the full sufficiency economy, it would be like returning to the Stone Age, to that age where humans lived in grottos or in caves." Instead of full implementation, Rama IX stressed that SEP should be partially applied in local practice. To be exact, the king explained, "50 percent sufficiency or even only 25 percent sufficiency would be enough."[110] The king also believed that SEP was not contrary to but compatible with global capitalism. "As we are in the 'globalization' era," he emphasized, "we also have to conform to the world because, if we do not comply with the existing agreements, there could be discontentment."[111] Given its ambiguity and moral tone, the king's economic model might be, as Handley put it, "at best pseudo-economics."[112] But the royal emphasis on self-sufficiency and constrained consumption could not have come at a better time, as the IMF was pushing the Thai government to implement an austerity program. As the government increased taxes, cut spending, and eliminated jobs in the public and private sectors, the king's words seemed to soothe the bourgeoisie's anxiety and helped them weather the worst economic crisis in the kingdom since the Great Depression.

The Bourgeois Alliance with the Crown

The rapid change in the Thai economy in the last two decades of the twentieth century transformed not only the mode of production but also the structure of social classes in the kingdom. Once manufacturing had decisively replaced agriculture as the most valuable component of national production, massive numbers of the working population shifted from the agrarian to the manufacturing, commercial, construction, and service sectors. In 1960 the working population in agriculture was 5.7 times greater than that of the manufacturing, commercial, construction, and service sectors together. In 1990, however, the former was merely two times greater than the latter. Eventually, in 2010, the peasantry was no longer the dominant class in Thailand; it was 1.2 times smaller than the classes that worked in the industrial economy.[113] Against the backdrop of these changes in the working population, the middle class in urban areas came into its own and grew rapidly. In 1960 the total number of professionals, administrators, managers, clerks, and salesmen made up merely 7.9 percent of the working population. In contrast, in 1990 and 2010 middle-ranking employees constituted 16.3

and 32.7 percent of the working population respectively.[114] In addition to its rapid growth, what is remarkable about the rise of the middle class in Thailand is its geographic concentration and economic power. In 2000, for example, Bangkok—the primary locus of the concentration of industrialists, businessmen, and white-collar workers—had 10.4 percent of the national population and produced 35.2 percent of GDP. In contrast, the Northeast, the poorest region, where the population was still mostly engaged in agriculture, accounted for 34.2 percent of the country's population but only 11.1 percent of GDP.[115] Besides its enormous contribution to GDP, the urban bourgeoisie made its presence felt in the realms of consumption and the adoption of modern lifestyles.

Barely existing before the economic boom, shopping malls have mushroomed in Thailand since the 1980s. While the three biggest Thai department stores—Central, Robinson, and the Mall—had merely 4 branches in total at the end of the 1970s, they opened 37 new stores from 1980 to 2000.[116] Even after the economic crisis, the bourgeois obsession with shopping did not abate. In the late 1990s Thailand became the only country in East and Southeast Asia to welcome all four giant retail corporations from Europe—Makro (Dutch), Tesco (British), Casino Group (French), and Carrefour (French)—and they instantly introduced Thais to a new type of consumption, the shopping spree in cash-and-carry and hypermarket superstores.[117] In 2006 the Big Four owned 177 stores in Thailand.[118] American and Japanese capitalists also jumped on the bandwagon of expanding Thai consumerism as they introduced convenience stores to the kingdom. Although the first twenty-four-hour convenience store opened in Thailand only in 1988, the kingdom in 2016 had 5,055 and 1,109 7-Eleven and FamilyMart stores respectively.[119] The popularity of twenty-four-hour consumption among Thais makes the kingdom the location of the world's second-largest number of convenience stores for both global franchises.[120]

Like shopping, the bourgeois culture of possessing automobiles, private telephones, and university degrees was a late but spectacular phenomenon in Thai society. Once perceived as rare and luxurious commodities, sedans, vans, and trucks became an everyday means of transportation among the bourgeoisie after Thailand industrialized. In 1960 the number of automobiles in Thailand was a mere 58,700. At the beginning of the economic boom in the 1980s, this number multiplied ten times, and once the millennium came the number of automobiles in the kingdom was a hundred times larger than it had been four decades earlier.[121] Bangkok, unquestionably, is the place where the majority of private vehicles are concentrated. At the peak of the economic boom in the late 1980s, more than 50 percent of them were in the capital city.[122]

Likewise, private telephones were no longer a privilege of the few but a mundane necessity for the bourgeoisie's businesses and lifestyles. In 1960 private telephone number subscriptions in Thailand were a mere 40,600. Beginning in 1980, the government responded to the public demand for private telephones by expanding the number of landlines and phone numbers, and by the end of the decade the number of private telephone subscriptions had reached 1 million. The introduction of mobile phones in the 1990s escalated the conspicuous consumption of the Thai bourgeoisie even further. In 2000 private telephone number subscriptions in the kingdom were a hundred times greater than they had been four decades earlier.[123]

Once the privilege of a handful of royalty and nobility, higher education also has become heavily dominated by the nouveau riche since the late 1970s. The annual number of students enrolled in and graduated from institutions of higher education in 2000, for example, was 42 and 152 times higher, respectively, than those in the same categories in 1950.[124] As a metropolis that hosts 45 percent of Thailand's colleges, universities, academies, and technological institutes, Bangkok has long been an educational destination for most Thais.[125] At the turn of the twenty-first century, there was no doubt that the multitudes of well-educated, urban, cosmopolitan, and consumerist bourgeoisie had become the most dominant class in the kingdom's economy and society.

During the late phase of Rama IX's reign, members of this flourishing bourgeoisie became mass supporters of the monarchy. Seeing the king in a business suit addressing the problems of rapid industrialization and urbanization, the nouveau riche in Bangkok started to appreciate their monarch, his works, and his vision for the Thai economy. During the economic boom, royal concerns about the problems of urban life resonated with bourgeois frustration about the government's failed urban planning initiatives. Similarly, the royal discourse on the sufficiency economy could not have come at a better time than during the critical period of the economic downturn that suddenly interrupted the bourgeoisie's long decade of capital accumulation.

In addition to his ability to calm bourgeois anxiety and insecurity amid the ebb and flow of the Thai economy, Rama IX soothed the bourgeoisie's resentments rooted in national politics. After holding a grudge against the palace for its role in state repression, radical students who joined the communist insurgency in the late 1970s gave up not only their weapons but also their antimonarchist sentiments when the government offered them a blanket amnesty in the early 1980s. Leaving the CPT behind, these former leftist students, as Anderson remarked, seemed to be enjoying a better "life after communism" than their counterparts in Southeast Asia were. Welcomed by their Sino-Thai parents, who were now wealthy members of the bourgeoisie, the defectors "returned home to join the family business, or went back to their universities, or studied abroad, mostly in Europe, America, and Australia, or decided to participate in parliamentary politics that began to take real roots in Thailand in the 1980s once the CPT was destroyed."[126] Most important, these ex-communists, as Somsak put it, eventually decided to "reconcile with the monarchy."[127] With the downfall of communism, the rise of bourgeois democracy, and the deep penetration of capitalism into Thailand, the former leftists began to view the monarchy from a new perspective. The palace was no longer a critical problem for Thailand but the last national bastion against "corrupt politicians" in the parliament, "lazy bureaucrats" in state offices, and "greedy capitalists" in the market.

The reconciliation between former leftist guerrillas and the former far right monarchy could be seen, according to Thongchai, in the dominant discourse of Thai intellectuals and social activists in nongovernmental organizations (NGOs).[128] Ignoring the wealth of the monarchy, the prominent role of royal enterprises in the market, and Rama IX's ambiguous statements about capitalism, the former leftist intellectuals and NGO activists in the 1990s strongly believed that the king's SEP should be widely acknowledged and implemented because it was compatible with their political campaign for a return to the "Thai village economy" (*setthakit chumchon*) as an antidote to western consumerism, capitalism, and imperialism.[129] By following the king's lead, they thought, all Thais could go back to living in a bucolic, agrarian, and communitarian society where capitalism had never left a mark—the primitive society that Rousseau, Marx, and Engels had mutually agreed was gone for good.[130] This romanticized and backward-looking vision of the former leftists and their willingness to follow royal discourse in the age of the "end of history" proved that the monarchy had finally achieved what seemed to be unachievable during Rama IX's early reign: the royal domestication of the radical segment of the bourgeoisie. As a result, when the twenty-first century dawned, the prospects of the monarchy could hardly have been brighter. As Somsak summed it up, the crown had successfully transformed itself from the "head of a ruling clique to the head of the ruling class."[131]

MARKET, MONEY, AND MONARCHY

How solid was royal hegemony in millennial Thailand? Answering this question should not stop at the examination of active consent to the royal leadership among the bourgeois intellectuals and activists but requires investigating further a consensus among the other two segments of the bourgeoisie: businessmen in the market and politicians and bureaucrats in the state apparatus. The examination of active consent to royal leadership among these members of the bourgeoisie, however, should not merely focus on their verbal homage to the monarchy. Doing this overlooks their material relations with the crown, relations that became stronger once the Rama IX's reign entered its later stage. Since the 1980s, wealthy businessmen had frequently visited the court, donated money and merchandise to the royal family, and appointed courtiers to the boards of directors of their conglomerates. Likewise, politicians and bureaucrats not only frequented the royal family but also financed their charitable projects annually and progressively. This phenomenon indicated that the crown in the late reign of Rama IX successfully secured popular consent from the bourgeoisie in the market and the state. With his leading status among the ruling class, Rama IX had finally achieved what previous Thai monarchs failed to accomplish in the face of capitalism: the royal accumulation of capital with popular support from a bourgeois class that might well have been expected to compete and tame the monarchy. Unlike Marx's vision of ideal conditions in capitalist society, the king, millionaires, and workers are not equal in the Thai market.[132] Splendidly eating first at the table of capital appreciation was noticeably His Majesty.

CORPORATE DONATIONS TO THE MONARCHY

Even though the tradition of private donations to royal charities was revived by the military government in Rama IX's early reign, its main features significantly changed during the late reign in various respects.[133] From the 1980s on, there was an enormous increase in the number of occasions when royalty met with businesspeople and received their donations to royal charities. As table 1 shows, Rama IX and the royal family increasingly granted audiences to businessmen during his early reign,

Table 1. Total number per decade and average number per year of
royal audiences granted to members of various business sectors,
1946–2010

Years	Total number	Average per year
1946–50	2	0.4
1951–60	15	1.5
1961–70	150	15
1971–80	379	37.9
1981–90	591	59.1
1991–2000	1,157	115.7
2001–10	1,814	181.4

Source: Data adapted from OHM, Yearbook of Royal Activities, various years.

from meeting them a couple of times a year during the 1940s and 1950s
to greeting them fifteen and thirty-eight times a year during the 1960s
and 1970s respectively. The frequency of these meetings with people
active in the private sector dramatically increased during the 1980s and
reached a new peak in the 1990s. In that decade royalty greeted capitalists in the palace at least one hundred times a year. This sharp increase
can be explained by Thailand's political and economic changes during
the late reign of the king. With the end of the Cold War, Thai royalty no
longer needed to travel to the Free World or make a rough passage to
rural provinces in order to promote themselves as the nation's fighters
against communism. Instead, they could spend more time in the palace
and welcome the crowd of capitalists and their donations in the era of
economic growth and expansion.

Moreover, in Rama IX's late reign, private donations to the monarchy were no longer accountable to the public. In the early reign of the
king, the palace usually provided information to the public regarding
not only the amount of money it received as business donations but
also the type of royal charities on which the money would be spent.
Studying business donations to the monarchy between 1960 and 1970,

Thak was able to show how much money businessmen poured into royal projects and how much of it was used in each category of royal expenditures: religion, social welfare, education, the Thai Red Cross, health care, anticommunism, disaster relief, and royal discretion.[134] Since the 1980s, however, scholars have no longer had access to the data that Thak once obtained because the palace decided to provide only two types of information about private donations: the way they would be used for royal charities (*phraratcha kuson*) and the identification of those that were subject to the king's discretion (*phrarat atthayasai*). The latter was the most popular type of donation among Thai billionaires. For example, the Chearavanont and Sophonpanich families—owners of Thailand's biggest agribusiness and financial conglomerates respectively—usually donated money to Rama IX without any specific instructions except the vague message "up to the king's discretion."[135] In this regard, a new consensus was formed among Thai businessmen when they decided to donate money to the palace in the late reign of the king. It did not matter how their money would be spent because once it was transferred to the king's hands they simply trusted the personal judgment of His Majesty. The lack of royal accountability was the price the public had to pay for the revival of the monarchy and a closer relationship between the crown and capitalists in the late reign of the king.

From the 1980s on, the monarchy also welcomed many new capitalist donors. In the face of the rapid transformation of the Thai economy, the crown remarkably continued to draw massive donations from different businesses in different eras (see appendix). In the 1960s, as western and Japanese capital was transferred to Thailand and instantly triggered national industrialization, the corporations that were the most frequent recipients of audiences with the crown included both foreign companies—Philips (Dutch), Shell (British-Dutch), United Artists (American), and National (Japanese)—and Thai enterprises such as the Bangkok Bank and SCG, the biggest bank and cement producer in the country respectively. In the 1970s, as Thai capitalists enjoyed both the technological transfers from foreign companies and the ISI policy, the most familiar faces at the royal hall were not foreign capitalists but local businessmen. In addition to the Bangkok Bank and SCG, the crown frequently welcomed millionaires and their donations from the Charoen Pokphand Group (CP), Siam Motors, and Boon Rawd Brewery, Thailand's biggest agribusiness, automobile, and brewing companies respectively. These local tycoons got richer and visited the palace even more frequently in the era of the economic boom and EOI policy in the 1980s. This decade also saw Japanese capital rapidly pouring into Thailand and Japanese conglomerates such as Toyota, Kyocera, Mitsui, and Honda paying homage to Thai royalty via private donations. In the 1990s and 2000s, although some Thai conglomerates, such as the Bangkok Bank and CP, still maintained the privilege of standing before the king, the crown also frequently welcomed donations from postindustrial enterprises such as the Shin Corporation and the Central Group, the biggest telecommunications and retail enterprises in the kingdom respectively. Despite the fact that the 1997 crisis ushered foreign capital into Thailand at the expense of domestic industries, private donations to the crown did anything but dwindle. In the 2000s the palace attracted donated money and materials from both familiar Thai firms and foreign newcomers. The latter included Microsoft (American), Nestlé (Swiss), and Cerebos (Japanese). In the millennial Thai economy, capitalists may quickly come and go. What they never fail to do, however, is frequent the palace and donate money to Thai royalty.

Further, instead of being conducted as hidden and private ceremonies at the court, private donations to the monarchy have been highly publicized and commercialized since the 1980s. In Rama IX's early reign, business sectors tended to donate their money to the palace merely for royal recognition. Private donors usually came from a small group of businessmen whose enterprises were under royal patronage, and their donations were unpublicized except in the palace's annual yearbook. The expansion of mass communications since the 1980s, however, significantly changed the traditional form of donations. In every Thai newspaper, a special section is devoted to a daily report on royal activities and charities. On television the government requires every channel to broadcast royal family news during prime time, 7:00 to 8:30 p.m.[136] The palace also provides websites and mobile applications that display current royal activities and those of the past.[137] With the mass publicity machine behind the monarchy, the act of visiting, socializing, and donating to the court became a valuable way for businesses to promote their new commodities to Thai consumers. Consequently, in the late reign of the king, the royal family often welcomed big capitalists from both inside and outside the kingdom who waited for hours in line to present not only money but also their merchandise to the palace. Instead of once in a while, it became an annual routine for Toyota, Honda, Isuzu, and Siam Motors to donate new automobiles to Thai royalty. Shin Corporation and Samsung donated the latest cellphones, Microsoft and

Apple innovative computers and software, Seiko luxury watches, Canon digital cameras, and Pernod Ricard Scotch whiskey.[138] Instead of movie stars, television celebrities, or famous athletes, the most valuable brand ambassadors for giant corporations in Thailand's expanding market seemed to be the king and members of the royal family.

Finally, in spite of the large number of representatives from different business sectors that visited the royal family in the late reign of Rama IX, royal audiences became highly concentrated among elite capitalists who normally introduced their business partners, parent companies, or subsidiary firms to court society. In the early reign of the king, small and medium-sized entrepreneurs in Bangkok still had a chance to meet and donate their money to the monarch. In turn, the palace acted, as Thak put it, as a "broker" in transforming private sector funds into state treasury or public project income.[139] In the late reign, however, both national and global capitalists pushed the petite bourgeoisie to the margins of the royal hall as the palace acted more like a broker for creating and strengthening business networks among big capitalists. From 1980 to 2010, royal audiences were highly concentrated among five giant corporations — the Bangkok Bank, CP, Shin Corporation, Toyota Motor Thailand, and the Central Group. Each of them had visited the court at least once a year. The Bangkok Bank and CP, in particular, had frequented the palace at least two times every year for three decades (table 2). Rather than visiting the royal family alone, the representatives of elite conglomerates normally entered the court with their business partners. In 2007, for example, Honda Automobile Thailand introduced its Japanese parent company, Honda Motor Company, to the king; Microsoft Thailand introduced its local partner, Hewlett-Packard Thailand; and CP introduced its numerous subsidiary companies, including 7-Eleven Thailand and True Corporation.[140] Occasionally, the "king's men," such as privy counselors or royal secretaries — some of them also serving on the boards of directors of elite enterprises — acted as introducers and moderators during the meetings between big capitalists and the royal family.[141] Besides the latest merchandise, the annual performance reviews and future projects of giant corporations — such as BMW, General Electric, and Guardian Industries — were normally presented to Rama IX, who was perceived as an experienced observer of the Thai economy.[142] On top of that, whenever a new factory, corporate building, or shopping mall was opened in the kingdom, it was the king and members of the royal family who were invited by big corporations — such as Toyota, the Central Group, and Nestlé — to preside over a grand opening and

Table 2. Frequency of royal audiences granted to five giant
corporations, 1980–2010

Year	Bangkok Bank	Charoen Pokphand	Shin Corporation	Toyota Motor Thailand	Central Group
1980s	16	7	—	11	7
1990s	29	21	19	18	10
2000s	29	36	33	19	26
Total	74	64	52	48	43
Average per year	2.46	2.13	1.73	1.6	1.43

Source: Data adapted from OHM, Yearbook of Royal Activities, various years.

ribbon-cutting ceremony.[143] In this regard, the boundaries between the monarchy and the market, the monarch and merchants, and the crown and capital became blurred.

STATE BUDGETS AND THE MONARCHY

Like their counterparts in the market, members of the bourgeois class who occupied the state apparatus were tamed by the monarchy during the late reign of the king. Once a political nemesis of royalty, bureaucrats and politicians no longer disrespected but rather supported the monarch, the royal family, the royal household, and royal development projects within the state budgets. In the early reign of the king, only two types of royal activities were financially supported by the government: hosting guests of the state and performing royal ceremonies. Both were organized by the royal household and the OHM.[144] In the late reign of the king, however, the government not only increased the funding that supported the routine activities of royalty but also unprecedentedly created two new types of budgets, which aimed to keep the king's development projects running: the budgets for royal development projects and the ORDPB (table 3). First introduced in 1993, these two types of state sponsorship sharply increased the annual budgets

Table 3. Annual budgets of the Thai monarchy, 1960–2015 (millions of baht and millions of US dollars)

Year	Royal household	OHM	Guests of the state	Development projects	ORDPB	Total
1960	40.3 (US$1.9)	0.6 (US$0.03)	—	—	—	40.9 (US$1.93)
1965	32.5 (US$1.5)	1 (US$0.05)	—	—	—	33.5 (US$1.55)
1970	46 (US$2.2)	1.6 (US$0.07)	12.5 (US$0.6)	—	—	60.1 (US$2.8)
1975	89 (US$4.4)	3.2 (US$0.15)	10 (US$0.5)	—	—	102.2 (US$5.05)
1980	141 (US$6.8)	7.8 (US$0.38)	16 (US$0.78)	—	—	164.8 (US$7.9)
1985	281.4 (US$10.4)	20.6 (US$0.76)	20 (US$0.74)	—	—	322 (US$11.9)
1990	450.4 (US$17.5)	14.6 (US$0.56)	40 (US$1.5)	—	—	505 (US$19.5)
1995	933.2 (US$37.2)	174.8 (US$7)	200 (US$7.9)	2,000 (US$79)	—	3,308 (US$131.1)
2000	1,028.3 (US$27.2)	251.2 (US$6.6)	200 (US$5.3)	2,000 (US$53)	—	3,475.9 (US$92.1)
2005	1,501.5 (US$38.5)	496.3 (US$12.7)	400 (US$10.3)	2,000 (US$51.4)	33 (US$0.85)	4,430.8 (US$113.7)
2010	2,578 (US$77)	1,190 (US$35.7)	500 (US$15)	2,300 (US$69)	83 (US$2.5)	6,651 (US$199.2)
2015	3,435.4 (US$104.5)	641.8 (US$19.5)	900 (US$27.3)	2,500 (US$76)	687.4 (US$20.9)	8,164.6 (US$248.2)

Source: Data adapted from OHM, *Yearbook of Royal Activities,* various years.

for the monarchy at the turn of the twenty-first century. While the monarchy was financed by the government at the rate of approximately US$2 million a year in the 1960s, the state budget for the crown increased a hundredfold when Rama IX reigned over his kingdom in the early 2010s.

The parliament's decision to allocate a significant part of the state budgets to royal projects was expected to arouse political resentment among bureaucrats for two reasons. First, their annual budget was proportionally cut to fulfill the new budget requirements of the monarchy, and, second, they would never see their names in lights since any achievement of theirs in national development would be overshadowed by what the monarch and his personal staff had accomplished. However, like politicians in the parliament, the bureaucrats tended to believe that the king's projects were worth every baht the government provided. In fact, since 2011 many state departments have foregone a significant part of their budget to create events and campaigns that promote the public image of the monarchy. The Ministry of Defense, army, navy, air force, Ministry of Justice, police, and Ministry of Labor all spent part of their budgets on a campaign to create the "social values of revering, protecting, and preserving the monarchy." The office of the prime minister and the Ministry of the Interior, meanwhile, added to that campaign another one, "empowering the grassroots economy by applying sufficiency economy philosophy."[145] What seemed to be gone for good in the Thai kingdom were those rebellious segments of the bourgeoisie—the bureaucrats and politicians who dared to challenge royal prerogatives and tame the monarchy under a bourgeois constitution.

THE UNQUESTIONABLE WEALTH OF THE UNQUESTIONABLE

In addition to private donations and state sponsorship, Thai royalty personally accumulated wealth in the stock market. According to the stock exchange of Thailand, Rama IX was the shareholder of significant percentages of the stock of several companies in different business sectors: Thai Insurance (22.91 percent) in insurance, Sammakorn (8.26 percent) in property development, Minor International (2.19 percent) in food and beverages, Amarin Printing and Publishing (1.58 percent) in media, and Singer Thailand (0.51 percent) in manufacturing and commerce.[146] In 2016 the king's stocks in those enterprises could have been sold for 171.3 million baht (US$4.7 million), 125.4 million baht (US$3.4 million), 3.81 billion baht (US$105.6 million), 26.9 million baht (US$0.7 million), and 14.3 million baht (US$0.4 million) respectively. Like her father, Princess Sirindhorn holds stocks in Thai Insurance (1.39 percent), Sammakorn (1.61 percent), and Amarin Printing and Publishing (0.63 percent), and their market values in 2016 were 33.3 million baht (US$0.9 million), 10.6 million baht (US$0.3 million), and 7.7 million baht (US$0.2 million), respectively.[147] Additionally, the princess is the major shareholder of Siam Piwat (25 percent), a retailing and development company that manages five shopping malls in Bangkok: Siam Center, Siam Discovery, Paradise Park, Icon Siam, and Siam Paragon.[148] The last one is the third-largest shopping mall in the kingdom but the first in terms of energy consumption. It consumes, as one report revealed, "nearly twice as much power annually as all of Thailand's underdeveloped Mae Hong Son province, home to about 250,000 people."[149] In 2010, the princess's share in Siam Piwat's net income amounted to 145 million baht (US$4.7 million).[150] In this regard, in the stock market— a place where money is "thrown into circulation as capital without any material basis in commodities or productive activity"—Thai royalty are clearly the frontrunners in the accumulation of what Marx called "fictitious capital."[151] Similar headlines from Bloomberg in 2007 and CNN in 2010 said it best: "Thai King Strengthens Grip on Stocks as Nation's No. 1 Investor."[152]

The wealth of the Thai monarchy, nevertheless, goes beyond royalty's personal investments in the stock market. Above all, the major source of royal wealth comes from the CPB's investments in land, banking, and manufacturing. As the landlord of the most valuable properties in Bangkok, the owner of one of the largest banks in the kingdom, and the owner of the biggest industrial conglomerate in Southeast Asia, the CPB had a net worth of US$27.4 billion in 2005.[153] Confirming the spectacular wealth of the Thai crown, *Forbes* crowned Rama IX the world's richest royal in 2008 thanks to his estimated fortune of US$30 billion.[154] In the rankings of the richest royals in 2009, 2010, and 2011, no royals on earth could dethrone the Thai monarch. In 2011 the "constitutional" monarch of Thailand was 66 and 150 times wealthier than Queen Elizabeth II of Britain and Queen Beatrix of the Netherlands, respectively. Even the assets of absolute monarchs and oil-rich royals in Brunei and the Middle East were easily outranked by the Thai king's accumulated capital.[155] If Rama IX had been included in the ranks of the world's richest (nonroyal) billionaires in 2011, he would have finished in sixth place, after magnates like Bill Gates and Warren Buffet but standing above members of affluent families in America such as the Waltons and Kochs.[156] Inside the Thai kingdom the king outranked the richest magnates, Dhanin Chearavanont of CP, Chaleo Yoovidhya of Red Bull, and Charoen Sirivadhanabhakdi of ThaiBev, whose total personal assets in 2011 were US$7.4 billion, US$5.0 billion, and US$4.8 billion respectively.[157]

Consistently keeping Rama IX at the top of its ranks of the world's richest royals, *Forbes* rubbed the Thai government the wrong way. Just two days after the magazine published its 2008 ranking, the Ministry of Foreign Affairs released an official statement that refuted the report on the wealth of the Thai monarch. According to the statement, the information that *Forbes* published about Rama IX was "a distortion of the fact" because its estimation of his wealth was based on the total assets of the CPB, which, "in fact, are not the private property of the king but the property of all the Thai people in the nation."[158] The government, however, did not tell the whole truth about the CPB and its problematic status in the Thai state. Even though the Crown Property Act of 1948 proclaimed the separation of the CPB from the king's private property, this act also stated that the use of the CPB's resources and income "can be expended in any way at the king's pleasure."[159] Moreover, whenever the CPB has faced legal disputes with private citizens, the Council of State has persistently provided ambiguous verdicts regarding the bureau's official status. On four different occasions, the council defined the CPB differently. It was categorized as a private company in 1975, a government department in 1990, a state enterprise in 1993, and most recently "a unit of the state" (*nuai-ngan khong rat*) in 2001.[160]

Seeking maximum profits for royalty instead of the public good while being totally exempt from taxation, the CPB is indeed a problematic institution that is legally protected like a state enterprise while relentlessly accumulating wealth like a private company. Unlike its counterpart in Britain, the CPB is not accountable to the parliament, as its annual report is made exclusively to the monarch and its annual revenues are not transferred to the state treasury for the benefit of the nation.[161] Rather than questioning the dubious status of this institution, members of the Thai bourgeoisie in the parliament, the government, and the market mutually consent to the crown and its special means of capital accumulation. As the Council of State made clear in its 2001 verdict on the status of the CPB, any investigation into the bureau's wealth "must consider the special status of the CPB," and the investigation should "rest upon royal discretion and should not bother His Majesty." People, the council warned, "should not pursue any investigation that disturbs the royal prerogatives since the monarchy holds its revered status, which cannot be insulted."[162] In other words, the royal accumulation of capital, on whose threshold there virtually hung the notice "No admittance except on business with royalty," has been widely accepted by the Thai bourgeoisie as an institution that should be highly respected and left intact.

CONCLUSION

In the kingdom of Thailand, there has been a novel form of monarchy. Since the 1980s, the Thai monarchy has embodied and embraced bourgeois activities, ethics, and appearances. Prior to that, the crown was closely associated with the extraeconomic forces of the military and royalists. The revival of its power, wealth, and prestige depended on violent coercion, and its symbolic role in fighting communism and rural underdevelopment was the royal priority. Thailand's political economy after the 1980s, however, provided a great opportunity for the monarchy to dramatically remake itself. With the rise of parliamentary democracy, the crown distanced itself from violent forces, jumped on the bandwagon of democratization, and informally intervened in national politics via its proxies and networks. Thanks to the economic boom, the crown enjoyed its accumulation of capital, its joint ventures with bourgeois enterprises, and its business connections, which were cultivated through corporate donations to royal projects. Instead of a hindrance, the economic crisis allowed the monarch to guide his subjects and show them how his personal ethic of hard work, self-reliance, and austerity could soothe and solve the bourgeoisie's anxiety and bankruptcy. The shift of the king's focus from the Cold War's agendas to the contemporary problems of rapid industrialization and unplanned urbanization even made the monarch a popular figure among members of the bourgeois class. Armed with royal hegemony over bourgeois democracy, enormous wealth from the capitalist market, and the active consent of elite businessmen, bureaucrats, and the middle class, the crown during the late reign of Rama IX transformed itself into a new form of monarchy, one that not only survives but thrives in a kingdom where industrial capitalism prevails. It is the "bourgeois monarchy" proper.

 **3**

THE KING AND (BOURGEOIS) EYES

On December 11, 2015, the streets of Bangkok were packed with hundreds of thousands of energetic urbanites all dressed in yellow. In contrast to the so-called Yellow Shirt movement of a few years before, during which political activities were punctuated by the seizure of Thailand's international airports, government offices, and parliament buildings, this new yellow mob did not gather on the streets to protest or voice their political demands. Riding their trendy bicycles from their homes, these urbanites were instead eager to participate in the country's biggest event of the year, a tribute to the then reigning monarch, King Rama IX, whom they commonly called "Dad." Presided over by Prince Vajiralongkorn, the heir apparent to the throne at that time, this collective action of mass biking aimed not only to promote a healthy lifestyle for all Thais but also to give Thai subjects an opportunity to show their loyalty to both the monarchy and the eighty-eight-year-old monarch, whose birthday had passed just a few days before.[1] Although the name of this event was not as extravagant as the government's expenditures for it, it perfectly captured the purpose of the celebration in three simple words: "Bike for Dad."

Since yellow was recognized by Thais as the symbolic color of Rama IX, not only did the bikers in this event dress in it but the streets, government offices, and businesses in Bangkok were also widely decorated with flags, Chinese lanterns, arches, and billboards, all in yellow.[2] Starting at the Royal Plaza and snaking through most of the urban and commercial districts of Bangkok, the eighteen-mile parade of bikers was strictly arranged. The crown prince and other members of the royal family led the pack, followed by the prime minister, military officers, senior bureaucrats, politicians, businesspeople, celebrities, and commoners, respectively. Along the yellow pageant's route, thousands of urbanites waved the national and royal flags while shouting "Long live the King!" Some even prostrated themselves and were moved to tears as the biking royals passed. The massive turnout of Thai people for this event was considered an accomplishment of the prince's.[3] Four months before, he had led a mass of bikers around the capital city in order to pay tribute to his mother, Queen Sirikit, in a similar public spectacle called "Bike for Mom."[4] These two events not only showed the enduring popularity of the monarchy in Thailand, especially among the urban middle class, but they also reaffirmed the observation of a French visitor to the country more than two centuries previously, when foreigners still called it the Kingdom of Siam. "In the Indies," he asserted, "there is no state that is more monarchical than Siam."[5]

The popularity of the Thai monarchy is even more remarkable if we see how some images and products that were associated with Rama IX were widely commodified in the mass market in the millennial era. *The Story of Thongdaeng*, for example, is the biography of a female stray dog adopted by Rama IX. Penned by the monarch, it was published in 2002 and became the national best seller of the year.[6] It was adapted as a comic book two years later and then an animated film released in 2015.[7] Likewise, when Rama IX finally appeared on November 2007 after a long period of seclusion due to illness, the appearance of the recovering king sporting a pink blazer set a trend in the retail apparel industry in the Thai kingdom. In addition to the previously ubiquitous yellow polo shirts, pink ones, too, became the hot retail items of the year.[8] Not even the biggest celebrities and fashion moguls in the country could rock the industry the way "the king's new clothes" did.

What makes the monarchy so popular in Thailand? Contemporary scholars cite religious beliefs deeply embedded in Thai society for centuries—a combination of Buddhism, Hinduism, and animism—as the main forces that not only elevate the monarchy above other social and political institutions but also connect the palace to the mass of the Thai people.[9] Since during his seven-decade reign Rama IX successfully played a role that fitted those religious beliefs, it is understandable that the monarchy is still relevant, revered, and even worshipped by the 68 million Thais, 95 percent of whom are officially Buddhist.[10]

This train of thought, however, treats Thailand as if it were an ancient society forever trapped in the feudal past. It overlooks the way the kingdom has rapidly changed into a capitalist society in recent decades and how bourgeois ideology—instead of religious beliefs embedded in the kingdom for centuries—plays a significant role in the relationship between the monarch and the masses. Going against the grain, we must look at the Thai crown through a new lens. The primary reason for the monarchy's popularity among many Thais, especially those in the urban bourgeoisie, is the institution's successful rebranding of itself by embracing ideological values and images that are well suited to the kingdom's transition to capitalism. What makes the bourgeoisie obsessed with the monarchy, therefore, is not simply ancient beliefs in Buddhism, Hinduism, and animism among Thai people generally. In fact, the nouveau riche in millennial Thailand perceived Rama IX less as a divine and religious figure and more as a beloved and ordinary father figure who embraced the bourgeois ethic of hard work, frugality, prudence, and self-reliance. The rising class also promoted this particular ideology just as global capitalism was finally making a deep impact on Thailand at the turn of the twenty-first century.

During the seven decades of Rama IX's reign, Thai royalty had drastically changed their public image. They went through an experimental process of reinventing, rebranding, and reconstructing the visual presentation of their bodies, manners, and costumes in the mass media. In other words, under the long reign of Rama IX, the corporeal bodies of royalty had become the battlefield of ideological production, contention, and reproduction for the Thai monarchy. From the mid-1940s to the late 1970s, Thailand was still deeply engaged in the Cold War; industrial capitalism had just been introduced, and the formation of the bourgeois class was still in a nascent stage. Against this background of the early reign of the king, the palace promoted Rama IX in public using three major themes: the religious king, the cosmopolitan king, and the warrior-king. However, from the 1980s onward, with the rapid transformation of Thailand into a newly industrialized country and the rise of the urban bourgeoisie, royal presentation in the late reign dramatically changed. It was now based on three new themes: the developer king, the economist king, and the jubilant king.

The new images of royalty, however, were not single-handedly constructed by the crown. In fact, the urban middle-class and business sectors had been actively engaged in popularizing royal images. The masses of the bourgeoisie in the market, nonetheless, were not a passive audience; they interpreted and reproduced royal images in their own way. Barely seeing how the monarchy and its images were relevant to their economic activities in the early reign of the king, the bourgeoisie changed its perceptions of the crown in the later period. Facing the ebbs and flows of Thailand's rapid transition to industrial capitalism in the last two decades of the twentieth century, they began to appreciate the monarchy. They selectively memorialized and glorified those royal images that were compatible with their class ideology, creating their own versions of royal discourse. These could be divided into four themes: the hardworking king, the frugal king, the father king, and the cosmopolitan king. Like their counterparts in the market, members of the bourgeoisie who occupied the state apparatus—bureaucrats and politicians—were attracted to royal images only during the late reign of the king. They responded to only those images that were associated with their class ethic of hard work, parsimony, and meritocracy. In light of this phenomenon, which had just emerged in Thai society in the late twentieth century, the popularity of the Thai monarchy should not be regarded simply as a byproduct of religious zeal embedded in the ancient kingdom but as a recent and invented construct in newly industrialized Thailand, the symbiosis between the rebranded images of the palace and bourgeois ideology.

THAI ROYALTY THROUGH THE LOOKING GLASS

Rama IX was born on December 5, 1927, in a Cambridge, Massachusetts, hospital while his father studied medicine at Harvard University. Spending his early years in Brookline, a prosperous suburb of Boston, he moved with his mother, sister, and brother to Lausanne, Switzerland, after his father's death. Growing up in the bourgeois environment of Europe before World War II, Rama IX was a renaissance man.

According to Handley, the king "studied French, Latin, and German instead of Thai and Pali, the language of Buddhism." When he was young, he "spoke Thai with a slight foreign accent" and spoke French with his brother.[11] Majoring in French literature, Latin, and Greek in high school, Rama IX studied political science, government, and law at the University of Lausanne.[12] While his western education was noteworthy, his cultural upbringing was as elegant as any bourgeois in Europe could ask for. Jazz music, motorsports, skiing, ice hockey, abstract painting, photography, and sailing were his leisure pursuits. Among these hobbies, jazz was his favorite. With a talent for playing clarinet, trumpet, piano, piccolo, and saxophone, the king formed a jazz band in Lausanne, which was, as *Life* magazine reported, "probably the most intricately gadgeted orchestra in Europe."[13] Jazz also led the young monarch to meet his future wife and queen. Studying at a music academy in Paris, Sirikit, a royal herself and a fan of Beethoven and Mozart, drew His Majesty's attention when she dared to disagree with his taste in bebop the first time they met.[14] They may have had a rocky start, but their relationship eventually ended with romantic love and a royal engagement celebration at Switzerland's Windsor Hotel.[15]

This kind of luxury and bourgeois lifestyle, however, had to be adjusted when the king left Europe and returned to the Thai kingdom permanently. Since the reputation of the monarchy had been tarnished by the 1932 revolutionaries, who publicly criticized the idle, spendthrift, and selfish lifestyle of royalty, Rama IX and his courtiers faced the uphill task of bringing royal prestige and dignity back into popular consciousness. To do so, the palace needed to develop a new visual presentation of the young sovereign of the Thai kingdom. As Susan Buck-Morss points out, the visual image of a sovereign figure is instrumental in creating political legitimacy in a modern state: "The sovereign figure as personification of the collective demonstrates the power of the visible image to close the circle between constituting and constituted power. . . . The closing of the circle demands a miracle, and the icon of the sovereign figure provides it."[16] In this section, I examine how the Thai monarchy performed its task of presenting Rama IX as a sovereign figure who could bridge the gap between the collective of Thais and their abstract idea of the Thai nation. This examination of the palace's economy of images—its construction, branding, and rebranding of images associated with Rama IX and the royal family—is divided into two subsections according to the two periods of Rama IX's reign: the early period (1946–80) and the late one (1981–2016). This historical categorization is

crucial for an understanding of how royal images, instead of being permanent and static, were dramatically transformed over time. Since the
royal images discussed here were primarily selected from the *Yearbook
of Royal Activities* published annually by the OHM, we should get a
glimpse of how Thai courtiers, to use Buck-Morss's terms, acted as
"image managers" or "iconocrats" by popularizing the public image of
Rama IX as the sovereign of the Thai kingdom.

EARLY IMAGES OF THE KING

The royal images that the palace promoted during Rama IX's early
reign can be categorized under three themes: the spiritual king, the cosmopolitan king, and the warrior-king. Realizing that the portrait of
Thai monarchs as the carriers of western modernity, high culture, and
conspicuous consumption to Thai society did not widely resonate with
the populace, when Rama IX returned from Switzerland to be officially
crowned in 1950 the palace returned to its roots by portraying him as
the spiritual head of the kingdom. On his return to Thailand, the young
monarch was tutored in courtly etiquette and archaic royal languages.[17]
Once he landed, the king had to attend the three biggest royal ceremonials of that year: the coronation, his royal wedding to Sirikit, and the
cremation of his brother, Rama VIII. These events were saturated with
costumes and mystical rituals performed by the court's Brahmins. At
the coronation, Rama IX was dressed in full regalia, with a white robe
and a gold-trimmed cloth over his body, the "Great Crown of Victory"
over his head, and the "Sword of Victory" in his hand. He was displayed to the public as *devaraja*, in accordance with religious belief in
Thailand that the monarch is a Hindu god named Rama, an avatar of
the god Vishnu (figure 1).[18] This over-the-top spectacle was a crucial
strategy of the palace. Formally addressing their monarch as "the excel-
lent feet of the supreme Lord above my head" or "May the power of the
dust on the soles and the dust under the soles of your royal feet protect
my head and the top of my head," all Thai commoners needed to be
reminded that their lord had returned from the West to claim his
kingdom.[19]

Devaraja, however, was not enough for the visual presentation of
Rama IX as the spiritual king. While Brahmanism is influential in the
Thai court, Buddhism is more popular among Thai commoners. As a
result, to revive a religious base among these commoners, the palace
also needed to depict the young monarch as *dharmaraja*, the Buddhist

Figure 1. King Rama IX as *devaraja*. The coronation of Rama IX took place at the Grand Palace on May 5, 1950. (Photo from OHM)

Figure 2. King Rama IX as *dharmaraja*. Rama IX entered Buddhist monkhood from October
22 to November 5, 1956. (Photo from OHM)

king who practices the ten kingly virtues of munificence, moral living,
generosity, justice, compassion, absence of bad ambition, suppression
of anger, nonoppressiveness, humility, and upholding dharma.[20] In
1956 Rama IX followed a religious tradition that Thai men normally
undertake by entering Buddhist monkhood for fifteen days at a Bangkok
temple. During this time, instead of a mystic godlike monarch in the
Hindu tradition, Rama IX appeared in public simply as an ordinary
monk with his head shaved and his body clothed in saffron robes (figure 2). Every day he made his morning alms rounds, walked the streets
barefoot, and received offerings from ordinary people. As one observer
described it, "He was just one among many thousands of monks performing the same simple, age-old ritual in the capital."[21]

This theme of the spiritual king, however, was constrained in the 1950s by the government of Field Marshal Plaek, a key member of the People's Party and the prime minister who tried to block the revival of the monarchy. The fortunes of the crown would be reversed when Field Marshal Sarit staged double coups in the late 1950s, which not only ousted an elected government but also marked the beginning of the age of military despotism in Thai politics. Unlike Plaek, Sarit was not a member of the People's Party and had no antimonarchist sentiments. Instead, as a staunch royalist, Sarit supported the publicity that depicted Rama IX as the spiritual king by restoring several royal ceremonies that had been abolished in former reigns.[22] On top of that, he also endorsed the public images of the young monarch as the cosmopolitan sovereign by authorizing the king and queen's official visits to several countries in the early 1960s. Taking over state power in the critical period when the Vietnam War and the communist threat in the region were beginning to escalate, Sarit received strong financial and military aid from the United States.[23] As a result, among the countries that were included in the royal "World Tour," there was no better place for the king and queen of Thailand to spend most of their time and show their political position than in the United States. The only monarch who was ever born in America, Rama IX seemed to have an emotional attachment to this republic. "I was born here in this country," the king remarked when he landed, "so I can say that the United States is half my motherland."[24]

In America the king and queen were free to be themselves again, and they showed the public how well they embodied western bourgeois culture. A meeting between Rama IX and President Dwight Eisenhower at the White House attracted a lot of attention from Thais as their monarch was warmly welcomed by the American leader. Nonetheless, it was the royal blending with American culture that cemented the public image of Thai royalty as cosmopolitan figures. During this 1960 tour, the king and queen met Elvis Presley on the set of *G.I. Blues*, toured Paramount Pictures studios, traveled with their children to Disneyland escorted by Walt Disney himself, visited the IBM Corporation, marched in downtown Manhattan in a ticker tape parade to City Hall, partied at night with New York governor Nelson Rockefeller, and paid a visit to Benny Goodman's apartment, where Rama IX participated in a two-hour jam session with Goodman and other top jazz musicians (figure 3). While the king, with his suit, tie, and sunglasses, looked calm and cool when he met American celebrities, the queen was

Figure 3. The "King of Jazz." Rama IX (*right*) in a jam session with Benny Goodman (*left*) in New York City, July 4, 1960. (Photo from OHM)

celebrated by the American media because of her youth, beauty, and taste in colorful and fashionable dress.[25] By the time the Thai royals finished their World Tour of fifteen countries in seven months, the king was being called the "King of Jazz" by the western media, while the queen was included among "the world's ten best-dressed women" and dubbed "Asia's Jackie Kennedy."[26]

Developed in the 1960s but flourishing in the 1970s, the warrior-king is the last theme of royalty's presentation during Rama IX's early reign. As Thailand became more involved in the Vietnam War, both the Thai and American governments shared an idea that the Thai monarch should be promoted as a symbolic figure fighting the communist threat in Southeast Asia.[27] Therefore, in addition to cultivating a cosmopolitan look, Rama IX also donned a military uniform as the commander in chief of the Thai army when he officially visited the Free World. Moreover, in the late 1960s, the palace started to downplay the public image of Rama IX as a man of leisure while promoting him more as the guardian of the nation in the fight against the communist insurgency. Instead of pictures of Rama IX playing the saxophone, painting an expressionist portrait, sailing a boat on a sunny day, or smoking Lucky Strikes while enjoying his leisure time, the palace turned to portraits of the king,

Figure 4. Battle royal. Rama IX visited a military camp and tested assault rifles on May 12, 1970. (Photo from OHM)

queen, and crown prince in battle dress with assault rifles in their hands visiting rural provinces where communist guerillas had started to gain the political support of local Thais (figure 4).

Moreover, as the right-wing paramilitary movement called the Village Scouts emerged in the 1970s to fight the communist insurgency in the kingdom, pictures of royalty in Scout uniforms were also widely circulated (figure 5). Although the Village Scouts played a crucial role in the massacre of Thai leftist students in 1976, the visual presentation of the king and queen as the patrons of this violent movement was still continually promoted by the palace in the late 1970s and early 1980s. In this regard, the palace brought the king back to his roots because the term *king* in Thai history was originally associated with the monarch's "martial prowess, and his ability to discern skilled warriors, build camaraderie, and inspire their loyalty."[28]

Although the visual presentation of Rama IX in the early stage of his reign was based on the ancient themes of Thai kingship, what evidently

Figure 5. The patron of the Right. Rama IX presiding over a Village Scout ceremony on December 11, 1971. (Photo from OHM)

had been absent from the royal publicity during that time was a depiction of the monarch as a merchant-king, a visual theme that was prevalent in the age of Thai feudalism. But it looked as though the palace had learned from its past mistakes; a visual presentation of the king as a wealthy, proliferate, and extravagant person could have alienated the masses. As a result, although the business successes of the capitalist body of the monarchy during Thailand's transition to industrial capitalism made Rama IX a wealthy king, the public images of the corporeal bodies of the king and the royal family told a different story. It was a series of new images during the later phase of Rama IX's reign that were instrumental in distracting the crowd from an awareness of the fortune of the wealthiest crown on earth.

THE KING'S NEW CLOTHES

Even though the visual themes of the spiritual king, the cosmopolitan king, and the warrior-king would still be promoted by the palace in the later phase of Rama IX's reign, they were gradually played down and taken over by three new themes in the 1980s and afterward: the developer king, the economist king, and the jubilant king. Initiating thousands of development projects from the 1960s on in order to improve the living conditions of poor peasants, who tended to be drawn to communist ideology, Rama IX not only visited rural areas but also tried to apply his projects to the local environment. However, the king in his early reign was disappointed by bureaucrats and politicians because they did not take his development projects seriously.[29]

A turning point came with the emergence of Rama IX's right-hand man, General Prem. Occupying the premier's office from 1980 to 1988, Prem pushed the government to consider the king's projects as a model of national development. During this critical period, the king's images were also dramatically transformed. Rama IX began to wear reading glasses in public, which made him look more serious and intelligent, rather than the dark sunglasses that formerly had made him look "cool." Instead of battle dress, the king frequently donned a business suit and armed himself with his iconic "development gear." In place of an assault rifle, his hands were now filled with a map, a pencil, and a walkie-talkie, and a camera was normally slung around his neck (figure 6). Most important, the visual presentation of Rama IX in this period was usually highlighted by beads of sweat trickling down his face as he worked on his development projects (figure 7). According to Irene Stengs, each attribute of the monarch's new look has its own connotation. A camera signified his documentation of Thai subjects, a pencil his note of their suffering, a map his knowledge of their geography, beads of sweat how hard he toiled for them, and a walkie-talkie how remote and wild were the trips that took him from the capital city.[30]

The second theme promoted by the palace from the 1980s onward was that of the economist king. In Thai history, the economy was usually

Figure 6. The monarch's new look. Rama IX as the developer king (c. 1980) who always carried a pencil, a map, a walkie-talkie, and a camera when visiting provincial Thailand. (Photo from OHM)

Figure 7. The sweat of the king. The iconic picture of Rama IX (c. 1985) showing beads of sweat trickling down his face as he worked on his development projects. (Photo from OHM)

the Achilles heel of the king, and the three monarchs who reigned before Rama IX were no exception. Rama VI faced a rebellion led by young bureaucrats who resented his prodigal spending on new palaces and Shakespeare plays while his kingdom was in financial debt and crisis. Making teaching economics in school a crime, Rama VII was afraid that modern knowledge about the economy would instantly create class consciousness among his subjects. Nonetheless, the last absolute monarch of Siam was eventually forced to surrender to the 1932 revolutionaries as he was unable to solve the economic crisis of the kingdom triggered by the Great Depression. Living mostly in Europe, Rama VIII never touched economic policies, which were dominated and steered by the military, bureaucrats, and politicians in his home country.

In this regard, the new depiction of Rama IX as an economic expert was groundbreaking. Although Rama IX had expressed some of his anticapitalist sentiments long before the 1990s, his thoughts on capitalism were extensively promoted by the palace when the national economy, which had boomed from the mid-1980s to the mid-1990s, suddenly crashed in 1997. Rama IX's fragmented, ambiguous, and romantic visions of the Thai economy—a retreat to a bucolic, static, and self-reliant village economy in the age of global capitalism—were repackaged by the palace as the SEP and promoted as an alternative to the nation's pursuit of industrial capitalism. Seeing this philosophy as well suited to all Thais, especially after the economic crisis hit, the king led by example. Unlike other monarchs of the Chakri dynasty, Rama IX did not live in the Grand Palace, a complex of buildings, halls, pavilions, and courtyards at the heart of Bangkok, which was perceived as the center of Thai kingship and Buddhist-Brahmin cosmology. Instead the king resided at the less extravagant palace called the Chitralada Royal Villa, which is composed of a two-story building, farmhouses, paddy fields, and fish ponds. This residence was promoted in public not as a palace per se but as a "working base" where the royal philosophy of a village economy was being enacted.[31] Instead of an extravagant and prodigal monarch, Rama IX as the economist king was displayed as if he were an ordinary farmer who practiced his philosophy of a sufficiency economy by growing his own rice, milking his own cows, and farming his own fisheries.

The jubilant king is the last theme that was developed and attached to the visual presentation of Rama IX as his reign surpassed several milestones in the late 1980s. In 1988 he became the longest-reigning monarch in Thai history and was given the title "King Bhumibol the Great."[32] Previously, only six monarchs in the seven centuries of Thai kingship had been called "Great."[33] Besides the national celebration held that year, the golden and diamond jubilees were the biggest national events of 1996 and 2006 respectively. State ceremonies were also arranged to celebrate each milestone of Rama IX's age in accordance with a popular belief in the twelve-year cycle of the Chinese zodiac in Thailand. Consequently, his sixtieth, seventy-second, and eighty-fourth birthdays were celebrated nationwide in 1987, 1999, and 2011. In addition to titles, medals, and awards from foreign governments, Rama IX received numerous honorable doctorates in his late reign from both Thai and international universities. Those degrees were varied in terms of their disciplines: from science to economics, political science to the arts, and dentistry to engineering. In these ceremonies, which celebrated the historic reign of Rama IX, although the king dressed in full regalia, a military uniform, or a business suit interchangeably, the connotations of each costume were different from those of the past.

Rather than mysteriously hidden in the court and surrounded by Brahmins, Rama IX dressed in full regalia to greet thousands of his subjects shouting "Long live the King!" outside the palace. Instead of a right-wing fighter against communism, the king wore a military uniform as the supreme commander to welcome presidents and monarchs from other countries who came to celebrate his historic reign. Critically, from the late 1990s on, Rama IX seldom traveled to rural provinces or visited his development projects in remote regions but often stayed in either his palace or Siriraj Hospital in the capital city thanks to both the end of the Cold War and his ailing body. As a result, rather than arming himself with military gear suited to the rough weather and environment of rural provinces, Rama IX in the twenty-first century donned a suit, carried a walking stick, and stayed in either the air-conditioned court or the quarantined hospital to welcome guests of the state, politicians, privy counselors, senior bureaucrats, and businessmen who came to visit him, consult with him, or donate money to his development projects.

As a result, in the late phase of his reign, Rama IX was portrayed by the palace as a great monarch who had achieved everything in his life and was ready to retire from his long and demanding duties. The nationwide ceremonies arranged by the palace were not only a celebration but also a swan song for the Thai idol. Annually designed by Rama IX himself and released by the palace, the King's New Year Cards in the last few years of his reign say it best. The 2010 card, for example, featured Rama IX wearing a sports jacket and running shoes, carrying a walking stick, and sitting with his dogs—Mrs. Thongdaeng and Mrs. Thonglang—in the palace garden. In this card, the king is depicted as if he were a senior bourgeois who no longer sweated and toiled but was spending his retirement in leisure, comfort, and ease (figure 8). In the early 2010s, the number of public appearances by the king and queen dropped dramatically, as Rama IX was frequently ill and Sirikit had lost her youth and beauty. As a result, in the last few years of his reign, many royal activities were actually carried out by other members of the royal family. Although pictures of the king and queen were still released by the palace, they seemed to be mere relics of the past. The corporeal bodies of the king and queen had long deteriorated and thus were absent from the public eye.

Figure 8. The king and royal canines on a lazy day. The 2010 King's New Year Card depicted Rama IX relaxing and sitting with his dogs, Thonglang (*left*) and Thongdaeng (*right*), in the palace garden. (Photo from OHM)

THE CROWN IN THE EYES OF THE BOURGEOISIE

Although royalty and courtiers played a crucial role in the visual economy of the Thai monarchy, they were not the only ones who popularized the new look of the crown. In fact, as Buck-Morss points out, the most influential "iconocrats" in modern society are the mainstream media, which shape the mass audience by "the manipulation of media simulacra." In today's "iconocracy," she notes, "we move from believing what we see to believing *in* what we see, not only when we see it, but when we don't."[34] To investigate how members of the Thai bourgeoisie interpreted the monarchy's self-presentation and popularized royal images via the mass media, we should look at a particular source that could be found annually in Thailand's daily newspapers during Rama IX's reign: print advertisements created to celebrate his birthday on December 5. These ads were typically the product of a collaboration among three groups: the businessmen who paid for the advertisements, the admen who designed them, and the literati who wrote prose or poetry to describe the visuals. With these ads, we can get a glimpse of what capitalists, the mass media, and intellectuals in Thailand thought about the crown. Like the periodization of royalty's self-presentation, the bourgeoisie's interpretation of royal images can be categorized in two phases, the early period of Rama IX's reign (1946–80) and the late one (1981–2016). It was only in the latter era that the invented images of the crown finally clicked with the crowd.

THE BOURGEOISIE'S FIRST IMPRESSION OF THE KING

In the early phase of Rama IX's reign, the palace's attempt to construct the new public image of Thai royalty received a mixed response from bourgeois audiences. On the one hand, the bourgeoisie did embrace two thematic portraits promoted by the palace: the spiritual king and the warrior-king. In corporate print advertisements produced to celebrate Rama IX's birthday, it was typical to see pictures of the king dressed in either full regalia or a military uniform. Similarly, prose and poetry composed to describe those pictures saluted not only the king's religious power but also his symbolic role as a fighter against the nation's threats. Written in an era when communism had penetrated provincial Thailand, a 1970 poem, for example, reflected how the bourgeoisie perceived its monarch at that time. In this poem, Rama IX is deemed the Hindu god, the nation's warrior, and the king all in one.

> When the land and provinces are invaded by enemies,
> People are suffering.
> With no one can they lean on,
> They are desperate and hopeless.
>
> But like the avatar of Vishnu flying over their heads,
> Royally marching into the wild forest,
> His charismatic power protects them from the menace.
> Men and women no longer suffer from anything.[35]

On the other hand, the bourgeoisie in this period had not yet seen how the monarchy and its images were relevant to its economic activities of production and consumption. In terms of quantity, print advertisements produced to celebrate the king's birthday were rare in the 1950s and 1960s but became more noticeable in the late 1970s. In terms of

Figure 9. The warrior-king and sacred king in the newspapers. In the early reign of Rama IX, it was typical to see images of the king in either full regalia or a military uniform, and they were juxtaposed to corporate logos, trademarks, and a phrase, "Long live the King." (*Siam Rath*, December 5, 1980)

content, two trends can be seen in the visual display of those ads. First, the pictures of the king and the royal emblem were juxtaposed against corporations' logos and trademarks, and there was no prose or poetry to explain the connection between them except a simple phase written in either Thai or Pali, "Long live the King" (figure 9). Second, in the few cases in which royal images were juxtaposed against merchandise in the advertisements, the former were small and normally located at the margins of the advertising space, which was dominated by a large product image in the central position (figure 10). In this regard, during the early phase of Rama IX's reign, royal images and discourse had not yet become popular or marketable from a businessman's point of view.

Figure 10. The monarchy at the margins. In the early reign of Rama IX, it was typical to see the royal emblem located at the upper margin of an advertising display while merchandise such as films was placed at the center. In this 1974 advertisement, the focus is on a newly released film, *Thip Chang*. Note the royal emblem at the upper left. (*Thai Rath*, December 5, 1974)

In other words, besides the traditional themes of the spiritual king and the warrior-king, there was nothing much about the king for advertisers to say and sell in the Thai market.

Among the few poems that could be found in the print advertisements of this period, two trends highlight the fact that Thai poets at that time still perceived the monarchy as an irrelevant institution in their daily lives. First, the poets normally wrote about Rama IX as if he were a divine god who was supposed to live in heaven with the angels and had nothing to do with the profane ethics and vulgar practices of commoners in the market and civil society. Two poems from the 1970s, for example, illustrate this perception among the bourgeois literati.

[1] O, all Thais are so lucky to have a god.
He takes care of them all the time.
His two royal hands support their hearts,
To not be scared and fearful.

Every hot house and heated province, burnt by the sun,
The god-lord marches everywhere.
So courageous, yet so torturing his royal body,
His Majesty's kindness is too much to be elaborated.[36]

[2] Wishing the virtual god to be great as a raja.
His Majesty progresses with joy and happiness.
All Buddha's blessings are given to His Majesty.
Long, happily, and magnificently live more than hundred
and thousand years.[37]

Another trend among Thai poets in the early reign of Rama IX can be found in their style of writing. Not only were the poems pretentious and exaggerated, but most of those published in the print advertisements were difficult for most Thai readers to understand. The language in these poems featured two elements. The first is the use of *rachasap*, a Thai language of reverence that is used on special occasions when commoners refer to royalty. The second is the use of ancient Indian languages—Pali and Sanskrit—which were imported into Thailand and used mostly in royal, Brahmin, and Buddhist ceremonies. Pali and Sanskrit became outdated in Thailand and are barely used today in school or the marketplace, as opposed to the contemporary and everyday language of the kingdom, which had long incorporated and mixed those ancient languages along with Thai, Lao, Khmer, and Chinese.

THE NEW RICH AND THEIR ENCHANTMENT WITH THE KING

From the 1980s on, the bourgeoisie's interpretation and reproduction of royal images in the mass media was transformed. While the print advertisements that celebrated the king's birthday were sporadic in Rama IX's early reign, they became more frequent, widespread, and established in the late reign. Moreover, their style of presentation dramatically changed in many ways. First, instead of juxtaposing royal images against their merchandise and simply stating "Long live the King," the advertisements from the 1980s on frequently elaborated on the greatness and legacy of Rama IX and how they were related to the business world. In these new advertisements, some of the biggest conglomerates in Thailand not only praised the king's SEP but also claimed that their companies would strictly follow that royal philosophy. As a result, in the later phase of the reign, it became normal for Thai newspaper readers to be bombarded by the advertisements of giant corporations such as Toyota Motor Thailand, Nestlé Thailand, CP, Amway Thailand, and the Central Group, all of which claimed to promote the king's ideal of a return to self-sufficient production and moderate consumption in a village economy.[38] That claim, however, contradicted the fact that these corporations were Thailand's biggest conglomerates in their industries—automobiles, food, agribusiness, direct sales, and retailing respectively. In spite of the assertion that these corporations took the king's model of a precapitalist economy seriously, they actually pursued advanced and industrial capitalism.

Moreover, in the post-1980 advertisements, royal images were usually located at the center rather than the margin of an advertising space, and they were treated as the focal point of the ad. More often than not, newspaper readers would not even have been able to see the marketed products since Rama IX's images and the royal emblem normally occupied the whole space of the visual presentation (figure 11). In this regard, corporations and advertisers in the late reign of the king seemed to have had much more to say and present about the monarch, his images, and his legacies than they did about their merchandise. Further, instead of the traditional images of Rama IX dressed in full regalia or a military uniform, print advertising at the turn of the twenty-first century usually appropriated pictures of the king wearing a business suit, a button-down shirt, and a necktie (figure 12). Unlike his image in the past, the new portrait of Rama IX in the eyes of Thai capitalists had a business-friendly appeal and became more bankable to bourgeois consumers in the market.

Finally, in the late phase of the reign, the language used in either prose or poetry celebrating the king's birthday became simpler and easier to understand. Instead of ancient and elegant Pali or Sanskrit, casual and ordinary Thai words were applied to describe the visual display in the advertisements. As a result, the print advertisements in the late reign of the king had the power to target a wider range of the audience.

While the increasing numbers and new style of the visual presentation of Rama IX in print advertisements were notable, the transformation of

Figure 11. The king
takes center stage. This
1987 advertisement made
Rama IX the focal point
while the merchandise,
fifteen newly released
films, was condensed at
the bottom of the page.
(*Thai Rath*, December 5,
1987)

the content of those ads was nothing short of spectacular. Unlike the
former era, when the bourgeoisie tended to be merely the passive fol-
lowers of thematic narratives that the palace attached to Rama IX, the
millennial bourgeoisie became more active, innovative, and selective
about royal images and discourses. Armed with several means of mass
communication that had been introduced in Thailand during the previous three decades—cell phones in 1986, personal computers in 1987,
cable television in 1989, the internet in 1996, and digital television in
2014—the Thai bourgeoisie had more virtual spaces not only to trans-
mit and reproduce royal discourses but also to create their own versions, which might deviate from the official version of the palace yet
were more compatible with their daily lives. In this era of mass communication, four major themes associated with the Thai monarchy
emerged and became the main narratives that dominated the bourgeoisie's class consciousness in the early twenty-first century. These were

Figure 12. The king with a business-friendly look. Four advertisements in 1993 depicted Rama IX wearing a business suit, a buttoned-down shirt, and a necktie. (*Thai Rath*, December 6, 1993)

the hardworking king, the frugal king, the father king, and the cosmopolitan king.

The Hardworking King

Hard work is one of the cardinal virtues of the bourgeoisie not only in western countries but also in Thai capitalism. While Chinese immigrants in the early twentieth century were alienated by Rama VI, as the king stigmatized their work ethic as a selfish drive for private profits instead of the national interest, the descendants of those immigrants found Rama IX and his images more appealing and compatible with their ethic of hard work. Thanks to the economic boom from the mid-1980s to the mid-1990s, the new generation of Sino-Thais became crucial actors in the kingdom's transition from an agriculture-based economy to an industrial one. Filling several occupations—industrialists,

financiers, businessmen, white-collar workers, and entrepreneurs—
Chinese descendants no longer worked as unskilled laborers as their
forefathers had done in the early twentieth century. Instead, they were
integral members of the urban bourgeoisie at the end of the century. As
the driving force behind the kingdom's rising capitalism, they seemed
to be more confident and proud of their Chinese ethical and cultural
roots than their ancestors were. Coincidently, the palace's attempt to
depict Rama IX as the developer king drew attention from this rising
class. Rather than passively accepting royal narratives, however, members of the bourgeoisie selected only some elements of them, those that
were compatible with their class ideology. The iconic picture of Rama IX
sweating while laboring on his royal projects was one of the royal images
that enchanted the newly prosperous members of the Thai economy.
Titled "The Royal Sweat That Bathes His Royal Body Feeds All Thais,"
a 1996 poem saluted Rama IX's fifty years on the throne by focusing on
his sweat as a symbol of his labor and sacrifice for all Thais.

> Fifty years of royal activities,
> Fifty years of thinking about everywhere he goes,
> Fifty years of enduring and building,
> Fifty years of the royal sweat that has been overflowing.
>
> The royal sweat floods over the desert.
> The royal sweat binds the cleavages in the dry land.
> The royal sweat is the miracle that makes plants flourish and grow.
> The royal sweat that bathes his royal body feeds all Thais.[39]

Similarly, this theme of the sweating monarch was used in a 2005
advertisement for Epson Corporation Thailand. Instead of an image of
its merchandise, Epson showed a portrait of Rama IX sweating while
working on his development projects. In a poem attached to this visual
presentation, Epson also tried to connect that royal image to its merchandise, a brand new color printer, by emphasizing the words *picture*
and *print*. This was a marketing strategy rarely found during the early
reign of Rama IX. As the poem states:

> A picture of His Majesty working everywhere he goes,
> A picture of his face that is saturated by the river of sweat,
> A picture of his hands that cool down the heat and create comfort,
> Dad's benevolence has been printed over the hearts of all Thais.[40]

Figure 13. A drop of sweat and dry land. This 1994 advertisement featured an image of a sweating Rama IX within a frame that looks like a drop of sweat. With cracked dry land in the background, the ad proclaimed that "a drop of water from His Majesty's heart solves the problems of all Thais." (*Thai Rath*, December 5, 1994).

Figure 14. The obsession with the sweating monarch. In this 2011 advertisement, images of Rama IX are circumscribed within many drop-shaped frames. The ad proclaimed "Long live the King" and "every drop of sweat is for the people's happiness and benefit." Below these messages, the ad also invited the audience to follow the ten kingly virtues in order to celebrate Rama IX's birthday. (*Thai Rath*, December 5, 2011).

From the 1980s on, sweat became the most popular symbol used to elaborate the work ethic of Rama IX. In addition to poems, the theme of the sweating monarch was used in print advertising. For example, two advertisements from 1994 (figure 13) and 2011 (figure 14) not only featured the iconic portrait of Rama IX sweating but also circumscribed it with a frame that looked like a bead of sweat. Putting a spotlight on this sweatlike frame, this ad had a semiotic message that every royal project the palace initiated came at a high price: the painstaking labor from the king's body.

According to many print advertisements in the early 2000s, Rama IX was undoubtedly the "hardest working monarch in the world" due to the popular perception in Thai society that during his reign the king had never stopped working for his subjects.[41] This perception, however, was at odds with some historical facts: Rama IX actually spent the first few years of his reign in Switzerland; he engaged in various recreational activities when he was not working; and, from the late 1990s on, he rarely worked on his development projects or visited remote provinces of the country.[42] The bourgeoisie, nevertheless, did not much care about those facts. For the nouveau riche, from the cradle to the grave, Rama IX always worked and toiled for his subjects. As Somsak remarked about the irony of the Thai bourgeoisie's mentality, its members strongly believed in Rama IX's work ethic, even though they never saw the king work with their own eyes or seriously measured how much he actually worked and whether his projects succeeded as advertised.[43]

The bourgeois obsession with its continually working monarch seemed to be well matched to this rising class, which relentlessly worked to accumulate capital and keep Thai capitalism expanding during the economic boom from the mid-1980s to the mid-1990s. Work, labor, and perseverance are ethical values that became even more important among the Thai bourgeoisie when the economic crisis hit the country in 1997. Despite the loss of wealth and jobs during the crisis, it looked as though the bourgeoisie would never fail to look up to its monarch as a role model. Titled "The King Makes Me Realize That I Have Not Lost Yet," a 1997 advertisement presented by UCOM, then the second-largest telecommunications corporation in the country, captured the spirit of the bourgeoisie during that time. It juxtaposed a picture of Rama IX relaxing while composing jazz music against the testimony of a white-collar worker who had just lost his job because of the economic crisis. As he told his story:

> *I am so sorry* was what the manager said to me that evening. This feeling was totally different from the feeling I had five years ago. I used to be an awarded employee and got a lot of bonuses. At that time, I thought my life and my family would be better and more comfortable. But on that evening, what I never expected happened. I was laid off, like hundreds of thousands of people, because the economy was bad. At that time, I felt like my life was broken, and I worried about my children and my family. . . . Today I'm following the king as a role model. I will grin and bear it in every crisis, no matter how hard the obstacles are to overcome. I will always think about His Majesty, and I will never give up. *I have the King fighting together with me. His Majesty will never leave all of us behind.*[44]

The Frugal King

Like hard work, frugality is an ethic that is highly valued among Chinese immigrants and their descendants in Thailand. Thai royalty, on the contrary, have never been perceived as frugal people. Instead Thai monarchs before Rama IX seemed to follow the Buddhist tradition of ideal kingship. From this perspective the king is the most generous man in the kingdom as he is supposed to be a benevolent giver who donates and spends his money to support his subjects and maintain Buddhist monasteries.[45] Furthermore, as Thai monarchs in the late nineteenth century virtually embraced bourgeois culture from the West, they were socially perceived as the most spendthrift and extravagant men in the kingdom. Rama V, for instance, lived up to this stereotype when he traveled to Europe in the early twentieth century. In addition to Thais, even Europeans were amazed at how spendthrift the king was when shopping and dubbed him "the big spender."[46] Consequently, as long as Thai monarchs placed emphasis on their munificence, splendor, and luxury, they honored a set of ethical values different from those that Sino-Thai entrepreneurs in the kingdom practiced daily. This ethical gap, however, was virtually bridged during the late reign of Rama IX.

Frugality was the ethical theme that the bourgeoisie drew from the palace's portrait of Rama IX as the economist king. While the palace attempted to promote the king's SEP as a complicated economic theory or even a modern science, the bourgeoisie selectively focused only on a trivial and simple aspect of this royal philosophy that was well suited to their class ideology. Namely, in the eyes of the bourgeoisie, the king's ideal of SEP was nothing but a way to be thrifty. Consequently, this class was obsessed with how Rama IX practiced the ethic of frugality and how this frugal king could help them bear the high cost of urban living. Without formal approval from the palace, four stories associated with Rama IX's frugality spread as urban myths among the bourgeoisie, dating from the late 1990s. Four mundane commodities that Rama IX allegedly consumed—toothpaste, shoes, pencils, and fried rice—are the focus of these stories.

Toothpaste is a focal point of the first story, which was narrated by a female dentist who had long served Rama IX. After checking the king's oral health, the dentist complained to him about the spendthrift ways of Thai youngsters. The king not only agreed with her but also shared a story about his frugal lifestyle. As the king put it, there was a time his servants recognized that a toothpaste tube in his bathroom was almost

Figure 15. The king's toothpaste tube. This toothpaste tube was allegedly squeezed by Rama IX until it was completely flat. (Photo by the author)

empty, so they replaced it with a new one without his permission. Disappointed by their uneconomical attitude, the king asked them to bring the old tube back. By pressing the tube with the handle of a toothbrush, the king claimed that he could squeeze every drop of toothpaste from that old tube for several more days. Fascinated by the monarch's ethic of frugality, the dentist asked permission to present that empty tube to her students in a dentistry class.[47] Today, in addition to the visual presentation in television commercials, Thai subjects can have a firsthand experience with the king's toothpaste tube, as it has been put in a glass display case and permanently exhibited in the Museum of Dentistry in Bangkok (figure 15).[48]

The second story is the tale of a male shoemaker and his memorable experience with the king's shoes. Surprisingly visited by courtiers at his small shoe repair shop in Bangkok, the shoemaker was asked to do a job he could only dream of—fixing the king's shoes. Seeing how worn and torn Rama IX's shoes were, the shoemaker at first was not sure that these really were the king's shoes since he assumed that they would be brand new and deluxe. On second thought, however, he realized that these damaged shoes must be Rama IX's since he believed that the king not only visited poor Thais in remote areas frequently but also promoted and practiced the ethic of frugality. After replacing the old soles

Figure 16. The king's old soles. The alleged soles of Rama IX's old shoes sealed in a glass display case. (Photo by the author)

with the new ones, the shoemaker asked for the king's permission to keep the old soles. Like the king's toothpaste tube, the Thai people today can visually appreciate the king's worn soles through both the mass media and personal experience. Sealed in a glass display case by the shoemaker, the royal soles are permanently exhibited in his shop, where any Thai who wants to can catch a glimpse of Rama IX's frugality (figure 16).[49]

The third tale focuses on Rama IX's frugal use of his pencils. There was a time, as the story is told, when a rookie page boy had a chance to clean His Majesty's office, and he threw away a worn-down wooden pencil stub of the king's. When the king entered his office and realized that his pencil had disappeared from his desk, he asked, "Where is my pencil?" After the page confessed to the king that the pencil was now in a bin, the king himself walked to the bin, picked up his pencil, and said to his servant, "Although this pencil stub looks very short, if we extend it by gluing it to a new one, we can still use the old pencil until it is completely consumed." Rumor has it that Rama IX used only pencils that were produced domestically because they were cheaper than

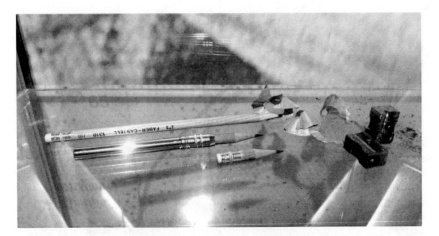

Figure 17. The king's pencils. Pencils and pencil sharpeners that were allegedly used by Rama IX were sealed in a glass display case. (Source: Photo by the author)

brand-name pencils imported from overseas. Although the king frequently used his pencils to take notes and make sketches for his development projects, he was praised by his servants for using only twelve pencils annually—one per month—and would never throw any pencil stub away until there was no graphite left in it.[50] Like the royal toothpaste tube and soles, Thai subjects today can have a firsthand experience of the king's wooden pencil stubs. They were put in a glass display case and are permanently exhibited in the Doi Tung Royal Villa (figure 17).[51]

Unlike those three commodities, the king's fried rice did not leave any remnants for the Thai audience to personally encounter and experience. The last legendary story about the frugal king, however, has been as popular among the bourgeoisie as the first three. Narrated by a male bureaucrat who had a chance to serve Rama IX in his development projects, this story begins with a scene of the king visiting rural areas with his staff members. Exhausted and hungry, as they had worked all day long, the staff quickly devoured Thai fried rice, a staple food for Thais when they traveled to remote and rough provinces. Seeing that one dish of fried rice had been left uneaten, the bureaucrat asked who would take that dish. When he got the answer that the king himself would eat the dry burned rice on that dish, the bureaucrat was shocked and could not believe what he had just heard. "His Majesty is the Lord of the Land, and he could have ordered anyone to cook a new dish of

Figure 18. The king's fried rice. This 2011 advertisement depicted the dish of fried rice that was allegedly devoured by Rama IX. Alongside the dish, a diagram explains that each ingredient in the fried rice required a lot of energy to produce. The ad read, "A great deal of energy goes into making a dish of fried rice. Is the way we eat it worth the energy that is used?" Below this message, a story describes how Rama IX frugally ate his fried rice. (*Thai Rath*, December 5, 2011)

fried rice anytime and anyhow," he said to himself, while looking at a portrait of Rama IX hung on a wall in the dining hall, "but he didn't do it."[52] Realizing how frugal the king was, all of royal staff followed the king's example by finishing their meal without any grains of rice left on their plates. Although the royal fried rice was allegedly devoured by the king and left no trace behind, its legacy has been immortalized since the late 1990s by the mass media in both print advertisements and television commercials (figure 18).[53]

The Father King

It is arguable that there is nothing new about the notion that the sovereign of a state is socially perceived as the father of a nation. In both monarchical and republican regimes, a head of state is conventionally portrayed as a father figure. The popular notion among the Thai bourgeoisie that Rama IX was a father king, however, is distinctive in terms of its divergence from the history of Thai kingship and its degree of informality. For most of the history of Thai kingship, monarchs were revered by their subjects as *devaraja*, whose absolute power and divine status are identical to those of a god in the Hindu cosmology instead of the head of a household. By comparison, starting in the late 1980s, Rama IX was informally called "Father" and "Dad."[54] A 1989 advertisement, for example, celebrated the king's birthday by displaying a poem that used the term *dad* as its theme and praised his greatness, sacrifice, kindness, and genius. As this poem expresses, Rama IX was:

> One dad who unites and unifies,
> One dad who is a perfect role model,
> One dad who makes the nation prosper,
> One dad whom the world remarks on and refers to,
>
> One dad who greatly sacrifices,
> One dad who is the great genius,
> One dad whom his children can depend on,
> One dad who has pure kindness, this dad "Bhumibol."[55]

Another example is a poem that was used in a 2005 ThaiBev commercial. In this poem, the writer referred to Rama IX using not only a formal term, *father* (*bida*), but also a casual word, *dad* (*pho*), which is more frequently used in the daily lives of Thai people. As this poem states:

> Dad is like water pouring over Thais, so they do not suffer.
> Dad is a role model through his teaching.
> Dad embraces all Thai hearts with his benevolence.
> This is the father, "Bhumibol," of the Thai people.[56]

In addition to the term *dad*, other casual words that Thai subjects were historically forbidden to use in reference to their monarchs have been popularly attached to Rama IX and depictions of him in the media. *Love, smile, home,* and *happiness*—popular catchwords among the bourgeoisie in both western and Thai capitalism as they connote bourgeois sentiments of romanticism and comfort—are unprecedentedly used by many Thais to express their personal feelings about Rama IX. Instead of worship, loyalty, respect, and fear, a 2010 advertisement presented by Thai Life Insurance—one of the three biggest life insurance corporations in the country—employed the word *love* to explain what all Thais felt about their monarch. Putting a spotlight on a diary written by anonymous children at the center of its advertising space, the commercial

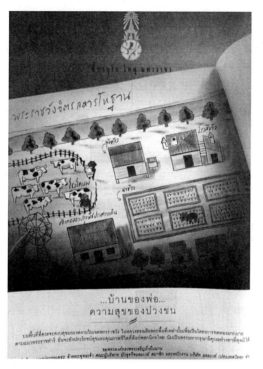

Figure 19. Dad's home. This 2006 print advertisement featured a sketch of Rama IX's residence, the Chitralada Royal Villa. (*Thai Rath*, December 5, 1999)

displayed several messages from them: "We Love Great Dad," "Love His Majesty," and "We Love the King." Alongside these words of affection were heart-shaped sketches drawn by the kids.[57]

Moreover, instead of a splendid palace, post-1980 advertisers often portrayed Rama IX's residence not only as a "working base," an image the palace worked to promote, but also as "Dad's home." For example, a 1999 advertisement presented by the Central Group—the biggest merchandizing and retailing corporation in Thailand—featured a picture of the Chitralada Royal Villa, which it called "dad's home." The ad asserted that this place had "rice barns, mill houses, milk houses, [and] fishery pools" and "We have a dad who never stops experimenting, never stops solving problems for his children, and continues to be a great role model for his 60 million children."[58] Similarly, a 2006 advertisement presented by Amway Thailand—the biggest direct sales company in the country—displayed a sketch of the Chitralada Royal Villa that depicted it as a combination of a paddy field, barn, dairy farm, and mill house. "Dad's Home, People's Happiness" was a slogan that this advertisement attached to the sketch (figure 19).[59]

Finally, the body of the Thai monarch—the corporeal figure that was traditionally untouchable and highly revered by his subjects—became less sacred among the contemporary bourgeoisie. The most outstanding example of this is the way this class referred to Rama IX's smile. In a traditional model of Buddhist kingship, the monarch is not supposed to express his emotions in public by smiling, laughing, or crying, but he should rather control and conceal those feelings under a calm and peaceful appearance. According to Handley, Rama IX, who was usually stoic and rarely smiled in public after the tragic death of his brother, followed this tradition and thus epitomized Handley's book title, *The King Never Smiles*. Advertisements in millennial Thailand nevertheless diverged from this tradition. Revealing a rare image of Rama IX smiling, a 2004 advertisement promoted the idea that all Thais must "unite and come together and be good citizens in order to keep His Majesty's smile with us forever."[60] Similarly, a 2010 ad asserted, "Wish to see dad able to smile . . . Wish him happy, living with Thais for more than a thousand years. Wish to have dad's smile for a long time."[61] The bourgeoisie's obsession with the king's smile and its love for "dad" were vividly reflected in the lyrics of a popular Thai song, "Thais' Smile Is Dad's Smile," which were used in a 2009 advertisement by ThaiBev. As the song rejoices:

> Smile. Dad's hands create smiles, for Thais to smile wherever they live.
> Love. Dad's heart has love, and shares love with every heart.
> Days and nights, no matter how long they are.
> We can still smile because of dad.
>
> So, we would like to continually follow dad's footsteps.
> To follow love, to follow the philosophy that dad offers.
> To always do good things, regardless of whether anyone recognizes them
>   or not.
> To give back every smile, happiness, and love that dad gives to us.
> From our hearts. After our hearts.[62]

The Cosmopolitan King

Even though the palace tried to promote Rama IX as the cosmopolitan king in the early period of his reign, the bourgeoisie at that time failed to find this royal theme appealing. Prospering during the economic boom and solidifying its position as the dominant class of the Thai economy since then, the bourgeoisie in Rama IX's late reign appreciated the monarch's multiple talents in art, music, literature, sport, and technology more than it had in the past. In 1982 the National Gallery of Thailand exhibited Rama IX's forty-seven abstract paintings. In this exhibition, for the first time, members of the bourgeoisie had a chance to see with their own eyes those royal paintings, which were the products of the king's short passion for art during the 1960s.[63] In addition to his artistic talent, Rama IX's writing skills were warmly welcomed by the bourgeoisie. His translations of *A Man Called Intrepid* and *Tito* in 1994 and *The Story of Mahajanaka* in 1996 were solid successes for the publishing industry, while his original writing, *The Story of Thongdaeng*, was a national best seller in the 2000s.[64] As the "King of Jazz," Rama IX also wrote forty-eight songs, most of them composed during the early phase of his reign.[65] The Thai bourgeoisie, however, was a late admirer of royal music since it began to appreciate and popularize those songs only in the millennial era. Although an anthology of Rama IX's songs had been produced in the 1980s, *H.M. Blues*, a 2006 anthology, was the first album on which those songs were sung by the kingdom's contemporary rock, country, jazz, reggae, rhythm and blues, and pop singers.[66] The king's songs also motivated Thailand's four prominent film directors to produce four short movies in 2015 inspired by the lyrics of four popular songs: "Smiles," "H.M. Blues," "Falling Rain," and "The Impossible Dream."[67]

This theme of the cosmopolitan king was also evident in the print advertisements that celebrated Rama IX's birthday. In addition to the iconic portrait of the king wearing a business suit, carrying a map and camera, and sweating, pictures of the king showing his multiple talents in bourgeois culture and knowledge were popularized in several advertisements during his late reign. A 1997 advertisement presented by UCOM, for example, showed a picture of young Rama IX composing a jazz song, "Smiles." Demonstrating how comfortable he was with music composition, the advertisement depicted Rama IX sitting with his Siamese cat, "Mr. Tito," and using his right hand to write a note on a manuscript while his left hand was on a piano keyboard.[68] Likewise, a 1991 advertisement presented by the Shin Corporation and a 2013 ad by PTT similarly presented Rama IX as a "genius monarch" who had a wide range of knowledge, from telecommunications to energy development.[69] In addition to music and technology, Rama IX's passion for sports was a popular topic in post-1980s advertisements. While an ad

presented by the Central Group in 1994 displayed an image of young
Rama IX skiing in Europe, a 2000 ad by Nestlé Thailand showed that
the young monarch was at ease sailing a boat near his summer villa in
Thailand.[70] Quoting a speech by Rama IX's that revealed how meticulously he took care of his body, the latter advertisement asserted that all
Thais should follow the king's example by paying more attention to
their bodies. This obsession with youth, fitness, and good health among
the Thai bourgeoisie, however, is based mainly on a fantasy about a
forever young monarch because Rama IX in the 2000s—like any senior
born in the 1920s—was no longer fit and firm.

These four new themes about Rama IX in the mass media reveal
some characteristics of the Thai bourgeoisie that, far from being unique,
share several features with their counterparts in other capitalist societies.
First, like the European and American bourgeoisies, the nouveau riche in
Thailand embody two contradictory types of ideology; to put it bluntly,
they have "two souls."[71] On the one hand, the Thai bourgeoisie, which
is mainly composed of and dominated by the descendants of Chinese
immigrants from an earlier period, highly values the ethic of hard work,
frugality, asceticism, rationality, self-motivation, and self-confidence.
On the other hand, members this rising class are mentally insecure,
anxious, and even ashamed of their alienated and low status, as their
Chinese ancestors formerly faced discrimination as "non-Thai" or the
"Jews of the Orient." With this psychological insecurity, the bourgeoisie
not only admire the splendid and luxurious lives of Thai royalty but
also seek their recognition, decoration, and incorporation into court
society. This intrinsic tension between two contradictory mentalities
of the bourgeoisie was virtually relieved by the visual presentation of
Rama IX, a natural-born Thai royal who was supposed to spend a privileged life in a splendid court but decided to dedicate himself to work
and labor just as ordinary Sino-Thai entrepreneurs do. Thanks to this
ideological fulfillment, which soothes the tension between the bourgeoisie's "two souls," Rama IX became a popular figure among members of this rising class.

Moreover, the Thai bourgeoisie selectively remembers only some
images of Rama IX while disregarding others that are incompatible
with its class ideology. This characteristic of the Thai bourgeoisie is
similar to the way the Japanese bourgeoisie treated its monarch. According to Takashi Fujitani, after World War II the Japanese bourgeoisie
tended to remember Emperor Hirohito only as a simple and humble

monarch while neglecting his wartime images, which were closely associated with imperialism, violence, and war crimes.[72] Like their Japanese counterparts, members of the Thai bourgeoisie today tend to ignore Rama IX's former images, which are closely associated with military despotism, right-wing movements, and state violence directed at the communist insurgency during the Cold War. As a result, two types of Rama IX's images are noticeably less publicized or have even vanished from the mass media today. First are the portraits of the warrior-king carrying an assault rifle or wearing a Village Scout uniform. In place of the violent and bloody monarch, the theme of the warm, caring, smiley, fatherly king became more popular among the nouveau riche, who are obsessed with bourgeois sentiments of romanticism, comfort, and family values. Another one is a portrait of the aged and ailing monarch. While the corporeal body of the king deteriorated in the early twenty-first century, the Thai mass media tended to present only images of Rama IX in his prime, a specific period when the king relentlessly traveled to remote provinces with beads of sweat trickling down his face.

Finally, the Thai bourgeoisie is an active class that frequently overdoes its interpretation of royal images. Studying the French bourgeoisie's attitudes and behaviors, Pierre Bourdieu argued that the nouveau riche are normally insecure and anxious when they encounter the upper classes. Therefore, they tend to "overshoot the mark for fear of falling short" by overdoing their manners in order to give the impression to the public that they belong to the noble class.[73] Like their French counterparts, the Thai bourgeois are indeed, as Thongchai put it, "hyper-royalist."[74] While the palace provided the public with subliminal messages that Rama IX was the humble and diligent father figure of the Thai nation, the bourgeoisie interpreted those messages in its own way. Exaggerating Rama IX's virtues, this impassioned class idolized him as a "dad" who always smiled, as a frugal man who parsimoniously used every bit of his toothpaste, and as a diligent worker who constantly sweated and toiled. This over-the-top interpretation of the Thai bourgeoisie was encapsulated in a 2008 pop song titled "Dad's Song," which perfectly reflects the spirit of the bourgeoisie in twenty-first-century Thailand whenever this class looks upon a portrait of Rama IX. All the keywords that define Rama IX's personality—*smile, love, comfort, labor, sweat, shoes, toothpaste tube, music, self-sufficiency,* and *dad*—are impressively packed and presented in the first few verses of the song, which celebrates:

An image of dad smiling, an image of dad laughing, an image
      of dad playing music,
An image of dad walking through mud, an image of dad enduringly
      going everywhere . . .
An image of dad laboring under the sun, sweating all over his face . . .
An image of the shoes that dad repairs again and again.

An image of the toothpaste tube that dad squeezes and grinds it
      until it is totally flat,
An image of a self-sufficient life that we observe from dad,
All of them we cannot remove from our hearts.
So, this is dad's song that we continually sing, for his kindness and
      love that never fade.[75]

CASH IS KING

Members of the Thai bourgeoisie in the business, media, and intellectual
sectors are not the only ones who were obsessed with the new royal images that had been constructed during the late reign of Rama IX. In fact,
another segment of this class, which occupied the state apparatus—
bureaucrats and politicians—was also enchanted by the rebranded
images of the crown. The emblematic case of this phenomenon is the
depiction of the monarchy on Thailand's banknotes. Designed by bureaucrats and approved by politicians, Thai paper money can help us
understand the common perception of those members of the bourgeoisie who run the state.[76] Furthermore, as an everyday medium of exchange, the banknotes also reflect how this stratum of the bourgeoisie
both shapes and is influenced by a dominant attitude toward the crown
among its counterparts in the market. With an examination of the historical transformation of royal portraits on Thai banknotes, it should be
possible to catch a glimpse of how the bourgeoisie as a whole—both in
the state apparatus and in the market—selectively memorialized its
monarch, his reign, and his legacy. As Chatri Prakitnontakan remarked
in his study of the history of Thai banknotes, "In my opinion, the design
of banknotes (especially in Thai society) is a process which is not so
different from the process of designing a collection of memories of the
nation's history."[77] Chronologically the history of Thai banknotes can
be categorized in three eras: the period before Rama IX's reign, that of
his early reign, and that of his late reign. As this history unfolded, the increasing eminence of royal images on Thailand's paper money paralleled

the successful revival of the monarchy under Rama IX's reign. The longer the reign continued, the bigger and more bourgeois the portraits of the monarch on the bills became.

THAI BANKNOTES
BEFORE RAMA IX'S REIGN

Due to the high demand for a medium of exchange after the rapid incorporation of Siam into the world market in the late nineteenth century, paper money was introduced in the kingdom for the first time in 1902 under the reign of Rama V. Since then, there have been seventeen series of Thai banknotes.[78] A tradition of displaying a portrait of the reigning monarch on baht bills, however, was invented and first practiced under Rama VII's reign. In 1928, Rama VII initiated a new visual presentation of banknotes which aimed to represent the prestige of the monarchy and traditional values of "Thainess."[79] But the king's desire was delayed and only actualized in the third series, which was released in 1934, two years after the overthrow of the absolute monarchy. Despite the fact that it was the first series of banknotes under the newly installed constitutional regime, the third series was designed in the age of the absolute monarchy, and thus it still reflected the political and cultural values of the old regime. These bills featured images of Rama VII and the Grand Palace on the front side and those of "Thai" and religious symbols such as the Royal Barge and the Temple of the Emerald Buddha on the back. This visual prominence of the monarchy on the banknotes, however, was about to decline once the government under the leadership of the People's Party successfully prevailed over the royalist reactionaries and domesticated the power of the palace.

With the abdication of the last absolute monarch in 1935 and the impromptu ascendance the throne of the nine-year-old Rama VIII, "the boy king," the revolutionary government found an opportunity to promote a new model of the Thai monarchy, the crown that was supposed to be restrained under the national constitution. In 1938, the groundbreaking fourth banknote series was released. While the front of the bills in this series still followed the tradition of displaying portraits of the reigning monarch and Buddhist temples, the back of the bills brought into light the Ananta Samakhom Throne Hall, a neoclassical building that was used as the king's reception hall under the reigns of Rama VI and Rama VII but later converted to the Parliament House by the People's Party.

Likewise, in the eighth series that was released in 1946, the same
year that Rama VIII was mysteriously shot dead and Rama IX unex-
pectedly ascended the throne, the visual presentation on the bills symbolically showed the rising status of the constitutional regime at the
expense of the monarchy's. According to Chatri, what is remarkable
about this series are the absence of "Thai" symbols such as temples and
palaces and the minimization of a portrait of the reigning monarch on
the front side. The back, meanwhile, featured the symbolic image of
the new regime as a focal point, Thailand's National Constitution. This
transformation of Thai banknotes during the first half of the twentieth
century makes clear that there was a historical period when the status
of the crown was subordinate to the constitutional regime that was
steered by bureaucrats and politicians. The status of the monarchy,
however, was soon to be reversed under the reign of Rama IX.

THAI BANKNOTES
IN RAMA IX's EARLY REIGN

In 1948, as young Rama IX was still in Europe and Thai subjects barely
knew their reigning monarch, the subordinate status of the monarchy
to the constitutional regime was still evident in the Thai banknotes that
were released that year. Just as had happened in the previous reigns,
the BOT designed the new bills, which primarily promoted the constitutional regime and parliamentary democracy at the expense of the
crown. However, the ninth series—the first under the reign of Rama IX—
was different from the others. The BOT broke its design tradition; there
was no portrait of the reigning monarch on either side of the fifty-satang
bill.[80] On the front of this bill—in the space that was conventionally reserved for the portrait of the reigning monarch—there were the names
of the currency and the Thai government with the image of the National
Constitution in the background. This trend toward depicting the constitutional regime rather than the monarchy, however, would fade after
the permanent return of the young monarch to his kingdom.

In parallel with the palace's attempt to promote Rama IX as the spiritual king and the warrior-king during his early reign, the BOT significantly changed its design of paper money by incorporating those royal
themes into the new versions of banknotes that were issued during the
1960s and 1970s. The visual presentation of Rama IX as the spiritual
king was vividly expressed in the eleventh series, which was released
in 1969. On the front, the bills unprecedentedly depicted the reigning

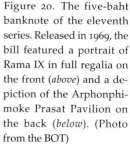

Figure 20. The five-baht banknote of the eleventh series. Released in 1969, the bill featured a portrait of Rama IX in full regalia on the front (*above*) and a depiction of the Arphonphimoke Prasat Pavilion on the back (*below*). (Photo from the BOT)

monarch in full regalia. More important, the back was no longer a space for the visual promotion of constitutional rule by bureaucrats and politicians but instead was used for the revival of a religious monarch who was traditionally revered as *dharmaraja* and *devaraja*. As a result, in lieu of images of Parliament House and the National Constitution, the back of the bills was occupied by royal and religious images such as the Royal Pavilion, the Royal Barge, and prestigious temples under the king's patronage (figure 20).

Similarly, the theme of the warrior-king that the palace had promoted in the Cold War era was reproduced by the BOT in the twelfth series, which was released in 1978. Showing a portrait of Rama IX in a military uniform as the commander in chief on the front, on their back the bills displayed portraits of the great monarchs of Thai history who defended the kingdom from "external enemies." The back of the hundred-baht bill in this series, for example, displayed King Naresuan riding an elephant in Siam's sixteenth-century war with the Burmese kingdom (figure 21). Portraying Rama IX as the spiritual and the warrior-king, Thai banknotes during the early reign tended to promote only traditional values and images of the monarchy. This trend, however, would gradually fade after Thailand was transformed into a newly industrialized country and an army of industrialists, white-collar workers, and

Figure 21. The hundred-
baht banknote of the twelfth
series. Released in 1978, the
bill featured a portrait of
Rama IX in the uniform of
the supreme commander
on the front (*above*) and the
monument of King Nare-
suan at the Don Chedi Me-
morial on the back (*below*).
(Photo from the BOT)

entrepreneurs rapidly arose and expanded during the late reign of the
king.

THAI BANKNOTES
IN RAMA IX'S LATE REIGN

Like their counterparts in the market, members of the Thai bourgeoisie
who occupied the state apparatus were enchanted by the images of the
crown during Rama IX's late reign, the particular images that were
compatible with their class values of hard work, self-reliance, and meritocracy. From the 1980s onward, while the monarchy was less inclined
to directly engage in national politics and less associated with the extraeconomic coercion of the military, the monarch was frequently outspoken on critical issues concerning the national economy and became
more active in development projects. The palace's attempt to promote
the king as an economic expert and hardworking developer was not in
vain. Indeed, it was recognized by bourgeois officeholders and commemorated in the new versions of banknotes that were released in the
late reign of Rama IX.

The new look of Rama IX as an ordinary father who tirelessly labored
for the common good of his children made its debut on Thai banknotes
in 1992. According to the BOT, the fourteenth series was intended to

Figure 22. The thousand-baht banknote of the fourteenth series. Released in 1992, the bill featured a portrait of Rama IX in the uniform of the supreme commander on the front (*above*) and an image of the king and queen's visit to the construction site of a dam and reservoir at Baan Bakong in Narathiwat on the back (*below*). (Photo from the BOT)

publicize the king's and the royal family's activities and "their contributions to the development of the country in various sectors."[81] With this intention, the depiction of royalty on the bills could not be those violent images that had shown the king and queen in battle dress or carrying assault rifles. Instead, pictures of royalty working on development projects were selected for the bills by the BOT. On the back of the thousand-baht bill, for example, there was the portrait of Rama IX in a business suit, carrying a map and a pencil and discussing the construction of a dam in a rural province with the queen (figure 22).

This theme was also reproduced in the fifteenth series, which was released in 1999, just two years after one of the worst economic crises in Thai history hit the kingdom. On the back of the new thousand-baht bill, for instance, there was a picture of Rama IX carrying his usual "development gear"—a camera and map—and this picture was juxtaposed against the BOT's short description of SEP (figure 23). As Chatri points out, the new look of Rama IX that appeared on Thai banknotes at the turn of the twenty-first century was innovative in two respects. First, instead of a formal uniform or sacred regalia, the monarch on the new banknotes was depicted as an ordinary man in a dress shirt and business suit. Second, instead of old temples and palaces, the new banknotes displayed images of the construction of dams and bridges under the king's guidance in the background. This depiction, Chatri

Figure 23. The thousand-baht banknote of the fifteenth series. Released in 1999, the bill featured a portrait of Rama IX in the uniform of the supreme commander on the front (*above*) and images of the king, the Pa Sak Jolasid Dam, and agricultural land, along with a short description of SEP, on the back (*below*). (Photo from the BOT)

notes, symbolically represented the modernity, science, and technology that were rapidly developed under Rama IX's reign.[82] What should be added to Chatri's observation, however, is a third aspect. For the first time, the reigning monarch's economic vision—the SEP model that bureaucrats and politicians in the past had not taken seriously—was incorporated in the visual display on Thai banknotes. Given these three aspects of the banknotes, it is clear that the graphic and ideological symbiosis between the crown and the currency had never been as seamless as that which occurred in Rama IX's late reign.

In addition to the circulating banknotes, the new look of the king made its presence felt in commemorative banknotes, which the BOT released only on special occasions during the reign of Rama IX. In 2011, while the corporeal body of the then eighty-four-year-old monarch had declined as he frequently became ill and mostly stayed in a Bangkok hospital, a new commemorative banknote was issued to celebrate Rama IX's seventh-cycle birthday anniversary. What is remarkable about this bill is that only selective portraits of the king in his prime were displayed and commemorated. On the back of the bill, there were four portraits of the king. The biggest one depicted Rama IX carrying a map and a camera while overseeing his development projects in the countryside. Juxtaposed against this portrait are three smaller pictures. The first depicted the king on his knees talking with his subjects, the second depicted the king using a sickle to harvest grain crops despite being in a business suit, and the last depicted young Rama IX as the

Figure 24. The banknote commemorating Rama IX's seventh-cycle birthday anniversary. Released in 2011, the bill featured a portrait of Rama IX in full regalia on the front (*above*) and images of the king overseeing his development projects, visiting people, harvesting crops, and playing the saxophone on the back (*below*). (Photo from the BOT)

cosmopolitan king playing the saxophone. The last picture, as the BOT put it, was included on the bill in order to show "His Majesty as the great musical genius."[83] In the background of these pictures, there were also images of the king's projects for artificial rainfall and irrigation, which represented, according to the BOT, "His Majesty, the genius of technology and science" (figure 24).[84]

As the twilight of Rama IX's reign was approaching in the early 2010s, this visual theme reflected how the Thai bourgeoisie wanted to memorialize Rama IX. Instead of the warrior-king with blood on his hands or the spiritual king wearing an exotic costume like the one that Yul Brynner wore when he comically portrayed the King of Siam in the 1956 musical film *The King and I*, the bourgeoisie seemed to appreciate the recently constructed look of the monarch as a father figure who had never lost his bodily strength and appeal, embraced the ethic of hard work and self-reliance, and was highly skilled in art, music, science, and technology. In other words, in the eyes of the bourgeoisie, only selective portraits of the "bourgeois king" should be forever immortalized on paper money. In this regard, royal images on Thai banknotes are distinct from those found in other capitalist kingdoms such as the United Kingdom. On the pound sterling banknotes, there has been a division of visual space since 1960, the year in which the tradition of displaying the British monarch on the bills was introduced.[85] While the portrait of Queen Elizabeth II regularly occupies the front of the bills, the back is a space for commemorating prominent commoners or members of the British bourgeoisie such as William Shakespeare, Isaac Newton, Adam Smith, Jane Austen, Charles Darwin, Charles Dickens, Florence Nightingale, and Winston Churchill. In Scotland and Northern Ireland this invented tradition does not exist, as the portrait of the British monarch is absent on those banknotes. On the baht banknotes, in contrast, there is no place for bourgeois heroes let alone commoners from the lower classes. Instead, both sides of the bills had recently been an exclusive space for honoring Rama IX, the monarch who successfully represented bourgeois appearance and ideology.

CONCLUSION

The popularity of the monarchy among the urban bourgeoisie in millennial Thailand cannot be understood simply as a byproduct of religious beliefs in Thai society. Instead that phenomenon must also be explained in terms of the kingdom's transition to capitalism and the bourgeois ideology that came with that transition. During the 1980s and 1990s, capitalism had a huge impact on Thailand by transforming its mode of production from agriculture to industry. Thanks to this transition, a class of Sino-Thai businessmen, industrialists, financiers, white-collar workers, and entrepreneurs rapidly emerged and became the vanguard of the Thai bourgeoisie, which played a dominant role in the national economy, politics, and pop culture. Before this critical transition, the monarchy had tried to popularize some images that were supposed to bring the institution back into mass consciousness. The palace's attempt to present Rama IX as the spiritual king, the cosmopolitan king, and the warrior-king, however, seemed to be detached from the mass of the Thai populace. Like new wine in old bottles, the images of Rama IX in his early reign were not essentially different from those of former monarchs; they were images of the divine, heroic, and splendid king, which tended to alienate the multitude of Sino-Thai subjects whose ethical values and daily practices were more banal, profane, and unheroic than those of royalty.

In the 1980s, the palace turned the tables on the cultural status of the middle class in the kingdom by rebranding Rama IX as an expert on the economy and development who relentlessly worked for the common good of his subjects. These rebranded images found a strong resonance among members of the rising bourgeoisie, who for the first time saw their monarch finally embrace the ideology that they had long valued. Consequently, a particular set of ethics that were attached to Rama IX in his late reign—hard work, frugality, and self-reliance—was highlighted, praised, and reproduced by the bourgeoisie in the mass media and the government's public relations. Meanwhile, Sino-Thai subjects, who were driven by two contradictory attitudes, a royalist ideology and a capitalist one, also appreciated images of Rama IX that were associated with bourgeois sentiments of love, comfort, family, and cultural indulgence. Embodying all the economic ethics and cultural values to which the bourgeoisie aspired, Rama IX became a role model for this class. This convergence between the invented images of the monarchy and the ideological satisfaction of the bourgeoisie is one of the main reasons why the Thai monarchy was successful not only in renovating its status from one of irrelevance to that of the most influential institution in the kingdom but also in securing the active consent of a huge army of capitalists, the urban middle class, intellectuals, bureaucrats, and politicians who were all loyal to instead of in rebellion against the throne. This bourgeois army indeed provided the mass-based support of the Thai crown in the early twenty-first century that would have made other monarchies in the history of capitalism green with envy.

 **4**

THE CROWN VERSUS THE CROWD

In 2006 the status of the Thai monarchy apparently reached its zenith. Celebrating King Rama IX's sixtieth year on the throne, the royal family hosted thirteen reigning monarchs from around the world and the close representatives of another twelve. The first diamond jubilee in Thai history was a rare assembly of global and endangered royalty. As an observer reported, it was a historic gathering of "the most exclusive club on earth in which membership arrives either by accident of birth or more occasionally through marriage."[1] From the absolute sultan of Brunei to the constitutional emperor of Japan, from the emir of oil-rich Kuwait to the king of the Swedish welfare state, and from the duke of York of postindustrial Britain to the crown prince of underdeveloped Bhutan, royalty around the world waited in line at the Ananta Samakhom Throne Hall to pay homage to the world's longest-reigning monarch. This was a remarkable success for Rama IX. Seven decades before, in this particular hall, his uncle—King Rama VII—had been forced by the People's Party to surrender his absolute power and accept a constitutional regime. That historical nadir of the monarchy was long gone. Once the place where commoners convened the National Assembly, the hall in June 2006 was packed with a crowd of blue bloods from Asia, Europe, the Middle East, and Africa. Outside the Hall, half a million Thais wore yellow shirts to honor their monarch and waited for hours in the hot, humid weather of Bangkok just to catch a glimpse of Rama IX and listen to his speech. While many repeatedly shouted "Long live the King!" and raised pictures of the royal family over their heads, some shed tears as their beloved monarch waved his hands to greet them. This mass excitement during the diamond jubilee was undeniably a sign of royal popularity among the Thai population, a sign that indicated how successfully the monarchy had been revived since it found itself on the brink of extinction in the mid-twentieth century.

At that historic moment, it looked as if the legacy of the ninth monarch of the Chakri dynasty was cemented. According to Handley's assessment of Rama IX's reign in 2006, the king "has sealed his own reputation, and it is unlikely to be undone. His prestige has survived unscathed, by the virtue of his sheer longevity and his personality—earnest, hard-working, [and] gentle, with an impeccably simple lifestyle."[2] It would sound like a fairy tale if his reign had come to an end at the diamond jubilee. The history of the monarchy under the reign of Rama IX, however, continued for one more decade, and it had an unsettling instead of happily-ever-after ending. In the last decade of his reign, the aged and ailing monarch had to witness an unprecedented upsurge of lèse-majesté charges and punishments, and he had to face the challenge of a prime minister who became a popular figure and stole the spotlight from the palace. Most important, his subjects were clearly divided into two antagonistic mass movements: the well-to-do, who revered and loved him as their hard-working and frugal "dad"; and the dispossessed, who begged to differ. While members of the first movement wore yellow shirts to signify their loyalty to the monarch, the latter dressed in red—the particular color that still haunted the crown since it was the symbolic color of the CPT. On the surface, the so-called Red Shirts might pay lip service to the crown, publicly claiming that they did not hold any antimonarchist sentiments. In songs, graffiti, and poems that were circulated among the participants of this movement,

however, there were political messages that showed signs of republicanism. Mocking the bodies of royalty, exposing the hypocrisy of the
world's richest monarch who presented himself in public as a frugal
man, and even wishing for the death of the ailing king, the Red Shirts
reminded the crown that not all Thais were monarchists. Their teasing
and taunting of the monarchy exposed a critical challenge to the bourgeois monarchy in industrialized Thailand. Although the monarchy
was popular among the "yellow" bourgeoisie, the "red" working class
and peasantry felt aggrieved by the crown, its massive wealth, and its
bourgeois supporters. These divisive views of the crown, which spread
along social class lines, tarnished the historic run of Rama IX on the
throne. Instead of a unified and peaceful kingdom, what the king left to
his heir apparent was an uphill task in conflict-ridden Thailand: to keep
enchanting the wealthy bourgeoisie while taming the multitudes of the
resentful underclasses in a kingdom where capitalism, inequality, and
class conflict prevailed. This is a tall order for any monarch, let alone an
unpopular one like King Rama X, to fulfill today.

What went wrong with the Thai monarchy during Rama IX's last
few years on the throne? In spite of all its successes during Thailand's
transition to industrial capitalism, the bourgeois monarchy embodied
some intrinsic contradictions that later developed into critical challenges to the monarchy in the last decade of Rama IX's reign. The crown's
success in accumulating capital and establishing monarchy-led capitalism in Thailand came at a price: socioeconomic inequality, uneven development, and capital concentration, which created a wide gap between
the rich and the poor and the city and the countryside. While the monarchy successfully developed an ideological, political, and economic
partnership with the urban bourgeoisie, their symbiosis alienated the
rural peasantry and urban working class, which constituted the majority of the national population. Furthermore, although the crown had
recently secured its hegemonic status in the government, the market,
and the mass media, it still relied on extraeconomic coercion as the last
resort to restore political order when royal ideology failed to maintain
public consent. Worst of all, the popular king who embraced bourgeois
ethics and images was anything but immortal, and it was uncertain
whether the unpopular prince who stood first in line of succession by
virtue of his birth—instead of the bourgeois ethic of hard work, frugality, and meritocracy—would be able to follow in his father's footsteps.
This was the anxiety that loomed large in the twilight of Rama IX's

years. Whether the bourgeois crown would be in good hands after the bourgeois king breathed his last was anything but certain.

THE KINGDOM OF INEQUALITY

At the end of the twentieth century, the monarchy was not only surviving but also thriving amid Thailand's rapid transformation into a newly industrialized country. Royal leadership of the national economy, royal investments in the capitalist market, and the relationship between the palace and the rising bourgeoisie had never been better. On top of their joint ventures in the major business sectors, the monarchy and the bourgeoisie developed their symbiotic relationship outside the market. The crown offered ideological inspiration and symbolic decoration to the nouveau riche, while the latter donated money to the crown, popularized royal prestige in the mass media, and served as a mass base for the palace. This symbiosis, nonetheless, planted the seeds of political conflict. While the monarchy and the bourgeoisie enjoyed their accumulation of wealth, the majority of the Thai population struggled with the kingdom's industrial revolution, which came with socioeconomic inequality, uneven development, and capital concentration. The masses of peasants, blue-collar workers, and unemployed people — the particular classes that were formerly the priority of royal charities — were not only poorer than their compatriots who belonged to the bourgeois class. Feeling alienated and neglected by the monarchy, they were also eager for an alternative to monarchy-led capitalism, which benefited the palace and its bourgeois partners.

It was this background that paved the way for a new political actor like Thaksin Shinawatra, a telecommunications tycoon who became prime minister. Promoting himself as the savior of the poor — the symbolic role that was formerly played by the royal family — Thaksin launched several groundbreaking policies that distributed welfare and capital to those who did not belong to the exclusive club of royalty and the bourgeoisie. The increasing popularity of Thaksin among these long-neglected classes apparently rubbed the palace the wrong way. From the palace's point of view, the energetic crowd of the peasants and workers needed to be tamed. Royal intervention, royalist protest and unrest, and a regally approved coup d'état were a series of events that undermined and eventually toppled Thaksin's government in September 2006, only three months after the diamond jubilee.

Inequality under Monarchy-Led Capitalism

As noted earlier, the industrialization, urbanization, and national development that began in the 1960s and the historic expansion of the economy from the 1980s on rapidly transformed Thailand into a newly industrialized country. This great transformation in the late twentieth century, however, came at a price: a broadening gap between the rich and the poor. Among Asian countries in the twenty-first century, Thailand has been ranked as one of the most unequal in terms of income distribution.[3] Using the Gini index to measure income distribution in Southeast Asian countries, Pasuk revealed that in the 1960s Thailand was a more equitable society than those of Malaysia and the Philippines. The economic boom in the mid-1980s, however, widened the income gap in the Thai kingdom, and today Thailand is head and shoulders above its neighbors when it comes to income inequality.[4] Inequality in Thailand becomes even clearer if it is seen through the lens of quintiles. Since the economic boom, the wealthiest 20 percent of Thais have earned more than half of all national income. In 2000, especially, they earned an all-time high of 57.42 percent of national income while the lowest quintile earned a mere 3.95 percent. In other words, the gap in incomes between the two strata was 14.54 times.[5] Not only do a few Thais earn more than others, but the top quintile of Thais also has the power to spend more money and acquire more consumer goods than others do. In the 1990s, for example, the wealthiest 20 percent accounted for 50 percent of national expenditures while the lowest quintile represented only 6 percent, and the gap in purchasing power between them was eight times, a record high.[6] In addition to incomes and expenditures, a few wealthy Thais own a disproportionate amount of land. In 2016, the top quintile of the Thai population owned 79.93 percent of all landed estates in the kingdom whereas the lowest quintile possessed merely 0.25 percent.[7] In the kingdom that is proudly called "the land of all Thais," the majority of land is ironically in the possession of a handful of its citizens.

Capital in Thailand has not merely been hoarded by a specific stratum of the population. It has also been highly concentrated in a specific region of the kingdom. That is, inequality in the kingdom can be illustrated through the differences in regional shares of the national population and GDP.[8] In 1960 Bangkok accounted for 8 percent of the national population and 24 percent of GDP, while the combination of the two poorest regions of the kingdom—the Northeast and the North—held

61 percent of the population and 33 percent of GDP. Four decades later the gap between the capital city and these two regions had widened. In 2000, 10 percent of the national population lived in Bangkok, and its share of GDP was 35 percent. In contrast, 53 percent of Thais lived in the northeastern and northern regions, but this majority of Thais accounted for merely 20 percent of GDP. While wealth has been increasingly concentrated in the Bangkok metropolitan area, where industrial factories, corporate buildings, and shopping malls are heavily packed, poverty has been spreading throughout the countryside. According to the NESDB, since the late 1980s, although the proportion of Thais who live in poverty has gradually decreased in general, some regions have higher concentrations of the poor. In 2000, for example, 6 percent of Bangkok residents lived in poverty whereas 60 percent of northeasterners and 50 percent of northerners were categorized as poor.[9]

For some scholars, the fact that capital in Thailand has been highly concentrated among the wealthiest 20 percent of the population and in the capital city is an oversimplification. According to Pasuk, Thailand, like the United States, has the "1 percent problem."[10] Behind the crowd of wealthy Thais stands the very wealthiest elite. In the early 2010s, the top four families alone owned 45 percent of the wealth of the fifty richest families in the kingdom.[11] The wealth of the kingdom's 1 percent, T. F. Rhoden contended, would be even more evident if the examination covered what scholars in Thai studies conventionally avoid—including the monarch and his wealth in the ranks of Thailand's wealthiest people. By doing this, Rhoden unveiled that Rama IX, thanks to his estimated wealth of US$41 billion in 2014, was the richest man not only in his kingdom but in all Asian countries. Measuring the inequality of wealth by the Material Power Index (MPI), Rhoden also showed that in 2014 Thailand's gap between the average wealth of the top fifty richest people (including the king at the top) and the average wealth per capita was the widest in Asia.[12] As a result, Rhoden concluded, "In materialist terms, there are oligarchs in Thailand and the Thai monarch is at the top of them all."[13]

These problems of socioeconomic inequality, uneven development, and capital concentration have been chronic in the kingdom since it became a newly industrialized country. Feeling that they had been left behind by the rapid train of socioeconomic changes, the majority of Thais desperately hoped to find an alternative to the dominant form of Thai capitalism in which the monarchy took the leadership role in the state and the market. Their hope was realized at a critical juncture in

Thai history at the turn of the twentieth-first century when the kingdom still struggled with the depression that followed the 1997 economic
crisis. As Pasuk and Chris Baker recapped the impact of the crisis among
the underclasses, "From mid-1998 onwards, the impact of the crisis
spread through rural society. The international price of rice dropped
sharply. The cost of imported inputs rose. Remittances from family
members working in the city shrank. Rural migrants lost their jobs and
were thrown back on the support of the rural family. The number in
poverty rose by 3 million, virtually all rural."[14]

At this historic juncture, the poor did not suffer alone. Indeed, the
crisis made its presence felt among Thailand's wealthy class. The
wealth of the CPB drastically shrank, and many conglomerates owned
by Sino-Thai moguls were taken over by multinational corporations.
On top of that, millions of middle-class employees lost their jobs. As a
result, even the urban wealthy desperately needed someone who could
rescue the national economy from the crisis. At that moment, the stage
was set for a new actor to enter the Thai political arena—the area where
the monarchy was normally hegemonic—and play the heroic role of
solving the nation's problems. In the 2001 general election, the first one
held after the crisis, Thaksin led his brand new party, Thai Rak Thai
(TRT), to a landslide victory with slogans such as "New Thinking and
New Action for Every Thai" and "The Heart of TRT is the People."
Living up to its slogans, Thaksin's party did something new in Thai
society. It set the politically inert masses of Thais into motion, motion
that Thaksin himself and even the monarchy could not control.

The Crown and the Contender

On the surface, the rise of Thaksin should have been anything but a
threat to the throne and the bourgeoisie. Above all, he was an elite member of the wealthiest class of the Thai population. According to his best-
selling biography, *Eyes on the Stars, Feet on the Ground*, Thaksin had a personal background that should have appealed to the bourgeoisie. He was
born into a Sino-Thai family and raised with the ethic of hard work and
frugality by his entrepreneurial father. Finishing at the top of his class
as an army cadet, he won a government scholarship to study abroad.
After earning a doctoral degree in the United States, he returned to his
home country to work as a police officer but later quit that job because
he had an ambitious vision of introducing a cutting-edge industry he
had learned about in America—wireless telecommunications—to the

domestic market.[15] Starting with a small business, going bankrupt after a risky investment but making a comeback with an innovative enterprise that made him an overnight billionaire, Thaksin personified the rags-to-riches story that Thai entrepreneurs had long hoped to experience. Like other Sino-Thai businessmen, he rapidly made a large fortune during Thailand's economic boom in the late 1980s. The crown jewel of his business empire—Shin Corporation—represented the new era in the Thai economy. Instead of heavy industry and landed property, Thailand in the millennial era would be driven by the service industries, and Thaksin's telecommunications conglomerate was the frontrunner. As the owner of an enterprise that promoted information technology, computerization, and digital innovation, Thaksin could be considered a visionary billionaire in the same league as capitalist icons such as Bill Gates, Steve Jobs, Mark Zuckerberg, and Jack Ma. On top of that, while many Thai corporations went bankrupt after the 1997 crisis, Thaksin's business empire successfully weathered the storm and was one of the few survivors among locally owned businesses.[16] As a result, when Thaksin declared in the 2001 campaign that he wanted to use his business experience to help the struggling domestic enterprises, revive the GDP growth, and take the country to the point where it could join the exclusive club of the Organization for Economic Co-operation and Development, his personal background and ambitious campaign resonated strongly with the urban bourgeoisie.[17] In Bangkok, the electoral district that had long supported royalist-conservative parties such as the Democrat Party, the TRT took twenty-nine of thirty-seven seats in the House of Parliament.[18] The urban bourgeoisie clearly gave Thaksin a chance to lead the country.

Likewise, in the beginning the relationship between the monarchy and Thaksin was not antagonistic. Even before Thaksin entered national politics, the Shin Corporation had been one of the major conglomerates that most frequently visited the palace and donated both money and commodities to the royal family. According to Handley, "Thaksin used his money to buy off the palace . . . [and] his generous donations reaped him entry into Queen Sirikit's circle . . . [where he also] used his wealth to get close to the crown prince."[19] Especially when the CPB was struggling after the economic crisis, it was Thaksin, Handley claimed, who bailed out royal businesses. In turn, when Thaksin faced a charge of corruption just a few months after he took office, according to McCargo, it was General Prem, the president of the Privy Council, who bailed him out by using the royal network in the

Constitutional Court to make a deal that called for Thaksin to keep the monarchy's loyalist associates in the army intact.[20] Even the monarch seemed to get along fairly well with the popularly elected premier. In his 2003 birthday speech, Rama IX praised one of Thaksin's policies, the "War on Drugs," despite the fact that it was criticized by the international community after a large number of drug dealers were extrajudicially executed.[21] As Kevin Hewison noted, what made the monarchy tolerant of the rise of Thaksin was the specific historical context after the economic crisis. Given his popular appeal to both the urban wealthy and the rural poor—plus his record of loyalty to and financial sponsorship of the royal family—Thaksin was not snubbed but rather accepted by the crown as the right person to prevent an uprising of the masses who had suffered severely in the crisis.[22] Meanwhile, Thaksin apparently knew how to pay lip service to the palace. While his government essentially aimed to revive and deepen capitalism in Thailand, he frequently declared in public that Rama IX's SEP would be the model for the national economy.[23]

This honeymoon period among the Thai wealthy—the richest monarch on earth, the urban bourgeoisie, and the billionaire prime minister—did not last long. Regardless of his personal intentions, Thaksin governed the country in a way that set the stage for a clash between him and the political alliance of the palace and the bourgeoisie. That is, his administration had several innovative and distinctive features that later developed into forces that challenged the hegemonic status of the crown. Unlike his forerunners, Thaksin was the first prime minister to secure popular support not only from the wealthy minority in the capital city but also from the underprivileged majority in the countryside. Taking 54 of 76 seats in the North and 69 of 138 seats in the Northeast, the TRT gained popular support from the rural poor because its 2001 campaign aimed to promote, in Jim Glassman's words, "populist Keynesianism."[24] Rather than following an IMF program of fiscal austerity, as former governments had done after the economic crisis, the TRT promised the lower classes that the new government would spend massively and quickly beyond the capital city. In a kingdom where rural peasants and urban workers had historically been neglected, burdened with debt, and unable to access health care, the TRT's three major policies—an agrarian debt moratorium, a grant of 1 million baht (US$22,700) to every village, and a 30 baht (US$0.68) per visit scheme of universal health care—were groundbreaking. Once in office, Thaksin not only delivered what his party had promised but also launched a series of other policies that later became trademarks of his populist government. These included affordable housing, supplies of low-priced computers, subsidized credit for buying taxis, loans of bicycles to young students so they could get to school, and a cheap life insurance plan that cost policyholders 1 baht (US$0.02) a day.[25] With these state-funded programs as part of the government's "War on Poverty" campaign, Thaksin quickly became a popular figure among the Thai underclasses. "We are in a state of economic war," he declared to his grassroots supporters. "The poor are like wounded soldiers. If we don't cure their injuries, where shall we find the soldiers to fight the war?"[26]

Despite his promotion of social welfare for the poor, Thaksin was neither a vulgar demagogue nor a democratic socialist. Above all, he was one of the richest capitalists in the kingdom, a member of "Thailand's 1 percent," and an ambitious billionaire who entered national politics not only to maintain and protect his business interests but also to do what capitalists do best, deepen capitalism. What drove Thaksin and his party, which was host to many business tycoons who entered politics for the first time, was a reaction to the damage inflicted by the 1997 economic crisis. Witnessing politicians, technocrats, an older generation of businessmen, and the palace all failing to steer the national economy and safeguard local businesses from takeovers by foreign capital, Thaksin believed that he could do a better job than those in office. Consequently, as Pasuk and Baker noted, Thaksin decided to lead "a group of the major domestic capitalists who had survived the financial crisis to capture state power with the explicit aim of using it to protect and promote domestic capital."[27] Furthermore, the invasion of Thaksin and his capitalist crew in national politics after the crisis, Hewison argued, was understandable if this phenomenon is viewed through a Marxist lens. "An important point in the Marxist approach," Hewison wrote, "is the recognition that a crisis is often a starting-point for a recomposition of capital, and new phases of investment. This reflects the tendency of natural competition between capitalists to become more intense and for capitalists to turn to each other in times of crisis."[28] The political rise of Thaksin, therefore, can be seen as the emergence of new capitalists who aimed to transform an outdated political and social arrangement that had long been dominated by Thailand's older capitalists. Likewise, Glassman argued that Thaksin tried not only to revive but also to deepen capitalism with a new approach.[29] Facing problems of overproduction, overcapacity, and capital concentration in Bangkok, each of which was among the main causes of the economic crisis, the TRT attempted to implement new policies, which could be described, in David Harvey's term, as a "spatial fix." Making it possible for Thai capitalists to survive the crisis and prolong the life of Thai capitalism required three initiatives: the creation of new urban spaces and built environments, the transfer of advanced technology, and the investment of capital in secondary cities in the countryside, which had lower production costs and cheaper labor.[30] Only through this geographic extension and decentralization of capital investment and the expansion of domestic consumption, all of which Thaksin and his fellow capitalists intended to do, could Thai capitalists temporarily overcome the problems of profitability in the domestic market. The TRT, as Glassman observed, "was promising a new sort of spatial fix for the Thai economy, with more wealth putatively to be invested and generated outside Bangkok."[31]

Driven by a crew of capitalists, the TRT was composed of Thailand's biggest enterprises in several business sectors: the largest telecommunications conglomerate (Shin Corporation), the biggest agribusiness empire (CP), one of the largest housing developers (Land and Houses), the fourth-largest telecommunications company (Jasmine), the largest auto parts company (Summit), and two of the largest media enterprises (Channel 3 and Grammy).[32] Armed with this crew of capitalists, Thaksin's government seemed to have an ambitious plan to administer Thailand not as a kingdom but as a company. Announcing to the public, "A company is a country. A country is a company. They are the same. The management is the same. It is management by economics. . . . Economics is the deciding factor,"[33] Thaksin had a tendency to treat his supporters, as Pasuk and Baker put it, "not so much [as] citizens with rights, liberties, and aspirations, but rather [as] consumers, shareholders, and factors of production."[34] In addition to the distribution of social welfare, what Thaksin's government unprecedentedly did to the kingdom was provide capital to the multitudes outside Bangkok. Promoting new entrepreneurs and consumers in Thailand's countryside, Thaksin's policies included a grand scheme to "turn assets into capital." The government advocated more productive use of local labor skills, capital reserves, and cultural assets; the elimination of rules and regulations, which raised the cost of starting a business; and the extension of government-directed credits to the grass roots. It also promoted small and medium-sized enterprises (SMEs) through the marriage of traditional craft skills and high technology, the stimulation of economic growth via private consumption, and the easing of age and income limits on credit card ownership. Even though these programs were panned by critics who claimed that they would eventually create household debt among the rural poor, Thaksin was not concerned but carefree. "Under the capitalist system," he proclaimed, "if villagers have no access to capital, they have no opportunity to get something going for themselves. And who will say it is debt? I will. If I had not been in debt before, I would not be where I am today."[35] Thailand's road to prosperity, for Thaksin, had only one route. It led to the engagement of all Thais with capitalism as both producers and consumers.

With this vision of Thailand as a company and Thai citizens as shareholders, Thaksin tended to see himself not only as a prime minister but also as the chief executive officer (CEO) of the country. Aiming to reform the Thai bureaucracy, which had a reputation for red tape, corruption, and loyalty to the crown instead of to the citizenry, Thaksin was politically ambitious and proposed a plan to implement the CEO system among the kingdom's civil servants. Governors, for example, were promoted by Thaksin as "CEO governors." Each had to draw up a provincial strategy on the model of a corporate business plan, and each was responsible for economic growth in his own province. Crucially, each could bypass the bureaucratic chain of command and report directly to the prime minister. "With this CEO Governor model," Thaksin stated in front of all the governors, who had been summoned to Bangkok to learn business management, "I'm challenging the governors [to find out] whether they are really managers."[36] The same kind of model was designed for the foreign ministry under the scheme of "CEO ambassadors." Summoned to Bangkok to attend seminars on business management and instructed to actively promote the country's economic interests overseas, Thai envoys got a signal from Thaksin, who warned, "This [CEO] system will be a test of the ambassadors' performance. And those who don't perform will be ousted, definitely."[37] In addition to civilian bureaucrats, Thaksin extended his power to the military and police by promoting his family members, in-laws, and former cadet classmates to key positions.

What made Thaksin the virtual CEO of Thailand in the millennial era, however, was not his power and influence over the state apparatus but the active consent he gained from the country's "shareholders." The first prime minister in Thai history to finish a four-year term in office, Thaksin led the TRT into the 2005 election with a campaign entitled "Four Years of Rebuilding, Four Years of Building." Even before this

election, the TRT was the dominant party, occupying 296 of 500 seats in
the House of Parliament thanks to its landslide victory in the previous
election and its merger with medium-sized parties after that. The 2005
election, however, was the high point of Thaksin's and his party's
achievements. Out of 500 seats, the TRT swept 377, while the Democrat
Party, the second-largest and then the opposition party, took a mere 96.
It was the first time in Thai politics that one party had gained a victory
of this magnitude, and it could have led to a single dominant party
system for years to come. Popular support for Thaksin and his party
was evident not only among the rural majority but also among the
urban minority—in the North, the TRT took 70 of 76 seats, in the Northeast 126 of 135, and in Bangkok 32 of 37.[38] Except for royalty, it is extremely rare to find anyone in Thai history who enjoyed as great a
popular appeal as Thaksin did in the early 2000s.

Although it seemed as though the aphorism "A rising tide lifts all
boats" rang true in Thaksin's Thailand, his personal boat was apparently
lifted higher than those of the others. After two years in office, Thaksin
did deliver what he had promised to his supporters: he revived the
national economy after the economic crisis. In 2003 his government
repaid an IMF loan two years ahead of schedule and staged a public
celebration of this event as "independence day."[39] By the time Thaksin's
first term of premiership came to an end, Pasuk and Baker noted, the
economy had completely recovered: "Most surviving firms had cleared
their debts, straightened their balance sheets, and begun to show a
profit . . . [while] banks ceased shrinking their commercial loan portfo-
lios and began to increase their lending to business. The overall level of
investment in the economy edged upwards."[40] During this phase of
national recapitalization, however, Thaksin's business empire seemed
to reap a larger share of good fortune than his capitalist rivals did. Before
Thaksin became a prime minister, Shin Corp's assets and market cap
were 37.8 billion baht (US$1 billion) and 46.1 billion baht (US$1.2 billion) respectively. Three years after Thaksin took office, the company's
assets were worth 60 billion baht (US$1.5 billion) and its market cap
had skyrocketed to 113.8 billion baht (US$2.8 billion). Likewise, in 2000
Advance Info Service (AIS), a subsidiary of Shin Corp, registered its assets and market cap as 59.1 billion baht (US$1.5 billion) and 97.2 billion
baht (US$2.5 billion) respectively. Just three years later AIS's assets had
increased to 125 billion baht (US$2.9 billion) and its market cap had bal-
looned to 250 billion baht (US$5.8 billion).[41] Despite the fact that before

taking office in 2001 Thaksin resigned from all positions in his companies and transferred his shares to his wife and children, the public had long been skeptical of the claim that he had given up control of his business empire and wondered whether he used his power to advance his own business interests at the expense of his rivals.

In 2006 the executives of Shin Corp shocked the nation by announcing the sale of the company's majority shares, held by Thaksin's family, to Temasek Holdings, an investment company owned by the government of Singapore. In the most lucrative deal in the history of Thailand's stock market, Thaksin's family netted approximately 73 billion baht (US$1.9 billion) and, in accordance with Thai tax laws, their business transaction was tax free. Although the sale of Shin Corp was legal and Thaksin claimed that the deal was done by his son and daughters in order to let him engage in politics without any accusation of a conflict of interest, the so-called Thailand's deal of the century drew heavy criticism and provoked frustration among the urban bourgeoisie. Once a national hero who promised to protect domestic enterprises from foreign capital, Thaksin was now seen as a traitor who sought only his own profits at the expense of the national interest and selfishly sold a Thai company to foreigners. "Corruption," "Thaksin sold the nation," and the "capitalist-absolutist regime" rapidly became catchphrases among members of the resentful bourgeoisie who took the streets of Bangkok to demonstrate against the prime minister, who was deemed unapologetic and arrogant in the face of a public backlash.[42] The bourgeois protesters, however, were not alone. Witnessing Thaksin's rapid accumulation of wealth, power, and popularity in millennial Thailand, the crown was ready to strike back at the contender who threatened both its popularity and its political dominance.

THE ROYALIST REACTION

Once Thaksin won his landslide election in 2005, it was just a matter of time before the monarchy finally intervened and toppled him. The palace was driven to oust Thaksin, in McCargo's words, "not because of the Temasek deal, or because of corruption or abuses of power, but because of his symbolic challenges to the monarchy."[43] The challenge of Thaksin to the hegemonic status of the crown, however, can be better understood if it is examined not merely as a symbolic clash but also as a product of the political, economic, and financial conflicts between them.

Royal resentments of Thaksin, which were essentially reactionary re-
sponses to distinctive features of his administration, had the following
elements.

To begin with, Thaksin competed with the monarch for popularity
among the lower classes. In the early reign of Rama IX, it had been
royalty who played a symbolic role as the saviors of the poor, and the
monarchy during the Cold War era had secured strong support from
the rural masses as the king and queen frequently visited remote provinces, provided donated goods to the underprivileged, and patronized rural artisans under royal projects. After the 1980s, however, the
poor majority felt that they had been left behind by the palace for several reasons. The aged and ailing king and queen lacked the physical
strength for rough travel and thus frequently stayed in the capital city.
Poverty among peasants and workers was no longer a critical issue for
the palace after the demise of communism in Thailand. Worst of all,
royal projects and charities were merely temporary panaceas instead of
systemic and permanent solutions to chronic problems of destitution,
underdevelopment, and lack of access to social welfare among the
poor. Instead, during the last two decades of the twentieth century, the
king and the royal family tended to prioritize urgent issues of rapid
urbanization and industrialization. In addition, the crown seemed to
enjoy a revered status among its new mass base, the nouveau riche in
the capital city, who not only promoted royal popularity in the mass
media but also financially sponsored the royal household and royal
charities.

The alliance between the monarchy and the urban bourgeoisie alienated the multitudes of rural peasants and urban workers further when
the palace attempted to preach the king's SEP to the lower classes.
Rama IX, according to Handley, had a history of attributing the poverty
of the lower classes to laziness, and the king usually viewed the poor as
children who did not know how to work.[44] Widely propagated by the
palace and the mass media after the 1997 crisis, SEP rubbed salt in the
wounds of the poor. Preaching to them to work harder, prudently save
and spend their money, and abstain from all consumerist activities, the
king's ethical code treated the poor as if they were not the ones who
actually worked and labored for the overclass. This attitude implied
that conspicuous consumption was not for them but was exclusively
the preserve of royalty and the bourgeoisie. Against this historical
background, it was understandable that Thaksin's policies toward the
poor would subvert the royal ideology. Instead of servile and childish

subjects, the poor were treated by Thaksin and his party as "share-holders" of the country with their own rights—a right to demand and receive social welfare from the state; a right to have a say in the allocation of the national budget; and a right to aspire, produce, and consume in a capitalist state as much as the bourgeoisie did. Pouring money into and providing credits, loans, and welfare to the poor, Thaksin's populist programs virtually liberated the multitudes from the royal ideology and replaced it with a new one. Instead of living in a self-sufficient economy, they, too, could lead wealthy and luxurious lives, as Thaksin did, if only they embraced capitalism, entrepreneurship, and consumerism. As Hewison put it, "Thaksin, the Porsche-driving modern entrepreneur, offered a different approach to [rural peasants]. Far from urging a return to the farm and being content with rural 'sufficiency,' Thaksin's policies emphasised 'getting ahead' [and] producing for the market and promoted entrepreneurism."[45] As Thaksin's policies strongly resonated with the poor and his popularity among them seemed impervious to his corruption scandals, there were growing concerns among the royalty and the bourgeoisie. For the crown, the symbolic role of royalty as the champions of the poor was seriously undermined by Thaksin. Similarly, among the bourgeoisie, the wealthy class that praised Rama IX as the "hardest-working father" of the nation, widespread feelings of insecurity sprang up, feelings that "there might be more than one ultimate core to the polity, more than one 'father.'"[46]

The conflict between Thaksin and the monarchy was also a consequence of their different visions of Thai capitalism. Under monarchy-led capitalist development, the role of the state was kept to a minimum. Business sectors had autonomy in the market, and royal charities were a prominent form of philanthropic relief for problems of inequality, uneven development, and capital concentration. For decades, the crown and the urban bourgeoisie had been the runway beneficiaries of this model of Thai capitalism. Without systematic and official programs of public welfare, social distribution, and state intervention, the royal business empire and bourgeois enterprises mutually enjoyed an uninterrupted accumulation and concentration of capital. Their appropriation of labor from the working class was not hindered by state regulations, and their incomes and assets were left intact, free of any form of progressive taxation that aimed to create public benefits for ordinary Thais. Instead the only form of public assistance in Thailand before the millennial era was the "welfare monarchy," a philanthropic practice through which the bourgeoisie donated money to royal charities and the royal family in turn acted as benevolent providers to the poor. Masking the inequality and hostility of underlying class conflicts in Thailand, the benevolent acts of the Thai wealthy were similar to what Marx and Engels said about the philanthropic and reforming tendencies of the bourgeoisie: "A part of the bourgeoisie is desirous of redressing social grievances, in order to secure the continued existence of bourgeois society . . . [but they] want all the advantages of modern social conditions without the struggles and dangers necessarily resulting from them. They desire the existing state of society minus its revolutionary and disintegrating elements. They wish for a bourgeoisie without a proletariat."[47]

As bourgeois proper, Thaksin's capitalist crew undoubtedly had as a primary goal the continued existence of bourgeois society, and thus a proletarian revolution was hardly in their master plan. What distinguished Thaksin's policies from monarchy-led capitalism, however, was that the former proposed a new model of the capitalist state that not only addressed the social grievances of the exploited classes but also initiated state programs that could delay a crisis of capitalism and a social uprising. According to Hewison, in order to maintain the social and political order, Thaksin attempted to construct a "new social contract" involving a number of policies that established "a higher level of social protection than ever considered possible in the past." The policies of soft loans to rural villages and a universal health care scheme, Hewison pointed out, exemplified how the "contract" was constructed and realized between the capitalist government and the poor majority.[48] Likewise, Glassman believed that Thaksin's notion of a "spatial fix," based on the geographic expansion of capital investment and domestic consumption, had a tendency to temporarily delay the next bout of economic crisis and a social uprising in the kingdom.

The monarchy and the bourgeoisie, nevertheless, did not buy Thaksin's grand schemes. For the crown, the Keynesian-oriented programs would not only undermine the symbolic role of royalty as the nation's philanthropists but also challenge Rama IX's long disapproval of a welfare state. Similarly, members of the bourgeoisie did not even consider Thaksin's redistribution programs to be a mode of welfare provision. Instead, they criticized those programs as demagogic politics that not only would waste their tax money on the poor majority, who were seen as idle and improvident, but would also cause a budget deficit and create national debt in the long run. The bourgeois resentment of Thaksin, therefore, was not mainly based on either his corruption scandals or his promotion of global capitalism's penetration into the domestic market. Instead, as Glassman noted, what this wealthy class strongly opposed was not neoliberalism per se but the Keynesian expenditures of Thaksin's administration.[49]

Furthermore, when it came to national politics, Thaksin and the monarchy were not on the same page. With unprecedented support from Thai voters, Thaksin was confident that he had a popular mandate to rule as the elected leader of the country. His CEO style of government, however, irritated the palace. For decades the center of the Thai polity was clearly the monarchy, and it was the unelected monarch around whom elected premiers and ministers had to orbit. In other words, Rama IX, especially in his late reign, had virtually acted as the CEO of the kingdom, and thus from the palace's point of view Thaksin not only disregarded the classic proverb "If two ride on a horse, one must ride behind" but also forgot the fact that he was a prime minister of the kingdom not the president of the republic. In Rama IX's provocative 2005 birthday speech, the king expressed his concerns about Thaksin's strong premiership, which many critics began to label "authoritarian" and "absolutist-capitalist." Given that Thaksin and his cabinet ministers were sitting in front of Rama IX in the royal hall, the king seemed to use his address to distinguish himself from the arrogant premier, who had a habit of not only neglecting but also silencing many critics of his government. "It is normal that a person wants to be praised and that no one likes to be criticized," Rama IX began his speech. Despite the fact that Thailand has the harshest punishment of lèse-majesté in the world, the king surprised his audience by encouraging all Thais to criticize him more often: "[The principle] 'the king can do no wrong' disrespects the king very much. Why can the king do no wrong? This argues that the king is not a human being. The king can do wrong. . . . The king must be offended and criticized. If there is no allowance for the king to be offended, it is bad for the king."[50] Broadcast on television and radio nationwide, this royal address seemed to invite the Thai audience to construct a binary opposition between the king and the prime minister—the former the humble "Lord of Life," the latter the lordly demagogue.

In addition to his strong and brash leadership, Thaksin was seen by the crown as a threatening figure because of cronyism in his administration. By appointing his cousins, capitalist associates, and former classmates to key positions in the cabinet, the bureaucracy, the police, and the army, Thaksin virtually created his own political network in the face of the "network monarchy" that had secured its hegemonic status in Thai politics at the turn of the twenty-first century. Thaksin, in McCargo's words, had a "determination to create a new super-network, centered entirely on himself, and characterized by a more hierarchical structure."[51] Thaksin's newly installed network made its presence felt in the royal establishment when some high-ranking officers who were critical of Thaksin but loyal to the throne were replaced with his associates. The king, in turn, signaled his disapproval by recruiting those sacked officers into the Privy Council.[52] Among the last ten privy counselors that Rama IX appointed during his reign, half had conflicts with Thaksin's administration or participated in the anti-Thaksin movement.[53] The relationship between the prime minister and the palace hit rock bottom in mid-2006 when the president of the Privy Council, Prem, publicly expressed his distaste for Thaksin to the military. As Thongchai recapped this incident, "Using a horse-racing metaphor, [Prem] told a military gathering that the elected government was merely a jockey assigned to ride the horse but not the owner of it. The military was reminded that they belonged to the monarchy, not to the jockey."[54] By arousing monarchist sentiments among the military—a sleeping giant that had withdrawn from national politics in the early 1990s—the monarchy clearly sent a message to Thaksin. The army was readily mobilized to protect the throne, and his days in office were numbered.

On top of that, a financial conflict between Thaksin and the monarchy inevitably set the stage for a clash between them. As capitalist enterprises normally do, Thaksin's conglomerates and the royal business empire both cooperated and competed with one another. Since the 1997 crisis, the CPB had become involved in Thaksin's enterprises, and their close relationship was exposed to the public by the sale of Shin Corp to Temasek Holdings. In this historic deal, the SCB, one of the three pillars of the CPB's capital accumulation, was evidently the deal maker. Having a longtime business relationship with the Singaporean corporation, the SCB was the broker that invited Temasek into the deal, even facilitating it and investing with the Singapore institution in the acquisition of Shin Corp. In this regard, if Thaksin was the "national traitor" who welcomed the penetration of global capitalism into Thailand, he was not a solo greedy capitalist but had partners in crime from the palace. Despite this close collaboration between Thailand's two business empires, the monarchy did not look upon Thaksin as a trustworthy partner. As Hewison noted, "It was the combination of Thaksin's wealth and political power that was most challenging for the managers of royal businesses. With

Thaksin controlling the government, the conflicts of interest involved could not have escaped palace scrutiny, as Thaksin and [the] TRT rewarded their supporters handsomely."[55] In this sense, Thaksin and his capitalist comrades inevitably shook the royal establishment to the core. For decades, business elites had passively allowed royal businesses to enjoy their privileged status in the market in return for royal patronage and honorifics. Thaksin and his capitalist associates, by contrast, undermined this royal patronage by creating a business clique that not only bypassed but also competed with the palace's business network. Thaksin's threat to royal businesses, Hewison concluded, was that he "not only competed economically with CPB firms but [he] challenged the CPB by apparently failing to protect its special status."[56] On top of marginalizing the political network of the monarchy, Thaksin twisted the knife in the royal wound by emasculating the business network as well.

The palace seemed to understand quite well that an attempt to topple Thaksin from power, unlike former royal interventions in Rama IX's reign, could not depend merely on royal and military powers. Instead, as parliamentary democracy had established itself in Thailand since the early 1990s without a military intervention, the political justification for unseating the popularly elected prime minister had to come from the Thai populace itself. The time could not have been better for the monarchy, as its bourgeois supporters, who initially seemed to be enchanted by Thaksin's policies, finally shared the crown's resentment. In addition to state-funded populism, the lack of fiscal discipline, the violation of human rights, and media censorship, the urban bourgeoisie increasingly condemned Thaksin's administration as an embodiment of greed, corruption, and crony capitalism. The final straw came with the sale of Shin Corp in early 2006. Rather than holding himself accountable by means of a parliamentary investigation and debate, Thaksin called for a snap election just one year after having been reelected. He was confident that, although he had lost the support of the bourgeoisie in Bangkok, the majority of voters in rural provinces would bring him back to power. His decision added fuel to the fire. Seeing that Thaksin had disregarded their resentful voices, hundreds of thousands of high-ranking bureaucrats, members of noble families, Sino-Thai businessmen, white-collar workers, and urban entrepreneurs took to the streets of Bangkok in early 2006 and rallied under the banner of the People's Alliance for Democracy (PAD). The PAD rallying point was obvious: the monarchy was the institution with which the Thai bourgeoisie had long been ideologically, economically, and politically allied. Alliance protesters sported yellow shirts to show their loyalty to Rama IX, and they were proud to call themselves "descendants of the Chinese (*luk chin*)" who rallied to "Fight for Dad." The most famous figure among their leaders was Sondhi Limthongkul, a Sino-Thai media mogul who was very talented when it came to the task of arousing royalist sentiments. In a landmark speech that launched the so-called Yellow Shirt movement, Sondhi motivated his supporters by reading "The Lost Sheep," a tale written by an anonymous royalist. While criticizing the titular character, a capitalist politician who is wealthy, corrupt, arrogant, and contrary to the king's vision of the sufficiency economy, this tale praises the protagonist "dad" who has long shepherded the nation. Vividly capturing the way the urban bourgeoisie reviled Thaksin but revered Rama IX as the father figure of the nation, the story begins with admiration for all Thais when they look to their monarch.

> Dad always offers love and warmth to his children . . .
> Dad always teaches us to be honest and industrious,
> So that we can have a good and sufficient life.
> Dad never teaches us to accumulate wealth in order to be happy.
> Dad always teaches us that we can be moderately happy without wealth . . .
> About his shoes, dad still frugally uses those old shoes.
> When they are worn and torn, he just repairs them.

The tale suddenly changes its tone, however, when the greedy capitalist—the titular "lost sheep"—enters the scene, steals the spotlight from the father king, and transforms Thailand into a capitalism-driven kingdom. As the turning point of "The Lost Sheep" reveals:

> But then, there is a stubborn child . . . [who] dares to fill dad's shoes . . .
> Dad tells us that we should practice the Sufficiency Economy Philosophy.
> The lost sheep questions: How can we feed ourselves?
> Go to live in a hut? Don't be stupid!
> Dad tells us to develop the country hand in hand;
> The lost sheep seeks the privatization of public goods for his own profits.

With a goal of arousing royalist sentiments among the urban bourgeoisie and mobilizing a street protest against the Thaksin government, the tale ends with a powerful declaration: all Thais must be loyal to their father king, not a capitalist demagogue like Thaksin. The tale ends with "All children. Awake! Open your eyes! Your life belongs only to dad and no laws are required to promulgate [this fact]. Let us prostrate ourselves before the feet of the Father of the Land."[57]

A binary opposition between Rama IX and Thaksin was brought further into play by Sondhi and other PAD leaders once they attempted to shift the Yellow Shirt campaign from protesting against an arrogant premier to protecting the monarchy from republican conspirators. Speaking on their protest stage, PAD leaders not only claimed that their anti-Thaksin movement was supported and funded by the royals, but they also alleged that Thaksin and his "communist associates" were conspirators who planned to abolish the Chakri dynasty and transform the kingdom into a single-party republic.[58] The climax of the Yellow Shirt movement came when its leaders decided to call for the crown to make a political intervention. They petitioned the king to end Thaksin's "tyranny of the majority" by using the royal prerogative of appointing a new prime minister and cabinet in Thaksin's place.[59] Nevertheless, as Kasian Tejapira remarked, the palace "[took] note perhaps of the scale of the pro-Thaksin mobilization and popular vote [and] ducked the open use of the Royal Prerogative."[60] Thanks to royal silence and a boycott of an election by opposition parties, Thaksin's party secured another landslide victory in April 2006 and set out to form a one-party government.

The new government under Thaksin's leadership, however, never came to power. After the election, the crown finally made a move. Just one day after winning the election, Thaksin announced that he would step down as prime minister and give way to other TRT members. According to Kasian, this decision apparently came after Thaksin received a message from the palace, the so-called whisper from heaven.[61] The power of royal speech became clearer a few days later when the monarch spoke to the country's judges and asked them to actively engage with the controversial election that TRT had just won. In this landmark speech, which launched judicial activism in Thailand, Rama IX not only asked "Should the election be nullified?" but also gave a clue to the answer to this question. "As far as I'm concerned," the king said, "a one-party election is not normal. The one-candidate situation is undemocratic." Ultimately the king demanded that the judges solve this political problem: "When an election is not democratic, you should look carefully into the administrative issues. I ask you to do the best you can. If you cannot do it, then it should be you who resign, not the government, for failing to do your duty."[62] Shortly after the king's intervention, the Constitutional Court ruled that the latest election was unconstitutional and void. As a new election was announced for October 2006, pundits and polls unanimously predicted that Thaksin and his party would still sweep into office. Subsequently, the crown made another extraconstitutional move to oust Thaksin for good.

The 2006 coup d'état, the first coup in Thailand since 1991, was the culminating point of the problems of the bourgeois monarchy. Despite securing the consent of the urban bourgeoisie, the crown had struggled to resonate with the majority of Thais, who felt alienated from the palace and its bourgeois alliance. Yet, rather than using an ideological means to win them back, the monarchy took a shortcut by returning to the use of extraeconomic coercion to oppress the disloyal. Instead of a neutral institution under a constitutional regime, the monarchy not only supported but also actively involved itself in the 2006 coup. The close collaboration between the monarchy and the military was gradually unveiled when Thaksin was ousted. Calling themselves the Council for Reforming the Democratic Regime of Government with the King as Head of State, the coup instigators received the king's blessing within hours of taking power. Portraits of the king and queen were overrepresented in the junta's announcement on television. General Surayud Chulanont, a privy counselor who was a political nemesis of Thaksin, was regally handpicked as a new prime minister. In addition to the military budget, the junta dramatically increased the budget associated with the royal household and its projects. While Thaksin's policies were denounced as corrupt and thus terminated, the king's SEP was adopted by the junta as the kingdom's development plan and incorporated into the new military-authored constitution. Most important, lèse-majesté charges unfortunately rose from an average of 5.5 cases per year between 1993 and 2005 to 23 cases per year between 2007 and 2009, with a conviction rate of 94 percent.[63]

Despite rule by decree and the abrogation of constitutional rights, elections, and freedom of speech, the urban bourgeoisie was supportive of the coup. Many Bangkokians not only asked the military to decorate tanks, rifles, and barricades with yellow ribbons and flowers, but they also took pictures and shared them on social media in order to show their solidarity with the junta.[64] With these joyful urbanites as royalist supporters, the king's man as the new premier, the military in charge of the government, Thaksin living in exile, and the TRT forcibly dissolved and its members banned from politics, the bourgeois monarchy assumed that the pecking order had been restored. Unfortunately for the monarchy, this assumption was wide of the mark.

THE CROWN AND THE COMMONERS

Dubbed by Giles Ungpakorn "a coup for the rich," the 2006 coup certainly left its mark on Thaksin's supporters who were economically inferior to the royals, generals, and urban bourgeoisie.[65] However, the poor resented the coup for more than the fact that it was planned and carried out by the rich. Thaksin's supporters were also aggrieved by the coup because it deprived them of their political right to vote for their favorite politicians who promoted policies that resonated with their needs. By taking away the electoral right that empowered rural peasants and urban workers in national politics, the coup was symptomatic of the cracks in royal hegemony. As Federico Ferrara pointed out, "What the royalist establishment appears to have now lost is the authority that once allowed unelected institutions to impose their will without the sustained application of physical coercion. The recent recourse to bullets and emergency rule, as well as the hundreds of arrests for *lèse-majesté*, are in this sense symptomatic of the diminished effectiveness of their myths, their ideology, and their moral authority."[66] Despite the restrictions, censorship, and punishment of Thaksin's supporters, the monarchy still failed to work its magic on the disloyal. In the 2007 election, the first one after Thaksin was toppled by the coup, the majority of Thai voters, especially those in the North and the Northeast, still voted Thaksin's proxy party—the People's Power Party (PPP)—into office instead of the Democrat Party, the monarchy's and the military's preferred choice.[67]

Once again, rather than accepting and listening to the voices of these resentful voters, the royalist bloc of the crown, the bourgeoisie, and the army repeated the same mistake it had made a few years before. It undermined the popularly elected government through a series of extra-parliamentary tactics. Inactive under the junta's rule, PAD members came back to life once Thaksin's proxy party was in power. They donned yellow shirts yet again, protested in the streets, and virtually paralyzed Bangkok by seizing Government House, the Parliamentary House, airports, and highways. Reinforcing its judicial activism, the Constitutional Court delivered two controversial decisions that ultimately unseated Thaksin's proxies. The first verdict disqualified the then prime minister Samak Sundaravej because he hosted weekly cookery shows on television while in office and thus allegedly created a conflict of interest. Another verdict ruled the PPP guilty of electoral fraud and led to the dissolution of the party. Finally, with the defection of former PPP members and the military's support, the Democrat Party was able to form a coalition government in 2008 led by Abhisit Vejjajiva, an Eton- and Oxford-educated prime minister who was widely supported by the urban bourgeoisie and the palace. Publicly endorsed by the palace, Abhisit was dubbed by the media "the *deva*-given premier."

Witnessing the tripartite coalition of the monarchy, the army, and the bourgeoisie seizing power back using any extraparliamentary means necessary, Thaksin's supporters and antijunta activists, who gradually coalesced after the 2006 coup under the banner of the United Front for Democracy against Dictatorship (UDD), finally made a countermove. From late 2008 to mid-2010, they initiated mass demonstrations in Bangkok and protested against political interventions by the monarchy, the army, and the judiciary. Ultimately they demanded that Abhisit dissolve the parliament and hold a new election. Dressing in red, UDD participants were commonly called the "Red Shirts," a color-coded nick- name that depicted them as a political nemesis of the "Yellow Shirts." Despite mobilizing the largest mass movement in Thai history, with hun- dreds of thousands of protesters in the capital city and millions of sup- porters in the countryside, the Red Shirts failed to overthrow Abhisit's government. Instead the government ordered the military to repress the Red Shirt protesters in 2009 and 2010. The latter crackdown was brutal, as ninety-two people were killed and more than seventeen hundred in- jured.[68] After this bloody repression, the Red Shirt movement never re- gained its strength. Its supporters largely disbanded under pressure. Some went underground, some lived in exile, and some were left to rot in jail.

In spite of their tragic defeat, the Red Shirts had a considerable im- pact on Thai politics, some of which was nothing short of revolution- ary. It was the first time since the overthrow of the absolute monarchy that the multitudes of Thai commoners not only expressed their resent- ment of the crown in public but also dared to profane and mock roy- alty. Who were the Red Shirts? What made them resentful of the mon- archy? How did they mock the royals in the kingdom where the charge of lèse-majesté was draconian and arbitrary? I investigate these ques- tions in order to show that there were more than just antimonarchist sentiments among commoners in the twilight of Rama IX's reign. In- deed, this investigation also reveals the critical challenges the bourgeois monarchy faced when it came to class conflicts in Thailand's capitalist society.

Unpacking the Underprivileged

Like any mass movement, the Red Shirts comprised a variety of participants with a wide range of backgrounds in terms of age, income, occu-
pation, education, and geographic residence. This diverse composition,
however, should not lead to the conclusion that attempts to conceptualize and classify this movement are fruitless, as some scholars tended
to do.[69] In fact the Red Shirt movement had prominent features that
were noticeably based on social class. According to a survey by the Asia
Foundation, the majority of the Red Shirt protesters did share some
common background. They lived in rural provinces, especially in the
North and Northeast, and their occupations were associated with farming, manual labor, and trades. Moreover, their monthly incomes were
below the national average, and they rarely held degrees beyond secondary school.[70] In comparison, the same survey presents the dominant
features of the majority of the Yellow Shirt protesters. They lived in the
capital city and worked for the civil service or in business. On top of
that, their monthly incomes were higher than the national average, and
they mostly held degrees from institutions of higher education.[71] In
light of this comparison, it is possible to make a sketch classifying who
the Red Shirts were. Even though they did not live in absolute poverty,
the Red Shirts were the underprivileged classes of rural peasants and
urban workers who had amassed relatively little wealth, worked for
lower wages, and had less job security and education than the urban
bourgeoisie.

In addition to the Asia Foundation survey, contemporary research
by scholars in Thai studies can help explain in depth not only the socioeconomic backgrounds but also the political views of the Red Shirts.
According to Naruemon Thabchumpon and McCargo, many Red Shirts
were not completely impoverished or led primitive lives as their urban
compatriots derogatorily alleged. Instead they were "urbanized villagers" who engaged in seasonal and market-oriented farming and owned
some land. While not well off, they were not especially poor, and some
migrated to Bangkok or surrounding provinces seasonally in order to
work as manual laborers or in the service sector. Most important, they
did not disdain capitalist development but looked for it, and thus they
widely supported Thaksin's policies such as the state funding of SMEs
and the promotion of a consumerist society.[72] Ethnographic accounts
by Charles Keyes and Andrew Walker illustrate further the daily lives

and political perspectives of the Red Shirts. Calling them "cosmopolitan villagers," Keyes studied the Red Shirts in the Northeast and found
that they had immersed themselves in global capitalism. Instead of traditional rice farmers, many northeasterners had joined the global labor
force by working not only in Bangkok but also in the Middle East, East
Asia, Europe, and North America. With savings from migrant work,
some became pioneering entrepreneurs in their own villages. Despite
their low level of education, they made up for that shortcoming with their
experience of cosmopolitan cultures and urban life overseas. Given their
immersion in global capitalism, these Red Shirts in the Northeast did
not feel alienated; they appreciated Thaksin's distribution of capital to
their villages.[73] Likewise, many Red Shirts in the northern provinces, as
Walker put it, were "middle-income peasants" who supported Thaksin
not because they had been "bought" or "brainwashed" by him but because they considered him the most attractive candidate on offer—the
one who delivered leadership, resource allocation, capitalist development, and administrative competence to their villages.[74]

In addition to studies that focused on the Red Shirts as the rural
peasantry, Claudio Sopranzetti and Glassman examined the Red Shirts
as the urban working class. Studying Red Shirt migrants who worked
as motorcycle taxi drivers in Bangkok, Sopranzetti reported that these
drivers often operated as mediators between members of the urban
bourgeoisie and their capitalist activities. As providers of transportation, they helped many white-collar workers beat the traffic with a quick,
flexible, and affordable means of commuting to corporate buildings or
high-end shopping malls in downtown Bangkok. They also often served
the urban bourgeoisie as personal assistants who were asked to pay
bills, deliver mail, and wait in line to buy brand-name commodities.
According to Sopranzetti, this daily interaction with a bourgeois lifestyle had long sown capitalist aspirations among the motorcycle taxi
drivers—the desire to have a better life in cities and enjoy conspicuous
consumption like an ordinary bourgeois—and Thaksin simply unleashed these desires with his capitalist-driven policies.[75] Capitalist
aspirations among the Red Shirts were vividly illustrated in one of the
interviews Sopranzetti conducted with those drivers. In response to a
question about why he had to migrate and work in Bangkok, one driver
confessed, "There is nothing to do [in the countryside]. I need to save
first to give a good education to my children. I have to buy them shoes,
uniforms for school, to have them study English, to buy a computer.
With what money? Should I just give them the same life I had, working

in a field for no profit, without the opportunity to study? What should I do?"[76]

Similarly, Glassman revealed that the Red Shirts were not merely concentrated in rural villages; they also could be found among the urban classes of "proletarian, lumpen-proletarian, and postproletarian workers, many from outside Bangkok, but many from Bangkok's peri-urban periphery, and even from the specific groups of workers in the city.[77] The latter included taxi drivers, paupers in Bangkok's slum communities, and poor women who labored in the sex industry. With the demise of communism and the rapid transformation of the kingdom into a newly industrialized society, capitalism became "the only game in town" in Thailand, and it strongly encouraged participation by the working class and even some of the most marginal social groups.[78] Touching on female Red Shirts, a particular group that is still under-studied, Glassman unveiled capitalist desires among these female dissidents. Migrating from rural villages to sell their labor in Bangkok, many poor women chose to work in the sex industry as prostitutes and showgirls because the money they earned in these jobs helped them improve their material prospects and class mobility. It was also this kind of capitalist aspiration that drove the poor women to work in Thailand's sweatshops, whose work forces had recently been feminized.[79] As a result, what made Thaksin appealing among these urban workers, Glassman concluded, was that he effectively invited millions of subaltern Thais to the electoral table to choose their preferred candidates, who not only promised but also delivered pro-capitalist programs that could improve their lives.[80] Unfortunately, these capitalist desires among the Red Shirts were seen by the palace and the bourgeoisie as less than desirable.

THE DISILLUSIONMENT OF THE DISILLUSIONED

In the early twentieth century, Prince Wongsanuprapat, a minister of agriculture under the absolute monarchy, had a chance to survey the daily lives of rural peasants in Siam. Observing that they all lived in destitution, the Bangkok prince with a degree from Denmark came to a simple conclusion: Siamese peasants were impoverished not because they had insufficient capital to undertake farming but because they were "irresponsible, wasteful, and lacking perseverance," "dissipated," "thriftless and uneconomical," and "unprepared with deplorable consequences."[81] A century later Thailand's socioeconomic changes had significantly transformed traditional life in rural provinces. What took the place of a primitive society and subsistence economy were capitalist-oriented farming, a seasonal migration of labor to industrial cities, and the mass inspiration of peasants and workers driven by political consciousness and capitalist aspirations. Despite these dramatic changes, the royal establishment still held the same kind of social prejudice toward the underclasses. In their view, what made the majority of Thais disadvantaged was not the history of uneven development, economic inequality, and wealth concentration but their intrinsic traits of idleness, prodigality, and improvidence. These traits were normally contrasted with what royalty and the bourgeoisie claimed they had long embodied and practiced: the ethic of hard work, frugality, and self-improvement.

Given this prejudice among the well-to-do, it is not surprising that there was a series of royalist attempts to force rural peasants and urban workers back into the elite's preferred image of humble, subordinate, childish, and primitive villagers instead of the aspiring entrepreneurs, unrestrained consumers, and politically active voters they had become in the Thaksin era. The king persistently reminded the poor about SEP, which simply asked the lower classes to work harder, consume less, and prudently save their money if they wanted to improve their material prospects. The queen publicly expressed her concerns about rural women who abandoned local handicrafts and went to work in the sex industry for "easy money" with which to indulge in rampant consumerism.[82] The Yellow Shirts arrogantly asked for the substantial disenfranchisement of the rural majority by proposing a model of "New Politics" that allowed 70 percent of parliamentary members to be appointed.[83] The military decided to topple Thaksin from power in 2006 simply because, as the coup leader later admitted, "It is our duty, as soldiers of the King . . . to win the grassroots back for the King [and] our most important aim is that all the masses in the territory must be ours."[84]

This series of desperate attempts to tame the multitudes of the lower classes in Thailand is similar to Marx's argument about the ruling class and its ideology in capitalist society; the bourgeois ideology preaches mythical ideas such as "ascetic sacrifice" and "original sin" to the working class. In the *Grundrisse*, Marx pointed to contradictions in the bourgeois virtues of asceticism, industriousness, and frugality, the particular ethics that classical economists promoted as the fountain of the wealth of nations. The first contradiction is that these ethics have long been promoted to legitimize the wealthy status of those who do not actually labor, sacrifice, or withdraw their money from an investment in the market, that is, the bourgeoisie itself. Preaching to the working class that the practice of self-denial, hard work, and thrift is the only path to enrichment, the bourgeoisie, according to Marx, justifies its wealth by claiming that "the capitalist too brings a *sacrifice*, the sacrifice of *abstinence*, in that he grows wealthy instead of eating up his product directly."[85] What has been distorted under this ideology is the fact that it is labor instead of ascetic sacrifice that begets wealth for the bourgeoisie. "Someone may castigate and flagellate himself all day long like the monks etc.," Marx sarcastically noted, "and this quantity of sacrifice [that] he contributes will remain totally worthless."[86]

Another contradiction is that bourgeois ethics are never meant to be universally practiced by the working class. As Marx argued, if all proletarians did what the bourgeoisie asks them to do—working tirelessly and saving money by abstaining from consumption in order to invest their savings in production as new entrepreneurs—they would become capitalists instead of laborers, and therefore labor would become capital. For Marx this scenario is contradictory because under capitalism capital "can posit itself only by positing labour as not-capital," and once labor is no longer not-capital but capital itself, "the concept and the relation of capital itself would be destroyed."[87] Instead bourgeois ethics, according to Marx, ask workers to be abstinent, industrious, and frugal only to the extent that they can reproduce their labor for production and survive capitalist crises at their own expense. In other words, the actual function of bourgeois ethics is to serve the capitalists' demands that workers "should save enough at the times when business is good to be able more or less to live in the bad times, to endure short time[s] or the lowering of wages," and that they "should always hold to a minimum of life's pleasures and make crises easier to bear for the capitalists." Further, they should "maintain themselves as pure laboring machines and as far as possible pay [for] their own wear and tear."[88]

Marx's critique of bourgeois ethics is also manifest in volume 1 of *Capital*. Drawing a parallel between the story of original sin in theology and the theory of inequality in classical economics, Marx pointed out that, while the former clearly provides the origin of "how man came to be condemned to eat his bread in the sweat of his brow," the latter never tells the audience exactly how inequality or poverty arises in the first place.[89] The history of economic original sin, Marx noted, has been narrated as if "Long, long ago there were two sorts of people; one, the diligent, intelligent and above all frugal élite; the other, lazy rascals, spending their substance, and more, in riotous living." Thus, "the former sort accumulated wealth, and the latter sort finally had nothing to sell except their own skins."[90] As a result, some of the most noticeable con- tradictions in capitalist society have never been explained but remain concealed by bourgeois economists. These are the contradictions that in this society there is not only "the poverty of the great majority who, despite all their labour, have up to now nothing to sell but themselves" but also "the wealth of the few that increases constantly, although they have long ceased to work." What is left untold by this tale of natural- born differences between the rich and the poor, Marx highlighted, is a history of primitive accumulation in which "conquest, enslavement, robbery, murder, in short, force, play the greatest part," and in which "great masses of men are suddenly and forcibly torn from their means of subsistence, and hurled onto the labour market as free, unprotected and rightless proletarians."[91] Despite this violent history of expropria- tion, the bourgeoisie hypocritically credits its self-proclaimed virtues of self-sacrifice, diligence, and thrift as the origin of its fortunes.

Armed with Marx's critiques of bourgeois ethics, no one should be surprised to see that the bourgeois monarchy in Thailand desperately attempted to defend its ruling ideology. The stakes were high for the monarchy. It was a matter of whether the subordinate classes still bought into what had long been preached—the royal ideology that there are intrinsic differences in traits between the alliance of the wealthy group of royalty and the Sino-Thai middle class in Bangkok and the under- privileged majority in the rural provinces. That ideology maintained that the former enriched themselves through industriousness, parsi- mony, and abstinence while the latter still lived in destitution because they lacked those traits. Instead of demanding the provision of welfare and capital, the royal ideology went, the poor majority should follow the king's supposed example by abstaining from consumption and taking care of themselves at their own expense. This same ideology also maintained that the origin of the monarchy's wealth was nothing like its actual history of exploitation, royal monopoly, and military oppres- sion in the feudal era. If all these firmly established myths still worked their magic on the underclasses, the status quo that had maintained the monarchy at the top of the politico-economic hierarchy in Thailand would have been left intact. With this concern about the defense of the ruling ideology, one of the most urgent policies that the junta leaders launched after they took power from Thaksin was the indoctrination of SEP in rural provinces, especially those in the North and Northeast. The junta's attempt to "win the grassroots back for the King," however, did not alleviate but actually aggravated the provincial alienation from the crown.

With the exception of Daniel Unger, who praised SEP as "a sort of survival guide for poor Thais enmeshed in globalized markets," most scholars in Thai studies mutually agreed that the king's vision of the Thai economy was out of touch with the daily lives of the lower classes.[92] Again ethnographic research that examines the everyday lives of the Red Shirts is helpful for understanding why SEP failed to resonate with the grass roots. According to Keyes, SEP was based on the elitist depiction of the subsistence economy of the Northeast in the 1960s. As northeasterners since the economic boom had "reoriented their economic life away from self-subsistence to producing cash crops for the market and then to dependence on earnings in urban Thailand and overseas," Keyes revealed, these "cosmopolitan villagers" felt that they had not only been misunderstood but also humiliated by a bygone image that the crown and the urbanites tried to impose on them.[93] Also studying the Red Shirts in the Northeast, Pattana Kitiarsa argued that "the political world of rural Thai villages has been closely intertwined with both the national and global economies" and rural villagers are not only "consumers, not different [from] urban dwellers" but also "sophisticated political entrepreneurs . . . [with] greater awareness of their rights as active citizens."[94] As a result, Pattana concluded, "it would be a grave mistake to view [the rural village] as a self-sufficient moral-economic unit, embedded in traditional ways of economic and political life."[95]

Furthermore, Phruek Thaothawin provided an insight into how the implementation of SEP in a rural village in the Northeast eventually ended in disaster. The junta's budget of 10 billion baht (US$336 million) for an application of SEP nationwide had been spent by local Thais to create not the common good but the Potemkin villages that were designed to please the royals and bureaucrats who came to visit them once in a while. Given its moral tone and detachment from the local practice, SEP was not embraced by local villagers but was considered by them, as Phreuk put it, to be "a political tool to control people in the countryside instead of improving their lives."[96] Walker came to a similar conclusion when he studied northern villagers. Although these "middle-income peasants" obtained their subsistence via market transactions, continually withdrew from agricultural activities, migrated to labor in cities and overseas, and even owned nonagricultural enterprises, SEP still depicted them using an image from the agrarian past, one that insisted that they still lived in a precapitalist community where there "are no neighbors, and no sign of a road, village or market, let alone an electric line, mobile phone tower or satellite dish!" For Walker, this royal vision of "Adam and Eve in Eden" was "simply not consistent with the economically diversified livelihood strategies pursued by rural people in contemporary Thailand."[97]

As if the elite's prejudice toward their economic activities were not enough, the Red Shirts had to endure the political prejudice of the monarchy and urban bourgeoisie. A series of events after the 2006 coup are recapped here to highlight how that political prejudice shaped the Red Shirt worldview. On October 13, 2008, Queen Sirikit, accompanied by Princess Chulabhorn, presided over the funeral of a Yellow Shirt protester and remarked that the deceased was "a good girl who had helped to protect the country and the monarchy."[98] For the Red Shirts, this event was significant, as the royals, who had been indifferent to the political demands of the grass roots, had finally shown their true colors by standing firm with the bourgeoisie. October 13, consequently, was remembered by the Red Shirts as the day on which their political consciousness was awakened. They dubbed it the Eye-Opening Day (*wan ta sawang*).[99] Another insult was added to the injury when the Red Shirts mobilized a protest in downtown Bangkok during April and May 2010. Asking for a dissolution of the royalist government and a new election, the Red Shirt demonstration, which drew as its participants both rural peasants and urban workers, was widely reviled by the urban bourgeoisie. Dehumanizing the Red Shirts by calling them "red water buffaloes [*khwai daeng*]," the bourgeoisie was irritated by the masses of protesters who not only disrupted their urban rounds of working and shopping in downtown areas but also showed signs of disobedience to royal hegemony.[100] On May 16, 2010, just three days before the brutal crackdown on the Red Shirts, Pongpat Wachirabunjong, a Thai actor who was actively engaged with the Yellow Shirt movement, gave a speech that not only spoke the bourgeoisie's mind but also implicitly gave a license to the army to crack down on the Red Shirt protesters. Echoing a popular discourse among the bourgeoisie that Rama IX was the father figure of the kingdom, Pongpat warned those "children" who no longer loved their "dad" to get out of "dad's house."

> Dad is a pillar of a house. My house is very big. We have many people living together. Ever since I was born, this house has been very beautiful and homey. For it to be like this, the ancestors of our

dad lost sweat and blood and sacrificed their lives to be able to build this house. Up to this point, dad is still working tirelessly to look after this house and to care for the happiness of anyone under this roof. If someone is angry at another, whoever that may be, and then transfers that anger onto our dad, hates our dad, insults our dad, and has thoughts about chasing our dad out of this house, I would have to go out to that person and say, "If you hate our dad and do not love our dad anymore, you should leave because this is our dad's house, because this is our dad's kingdom."[101]

Like the bourgeoisie, the monarchy apparently had no mercy for the Red Shirt dissidents. Although the royals normally conducted a political intervention when military repression of civilians was out of proportion, they were silent during the 2010 crackdown. What seemed to hurt the Red Shirts most was the absence of public condolences from the palace on the deaths of their comrades in the streets. Instead what the monarchy did after the crackdown simply aggravated them further. Accompanied by the crown prince, the queen presided over the funeral of a colonel who was killed during the crackdown, praised him as "a good soldier who protected the nation," and gave the fallen soldier one of the most prestigious chivalric orders.[102] A year later Princess Chulabhorn gave an exclusive interview on a popular talk show and unveiled what the Red Shirts had suspected: the crown was not indifferent to but was instead resentful of their mass demonstration in Bangkok. In the interview, the princess openly blamed the Red Shirts for the deepening crisis in Thailand and claimed that their political actions had brought sorrow to the king and queen.[103]

According to Khorapin Phuaphansawat, it was this series of expressions of royal prejudice that the Red Shirts had to endure during their political movement that radically transformed their political consciousness. In the early stages of their formation, Thaksin's supporters and antijunta activists still dressed in yellow to please the crown. They criticized the extraconstitutional role of the privy counselors but never went as far as to criticize the royal family. Later they switched their dress code from yellow to red—the color formerly associated with Thai communists—and became more critical of the monarchy as an institution, making no exception for the monarch and other members of the royal family.[104] Disillusioned by the royal ideology, the Red Shirts were indeed the crown's worst nightmare. They did not simply criticize and mock royal hypocrisies but also revived and spread what the monarchy had long attempted to bottle up—antimonarchist sentiments and re-publican ideas. Unfortunately for the crown, the Red dissidents apparently let the genie out of the bottle.

THE MOCKED MONARCHY

The act of discussing, criticizing, or mocking the monarchy has long been prohibited by the law of lèse-majesté in Thailand. Based on Thai Criminal Code, section 112, which states, "Whoever defames, insults or threatens the King, the Queen, the Heir-apparent or the Regent, shall be punished with imprisonment of three to fifteen years," the lèse-majesté law has been arbitrarily applied beyond its legal limits. It is used to protect all members of the royal family and even privy counselors against insults. With no legal definition of what actions constitute a defamation, insult, or threat against the monarchy, the law leaves plenty of room for interpretation, and the judges normally use it to cover any debates, criticism, or mockery of the monarchy. Since lèse-majesté complaints can be filed by any person against anyone else, it has become a political tool through which not only the state but also ordinary people in civil society can silence those who appear to be critical of the crown. As a result, what makes Thailand unique among other states today that still have a law of lèse-majesté, Streckfuss remarked, is that in the Thai kingdom lèse-majesté is "not merely a crime against the reputation of the royals but a national security offense" and that the lèse-majesté law is aggressively applied "to defend the institution of the monarchy rather than the person of the monarch."[105]

Despite this draconian law and its arbitrary implementation, the Red Shirts still found a way to express their resentment of the monarchy, and the royals had no one to blame but themselves. As the crown had played down its traditional images, which were associated with religion, national security, and courtly extravagance, during the last two decades of the twentieth century while building up its bourgeois images in public, the bourgeoisification of royalty's natural bodies turned out to be a double-edged sword. On the one hand, the transformation of the Thai royals from untouchable, mysterious, and holy beings in public to more industrious, frugal, and down-to-earth people widely resonated with the urban bourgeoisie. On the other hand, this desecration of and disenchantment with the crown brought the royals, who were traditionally treated like gods in the heavenly sky, down to the vulgar affairs on earth and provided an opportunity for the grass roots to monitor, expose, and mock the differences between what royalty pretended to be and what they actually were. In other words, once the king no longer acted like the "Lord of Life" and "Lord of the Land" but an ordinary "dad" who was beloved by his bourgeois "children," he became an easy target whom the Red Shirts could mock whenever they found that his life was not as mundane as advertised.

Furthermore, the popularization of the monarchy through the mass media turned out to be a mixed blessing. Through the culture industry of print advertising, television, film, music, the internet, and mobile applications, the mass advertising of the monarchy successfully created the passive and royalist army of the bourgeoisie in Thailand's capitalist society. However, it was precisely this new means of communication that empowered what James C. Scott called "weapons of the weak" among the lower classes. With the advent of affordable printing and accessible social media sites such as Facebook and YouTube, the Red Shirts could share their gossipy tidbits, nicknames, rumors, jokes, and criticisms of the monarchy with a mass audience in a short period of time.[106] These everyday arts of resistance among the Red Shirts can be categorized into the following four major themes—the themes that clearly negated the bourgeois perception of the monarchy in the mainstream media.

The Negation of the Hardworking King

While Rama IX and the royal family had been praised by the bourgeoisie as hardworking royals who tirelessly labored for the country, derogatory and satirical remarks about the monarchy that were shared among the Red Shirts offered a different account. Royalty only appeared to be diligent in public, they claimed, and the ones who had long industriously labored for the nation were actually the commoners. As a dialectical response to the bourgeois obsession with Rama IX as a hardworking king, one that could be seen through the popularization of the iconic portrait of Rama IX raising a finger to the tip of his nose to wipe away a drop of sweat, the rallying point of the resentment among the Red Shirts was the overstatement of the king's sweat in the mass media. In the song "One Drop of Sweat," a Red Shirt rock band, Faiyen, kills two birds with one stone. It mocks the king's work ethic, which was advertised as if a drop of sweat from him alone could improve the material prospects of all Thais. In addition, the band turns the ruling ideology upside down by asserting that it was the sweat of Thai peasants that built the nation and that such commoners still live in poverty because of the exploitation of the kingdom's "parasitical feudalists." The song ends with passages that challenge what was widely perceived as a given in Thai society, that instead of helping, the king's drop of sweat hurt the commoners because it stole the limelight from their hard work and distracted the public from its struggle with poverty. As the song goes:

> One drop of sweat cannot build the nation.
> Whose drop of sweat? That drop of sweat is well remembered.
> The sweat of peasants has flowed for hundreds of years,
> Pouring through this land more than the Chao Phraya River ever does.
>
> The sweat of Thais founded their land,
> But it is claimed by parasitical feudalists.
> The Thai homeland has been built from blood and tears,
> But it has become a land which is sucked and eaten by feudalists.
>
> The country belongs to all the people.
> The rights of Thais thus belong to all Thais.
> Don't claim that you are superior to the people in this land.
> All property in this land must belong to all Thais.
>
> One drop of sweat makes the nation underdeveloped.
> Thailand has to face the vice of poverty.
> One drop of sweat hurts all Thais.
> The country has been poor and frustrated because of one drop of sweat.[107]

This seditious theme of diminishing the value of the king's sweat while highlighting the contributions of hardworking commoners was also emphasized by a Red Shirt poet, Phiangkham Pradapkhwam. In the poem "The Ones Who Work Industriously Are the People," Phiangkham undermines the bourgeois perception that Rama IX was the hardest worker in the kingdom by asking a provocative question: "Who actually are the hard workers?" As the poem reveals, it is the masses who not only develop the country but also feed the ruling class. As a result, it is the sweat of ordinary people that should be saluted.

> Drops of sweat that flood the saturated land . . .
> Originated from no one else but the people . . .

Who actually are the hard workers?
Who are the enduring and suffering ones?

Who actually carries whom on their shoulders?
Who sacrifices with their blood soaking the land?
Who actually are the ones standing firm and fighting?
No one else but the people, the people, the people!!![108]

In addition to songs and poems, seditious messages among the Red Shirts regarding the "royal sweat" also found visual expression. In a mass rally of the Red Shirts on September 19, 2010, the first rally after the military crackdown, antiroyal graffiti were found on construction fences and walls near the rally site in downtown Bangkok. Even though the graffiti were quickly removed by the police, some observers took pictures and circulated them online. According to Serhat Ünaldi, "One of the most daring graffiti depicted the king as Hitler wearing an eye patch. Someone added to the picture a drop falling from the figure's nose and the expression *phra-setho saksit* (holy perspiration). This was a reference to a famous photo that shows the king sweating from the tip of his nose."[109] What should be added to Ünaldi's account is that this visual mockery of the king has a double meaning. It teases not only the bourgeois obsession with the king's sweat and the totalitarian-oriented regime that the monarchy and the military tended to establish. In fact, as someone added another expression to the graffiti, "the blind who never smiles (crippled)," the Red Shirts also mocked the corporeal body of the king. While the bourgeoisie admired the physical strength of Rama IX as he relentlessly traveled to many rural villages in the Cold War era, the Red Shirts mocked his physicality in three ways. He was mocked as a one-eyed man, an image derived from a report that he lost his right eye in a car accident when he was young; as the monarch who never smiled because of his stoic look in public; and as a crippled man since the octogenarian monarch barely worked in the late years of his reign but struggled with sickness and mostly stayed in a hospital. In light of these examples, it is clear that there were signs of a breakdown in the royal ideology among the Red Shirts. The king was no longer seen as the hardest worker in the kingdom but as a crippled royal who no longer worked. The popular image of the hardworking king was debunked as it overshadowed the contributions of ordinary people who actually worked and fed the royals. Most important, a work ethic was considered a virtue that belonged to commoners rather than royalty.

The Negation of the Frugal King

While Rama IX was praised by the bourgeoisie as the frugal king due to his ascetic lifestyle and his SEP model, the king's ethic of frugality was ridiculed by the Red Shirts. In a song titled "Advertising Gone Wrong," Faiyen mocks the monarch in various ways. The bourgeois obsession with Rama IX's empty toothpaste tube, which was popularly promoted as a symbol of the king's ethic of frugality, is ridiculed as nonsense. The royal news at 8:00 p.m. that daily promotes SEP is criticized as a brainwashing program. The king's self-sufficient lifestyle is lampooned as pretentious because his medical, electric, and water bills were all paid by the people's taxes. Critically, this song also exemplifies the way "weapons of the weak" were cunningly practiced by the Red Shirts. Instead of referring to the king directly, the song evasively gives him the nickname of an average Thai male, "Uncle Somchai." As the lyrics go:

[Introduction]
Son: Mom! The toothpaste tube is empty.
Mom: If it's empty, just go to buy a new one.
Why in the world would you let it become completely empty?

[Verse]
That particular toothpaste tube, I have seen it for a very long time.
Who lampoons it?
I'm so annoyed with it. Damned!

Once it's 8:00 p.m., oh! It's time to be wide awake.
Folk drama is coming. To save electric energy, just turn off your TV.
Be self-sufficient!

Want to stay in the hospital? Want to stay in the hospital?
You must feel good, must feel great.
No need to pay for electric and water bills?
Uncle Somchai feels good and great.[110]

This theme of mocking the king's pretentious display of a frugal lifestyle could also be found in the Red Shirt graffiti. Based on Ünaldi's observation, there were three graffiti that revealed how Rama IX's promotion of an ascetic lifestyle and a self-sufficiency economy were derided by the Red grass roots. Contrasting the popular perception that the king was frugal with the fact that he was the richest royal on earth, the first street artist sarcastically wrote, "You have millions but preach sufficiency to me."[111] Skeptical of the king's SEP as a means of improving the material prospects of ordinary people, the second artist asserted, "Sufficiency, but I didn't have enough to eat."[112] The last artist gave a longer statement about the crown: "The country does not progress because there are no good people. Bad people were taken to rule the land because heaven has no eyes, because the eyes are blind. [They] see damn animals [*ai sat*] as good people. I ask for real, you damn blind man [*ai bot*], when will you die?"[113] The latter statement is iconoclastic in many ways. It ridicules the king's lack of a corporeal vision because he was a one-eyed man. It criticizes the king's lack of an economic vision as his kingdom did not progress as it was supposed to have done. Most symbolically significant, it implicitly refers to the royals as subhuman animals instead of superhuman *devas*, and it even dares to wish for the death of Rama IX—the king whom the bourgeoisie wished could have lived for a thousand years.

The contradiction between the public appearance of Rama IX as the frugal king and the reality that he was extremely wealthy was also picked up by one of the most prominent Red Shirt poets, Mainueng Ko Kunthi. Instead of simply echoing the Red Shirt sentiments against the monarchy, Mainueng broke the Thai taboo by advocating republicanism in his masterpiece, "Constituting the People's Constitution." In this poem, what the monarchy had tried to silence in public is spoken aloud. Rama IX was wealthy because of his profits from business investments and partnerships with elite capitalists. He was a billionaire who pretended to work hard while many Thais who labored day and night still lived in destitution. The royals took all the credit for national progress despite its having been created by ordinary people. While standing firm with the wealthy Yellow Shirts, the palace never showed any support for but rather despised and undermined the political movements of the poor Red Shirts. Above all, Mainueng urged, Thai commoners must make a revolution one last time to abolish all remnants of Thai feudalism and constitute a republic of the people—the revolutionary mission that a new generation of Thais had failed to carry out after the 1932 revolution ended the absolute monarchy in Thailand. As the poem states:

> We did not protect the revolution.
> The reactionary wind consequently came back.

The deconstruction cannot be done gently.
Everything must be audaciously rebuilt from scratch . . .

We did not protect the revolution.
State power and the economy consequently went backward.
Money in the house of peasants is so insufficient,
But money is packed in a white letter above the golden tray . . .

Land is actually the property of all Thais.
It has nourished slave owners and lords for generations.
1932 was the end of absolute power.
You originate from the generous people. Remember that, O King.

You are virtually the partner of every company,
Seeking profit regardless of the mode of production,
Devouring until becoming overweight,
While the multitudes of people have nothing to eat.

All the drops of sweat of your labor
Are just dampness compared to those of the lower classes
    in the whole country.
Those who are dirt poor and suffering
Are the real producers of the wealth of the nation.

Which ones are your people?
The prosperous and nice-looking Yellow Shirts?
The dirty and penniless Red Shirts?
The hopeless and homeless with no clothes?

Where do you see yourself in the nation?
At the top of the shining mountain?
We are the base of the population's pyramid.
If you undermine us, you will damnably crumble . . .

Unite hand in hand in this land of history!
Rise up for one more revolution![114]

The Negation of the Father King

Dad was an informal term that members of the urban bourgeoisie used
to refer to Rama IX. Instead of emancipated citizens, the nouveau riche
usually saw themselves as the "children" of their beloved father king

and mother queen. The Red Shirts, on the other hand, challenged this ruling ideology by asserting that they had only one father in their lives and he was obviously not the monarch. In the song "Dad," Faiyen mocks the bourgeois exaggeration of Rama IX as the flawless father of the nation and wonders if an ideal of the king as the perfect father would still be intact if there were no state censorship and propaganda. Furthermore, the Red Shirt rock band states that the king should not be considered the father of all Thais since each person already has a biological father. As the song satirically remarks:

> My dad teaches me well,
> Teaches me to use reason.
> My dad may not be a good man,
> But he is good from my point of view.
>
> I have only one dad.
> Other men are not my dad.
> My dad can be criticized.
> He is not like someone else's dad.
>
> Who claims to be a perfect and noble prophet,
> But cannot be criticized, questioned, and interrogated,
> So, I wonder how I would know if
> He is as good as advertised.[115]

Likewise, the Red Shirt street artists ridiculed the bourgeois perception of Rama IX as the father king. According to Ünaldi's account, there were two graffiti that clearly made fun of the "dad" who was so widely beloved by the bourgeoisie. The first lampooned the bourgeois attempt to propagate the notion that Rama IX was the father of all Thais despite the fact that many Thais had already lost their biological fathers: "My father is already dead, why do you claim to be my parents? Damn you!"[116] The other revealed the ideological shift among many Red Shirts, who used to see themselves as children of the father king but now bore him only hate: "Before I used to love you . . . but now I hate you—go to ruin! Today, Thais everywhere in the country have their eyes open."[117] This Red Shirt's resentment of the father king was echoed by an outspoken Red Shirt leader, Jatuporn Prompan. Witnessing many Red Shirt protesters killed in the crackdown, he reaffirmed a conspiracy theory among the Red Shirts that the monarchy was behind the military action. Jatuporn apparently expressed his grievances directly to the crown. "Which countries in this world," he said, "kill the children for the father, kill the children for the mother? Only in this country!"[118]

Instead of romanticizing their social status as children of the father king, the Red Shirts usually saw themselves as "servants" or "serfs" who had been exploited by the ruling class, of which the king himself was the leader. One of the most crucial discourses that the Red Shirts developed in their movement was a feudal theme of class struggle between the traditional elite (*ammat*) and serfs (*phrai*). While the former was composed of the monarchy, aristocratic landlords, high-ranking civil servants, and businesspeople, the latter were the Red Shirt peasants and workers. Yet, instead of shame and disgrace, the Red Shirts identified themselves as *phrai*, as Nick Nostitz noted, to instill pride and empower the lower classes in their "class struggle in which *phrai* tried to free themselves from the oppression by the *ammat*."[119] This theme of class struggle is manifest in a Red Shirt poem, "God Gave Birth to Me, the Free; This God's Name Is the People." Powerfully composed by Phiangkham, the poem seems to retell Hegel's master-slave dialectic in a Thai version. It begins with a story of Thai servants who are suffering as their labor is appropriated by their Lord of Life and they start to question the legitimacy of this divine ruler, who does not work but "farms on the people's back." It ends with a republican message of hope that someday these servants will rise up with their political consciousness raised not only to end the regime of a false god, the "*deva* of exploitation," but also to establish a new regime of "God, the people."

> Who gave birth to me, a servant below his feet?
> Just a slave, a natural-born serf. No wings of dream . . .
> We dream of a turn of fate and the world turned upside down . . .
> Who farms on the people's back for so long?
>
> When the wind of change is coming,
> All the people rise up together . . .
> Let's damn the *deva* of exploitation.
> As God gives birth to me, the free,
> This God's name is the "people"!!![120]

The Negation of the Cosmopolitan King

Rama IX was widely praised by the urban bourgeoisie as the cosmopolitan king. His talents in art, music, literature, photography, sports, science, and technology were portrayed in the mass media as if they were universally recognized and second to none. During his trips overseas in the Cold War era, he was warmly welcomed by cultural icons such as Elvis Presley, Walt Disney, and Benny Goodman and political figures such as Dwight Eisenhower, Richard Nixon, Charles de Gaulle, and Queen Elizabeth II. On top of that, the king's SEP was saluted by the United Nations and included in its list of sustainable development goals. By contrast, the Red Shirts challenged the bourgeois perception of the king with a different narrative. Instead of cosmopolitan, sophisticated, and universally recognized, Rama IX was parochial, narrow-minded, and intolerant of universal values such as democratic elections, political accountability, human rights, and the rule of law. In the poem "Full Democracy . . . Not!" Rangsan Haruehanroengra sarcastically states that as long as Rama IX was still alive a democratic regime would never be found in Thailand because the king never supported the elected government and majority rule; he preferred the rule of wealthy oligarchs, which allowed him, the world's wealthiest king, to accumulate more wealth. Nor did the king hesitate to use brutal force to maintain his power and suppress those who were deemed disloyal to him. In fact what the king wanted was for the poor majority to be tamed by SEP. Speaking from the king's point of view, the poem satirically says:

> Democracy? It belongs to my dynasty . . .
> For antimonarchists, they will be chained with chuckles and
>   endlessly imprisoned . . .
> I will deceitfully eat you alive and become the world's wealthiest.
> I will exploit until you have no cents in your pocket . . .
>
> Hey! Democracy that you ask for.
> Must beware, as I'm still alive, don't you dream of it.
> Just go live sufficiently on a daily basis . . .
> Don't you ask for more than what is royally granted . . . Wrap your brain
>   around it.[121]

Likewise, in the poem "Big Boss," Anon Nampa shatters the cosmopolitan image of Rama IX. The king is depicted as if he were American imperialism's running dog who has no talent in war beyond holding the highest of military ranks. His accumulation of wealth is criticized because it is unaccountable, and his popular support is mocked because it is merely based on favoritism. Furthermore, the king is panned in this poem for preferring the military junta over the rule of law and the elected government and for trying to intervene in the kingdom's legislative, executive, and judicial affairs. Worst of all, the king is unsympathetic to his own subjects who were brutally killed in the military crackdown. With this train of thought, Anon audaciously ends his poem with an antimonarchist statement, "I have to dethrone you." Calling the monarch "Big Boss," the poem reads:

> Big Boss . . . though America is not your father,
> You are obedient to it and sell your soul . . .
> You are not talented in war,
> But you still hold ranks and decorations . . .
>
> Big Boss . . . Your wealth reaches the sky . . .
> You are influential in the stock market.
> Your businesses do not have to pay taxes,
> While those of your subjects do. I see . . .
>
> Big Boss . . . You run the country but have never been elected . . .
> I remember, you were the cause of the coup . . .
> The death of ordinary people during April–May 2010 was your
>   responsibility . . .
> A corpse of a bare-handed woman and that of a man with his brains
>   shot out. I see . . .
>
> Big Boss . . . You even kill my fraternal comrades, the people . . .
> My eyes are open.
> Big Boss . . . I have to dethrone you,
> For a full democracy. I swear![122]

In addition to the all-around and universally recognized king, the bourgeois obsession with Rama IX was based on the fantasy of the forever-young king whose physical body is always fit and firm and whose ageless body will help him reign in the kingdom and "live with Thais for a thousand years." This bourgeois obsession with the king's fitness did not escape the seditious eyes of the Red Shirts. As Rama IX during his late reign suffered declining health and spent extended periods in a hospital, many Red Shirts acknowledged that the death of the aging monarch was imminent and his immortality was merely a bourgeois fantasy. In the song "Black Shirts," Faiyen half-jokingly states that all Red Shirts look forward to dressing in black to attend the funeral of Rama IX, whose death would seem to be imminent. The end of Rama IX's reign, the rock band predicts, would be one man's meat and another man's poison. While the Red Shirts would widely celebrate the passing of their oppressive monarch, the "feudal elite" and the Yellow Shirts would break down in tears because the head of the ruling class was gone. As the song rejoices:

> Black, Black, Black. Prepare to dress in black countrywide.
> Feudalism weeps. Feudalists weep.
> All people in the land prepare to wear black shirts.
>
> Wait for so long. Wait for a change.
> The Red Shirts prepare to wear black shirts.
> All of our lives, we have been abused.
> It is karma. When will he die?
>
> Complain about when he will die.
> So bored with the moralist who oppresses the people.
> The longer we live, the more we become poor.
> The Red Shirts complain: When will he die?
>
> Find black shirts.
> Prepare for a change that brings prosperity to Thailand.
> Change from red to black countrywide.
> Change from red to black. Black countrywide.
> Then, the Yellow Shirts will have to wear black shirts too.[123]

TWILIGHT OF THE IDOL

In spite of the development of seditious, antimonarchist, and revolutionary messages in their movement, the Red Shirts were not able to translate their resentment and grievances into political action but kept their critical views of the crown underground. As Vincent Boudreau pointed out about the historical trajectory of repression and protest in Southeast Asia, the history of state repression shapes the patterns of political contention: "Regime opponents anticipate state activity, search out its pattern, and in light of that pattern, calibrate movement practice to navigate between the innocuous and the suicidal. Some movements abandon activist forms crushed by surveillance and violence, others challenge prohibitions, or act evasively."[124] In the Thai case, the history of state oppression over political contention, especially that of anti-monarchists, was brutal and bloody, and what the Red Shirts faced in the 2010 crackdown was no exception. As a result, it was understandable that after the crackdown the Red Shirt movement decided to content itself with circulating its antimonarchist ideas via cultural media such as songs, poems, and graffiti instead of actively mobilizing a political movement or organizing a party to openly challenge royal power. The latter action would not be innocuous but suicidal. With an exceptional case of some daredevil dissidents who eventually ended up in jail, the majority of the Red Shirts disbanded after the crackdown, went back to work on farms and in factories, and evasively shared their grievances against the royal establishment not on the streets but in social media and underground art, music, and literature.

Despite being politically demobilized and emasculated, the Red Shirts left a mark on the minds of the royals and the bourgeoisie, which had become ultraconservative after facing the largest movement of the lower classes in Thai history. As Corey Robin notes, what the conservatives fear is the attainment of political agency among the subordinate classes: "Every once in a while . . . the subordinates of this world contest their fates. They protest their conditions, write letters and petitions, join movements, and make demands. Their goals may be minimal and discrete . . . but in voicing them, they raise the specter of a more fundamental change in power. They cease to be servants or supplicants and become agents, speaking and acting on their own behalf."[125] In the Thai case, what the royal establishment feared was the specter of a radical change that grassroots activists such as the Red Shirts could bring to Thailand—a change that might entail the political parricide of the father and mother figures of the kingdom and the political emancipation of all the "serfs" from their "Lord of Life." Given this fear of an uprising of their subordinates, Thai conservatives in turn used fear as a political tool to prolong their regime. One of the most crucial strategies the conservatives use to arouse political fear in their polity, according to Robin, is to construct foreign, empty, and nonpolitical objects of fear, the intractable foes of the regime, for "Nothing can be done to accommodate them: they can only be killed or contained."[126] In the case of the conservative elites in Thailand, they aroused political fear in public by creating a Thai version of a "Red scare." The military promoted the idea that the Red Shirts were terrorists who had organized an army to overthrow the monarchy. The Red Shirts were portrayed by the government as empty nonpolitical villagers who were driven not by political grievances but by Thaksin's money. The mass media spread a rumor that they were separatists who wanted to create a new republic in the northern and northeastern regions of the kingdom. The urban bourgeoisie not only created a witch-hunt that pursued the Red Shirts in social media but also popularized derogatory attitudes that defamed the latter as "red water buffaloes," "Thaksin's slaves," and "idiots" rather than politically conscious Thai citizens.[127]

It was this invented fear of the Red Shirts that played a vital role in the twilight of Rama IX's reign, a turbulent period that saw a series of reactionary actions emanating from the palace. The monarchy and the bourgeoisie revived ancient concepts of Thai kingship and mixed them with the popular discourse of the bourgeois crown. Further, the monarchy frequently relied on extraeconomic coercion in order to repress political dissidents. Finally, the monarchy also relied on state censorship and repression to cover up erratic and notorious acts of the crown prince, who stood first in line of succession but was deemed unfit to reign.

THE RETURN OF THE CELESTIAL CROWN

During the last few years of Rama IX's time on the throne, there was a tendency of the monarchy and bourgeoisie to revive the ancient concepts of the spiritual king and warrior-king. It was a reactionary move intended to remind the Red grass roots about the proper order of things in the kingdom. For the monarchy and its bourgeois allies, Rama IX was above all the monarch, and therefore he could not be compared to a commoner like Thaksin. They also preached that the divine right of the king was superior to Thaksin's vulgar populism and that, although the monarchy had recently been indulgent to the urban bourgeoisie, Rama IX was the king of all Thais regardless of their social class, political views, and geographic residence. Most important, they maintained that, despite the mortality of the natural body of Rama IX, the monarchy as a political body was immortal and would endure. This counterstrike against the specter of the Red Shirts using traditional concepts of Thai kingship was manifest in the mass media. According to Sarun Krittikarn, in the last decade of Rama IX's reign there was a "trend in the popular media, such as in commercials, TV dramas, movies, and national and royal anthem music videos, to render the king as *invisible*." Instead,

Sarun revealed, Rama IX appeared "as various symbolic avatars such as drops of rain for people in a drought region . . . the sun above a vast space of green hills . . . or in shadows to which people would prostrate or cry with utmost respect and admiration—all without a single familiar image of the king."[128] For Sarun, this trend was indicative of a shift of royal images in the mass media "from the overexposed king-as-logo" in previous decades to "the more mysterious and sacred king-as-shadow," "from spectacle to surveillance," and from the mundane and popular king to the panoptic and godlike king who has the power "to see without being seen."[129]

In a 2008 song composed for a royal celebration, "The Picture That Every Home Has," sung by Thailand's "King of Pop," Thongchai McIntyre, this theme of the god-king who oversees his subjects despite the absence of his physical body is cunningly mixed with the bourgeois obsession with Rama IX as the hardworking father of the nation. In addition to some bourgeois catchwords such as *self-sufficiency, hard work, dad, children,* and *love,* this song revives archaic concepts of Thai kingship by describing the king as a "breathing *deva*" and promoting the prostration of all Thais before the portrait of the king. The song rejoices:

> When I was young, I asked mom,
> Who was the man in the picture hung on our home's wall?
> She said we should prostrate before that picture every day because
>   he is a breathing *deva.*
> We have enough to eat and live because he has overseen us
>   for so long. Remember that.
>
> It is the picture that every home has,
> Whether it be a rich, poor, remote, or urban home . . .
> I see the picture of him working every single day . . .
> I will follow dad's footsteps and learn by heart the idea of sufficiency.[130]

The attempt to mix the bourgeois ethic of Rama IX with the ancient notion of a sacred, immortal, and celestial monarch is also evident in a 2011 song written for another royal celebration, "To Be a Servant under His Feet in Every Afterlife." Sung by Thailand's popular rockers Asanee and Wasan Chotikul, this song not only reproduces a common perception among the Thai bourgeoisie that Rama IX worked hard every single day of his life but also emphasizes the traditional notion of Thai kingship that a monarch is not a "dad" but the "Lord of Life," that his subjects are not his children but his servants, and that this hierarchical relationship is a bond forever due to the eternal recurrence of both the king's avatars and the rebirth of his subjects on earth. Negating the Red Shirt rhetoric of emancipating Thais from royal bondage, this song reminds the grass roots that they should be proud to be born as servants under His Majesty's feet not only in this present life but also in every afterlife.

> Prostrate before Him. Promise in your heart that,
> No matter how many afterlives, "I will follow Him.
> To be a servant under His Feet in every afterlife,
> No matter how hard and exhausted, I will be loyal."

> While a king in a fairy tale for children has a beautiful and happy life,
> This King over here industriously works and works . . .
> Wish that the King will live forever and after,
> Forever live until the end of time.[131]

In addition to pop songs, the ancient concept of a godlike, invisible, and immortal king was also revived in graphic novels written for royal celebrations. Published in 2011 by Amarin Printing and Publishing, a Thai enterprise in which Rama IX and Princess Sirindhorn were among the major stockholders, *The Comics for Celebrating King Rama IX* is a graphic biography of Rama IX that tells the story of the king from the time he was born to the diamond jubilee.[132] What is unique about this graphic novel, which targets young readers, is that it portrays the king in an unorthodox style. Instead of showing Rama IX as a living person of flesh and blood, it depicts the king as a translucent and hollow being with an aura around his body. By contrast, Thai commoners are depicted as Asian men and women with yellow and brown skin; Thaksin, who is portrayed as a popular turned authoritarian prime minister, is no exception. Capturing all the major historical events in Thai politics from the 1940s to the 2000s, the narrative of the novel is simple. Thai commoners are by nature conflict-prone people, yet they were fortunate to have Rama IX, who normally stayed above vulgar conflicts but would sacrifice his labor and time to save the nation if those conflicts got out of hand. In this sense, the novel is not a biography of the king as a man but serves as a hagiography of the king as a saint. The transcendent image of the godlike king that this novel illustrates is a counterstrike against the Red Shirt grass roots, who not only mocked the ailing body of the king but also anticipated his death. For the monarchy and the bourgeoisie, the natural body of Rama IX might be mortal, but the legacy of his reign would certainly be memorialized and embedded in the kingdom forever.

The royalist reaction against the Red Shirts could also be found in a 2010 graphic novel, *The Celestial Couple: The Two Charismatic Royals*.[133] Published by the government's campaign to promoting SEP among Thai youngsters, this novel tells a story of a young boy from the Northeast who comes to Bangkok to attend the diamond jubilee. At this event, the boy has conversations with some senior northeasterners who are also attending the nation's biggest event, and he gradually learns why all Thais love and revere Rama IX as the elders recall historical events of the king's six decades on the throne. In contrast to ethnographic research on northeastern villagers, the novel depicts them as submissive, royalist, and nonpolitical. Social grievances, economic inequality, and political conflicts between Bangkokians and the rural poor are noticeably absent while social harmony and unity among Thais are overstated. Above all, northeasterners in the novel never dress in red but in yellow, the particular color that symbolizes both loyalty to Rama IX and the political nemesis of the Red Shirts. Reading between the lines, it is therefore difficult to miss the crucial messages that this graphic novel sends to its readers: Rama IX is the king of all Thais, and he transcends all differences of class divisions, political conflicts, and regional boundaries; there are no political dissidents in the poor Northeast but only royalist subjects of the crown; and Thailand has never been divided by a color-coded conflict because all Thais are united under one color, the yellow that is not the color of any political movement but the symbolic color of Rama IX.

Alongside the ancient concept of a divine and transcendent monarch, another ancient theme was revived as a reactionary move against the Red Shirt dissidents, the warrior-king. The revival of this theme could be seen in the last version of Thai banknotes issued under the reign of Rama IX. From the 1980s on, the popular theme for depicting the monarchy on banknotes had been that of Rama IX as the bourgeois king—the king who worked extremely hard; sacrificed his labor for the nation; and mastered science, technology, art, sport, and music. In 2012, however, the BOT released its sixteenth series, which dramatically changed the previous trend by returning to a theme that was widely used in the Cold War era—the monarch as the great warrior who fights national enemies. While the front of the bills in this series features Rama IX in full regalia as usual, the back portrays five Thai monarchs who are titled "the Great." Three had been saluted in Thai history as national warriors who either defended or liberated the kingdom from foreign foes. King Naresuan and King Taksin, both of whom liberated Thais from Burmese domination, are depicted on the fifty-baht and the hundred-baht bills, respectively, while King Rama V, who diplomatically protected Siam from European colonization, is featured on the thousand-baht bill. According to Chatri, the latest depiction of the monarchy on Thai banknotes was indicative of "a return of a theme of the warrior-king who fights against the national threat . . . which was used in the age of the War on Communism." The revival of this old theme, for Chatri, was a desperate attempt by the conservative-royalist elite to revive fear and anxiety among the people. In the past, it was the specter of communism that was propagated to create fear among Thais. Now, it turned out that the "absolutist-capitalist" regime of corrupt politicians and their grassroots supporters were the figures all Thais were supposed to fear.[134] With the invention of these new objects of fear and anxiety in contemporary Thailand, the monarch—whose formal title, *pramahakasatri*, literally means "the great warrior" in Thai—was undeniably a runaway beneficiary. Thus, the national hero who was set up to exorcise the specter of Thaksin and the Red Shirts from the Thai kingdom was none other than Rama IX.

THE RETURN OF EXTRAECONOMIC COERCION

In addition to the invention of fear, the use of force was manifest in the twilight years of Rama IX. Referring to Marx's insight that force is integral to capitalism, Ernest Mandel remarked, "Under capitalism, labour is fundamentally *forced* labour. Whenever possible, capitalists prefer hypocritically to cloak the compulsion under a smokescreen of 'equal and just exchange' on the 'labour market.' When hypocrisy is no longer possible, they return to what they began with: naked coercion."[135] Similarly, in the Thai case the royals and members of the urban bourgeoisie, who enjoyed their accumulated of wealth in the newly industrialized kingdom, attempted to use the royal ideology to tame the classes of rural peasants and urban workers. After the invasion of the Red Shirt protesters into downtown Bangkok, however, the bourgeois crown and its partners seemed to realize the fact that their subordinates in the kingdom no longer swallowed the tale of hardworking, frugal, and ascetic royalty but mocked and exposed royal hypocrisies instead. To force the multitudes of the dissidents back to work on farms and in factories, the bourgeois monarchy returned to extraeconomic coercion. In contrast to the monarchy during the 1980s and the early 2000s—the golden era of the crown as it secured its hegemonic status via its role in bourgeois democracy, the market economy, and the mass media— starting in the mid-2000s the palace became more dependent on the coercive forces of the government, the army and the police. In other words, to use Althusser's terms, there was a late shift at the palace from popularizing its status in ideological state apparatuses to repeatedly relying on repressive brute force.[136]

Having played second fiddle to the monarchy during the last two decades of the twentieth century, the military became more politically active from the mid-2000s on, as the royalist bourgeoisie demanded. Even the palace itself took up the cudgel to tame what became perceived as threats to the throne. The army toppled Thaksin from power in the 2006 coup and violently suppressed the Red Shirts in the 2010 crackdown. Despite military coercion, Thaksin and the Red Shirts were politically resilient. In the 2011 general election, the first one since the crackdown, Thaksin nominated his youngest sister, Yingluck Shinawatra, as a candidate for prime minister. A former executive of the Shin Corporation who lacked any political experience and a soft-spoken female who was seen as a political puppet of her brother, Yingluck was snubbed by the incumbent royalist government and political pundits, who were certain that she would end Thaksin's winning streak in general elections.

The Red Shirts, however, stood firmly with Thaksin and voted for his proxy party, the Pheu Thai Party (PTP), which came up with a simple slogan: "Thaksin Thinks, Pheu Thai Acts." In a landslide victory that made Yingluck the first female prime minister in Thai history, the PTP received massive support from electoral districts in the North and Northeast. The party took 35 of 36 seats in the North and 104 of 126 in the Northeast. On the outskirts of Bangkok, in the poor districts where urban workers were crowded, the PTP also performed very well.[137] As Keyes and Glassman noted, the voting pattern in contemporary Thailand was indicative of geographic and economic divisions in the kingdom. Political oppression, state censorship, and social humiliation did not shake the resolve of voters in relatively poor districts such as those on Bangkok's outskirts and in the North and Northeast. They remained true to their preferred party, the proxy of Thaksin. Voters in more affluent districts, such as inner Bangkok and the South, in contrast, still supported the conservative-royalist Democrat Party.[138]

Thai history repeated itself, however, and Yingluck not only followed in her brother's footsteps but also faced a similar reaction from the royal establishment. Holding 265 of 500 seats in the House of Parliament, the PTP tried to deliver what the party promised in its electoral campaign: an increase in the minimum wage, the implementation of rice subsidy programs, and the construction of national infrastructure such as high-speed railroads and highways. Just as her brother did, though, Yingluck faced the criticism that her government was the embodiment of the populism, corruption, crony capitalism, and tyranny of the majority. Her minimum wage and rice subsidy policies were condemned by the bourgeoisie, whose faction argued that they would waste the state budget on the "idle" working class and the "imprudent" peasantry. Judicial activism also played an important role in undermining Yingluck's government. The judiciary not only declared her rice subsidy programs corrupt but also terminated her plans to construct high-speed railroads. The latter verdict was based on the Constitutional Court's assertion that built environments in Thailand were "not necessary" and "incompatible with the king's SEP."[139]

The tipping point for Yingluck came in late 2013 when she attempted to pass an amnesty bill that would have pardoned not only the convicted protesters of the last ten years—the majority of them Red Shirts—but also her brother, who had decided to live in exile in 2008 after he was sentenced in absentia to two years in jail for abuse of power. Once the bill was passed by the PTP-dominated parliament, the urban bourgeoisie came alive and mobilized under a new banner, the People's Democratic Reform Committee (PDRC). Nevertheless, like old wine in new bottles, the PDRC was merely the political reincarnation of the Yellow Shirt movement as it embodied the same components and practiced the same strategies the Yellow Shirts had used before. The PDRC was composed of white-collar workers, businessmen, urban entrepreneurs, professionals, high- and midlevel bureaucrats, members of noble families, and media personalities. It took to the streets, shut down the commercial areas of Bangkok, and occupied government buildings. It condemned electoral democracy as unfit for "Thai-style democracy" and demanded the disenfranchisement of the rural majority, which it stigmatized as "uneducated," "poor," "antimonarchist," and "Thaksin's slaves." It also asked the military to intervene in the political conflict and topple the elected government.[140] In mid-2014, after Yingluck's snap election was obstructed by the PDRC and declared unconstitutional by the Constitutional Court, the military finally stepped in and launched its second coup in eight years. As many observers point out, the 2014 coup that toppled Yingluck was both similar to and different from the 2006 coup that toppled Thaksin.

What made this coup similar to the previous one was the political collaboration between the monarchy and the military. Shortly after the 2014 coup, General Prayut Chan-o-cha, who had led it, received a royal endorsement and was formally appointed by the king to run the country. Prayut in turn justified the coup as a political intervention to remind all Thais that sovereignty in the kingdom was always with the king, not elected politicians. "In the name of His Majesty the King," he said, "royal power [was presented] to us; today who among us considers this?" As he explained further, "From the point of view of the government, you are using the three powers [legislative, executive and judicial] that belong to Him. The power does not belong to you. You do not receive this power when you are elected. It is power that comes from His Majesty the King. His Majesty presented this power to us to form the government." Armed with this train of thought, Prayut concluded with his justification to lead the new government: "Today, the power that I have was presented to me by the King."[141]

The 2014 coup, however, had two major features that distinguished it from the one in 2006: the prolongation of military dictatorship and the scale of state repression. As Baker remarked about military rule after the 2014 coup, "The junta did not step back from the front line and install a normally civilian government to placate local and, more importantly, international opinion. Instead, the coup group installed themselves at the apex of the political system."[142] To Baker the latest coup had installed "a military government of a kind not seen in over 40 years," and it was possible to see the junta extending its rule in Thai politics for twenty more.[143] Similarly, Sopranzetti argued that the 2014 coup was symptomatic of "Thailand's relapse toward a dictatorial system of governance," a political system that used to be dominant in the Cold War era. Highlighting three components of the junta's rule since 2014—an administrative structure directed by military officers instead of elected politicians, state ideology based on the remystification of the monarchy, and a strong political alliance of the traditional elite, the military, and the urban middle class—Sopranzetti believed that the Thai people would have to live under military authoritarianism instead of democracy for years to come.[144] Calling the ruling junta the "monarchised military," Paul Chambers and Napisa Waitoolkiat made the bold prediction that when the reign of Rama IX came to an end the new monarch "will need a strong military to protect palace interests, but such strength will mean that the military will be a 'senior' partner and more difficult to control" and that "more likely, for the foreseeable future, military officers will continue to play a prominent role in Thailand."[145]

In addition to the prolongation of its state control, the ruling junta also used state violence on a scale that virtually returned the Thai polity to the age of military despotism. As Baker described political suppression in Thailand after the 2014 coup, "The junta used repressive regulations and techniques of intimidation to silence opposition in a more aggressive way than any coup since 1976. They retained martial law nationwide for over ten months. . . . A small number of people were subject to interrogation techniques and possibly torture (always strenuously denied), intimidating everyone."[146] Speaking to the public on television every week on behalf of the ruling junta, Prayut also "deployed a strong undertone of violence through semi-jocular threats to 'execute' persistent journalists, and references to 'getting rid of human garbage.'"[147] Most important, abuse of the lèse-majesté law became a trademark of the ruling junta. As Prayut himself declared, the persecution of lèse-majesté violators was one of the junta's top priorities because the "previous administration" had neglected to "enforce the law properly."[148] Thanks to this political motivation, the abuse of the lèse-majesté law under Thailand's military regime, according to the International Federation of Human Rights (FIDH), has reached alarming levels. As the junta has transferred the trial of lèse-majesté cases from the civil to the military courts, individuals accused of lèse-majesté are deprived of the right to a fair trial, the right to a public hearing, the right to counsel, and the right to bail. The rate of imprisoning lèse-majesté violators has experienced a ninefold increase over the rate before the coup. Furthermore, social media users who share any messages deemed critical of the crown face a lèse-majesté investigation and can be sentenced to prison with a harsh penalty, an average of seven years and nine months per message. On top of that, those who are specifically targeted by state authorities for a lèse-majesté violation have been mostly members, supporters, or sympathizers of the Red Shirt movement.[149]

As the FIDH unveiled in several cases of lèse-majesté charges, Thai authorities under the junta regime have lacked sensible reasons for them. They arbitrarily and absurdly charge anyone they deem critical of the crown. A Red Shirt factory worker was accused of posting a message online that mocked Rama IX's dog, famously known in public as Mrs. Thongdaeng. A renowned scholar faced a police investigation for criticizing Thai monarchs of the nineteenth century. A Red Shirt hotel worker was detained in a military camp for dressing in black on Rama IX's birthday. Two university students were sentenced to two and a half years in prison for staging a theatrical play about a fictional monarch that was deemed offensive to the monarchy. A US ambassador to Thailand faced a police investigation after he expressed his concerns about the abuse of the lèse-majesté law in the kingdom. A woman was arrested for merely showing the banner "Long live USA Day" on July 4, 2014, in front of the US embassy in Bangkok, which was considered a parody of the expression "Long live the King!" Even a news reporter was summoned by state authorities for reporting on lèse-majesté cases and trials.[150] In other countries, these legal cases might sound absurd and ridiculous. In the Thai kingdom, however, they were executed by authorities as a matter of life and death. The days when the subordinate classes could air their political resentment toward the monarchy through satirical songs, metaphorical poems, public performances, and critical posts on social media are gone. Under the ruling junta today, Khorapin remarked, even the "weapons of the weak" that the powerless evasively apply to sustain their political resistance are suppressed by state authorities.[151] In this kingdom, where fear and force prevail, the underclasses have been tragically dispossessed not only of their political and human rights but also of their arts of resistance.

THE RETURN OF THE PRODIGAL SON

What was the political motivation of the military to prolong its rule, violently suppress dissidents, and take the lèse-majesté law to extremes? Outside the palace, it was clear that the military had been summoned to repress the Red Shirt movement, whose scale of mass mobilization was deemed a threat to the throne. However, there was a critical problem that loomed large inside the palace itself, and it also played a role in the political return of the military: anxiety among the palace establishment over the royal succession. What became paramount was not the question of who would ascend the throne once Rama IX passed away. The Palace Law of Succession, the Constitution of Thailand, and Rama IX's appointment of Prince Vajiralongkorn as successor left nothing uncertain about that. The crown prince would be King Rama X of the Thai kingdom. What concerned the royal establishment, however, was whether the tenth monarch of the Chakri dynasty would be able to step into his father's shoes. This is an intrinsic problem not only for the Thai monarchy but also for monarchy in general.

Royal succession under a constitutional monarchy, as Marx pointed out, is not different from that of an absolute monarchy since they are similarly based on primogeniture—the right of a crown prince to stand first in line of succession due to the virtue of his birth instead of his talents, intellect, or ethical merits. "Birth," Marx remarked, "would determine the quality of the monarch as it determines the quality of cattle."[152] Despite his particular interest in the British monarchy, Bagehot provided an insight into several problems of succession under a constitutional monarchy in general. First, the populace should expect not greatness but mediocrity from an heir apparent because his rank and title are not earned but given and fixed after the queen gives birth to him. "It is idle," said Bagehot, "to expect a man whose place has always been fixed to have a better judgment than one who has lived by his judgment; to expect a man whose career will be the same whether he is discreet or he is indiscreet to have the nice discretion of one who has risen by his wisdom, who will fall if he ceases to be wise."[153] Moreover, the age of the crown prince when he ascends the throne matters: the younger the better. If he becomes the new king when he is old or middle-aged, Bagehot asserted, "He is then unfit to work. He will then have spent the whole of youth and the first part of manhood in idleness, and it is unnatural to expect him to labor."[154] Finally, kings who are willing to work, to Bagehot, are "among God's greatest gifts, but they are also among His rarest," and thus people in a kingdom should prepare for two possible scenarios in a new reign: they will get either "an ordinary idle king" who leaves no mark on his time or "an active and half-insane king" who is used as a political tool by others. If it turns out to be the latter case, Bagehot believed that a kingdom will have "one of the worst of governments."[155]

Bagehot's worst-case scenario of a newly crowned monarch might turn out to be a reality in Thailand. Inside the Thai court, the apple fell far from the tree. Unlike his father, Prince Vajiralongkorn grew up in the era of the revival of the monarchy instead of the dark time when the crown reached its nadir. Therefore, instead of acquiring a sense of urgency and insecurity, he was nurtured in the royal sanctuary of wealth, power, and prestige. While Rama IX surprisingly ascended the throne when he was a teenager, his son had been appointed the heir apparent long ago, in 1972. Yet, even when the crown prince turned sexagenarian in 2010, his octogenarian and ailing father did not show any signs of abdication. On top of that, while Rama IX seemed to embody personal ethics and public images that resonated with the bourgeoisie, the crown prince had struggled to follow in his father's footsteps. According to a BBC report that was banned in Thailand, as a young student in British private schools, the prince was anything but brilliant in science, technology, art, sports, or music because "by his own account, he struggled to keep up at school, blaming his pampered upbringing in the palace." Growing up, he gained a reputation for "womanizing, gambling and illegal businesses," and even his mother, Queen Sirikit, "alluded to these problems, describing her son as 'a bit of a Don Juan' and suggesting that he preferred spending his weekends with beautiful women rather than performing duties." Divorced three times, the crown prince dated and later married a former Thai Airways flight attendant who was appointed an officer of the Royal Household Guard with the rank of lieutenant-general. Most notoriously, he "promoted his pet poodle, Fu-Fu, to the rank of air chief marshal."[156]

In the twilight of Rama IX's reign, the crown prince's erratic and prodigal lifestyle not only tarnished the public image of Thai royalty as ascetic, diligent, and frugal but also exposed a critical problem in Thailand—the inability to distinguish between the property of the crown and that of the kingdom. On July 2011, a Boeing 737 of the Royal Thai Air Force was impounded at a Munich airport due to the Thai government's refusal to pay a debt to a German construction company. This would not have been big news in Thailand if that particular aircraft had not been normally piloted and used by the crown prince as his private jet. From the German authorities' perspective, the impounding of the so-called Royal Flight was justified because it was de facto the property of the Thai government. Thai authorities, to the contrary, asserted that the aircraft belonged to the prince and the Germans should immediately return it to him.[157] Another incident occurred in November 2014 when the crown prince wanted to divorce his third wife, formerly Princess Srirasmi, and have her relinquish her royal title. Even though the government has long claimed that the CPB is not the private property of the royal family but belongs to all Thais, a payment of 200 million baht (US$6 million) was given to Srirasmi in exchange for relinquishing the title. After days of rumors, the government finally confirmed that the money was paid by the CPB.[158] Thanks to this controversial divorce, Thai commoners finally had a chance to catch a glimpse of how the massive wealth of the CPB was spent. Instead of being dispensed for the common good, it was spent according to the private interests of the royal family.

Unlike his only son, Rama IX's three daughters would have been better candidates for their father's bourgeois crown. Princess Sirindhorn is the most popular member of the royal family, second only to the king. She has been praised in the mass media as down to earth, frugal, diligent, and brilliant in literature, art, and music. In addition to the languages that are closely related to Thai culture, such as Pali, Sanskrit, and Khmer, the princess has reportedly mastered English, French, Chinese, German, and Latin. Princess Ubolratana graduated with a bachelor's degree in mathematics from MIT and a master's degree in public health from UCLA, spent almost three decades in the United States, and recently launched a career as a movie star and television personality. Princess Chulabhorn is heavily involved in the promotion of scientific research and frequently receives awards and honors, the most prestigious of which is the Albert Einstein Medal of the United Nations Educational, Scientific and Cultural Organization (UNESCO). Besides these three female royals, Queen Sirikit would also have been a better candidate for the throne. Despite the loss of her physical strength, the octogenarian queen is still highly revered by many Thais since she is the one who stood side by side with Rama IX from the beginning of his reign. The possibility that the Thai kingdom might have had its first female sovereign, however, was shunned by the palace. Despite its modern and bourgeois appearance, the monarchy was conservative when it came to the issue of royal succession, and thus the ancient tradition based on male primogeniture was strictly followed.[159]

As it was certain that Rama IX was not simply ailing but dying and Prince Vajiralongkorn would reign as the next king, the monarchy had the uphill task of rebranding the prodigal and notorious prince, who was less popular than his siblings, had barely appeared in public for decades, and did not have royal charities and development projects under his belt. Consequently, having the military instead of popularly elected politicians in office did not hurt but helped the crown to carry out this task. That is, the ruling junta did not hesitate to divert state budgets from promoting the general welfare of the people to promoting the royal image. Extravagant events such as "Bike for Dad" and "Bike for Mom" were staged so that the crown prince could soothe any concerns about his personality. Instead of an old prince, he was depicted by the media as a healthy and sporty biker; instead of an estranged member of the royal family, he was shown as a family man who loved to pay homage to his father and mother; and instead of an unreliable and unstable man, he was promoted as a mature prince who could lead thousands of royalist participants in the nation's biggest events. In addition to these bourgeois images and values, the rebranding of the heir apparent was also based on the ancient concept of the warrior-king. To show that he was ready to reign as the great warrior of the kingdom, the military government brought back an old image of the prince that had not been seen in public for decades, a portrait of him dressed in a military uniform and fighting communist guerrillas. Furthermore, the military regime was instrumental in helping the palace wipe clean any royal scandals that were leaked to public. In 2015 several of the prince's close associates were accused of abusing his name for private gain and charged under the lèse-majesté law. While some mysteriously disappeared, others were put in jail and later found dead while in military custody. Police investigations into or public discussions about this scandalous purge, however, were silenced and prohibited under the military regime.[160]

The monarchy and the military might wish that they had more time to rebrand the public image of the crown prince and clean up his notorious past. Unfortunately, after seven decades on the throne, Rama IX finally passed away on October 13, 2016. Within hours General Prayut announced to the public, "The King is dead, long live the King!" in order to assure all Thais of the continuity of the monarchy.[161] The crown prince, however, broke royal tradition by asking for time to mourn and prepare himself before being proclaimed the new king.[162] After the longest interregnum in Thai history, the sixty-four-year-old prince was ready to fill the king's shoes. On December 1, 2016, he accepted the throne and was officially declared King Rama X. Whether the tenth reign of the Chakri dynasty will be led by a bourgeois king, "an ordinary idle king," or "an active and half-insane king" may still be uncertain. What is certain, however, is the type of Thai kingdom that his father left for him. It is a kingdom of industrial capitalism where royal conglomerates stand head and shoulders above those of commoners, where the "monarchised military" brutally rules politics, where sixty-eight million Thais are deeply divided by a color-coded class conflict between the yellow bourgeoisie and the red workers and peasants, and where royal wealth, power, and prestige have begun to rely on coercion rather than consent. How will the new king manage the enormous fortune of the bourgeois crown, continue enchanting the urban bourgeoisie, keep the military generals in line, and tame political resentment among the grassroots dissidents? This is a tall order for any monarch in the world today, let alone an unpopular king like Rama X.

CONCLUSION

Despite its successes during Thailand's transition to industrial capitalism in the late twentieth century, the bourgeois monarchy embodied some intrinsic contradictions that were disguised by the prosperity of the newly industrialized kingdom. Under monarchy-led capitalism, even though the crown was at the top of the kingdom's political and economic hierarchy, the gap between the urban rich and the rural poor had increasingly widened. As inequality, uneven development, and capital concentration showed no signs of diminishing, the alienation of the underclasses intensified. Although the monarchy successfully won the hearts and minds of the urban bourgeoisie and secured a symbiotic relationship with this wealthy class, it was this symbiosis that marginalized and alienated the masses of peasants and workers who constituted the majority of the Thai population. Furthermore, royal hegemony was based on the success of the bourgeois crown in establishing a ruling ideology, yet extraeconomic forces such as military intervention and the draconian law of lèse-majesté remained the last resort of the palace when the royal ideology failed to work its magic. On top of that, despite its bourgeois appearance, the monarchy was still conservative when it came to the issue of royal succession. Instead of hard work, frugality, and merit, the succession to the Thai throne was based on male-preference primogeniture, and thus it was the unpopular prince who became the next king after the bourgeois monarch passed away.

These contradictions had turned into critical challenges for the crown in the last decade of Rama IX's reign. Long exploited under monarchy-led capitalism, the multitudes of the subordinate classes gave electoral consent to a new political party that offered an alternative to Thai capitalism, the provision of capital and social welfare to the grass roots, and the extension of production and consumption to the countryside. In the face of this popularly elected government and the massive support of the poor majority, the monarchy and its bourgeois partners turned out to be more reactionary. Rather than accepting and listening to the resentful voices of the grass roots, the palace frequently intervened in political and judicial conflicts while the bourgeoisie undermined the popularly elected government with mass protests. Both also tried to revive ancient notions of Thai kingship in order to differentiate between the divine monarch and demagogic politicians. Yet, as the masses of rural peasants and urban workers stood firmly with their preferred government in spite of the royal intervention and bourgeois protest, the monarchy finally realized that its ruling ideology was no longer functional, and so it returned to the use of naked coercion. Having once retreated from national politics, the military was reactivated by the monarchy to topple not one but two elected governments, to force the politically active grass roots back to work on farms and in factories, to violently suppress anyone who was deemed critical of the crown, and to restore the order of monarchy-led capitalism in the kingdom. Since it was still uncertain whether the lower classes would reconcile with the monarchy and whether the heir apparent was ready to ascend the throne once the reigning monarch passed away, the ruling junta showed no sign of returning power to civilians and silenced political dissidents with the lèse-majesté law, state censorship, and brute force.

During the last decade of Rama IX's time on the throne, Thailand was plagued by political instability, class conflicts between the bourgeoisie and the lower classes of workers and peasants, and military oppression of civilians. Instead of remaining a neutral institution under a constitutional regime, the monarchy got deeply involved in these conflicts, sided with the bourgeoisie and the army, and further alienated the resentful masses. As a result, the legacy of the historic reign of Rama IX was far from cemented; rather, it was tarnished by this chaotic and violent decade. Unlike the golden age of the bourgeois monarchy from the late 1980s to the early 2000s, the twilight of Rama IX's reign saw the frequent reliance of the crown on extraeconomic coercion instead of active consent, the revival of ancient traditions of kingship that began to overshadow the crown's bourgeois image, and the undisguised partnership between the monarchy and the military—a partnership in which the latter seemed less content to play second fiddle to the former than before. It remains to be seen whether King Rama X will maintain or reverse these reactionary trends in the monarchy in the years to come. A look at the notorious and violent history of the newly crowned monarch of the Thai kingdom, however, led to an early prediction that the prospects of the bourgeois monarchy under his reign looked anything but bright.

 **5**

ALL HAIL THE KING

Even though everyone saw it coming, the death of King Rama IX still shook the Thai kingdom to its core. In early October 2016, there were several signs that the end of the king's seven-decade reign was imminent. The royal medical team announced to the public that the eighty-eight-year-old monarch was in critical condition due to a variety of ailments, including kidney, lung, and liver problems. Members of the royal family rushed to the hospital to visit the ailing king. Having lived mostly in Germany, the crown prince flew back to Bangkok and went immediately to his father's deathbed. The Privy Council called an urgent meeting, and the prime minister canceled his overseas trips. Most symbolically significant, the stock market of Thailand—the place where royal enterprises and the king's investments reigned supreme—quickly responded to the looming end of the reign. As the king, the hegemonic figure in Thailand's politics, economy, and society, showed no sign of surviving, the Thai stock market index plunged 6.5 percent, the world's biggest drop of the month. Uncertain about the kingdom's prospects, foreign investors pulled money from Thai stocks at the fastest pace of the year. The Thai currency also sank to the year's lowest rate.[1]

On the afternoon of October 13, after hours of uncertainty, all television channels went black and white at 7:00 p.m. and broadcast a brief announcement by the royal household: the ninth king of the Chakri dynasty had died at 3:52 p.m. A few minutes later the prime minister appeared on the television screen and officially announced the death of the king. "It is the greatest loss and despair in the lives of all Thais nationwide," the junta leader turned premier, General Prayut, said to the nationwide audience.[2] While Thai newspapers rapidly reported this breaking news to the public, *The Nation* stood out in terms of its visual presentation. It converted the iconic picture of Rama IX sweating from the tip of his nose while working on his development projects to black and white and printed this image on its front page with the caption "Kingdom Grieves."[3] The message the newspaper delivered to its readers was this: the father figure of the nation who had tirelessly worked for his subjects was finally at rest.

The morning after Rama IX passed away, hundreds of thousands of Thais donned black and waited along the procession route transporting the king's body from the hospital to the Grand Palace. Kneeling and praying for the late king during Bangkok's hot afternoon, many mourners wept while holding portraits of Rama IX and royal flags. Those who did not bring royal portraits from home took Thai banknotes from their pockets and held the bills overhead while waiting for the royal procession (figure 25).[4] The bills featured portraits of Rama IX on the front and those of the late king and other royal figures on the back. It was a spectacular event in Thai history. Instead of an official ceremony meticulously arranged by the royal household, a crowd of mourners expressed their loyalty to, grief over the death of, and familial love for the late king through the mundane medium of monetary exchange. Instead of religious items such as amulets, statuettes, and white cotton threads (*saisin*), which are normally used to reify spirits in Thai culture, it was cash that served as a mediator between the dead king and his living subjects. A few days later thousands of Thai mourners lined up at 2:00 a.m. in front of government banks in order to buy commemorative banknotes that featured Rama IX visiting rural citizens, overseeing his development projects, and playing the saxophone. First released in 2011, the banknotes were reissued by the BOT when they became the hottest items in the market following the king's death. Within hours the

Figure 25. King is cash. A crowd of Thai mourners raise Thai banknotes with images of Rama IX while waiting for the convoy that returned the body of the late king to the Grand Palace on October 14, 2016. (Photo by Rungroj Yongrit /Epa/Shutterstock)

entire first print run of ninety thousand banknotes sold out, and the government had to order a new stock of two hundred thousand bills to meet the demand.[5] In addition to the classic phase "cash is king," this craze for banknotes with images of Rama IX shows that the reverse, "king is cash," also rings true in the Thai kingdom.

KING IS CASH

During the long reign of Rama IX, the monarchy not only made its presence felt on Thai banknotes. In fact the crown had also become an invisible currency for political, business, and cultural relations in the Thai kingdom. In national politics, the monarchy's support and endorsement were political capital. Instead of parliament buildings or government offices, it was a trend in contemporary Thailand that politicians, civil servants, and high-ranking generals had to frequent the palace in order to secure political support from the king, the royal family, and the Privy Council. Without the green light from the crown, the prospect that a government—military or civilian—could administer the kingdom was bleak. In the market, business connections with the palace were capital. By donating money to royal charities, appointing privy counselors to a board of directors, or creating joint ventures with royal enterprises, both Thai and foreign investors could be business partners of the CPB—the corporate body that owns not only one of the largest conglomerates but also the most valuable collection of commercial land in the kingdom. In the mass media, anything associated with the crown was cultural capital. Songs, books, films, television programs, and photographs that were either composed by royalty or produced to salute the crown had the Midas touch, as they invariably became best-selling and award-winning merchandise. When Rama IX closed his eyes forever in 2016, he left a remarkable legacy behind. Rather than being a marginal institution in a capitalist state, the monarchy at the end of Rama IX's reign held a virtual hegemonic status in Thailand's national politics, economy, and pop culture.

The hegemonic status of the monarchy in Thailand, as this book has shown, is not a natural or inherited trait of the kingdom but a recent construct. It is the innovative construction and renovation of three bodies of the monarchy under the historic reign of Rama IX. When the reign began in 1946, the king's two bodies, the natural and the political, were in critical condition. Regarding the natural body, Thai kings and the royal family had been physically absent from the public for decades. Born in the United States and having spent his childhood and adolescence in Europe, Rama IX was an unfamiliar face to local Thais when he became king at age eighteen after the mysterious death of his elder brother. During the early reign of Rama IX, however, fortune seemed to smile on the crown. In the late 1940s, Thailand's constitutional regime, which had been unstable and vulnerable since the end of the absolute monarchy, was taken over by the military faction of the Thai bureaucracy, and for decades to come the army would maintain its authoritarian rule in Thai politics. Lacking legitimacy, the military turned to the king's two bodies and brought them back to life in the hope that they could be used as a political facade for military rule. Portraits of the king and the royal family were widely promoted among the public. Royal ceremonies that had vanished with the end of Thai absolutism were popularly revived. In the media, the king was depicted not only as the supreme commander of the Thai army but also as the religious ruler in accordance with Hindu-Buddhist beliefs.

It was also during this early phase of Rama IX's reign that the third body of the monarchy—the capitalist one—began to take shape. When Rama IX ascended the throne, the fate of the Thai crown seemed to be no different from that which other constitutional monarchies had to face. The monarchy's financial status was dependent on government aid, not its personal investments. Governmental control of wealth over that of the Thai monarchy nonetheless did not last long. Thanks to the end of the constitutional regime and the rise of the military's power in Thai politics, the crown was able to restore its financial situation to the status quo ante. With military backing, the monarchy took back control of the Privy Purse in the late 1940s and renovated it under a newly created office, the CPB. Unlike the Privy Purse in the old regime, the CPB did not accumulate wealth as a rentier by draining money from the kingdom's treasury and squandering it on unproductive expenditures. Instead, as the military government pursued the national project of industrialization in the 1960s and 1970s, the CPB actively participated in the expanding market by investing royal wealth in industry, finance, and property development. Thanks to the formation of the CPB as the capitalist body of the crown, the king and the royal family were able to get back on their feet. Instead of being at the mercy of the government, their financial security now rested on the crown's growing success in the market.

The attempt to bring the Thai monarchy back into politics and the market economy, however, was not a smooth road. In fact it backfired in the 1970s when the CPT and radical students began to rebel against the political alliance between the military and the monarchy. The publicity about the natural body of the king failed to resonate with the Left. The depiction of Rama IX as a religious ruler made him look like a conservative sovereign from the feudal past, while the portrayal of him as the commander in chief made him indistinguishable from the ruling junta. The political role of the second body of the king also fueled the fire. Thanks to the crown's involvement with the military crackdown on leftist students in the late 1970s, many young radicals decided to join the CPT in the deep jungle and unprecedentedly made the communist force a serious threat to the monarchy. Even the development of the third body of the king did not go unnoticed by the Left. The increasing wealth of the Thai monarchy in the kingdom, where inequality and poverty had been widespread, was intensely discussed and criticized by the CPT. In short, in the early phase of Rama IX's reign, the three bodies of the Thai monarchy, despite gaining influence, were still vulnerable to political threats, as the crown still relied heavily on ancient beliefs in Thai kingship and extraeconomic coercion.

The status of the three bodies of the monarchy dramatically changed as the reign of Rama IX entered its second phase in the 1980s. It was a critical decade when the Thai economy saw unprecedented growth; the bourgeoisie was on the rise; and consumerism, the mass media, and pop culture quickly penetrated Thai society. Against this background, the first body of the king started to embody new ideological features that came with capitalism: bourgeois ethics and appearance. Instead of being the divine Hindu king, the virtuous Buddhist king, and the ancient warrior-king, Rama IX became more visible in the public eye by means of the four themes of a "bourgeois monarch." That is, he was now popularly praised as the industrious king who never stopped working for the common good of his subjects, the frugal king who lived a humble and self-sufficient life, the father figure of the nation who provided familial affection and attachment to his childlike subjects, and the cosmopolitan king who was talented in the fields of art, music, literature, sports, science, and technology.

Rama IX also embraced a new public image that made him look more like an ordinary bourgeois. Rather than wearing a military uniform or religious regalia as he had done in his early reign, Rama IX dressed more often in public in a business suit, a buttoned-down shirt, a necktie, and reading glasses. In place of a regal sword and an assault rifle, which he had commonly carried during the first phase of his reign when he was being presented as a divine king and warrior-king, he usually carried a camera, map, pencil, and walkie-talkie when he visited his subjects in rural provinces. Thanks to this rebranding of the king's image, Rama IX became widely popular among the urban bourgeoisie, and this phenomenon distinguished him from previous monarchs of the Thai kingdom.

Like the natural body of the king, the political body was clearly bourgeoisified in the second phase of Rama IX's reign. During the last two decades of the twentieth century, a series of political events pushed the monarchy to make a significant adjustment in its political alliances and mass-based support. In the late 1980s, as the communist influence in the kingdom declined dramatically, the monarchy shifted its focus from the national security and political conflicts that had been its concern in previous decades to economic development and urbanization. Instead of visiting military camps, Thai royalty spent more time with their development projects. These were designed to solve the socioeconomic problems of inadequate urban infrastructure, traffic congestion, and environmental degradation—problems that resonated widely with the urban bourgeoisie. The royal attempt to create a political alliance with the bourgeoisie became clearer in the early 1990s when the power of this rising class could no longer be contained by the military. In the face of increasing demands for demilitarization and democratization by the bourgeoisie, the monarchy jumped on the bandwagon. The crown distanced itself from the military, intervened as a mediator between the military and urban protesters, and promoted itself as a democratic advocate. With the withdrawal of the military and the establishment of parliamentary democracy in Thailand from the mid-1990s onward, the monarchy adapted itself to the new political climate by applying two strategies that were more compatible with the new order steered by the bourgeoisie.

First, instead of using physical force against those he deemed to be a threat, the king gave speeches that became a political tool for the crown to put pressure on the government. Barely making himself heard in the early years of his reign, Rama IX was outspoken in his later period. The king frequently addressed not only the political problems of corruption among politicians, the political stalemate in the parliament, and the instability of the civilian government but also the socioeconomic problems of rapid industrialization, unrestrained capitalism, and conspicuous consumption. Echoing the frustration with the government among the urban bourgeoisie, the king's speeches appeared regularly in the mass media, and they became verbal requests by the crown to which the government had to give a positive response. Another strategy the crown employed was informal interventions in national politics via the monarchy's networks and proxies. Promoting itself as a neutral institution that stood above political conflicts, the crown often used its loyalists in the parliament, the bureaucracy, the army, social movements, and academia to deliver political demands to the government. Thanks to these masterful strategies, the monarchy could rebrand its image in Thai politics. Instead of being a partner in crime with the army and an advocate of despotic rule, the crown gained a new reputation as the guardian of the nation that oversaw, warned, and indirectly intervened on behalf of the fledgling order of bourgeois democracy.

The transformation of the first two bodies of the king was crucial to the status of the third. With the new look of the natural bodies of Thai royalty, the public tended to see the king and the royal family as frugal and industrious and indeed as ordinary people; it became unthinkable for many Thais to connect the dots between the economical royals and the massive wealth that the CPB accumulated from its investments in the thriving market. Therefore, when Rama IX was ranked the world's richest royal in the latter part of the first decade of the new millennium, thanks to his estimated fortune of US$30 billion from the CPB, it created a public backlash, as the king and capital were normally perceived as mismatched and incompatible.

The new status of the crown in national politics also helped the CPB to find business partnerships. Having withstood the end of the military regime and the rise of bourgeois democracy, the monarchy was seen by businesspeople as a stable, reliable, and resilient institution. As the monarchy distanced itself from the military and contentious politics but engaged more with the economic issues of industrialization, development, and urbanization, businesspeople also saw the crown, which could influence government policy, as the active overseer of the national economy. Thus, in the later years of the reign, it became popular among elite corporations in Thailand not only to seek partnerships with the CPB but also to appoint executives of the CPB, privy counselors, and royalist bureaucrats and generals to their boards of directors. Unlike the majority of Thai commoners, officials of these elite corporations recognized the deep connection between the monarchy and the market and understood that their partnerships with the crown could offer them not only honor and prestige but also political security and financial resources. Besides, by allying themselves with the capitalist body of the king, giant corporations could ride the king's public relations coattails. In addition to their business collaborations with the crown, most conglomerates frequently donated money to development projects and philanthropic organizations initiated by Rama IX and other members of the royal family. They also claimed that they took the king's concerns on rapid industrialization and unrestrained capitalism seriously, and they enthusiastically promoted the king's ethic of thrift, hard work, and self-sufficiency. In the shadow of the natural body of the king, the wealthy partnerships between the CPB and big corporations meant that they could pursue their promotion of free trade, industrial capitalism, and consumerism unhindered by serious public scrutiny.

In spite of all its successes during Thailand's transition to industrial capitalism, the monarchy had its Achilles heel. Under monarchy-led capitalism in Thailand, while the crown and the bourgeoisie enjoyed their accumulating wealth, the majority of the population struggled with the kingdom's industrial revolution, which entailed socioeconomic inequality, uneven development, capital concentration, mass dispossession, and environmental destruction. During the twilight of Rama IX's reign, their resentment could no longer be contained and became exposed to the larger public. Masses of peasants, blue-collar workers, and unemployed people protested in the streets and voiced their resentment toward the king, members of the royal family, and privy counselors, who all stood firmly with the wealthy bourgeoisie. Burdened with debt and unable to access social welfare, the underclasses took exception to the massive fortune of the king's capitalist body and its partnerships with national and global corporations. Most symbolically important, they mocked the natural bodies of the king, exposed the hypocrisy of the world's richest monarch, who presented himself in public as a frugal man, and even wished for the death of the old and ailing king.

As the three bodies of the king were on shaky ground in the eyes of the multitudes, the crown defended itself by turning to its last resort, the army and its repression of any sign of antimonarchial sentiments. The monarchy's recourse to the coup d'état and junta regime raised a red flag indicating that the crown had already lost its hegemonic status and headed south when Rama IX was on his deathbed. As a result, when the crown passed from the longest reigning and most popular monarch in Thai history to his heir apparent, the odds were stacked against the new monarch, King Maha Vajiralongkorn Bodindradebayavarangkun, or Rama X. Thanks to his prodigal lifestyle, erratic personality, and inexperience in politics, it was widely assumed that Rama X would be merely a playboy king, a political puppet of the junta, and an unskilled sovereign.[6] He would stand no chance of carrying on the royal power, wealth, and popularity that his father left behind. With an incompetent king on the throne, it looked as if the new reign was doomed right off the bat. Yet, against all odds, the royal succession was smooth. The new reign took hold without political chaos or mass uprisings. Most important, Rama X has shown to the public during the early stage of his reign that he is a much shrewder king than people expected, and he does not shy away from but engages with royal intervention in national politics and royal investment in the market. Once again the Thai crown is proving itself a resilient institution, surviving the death of one king and living to fight another day.

IN THE KINGDOM OF THE BLIND

Having ascended the throne at age sixty-four, Rama X is the oldest newly crowned monarch of the centuries-old Chakri dynasty. The aged Rama X, however, is not an inert king who has abdicated the management of royal power and wealth. In fact, during the early phase of his reign, he has been active and apparently more assertive than his father was when it comes to the interests of the monarchical bodies. A few months after his reign began, the junta asked the new king to sign off on the kingdom's latest constitution, a charter drafted by the military to prolong its rule as approved by a national referendum in 2016. Surprisingly, Rama X intervened and ordered the junta to revise some parts of the constitution of which he disapproved, and two of them are directly related to royal prerogatives.[7] First, while the constitutional draft required that the king appoint a regent when he is absent from the kingdom or unable to perform his duties, Rama X insisted that it is up to the king whether he should appoint a regent to represent him pro tempore. Recently spending most of his time in his luxury villa in Munich, Rama X could take advantage of this revision by reigning from the German republic instead of his home kingdom.

Another part in the draft of which the king disapproved is related to the role of the monarchy when there is a constitutional crisis. Expecting that the new king would lack leadership, charisma, and political skills, the junta drafted a charter that transferred the power to resolve a constitutional crisis, which included the right to dissolve the parliament and appoint an interim prime minister, from the monarchy to the Constitutional Court and the parliament. Rama X rejected this draft and demanded a restoration of the royal prerogatives in a constitutional crisis. After the junta complied with the royal requests, the king finally approved and signed off on the twentieth constitution of the kingdom. The promulgation of the new constitution was presented to the national audience in a royal ceremony, a historic moment during which the new monarch bestowed the new constitution on his subjects. The ceremony took place in the Dusit Palace on April 6, 2017, a special day for Rama X and the Thai monarchy, as the Chakri dynasty had been founded by King Rama I on this date 235 years earlier.

After ratification of the new constitution, Rama X made another move to consolidate the monarchical power of his reign. He asked the junta government to transfer the control of royal agencies from the state to the monarch. This included the Royal Aide-de-Camp Department, the OHM, the Bureau of the Royal Household, the Office of Privy Council's Secretary, the Royal Guard Command, and the Royal Court Security Police. Under the new royal acts and decrees, those agencies are no longer parts of the government but belong to the palace's newly founded agency, His Majesty's Bureau (*suan ratchakan nai phra-ong*). Those agencies are no longer staffed with state officers but with His

Majesty's personal officials (*kharatchakan nai phra-ong*), and the appointment or discharge of any of them is at the king's personal discretion.[8] Thanks to this political intervention, the monarchy under Rama X's leadership looks like an autonomous institution unchecked by the junta government let alone by the parliament. In the new regime, the political and natural bodies of the king are actively accumulating and centralizing political power to a greater extent than the palace did in the former reign. In other words, Rama X is driving the Thai kingdom even farther away from a constitutional monarchy than his father did.

Similarly, the capitalist body of the monarchy and its massive wealth have been centralized and are directly supervised by the new monarch himself. During 2017–18, the junta government terminated all previous acts that were associated with the CPB and announced the two new acts—the Crown Property Acts of 2017 and 2018—that were endorsed by the new monarch. Under these new acts, all royal assets were transferred to the full ownership of the king, and the management and investment of those assets are "up to the king's discretion." Those assets include not only land, stocks, and enterprises that the CPB had managed for decades but also palaces and royal residences, a type of property that used to be categorized as national treasures under the former laws.[9] In taking over the CPB, Rama X became the major stockholder in the SCG and SCB, the biggest industrial conglomerate and one of the biggest banks in Southeast Asia, respectively. With full control of the royal assets, which various analysts have valued at between US$30 billion and US$60 billion, Rama X is undisputedly the richest monarch and one of the wealthiest men on earth.[10] Moreover, unlike the former legislation, the 2017 and 2018 acts exclude the minister of finance from the CPB's board and allows the king to appoint all members of the board as he pleases. In other words, thanks to the new acts, the monarchy's wealth and its management are completely independent of the control of the government. A significant change of the CPB under the new acts also includes the replacement of its director. The former director, Chirayu Isarangkun Na Ayuthaya, was appointed by Rama IX in 1987. With his professional management and business connections, Chirayu successfully transformed the CPB from an inert, rigid, and deficient bureau into a moneymaking machine for the crown, and the late king never lost trust in him.[11] Under the new reign, however, Chirayu was replaced by Rama X's close aide, Air Chief Marshal Satitpong Sukvimol.[12] In this regard, unlike his father, the new king was eager to personally take charge of the monarchy's capitalist body. If the boundaries between a monarch and a mogul, a king and a capitalist, and the crown and a corporation were blurry under the former reign, they simply disappeared under the new one.

The centralization of royal power and wealth after the new reign began, however, can give the wrong impression and has led to the assumption among some observers of Thai politics that the kingdom is moving back toward monarchical absolutism.[13] This kind of assumption passes over the fact that, as this book has examined, Thailand has been transformed into a capitalist kingdom and the monarchy alone cannot maintain its power and wealth without the popular consent of the bourgeoisie and political support of the military and judiciary. Rama X and the palace seem to realize this fact, and thus they make any political move with a give-and-take approach. After ascending the throne, Rama X reshuffled the members of the Privy Council. While keeping half the privy counselors who served his father, including the president, General Prem, the new king handpicked his own men to occupy the other positions. Most are former judges and retired generals. The latter not only have a close connection with the junta leaders but also formerly served as ministers under the junta government.[14] Despite being discharged from serving as the director of the CPB, Chirayu was not left high and dry. Instead, he landed one of the most prestigious jobs in the kingdom, as Rama X recruited him to serve as a new privy counselor.[15]

Moreover, under the new reign, the tripartite relationship among the monarchy, elite capitalists, and the army remains strong. Although all of them publicly claim that they will follow Rama IX's SEP, they actually pursue new policies that facilitate capitalism's deeper penetration into the kingdom. The exemplar of those policies is the so-called civil state (*pracharat*) policy, which has been widely promoted by the military government since Rama X became king. On the surface, the government claims that it will promote the self-sufficiency economy in each province by forming a "social enterprise" (*wisahakit phuea chumchon*).[16] It is a provincial enterprise operated by three-way cooperation among local villagers, small entrepreneurs, and state officials. Instead of accumulating capital and seeking profits, this enterprise works to provide sufficient incomes for local villagers and thus alleviate their destitution. In fact this is a cooperative policy among royal enterprises, giant corporations, and the junta leaders. Among its advisers, there are not only ministerial generals but also executive managers from the SCG—the cement conglomerate that is now largely owned by the king himself—and several companies that have a close relationship with the crown. These include CP, the Central Group, ThaiBev, and the Mitr Phol Group, the country's biggest companies in agribusiness, retailing, beer, and sugar industries, respectively.[17] Rather than being initiated and controlled by local people, the "social enterprise" is run by these conglomerates in order to extract local resources and connect the local market with the national and global economies.[18] As a result, instead of alleviating poverty among the rural villagers, this flagship policy of the junta government is making the rich royals, generals, and tycoons even richer under the new reign.

This lucrative cooperation among the monarchy, elite capitalists, and the army is also symbolized by the planned construction of two Bangkok skyscrapers. Ambitiously designed as a new landmark of the Thai kingdom, the Bangkok Observation Tower is a US$138 million project. It is a collaboration among the junta government and two corporations, Siam Piwat and CP. The junta not only provided public land for this project but also bypassed a call for bids, claiming a concern about a delay and lack of interest from construction companies.[19] Rama X's sister, Princess Sirindhorn, is one of the major stockholders in Siam Piwat, Thailand's top development and retail company. Owning not only the largest agribusiness conglomerate in Asia but also several development companies in Thailand, CP has been one of the biggest donors to the royal family and among the most frequent visitors to the palace from the time of the former reign. When completed in 2020, the 1,505-foot tower will be the second-tallest building in Thailand and the world's sixth-tallest tower. On the top floor of the building there will be a museum commemorating the legacy of Rama IX and the history of the Chakri dynasty. The building will stand alongside luxury condominiums, entertainment complexes, and high-class retail outlets operated under the name Icon Siam, the US$1.6 billion project also owned by Siam Piwat and CP.[20]

The second skyscraper is the Grand Rama IX Tower, a US$540 million building and the center of a business complex composed of luxury hotels, shopping malls, and corporate offices. Located on Rama IX Road, the US$1.8 billion complex will honor the late king by naming its flagship hotel and shopping mall after him, the New World Grand Rama IX Hotel and the Central Plaza Grand Rama IX respectively.[21] When completed in 2021, the 2,018-foot skyscraper will be the tallest building in Thailand, one of the world's ten tallest buildings, and the center of a new commercial district in Bangkok. At the moment when

Rama IX passed away, the palace followed an ancient tradition of Thai kingship by announcing, "The Lord of the Land now leaves the worldly earth and 'goes back to the heavenly sky'" (*sadet sawan khot*). Capitalists in Thailand, however, did not take that phrase as a metaphor. Instead they elevated the legacy of Rama IX to reach the sky, literally.

In addition to elite capitalists in the kingdom, the monarchy under the new reign is attempting to maintain popular support among the bourgeois masses. Thanks to the notorious and violent history of Rama X when he was a crown prince, many Thais could not help but have feelings of fear and anxiety when the crown passed to him. The palace apparently recognizes this problem and is actively rebranding the public image of the unpopular king. Even though the palace widely promotes pictures of Rama X as a commander in chief in order to show the monarch's military prowess and the monarchy's solidarity with the junta leaders, the palace also balances those images with another theme of visual presentation: the new king as a grateful son and family man.[22] Instead of stepping out of the shadow of his late father, Rama X has been promoted in the mass media as if he were a loyal son who will follow in his father's every footstep. In the old photographs redistributed by the palace, Rama X, then the young Prince Vajiralongkorn, was depicted as a son who prostrated himself before his father, traveled with him to visit rural villages where communism was widespread, stood behind him to perform state and religious ceremonials, ate dinner with him as they fed one another with smiles, and even played the saxophone with him in a jazz band when they took a break from their official duties.[23] Likewise, despite his third divorce and the hushed gossip about his private life and conjugal visits, several new pictures of Rama X that depict him as a family man have been promoted in the media. In those pictures, instead of a playboy and a cruel and prodigal king, he is shown to be an ordinary dad who hugs and giggles with his children, rides a bicycle alongside his daughters in the streets of Bangkok, and taught his son how to swim and paddle on a sunny day in Germany.[24]

Even the king himself seems to recognize the importance of rebranding his image and relating it to the bourgeois values of a warm nuclear family, fatherly love, and visual fantasies. Following a tradition invented by his late father, Rama X did not miss a chance to give the King's New Year Card to his subjects during the early years of his reign. Produced by the king himself and released by the palace, the King's 2018 New Year Card is a combination of photographs and cartoons.

While the former show Rama X, his father, and his mother all smiling while greeting their subjects, the latter are the king's own drawings. They depict a nuclear family living happily together in a small house and owning a compact car, dad and mom hugging each other, their son playing with a poodle, their daughter hugging a snowman standing alongside a Christmas tree, and a Santa Claus giving Christmas gifts to the family. Although Thailand is a hot and humid country and the majority of its population are Buddhists, the king's cartoons visually echo capitalist fantasies among the Thai nouveau riche, who embraced consumerism, mass commodities, and western culture from the time of the former reign. In addition to the cartoons, the king provided a greeting on the card in his own hand: "Happy Heart. Happy Body. Bright Mind. Live a Self-Sufficient, Humble, and Reasonable Life."[25] With this rebranding of his public image, Rama X has a chance to show his soft side, hidden skills in art and sports, and devotion to his young children and his father's vision of the kingdom. Regardless of Rama X's scandalous lifestyle behind the scenes, which frequently sparked headlines in tabloids around the globe,[26] the visual presentation of the natural bodies of the royal family through bourgeois ideology remains one of the crucial themes of royal publicity under the new reign.

While seeking and securing popular support from the bourgeoisie remains one of the top priorities of the monarchy under the new reign, the crown also promotes itself as a champion of the underclasses. When he had a chance to grant a pardon for the first time in 2016, Rama X showed mercy toward his subjects. To celebrate the proclamation of his reign, the king granted a total or partial pardon to 150,000 prisoners. While 30,000 were set free right away, the rest had their sentences reduced but were not released. The latter included some inmates who had been jailed under the lèse-majesté law.[27] As a result, in contrast to his reputation as a ruthless person, the new king showed the public that he is capable of mercy and sympathy even toward those who offended the monarchy. Rama X's historic pardon, however, was a royal ceremony that distracted the public from the fact that the charges and punishments of lèse-majesté are still draconian and arbitrary under the new reign. In a southern province of the kingdom, a blind woman was charged and received an eighteen-month jail sentence after she reportedly shared a Marxist critique of the Thai monarchy on Facebook.[28] A young man from a northern province, meanwhile, was sentenced to thirty-five years in jail for Facebook posts that were deemed to insult the royal family. He was initially given a seventy-year sentence, a record breaker for an infraction of lèse-majesté, but his term was reduced by half after he confessed.[29] In a northeastern province, six teenagers were arrested after they set fire to the royal arches that celebrated Rama X. Thanks to their confession and juvenile status, their sentences were reduced by half. Yet most will spend seven years and eight months in prison, and one will be incarcerated for eleven and a half years.[30] In this sense, as during the former reign, lèse-majesté has been treated as a life-and-death crime under the new reign. The draconian use of this law makes Thai people, especially those from the lower classes, think twice if they want to speak publicly about—let alone criticize—Rama X's concentration of royal wealth and power and the close association among the crown, elite capitalists, and the junta government.

In October 2017, one year after the new reign began, the monarchy was ready to cremate to Rama IX's body and ritually send the king "back to the heavenly sky." The body of the late king had lain in a coffin at the Grand Palace for a period of one year to let Thai subjects pay their respects to their beloved king in person. They did not let the crown down. More than twelve million people viewed the king lying in state, which broke the record for public attendance at Thailand's royal funerals.[31] In spite of being the richest crown on earth, the palace received more than US$26 million in donations from those loyal attendees. The junta government also showed its loyalty to the crown by spending US$90 million of state budget funds on Rama IX's funeral and cremation.[32] The previous funeral and cremation of a Thai king, that of Rama VIII, took place in 1950, and they cost much less by comparison: a state budget sum of US$140,000.[33]

On Rama IX's cremation day, October 26, 2017, 157,000 people attended the elaborate ceremony around the Grand Palace, and 19 million nationwide paid their respects at different memorial sites provided by the government.[34] Like their compatriots in the middle and lower classes, elite capitalists did not miss the chance to pay their respects to their bourgeois king. They voluntarily paused in their capital accumulation by closing their businesses on the afternoon of the cremation day and even provided free transportation to their office employees, factory workers, and customers who wanted to attend the royal ceremony. Those businesses included banks, shopping malls, movie theaters, supermarkets, fast food restaurants, and even twenty-four-hour convenience stores. Many of these are owned by CP, ThaiBev, Bangkok Bank, and the Central Group, the billion-dollar conglomerates that have long been business partners of and loyal donors to the crown.[35] Thanks to the strong support and loyalty of the elite capitalists, the military government, and masses of the Thai populace, the prospects of the Thai crown did not look as gloomy as the smoke pouring from the burned body of the late king into Bangkok's sky on the night of his cremation. Despite the death of a bourgeois king, the bourgeois crown as a political institution and capitalist corporation is able to outlive one king and serve the next one so that he can reign supreme in the capitalist kingdom.

THe THRONe aND ITS TRUMP CaRDS

Although this book has focused only on a single case of the monarchy in Thailand, this case provides some lessons for rethinking the other monarchies around the world, their relationships with social classes, and their prospects in the age of global capitalism. There has long been an underestimation of the power of a monarchy to adapt itself to the forces of capitalism. Yet one of the major lessons that can be drawn from the Thai case is that monarchy is not necessarily the outmoded, static, and nonadaptive institution it is usually considered to be. Instead, against all odds, a monarchy can weather socioeconomic changes and transform its mode of political control, surplus extraction, and class alliance in concert with a kingdom's transition to a capitalist state. With a fusion of ancient beliefs and modern bourgeois values, reliance on both active consent and extraeconomic coercion, and an accumulation of wealth through corporate donations, business investments, and sponsorship by the state, a modern form of a monarchy—like the Thai crown—is able not only to survive but also to thrive in the age of global capitalism. As a result, a study of capitalism in the twenty-first century should not focus merely on capitalists while giving monarchies around the world a free pass. In the United Kingdom, the royal family remains popular, as it embodies both ancient beliefs and modern bourgeois values. In Scandinavia, the Low Countries, and Japan, monarchies still reign over some of the most advanced capitalist states and most stable polities on earth. In the United Arab Emirates, members of the royal family hold one of the largest oil reserves in the world, chair wealthy state enterprises, and have transformed Dubai into a global city and the business hub of the Middle East. Therefore, how kings, queens, princes, and princesses, from those in postindustrialist Europe to those in late capitalist Asia, still live long and large in the age of global capitalism is a puzzle that needs to be examined further based on the evidence that this single case of the Thai monarchy provides.

There has also been an overestimation of the power of the bourgeoisie and insufficient examination of the ideology of this capitalist class. As the Thai case reveals, the rise of a massive, wealthy, and powerful class of the nouveau riche does not entail a bourgeois revolution that can tame or abolish a monarchy. As a mass base of the monarchy, the Thai bourgeoisie and its symbiotic association with the crown should lead to a rethinking of the progressive and heroic ideals of the bourgeoisie. Instead of a full-time progressive, confident, and revolutionary class, the bourgeoisie frequently turns out to be a conservative, anxious, and reactionary class that seeks political, economic, and ideological support, all of which a new form of monarchy is able to supply very well. Even classical theorists who highly valued the revolutionary and progressive tendencies of the bourgeoisie still looked at this class with reservations. Adam Smith argued that the bourgeoisie tends not only to obsess over the spectacle, beauty, and greatness of royalty and nobility but also to aspire to become members of the upper class.[36] Marx accepted the fact that the nineteenth-century bourgeoisie in some countries, as in the German case, would not live up to their historical and revolutionary task because of their "timidity and cowardice" and inclination from the outset "to betray the people and to compromise with the crowned representative of the old society."[37] Weber acknowledged that, alongside the "cold skeleton hands of rational orders" and the "banality of everyday routine," bourgeois society is also driven by the sentiments of religious zeal and romantic love.[38] With the global rise of conservative, reactionary, and rightist bourgeoisies in the twenty-first century, it is time to explore what those theorists noted only in passing: the reactionary and illiberal mentalities of the bourgeoisie. As capitalism develops and penetrates further into their countries and daily lives, it becomes normal to see elite capitalists and the middle class today turn into the loyal supporters of right-wing ideologies such as nationalism, racism, Islamophobia, homophobia, misogyny, and, as the Thai case epitomizes, monarchism and royalism.

Moreover, if a monarchy is not necessarily the first victim of a bourgeois revolution, as has generally been believed, a rethinking of a theory of class struggle in some capitalist states where monarchies still reign, if not rule, is necessary. As the Thai case shows, the classes of peasantry and proletariat have struggled not only with the urban bourgeoisie but also with the monarchy—an ancient institution that can survive a national transition from feudalism to capitalism and successfully embed itself into the capitalist state, the market economy, and bourgeois ideology. As a result, in addition to a struggle with the bourgeoisie proper, the Thai grass roots face an uphill battle with a monarchy that operates more as a bourgeois enterprise than an ancient institution. This two-front war that the Thai underclasses struggle with demonstrates a new form of class struggle in capitalist kingdoms around the world. The Arab Spring uprisings seriously damaged the authoritarian regimes in the republics of Tunisia, Egypt, Libya, Yemen, and Syria; however, Arab monarchies and capitalist elites in Morocco, Jordan, Saudi Arabia, Kuwait, Bahrain, Qatar, Oman, and the United Arab Emirates helped one another to weather the uprisings and kept their power and wealth intact. For the lower classes in those kingdoms, their road to unchaining themselves from the fetters of capitalism appears to be as hard as, if not harder than, social emancipation in a capitalist republic.

This symbiotic relationship between the crown and capital, however, should not be perceived as a parochial phenomenon that is significant only for those who are interested in capitalist kingdoms. Instead, one can argue that it is a mirror image of what has been developed in capitalist republics in the twenty-first century. While the monarch in the Thai kingdom is indistinguishable from a mogul as he accumulates capital and owns massive fortune like a bourgeois billionaire, the forty-fifth president of the United States looks like his identical twin from afar. In the American republic, Donald Trump, a real estate developer and bourgeois billionaire, was elected president in 2016. He became the first billionaire president and thus the wealthiest person ever to assume the presidency.[39] He selected members of his family who are themselves successful and wealthy businesspeople—his eldest daughter, Ivanka, and his son-in-law, Jared Kushner—to serve as his senior advisers. While primarily residing in the White House, he took a break from his presidential duties to stay with his third wife, Melania, and their son, Barron, on the highest floors of his fifty-eight-story Trump Tower, which is located on Fifth Avenue in Manhattan in New York City. Inspired by the Palace of Versailles, his US$100 million penthouse is decorated with gold and diamond doors, lavish crystal chandeliers, Greek mythological statues, classical portraits, Louis XIV furniture, and an indoor fountain.[40] Never officially crowned, Trump lives a wealthy, powerful, and extravagant life that makes him look like no one more than a king.

Beyond the United States, other major capitalist republics in the world also see a trend that bears some similarities to the Thai kingdom: the decline of democracy and the rise of a political regime that allows

one man to serve as a sovereign of the nation for a long period of time—
if not for life. In Russia, China, and Turkey, political leaders strengthen
their executive power, prolong their time in office by changing the constitutional rules, and violently repress opposition parties and street
protests. Serving as the prime minister of Russia in 1999 and president
in 2000, Vladimir Putin has switched back and forth between those two
positions since then and remains the most powerful man in the Russian
republic. Despite corruption scandals, democratic backsliding, and the
violation of human rights under his regime, Putin secured a landslide
victory in Russia's 2018 presidential election. He has promised that he
will finally step down when his latest term as president ends in 2024, a
quarter of century after he rose to power.[41]

Likewise, in China, Xi Jinping has served as the general secretary of
the Central Committee of the Communist Party and chairman of the
Central Military Commission since 2012. He has also served as the
president of the People's Republic of China since 2013. In 2018, Xi removed presidential term limits; thus, he can rule open-endedly as
"president for life."[42] In Turkey, Recep Tayyip Erdoğan served as prime
minister from 2003 to 2014 and then as the president of the Turkish republic. Thanks to 2017 amendments to the Constitution of Turkey, the
post of prime minister was abolished, and the president became both
the head of state and head of government. Elected the first executive
president in Turkish history in 2018, Erdoğan will rule for five years
and be eligible for reelection. As president, he has lived in a new presidential residence in Ankara, the US$615 million building complex com-
monly known as the White Palace.[43] With their lengthy presidential
terms, the unchecked power of one-man rule, and even their grandiose
lifestyles, these leaders give the impression that they are less like republican presidents than monarchical rulers. They are the Russian tsar,
Chinese emperor, and Ottoman sultan of the twenty-first century.

Finally, if state power has been controlled and centralized in a
monarchical style in many countries, whether they are kingdoms or republics, capital accumulation in the world today also shows a similar
trajectory. According to Thomas Piketty, capitalism in the twenty-first
century is likely to create an economy dominated by capitalist elites,
the wealthiest people in society, who inherited their fortunes instead of
working for them or profiting from their own innovative production.[44]
Capitalism today, in other words, tends to be run by those who are lucky
enough to have been born into a position of economic fortune and inherited substantial assets from their parents. In this regard, the case of

the Thai monarchy fits neatly into this trajectory. Succeeding the wealthiest monarch on earth, Rama X inherited a multi-billion-dollar fortune from his late father and became the new richest king in the world. What makes him rich are not frugality, hard work, and entrepreneurship. He was simply born the only son of a rich king. As inheritance becomes a popular means of accumulating wealth in the twenty-first century, we live in an age in which a monarch's heir apparent and a magnate's offspring are virtually indistinguishable. Although the natural bodies of a monarch and a magnate cannot escape mortality, their legacies of wealth and power survive through inheritance in their flesh and blood. No matter of what type, be it a castle or a corporation, the inheritance of capital today is still mainly based on bloodline and birthright, a tradition that monarchies have used to decide the rightful heir to the throne for centuries.

Seeing that industrial capitalism was widespread throughout Western Europe in the nineteenth century, Marx predicted a foreseeable future for the lower classes in a capitalist state: they would suffer not only from the capitalist mode of production but also from the archaic modes of production and outdated institutions that would linger in a capitalist state. Showing his solidarity with the dispossessed, Marx wrote in the preface to volume 1 of *Capital* that a two-front struggle lay ahead of them: "Alongside the modern evils, we are oppressed by a whole series of inherited evils, arising from the passive survival of archaic and outmoded modes of production, with their accompanying train of anachronistic social and political relations." In short, Marx stated, "We suffer not only from the living, but from the dead."[45] One-and-a-half centuries after its publication, Marx's dystopian vision in his magnum opus seems to ring true beyond Western Europe. In Thailand, alongside the modern evils of industrial capitalism, the lower classes have struggled with the inherited institution, which has remained in the kingdom for centuries. What would have surprised Marx, however, is that this institution not only maintains its outmoded components but also embraces and embeds itself into the capitalist mode of production. Instead of the dead arising from the feudal grave, this institution is a living corporate body that plays an active role in the capitalist kingdom, the market economy, and the culture industry. Most important, the masses of the Thai bourgeoisie welcome, support, and even defend this novel form of monarchy. This institution is a double-headed leviathan—one monarchical, another bourgeois—that still reigns supreme in industrialized Thailand. It is still uncertain whether the bourgeois monarchy in the

Thai kingdom will survive the socioeconomic challenges of the twenty-first century. What is certain, however, is that the Thai crown does not walk alone in the uncharted territory. Domestically, the crown has been warmly escorted by elite capitalists, the urban middle classes, and multi-national corporations. Globally, what has unfolded in many kingdoms and republics suggests that the crown is not on the wrong side of history as is normally assumed. The surviving monarchies around the world still play a crucial role in capitalist expansion in their thriving kingdoms. Political leaders and bourgeois billionaires in capitalist republics have begun to live like kings and embraced monarchical features of government and inheritance. In this sense, monarchy is not dead, after all, in the age of global capitalism. Alive and kicking, it is here to stay.

Appendix

Table A1. Top 10 corporations most frequently visiting and donating money to the monarchy in the 1960s

Corporations	Nationality	Family or parent company	Type of business	Frequency
Philips Electronics Thailand	Dutch	Koninklijke Philips N.V.	Electronics	8
The Shell Company of Thailand	British-Dutch	Royal Dutch Shell	Petroleum, natural gas, petrochemicals	4
Thai Airways	Thai	State enterprise	Airline	4
United Artists Thailand	American	United Artists Corporation	Film and television	4
International Engineering	Thai	Siam Cement Company	Importer of industrial equipment	4
Bangkok Bank	Thai	Sophonpanich	Banking, finance, insurance, trading	3

(Continued on next page)

(Table A1—Continued)

Corporations	Nationality	Family or parent company	Type of business	Frequency
Siam Cement Company	Thai	Crown Property Bureau	Cement, steel, chemicals, construction	3
Sermsuk	Thai	Bunsuk	Soft drinks	3
Siew National Sales & Service	Japanese	Matsushita Electric Industrial Company	Electronics	3
Boon Rawd Brewery	Thai	Bhirombhakdi	Beverages	3

Source: Data adapted from OHM, *Yearbook of Royal Activities*, various years.

Table A2. Top 10 corporations most frequently visiting and donating money
to the monarchy in the 1970s

Corporations	Nationality	Family or parent company	Type of business	Frequency
Bangkok Bank	Thai	Sophonpanich	Banking, finance, insurance, trading	13
International Engineering	Thai	Siam Cement Group	Importer of industrial equipment	11
Charoen Pokphand Group	Thai	Chearavanont	Agribusiness	10
Toyota Motor Thailand	Japanese	Toyota Motor Corporation	Automotive	9
Siam Motors Group	Thai	Phornprapha	Automotive	9
Boon Rawd Brewery	Thai	Bhirombhakdi	Beverages	7
United Machinery	Thai	Chittkusol	Importer of industrial equipment	7
Bangkok Metropolitan Bank	Thai	Taechaphaibun	Banking, finance	6
Thai Airways	Thai	State enterprise	Airline	5
Channel 3	Thai	Maleenont	Commercial television station	5

Source: Data adapted from OHM, *Yearbook of Royal Activities*, various years.

Table A3. Top 15 corporations most frequently visiting and donating money to the monarchy in the 1980s

Corporations	Nationality	Family or parent company	Type of business	Frequency
Bangkok Bank	Thai	Sophonpanich	Banking, finance, insurance, trading	16
Kyocera Thailand	Japanese	Kyocera Corporation	Electronics	13
Toyota Motor Thailand	Japanese	Toyota Motor Corporation	Automotive	11
Siam Commercial Bank	Thai	Crown Property Bureau	Banking, finance, insurance	10
Siam Motors Group	Thai	Phornprapha	Automotive	10
Mitsui Group	Japanese	Mitsui & Company	Trading, banking	10
Bangkok Metropolitan Bank	Thai	Taechaphaibun	Banking	9
Boon Rawd Brewery	Thai	Bhirombhakdi	Beverages	8
Charoen Pokphand Group	Thai	Chearavanont	Agribusiness, retailing	7
Siew National Sales & Service	Japanese	Matsushita Electric Industrial Company	Electronics	7
Thai Airways	Thai	State enterprise	Airline	7
Honda Automobile Thailand	Japanese	Honda Motor Company	Automotive	7
United Machinery	Thai	Chittkusol	Importer of industrial equipment	7
Central Group	Thai	Chirathivat	Retailing, department store, real estate, hospitality	7
Bangkok Insurance	Thai	Sophonpanich	Insurance	5

Source: Data adapted from OHM, *Yearbook of Royal Activities*, various years.

Table A4. Top 15 corporations most frequently visiting and donating money to the monarchy in the 1990s

Corporations	Nationality	Family or parent company	Type of business	Frequency
Bangkok Bank	Thai	Sophonpanich	Banking, finance, insurance, trading	29
Charoen Pokphand Group	Thai	Chearavanont	Agribusiness, retailing, telecommunications	21
Shin Corporation	Thai	Shinawatra	Telecommunication, media, information technology	19
Toyota Motor Thailand	Japanese	Toyota Motor Corporation	Automotive	18
Isuzu Motors Asia Thailand	Japanese	Isuzu Motors	Automotive	17
Thai Airways	Thai	State enterprise	Airline	17
Bangkok Metropolitan Bank	Thai	Taechaphaibun	Banking, finance	16
Kyocera Thailand	Japanese	Kyocera Corporation	Electronics	13
PTT	Thai	State enterprise	Petroleum, chemicals, electricity generation	12
Siam Motors Group	Thai	Phornprapha	Automotive	10
Central Group	Thai	Chirathivat	Retailing, department store, real estate, hospitality	10
United Machinery	Thai	Chittkusol	Importer of industrial equipment	9
Bangkok Insurance	Thai	Sophonpanich	Insurance	9
Siam Commercial Bank	Thai	Crown Property Bureau	Banking, finance, insurance	8
Boon Rawd Brewery	Thai	Bhirombhakdi	Beverages	8

Source: Data adapted from OHM, *Yearbook of Royal Activities*, various years.

Table A5. Top 15 corporations most frequently visiting and donating money to the monarchy in the 2000s

Corporations	Nationality	Family or parent company	Type of business	Frequency
Charoen Pokphand Group	Thai	Chearavanont	Agribusiness, retailing, telecommunications	36
Shin Corporation	Thai	Shinawatra	Telecommunication, media, information technology	33
Bangkok Bank	Thai	Sophonpanich	Banking, finance, insurance, trading	29
Central Group	Thai	Chirathivat	Retailing, department store, real estate, hospitality	26
Thai Airways	Thai	State enterprise	Airline	25
Kyocera Thailand	Japanese	Kyocera Corporation	Electronics	22
Toyota Motor Thailand	Japanese	Toyota Motor Corporation	Automotive	19
PTT	Thai	State enterprise	Petroleum, chemicals, electricity generation	19
Siam Commercial Bank	Thai	Crown Property Bureau	Banking, finance, insurance	15
Cerebos Thailand	Japanese	Cerebos Pacific	Health supplements, food	15
Nestlé Thai	Swiss	Nestlé S.A.	Food and drink	14
Bangkok Metropolitan Bank	Thai	Taechaphaibun	Banking, finance	14
Microsoft Thailand	American	Microsoft Corporation	Computer software, personal computers and services	11
Novartis Thailand	Swiss	Novartis International AG	Pharmaceuticals	10
Amarin Printing and Publishing	Thai	Utakapan	Publishing	10

Source: Data adapted from OHM, *Yearbook of Royal Activities*, various years.

NOTES

Introduction

1. The Chakri dynasty is the current ruling royal house of Thailand. The dynasty has ruled the Thai kingdom since King Yodfa, or Rama I (r. 1782–1809), ascended the throne and established Bangkok as the capital city of Siam in 1782.

2. I borrow the term *bourgeois monarchy* from theorists and historians who usually refer to Louis Philippe I, the French king who reigned from 1830 to 1848, as the "bourgeois monarch" and the French monarchy under his reign as the "bourgeois monarchy," thanks to his close association with and political support from bankers, industrialists, and the middle class. See Karl Marx, "The Class Struggle in France," in *Karl Marx: Selected Writings*, ed. David McLellan (Oxford: Oxford University Press, 1977), 286–97; Friedrich Engels, *Socialism: Utopian and Scientific* (New York: International Publishers, 2015), 19; Jerrold Seigel, *Modernity and Bourgeois Life: Society, Politics, and Culture in England, France, and Germany since 1750* (Cambridge: Cambridge University Press, 2012), 106.

3. Aristotle, *Politics*, trans. Ernest Barker (Oxford: Oxford University Press, 1995), 100.

4. Plato, *The Republic*, trans. Desmond Lee (New York: Penguin Books, 2007), 192.

5. Niccolò Machiavelli, *The Prince*, trans. Harvey C. Mansfield (Chicago: University of Chicago Press, 1998).

6. Thomas Hobbes, *Leviathan*, ed. C. B. Macpherson (New York: Penguin Books, 1985), chapters 17–19.

7. William Spellman, *Monarchies, 1000–2000* (London: Reaktion Books, 2006), 7–22.

8. Adam Smith, *The Theory of Moral Sentiments*, ed. D. D. Raphael and A. L. Macfie (Indianapolis: Liberty Fund, 1982), 184; Adam Smith, *An Inquiry into the Nature and Causes of the Wealth of Nations*, ed. R. H. Campbell and A. S. Skinner (Indianapolis: Liberty Fund, 1981), Books III and V.

9. G. W. F. Hegel, *Elements of the Philosophy of Right*, ed. Allen W. Wood, trans. H. B. Nisbet (Cambridge: Cambridge University Press, 1991), 220, 308, 313, 377–79; G. W. F. Hegel, *Introduction to the Philosophy of History*, trans. Leo Rauch (Indianapolis: Hackett Publishing, 1988), 97.

10. Karl Marx, *Pre-capitalist Economic Formations*, ed. Eric Hobsbawm, trans. Jack Cohen (New York: International Publishing, 1965); Karl Marx and Friedrich Engels, "The Communist Manifesto," in *Karl Marx: Selected Writings*, ed. David McLellan (Oxford: Oxford University Press, 1977), 223.

11. The facts about the forms of government in the twenty-first century in this section come from Wikipedia, "Monarchy," accessed September 28, 2015, https://en.wikipedia.org/wiki/Monarchy; United Nations, "United Nations Member States," accessed June 12, 2018, http://www.un.org/en/member-states/.

12. The sixteen member states of the Commonwealth of Nations are Antigua and Barbuda, Australia, the Bahamas, Barbados, Belize, Canada, Grenada, Jamaica, New Zealand, Papua New Guinea, Saint Kitts and Nevis, Saint Lucia, Saint Vincent and the Grenadines, the Solomon Islands, Tuvalu, and the United Kingdom of Great Britain and Northern Ireland.

13. These twenty-two states are Andorra, Bahrain, Belgium, Bhutan, Cambodia, Denmark, Japan, Jordan, Kuwait, Liechtenstein, Lesotho, Luxembourg, Malaysia, Monaco, Morocco, the Netherlands, Norway, Spain, Sweden, Thailand, Tonga, and the United Arab Emirates. Among these twenty-two states, only the monarchies of Bahrain, Bhutan, Jordan, Kuwait, Liechtenstein, Monaco, Morocco, Tonga, and the United Arab Emirates still retain executive power.

14. These five states are Brunei, Oman, Saudi Arabia, Swaziland, and Qatar.

15. Friedrich Nietzsche, "The Greek State," in *The Nietzsche Reader*, ed. Keith Ansell Pearson and Duncan Large (Oxford: Blackwell, 2006), 88–100.

16. Joseph Schumpeter *Capitalism, Socialism, and Democracy* (New York: Harper & Brothers, 1975), 136–37; Karl Polanyi, *The Great Transformation: The Political and Economic Origins of Our Time* (Boston: Beacon Press, 2001).

17. Oxfam International, "Just 8 Men Own Same Wealth as Half the World," January 16, 2017, https://www.oxfam.org/en/pressroom/pressreleases/2017-01-16/just-8-men-own-same-wealth-half-world.

18. Christopher Hill, "The English Revolution," in *The English Revolution, 1640: Three Essays* (London: Lawrence & Wishart, 1940), 9–82.

19. Perry Anderson, "Origins of the Present Crisis," *New Left Review* 23 (January–February 1964): 28; Vivek Chibber, *Postcolonial Theory and the Specter of Capital* (New York: Verso, 2013), 56–66.

20. This theme, originally proposed by Perry Anderson and Tom Nairn, became known as the "Nairn-Anderson theses." See Anderson, "Origins of the Present Crisis"; Perry Anderson, "Socialism and Pseudo-Empiricism," *New Left Review* 35 (January–February 1966): 2–42; Perry Anderson, "Components of the National Culture," *New Left Review* 50 (July–August 1968): 3–57; Tom Nairn, "The British Political Elite," *New Left Review* 23 (January–February 1964): 19–25; Tom Nairn, "The English Working Class," *New Left Review* 24 (March–April 1964): 43–57; Tom Nairn, "The Nature of the Labor Party, part 1," *New Left Review* 27 (September–October 1964): 38–65; Tom Nairn, "The Nature of the Labor Party, part 2," *New Left Review* 28 (November–December 1964): 33–62; Tom Nairn, "The Fateful Meridian," *New Left Review* 60 (March–April 1970): 3–35; Tom Nairn, "Twilight of the British State," *New Left Review* 101 (February–April 1976): 11–91.

21. Ellen Wood, *The Pristine Culture of Capitalism: A Historical Essay on Old Regimes and Modern States* (New York: Verso, 1991), 33, 76; Ellen Wood, *The Origin of Capitalism: A Longer View* (New York: Verso, 2002), 47; Colin Mooers, *The Making of Bourgeois Europe: Absolutism, Revolution, and the Rise of Capitalism in England, France, and Germany* (New York: Verso, 1991), chapter 4.

22. Wood, *Pristine Culture of Capitalism*, 6; Wood, *Origin of Capitalism*, 63.

23. Chibber, *Postcolonial Theory and the Specter of Capital*, 66–76.

24. Marx himself acknowledged this problem and discussed it in "The Eighteenth Brumaire of Louis Bonaparte," in *Karl Marx: Selected Writings*, ed. David McLellan (Oxford: Oxford University Press, 1977), 300–325; Mooers, *Making of Bourgeois Europe*, chapter 2. Moreover, inspired by the French Revolution, the Haitian Revolution (1791–1804) also showed that it was not easy to abolish a monarchy. In the century after the revolution, Haiti suffered political instability as it changed its form of government back and forth between republic and monarchy.

25. See Benedict Anderson, "Modern Monarchies in a Global Comparative Perspective," keynote address delivered at the conference Democracy and Crisis in Thailand, Chulalongkorn University, Bangkok, March 9, 2012, published as Benedict Anderson, "Modern Monarchies in a Global Comparative Perspective" [ราชาสมัยใหม่ในมุมมองเปรียบเทียบระดับโลก], *Fa Diew Kan* 10, no. 1 (January–June 2012): 59–78.

26. On the first factor, see Theda Skocpol, *States and Social Revolutions: A Comparative Analysis of France, Russia, and China* (Cambridge: Cambridge University Press, 1979). On the second factor, see Anderson, "Modern Monarchies in a Global Comparative Perspective."

27. For the influence of the two world wars on monarchies in Europe, see Arno J. Mayer, *The Persistence of the Old Regime: Europe to the Great War* (New York: Verso, 2010); Denis Judd, *Eclipse of Kings: European Monarchies in the Twentieth Century* (New York: Stein and Day, 1976). For an example of colonial interference in monarchies, see Bernard Lewis, "Monarchy in the Middle East," in *Middle East Monarchies: The Challenge of Modernity*, ed. Joseph Kostiner (Boulder, CO: Lynne Rienner, 2000), 15–22.

28. Walter Bagehot, *The English Constitution* (Ithaca, NY: Cornell University Press, 1966), 97; Tom Nairn, *The Enchanted Glass: Britain and Its Monarchy* (New York: Verso, 2011), 316–17.

29. Mooers, *Making of Bourgeois Europe*, chapter 3; Reinhard Bendix, *Kings or People: Power and the Mandate to Rule* (Oakland: University of California Press, 1980), chapters 3 and 5.

30. See the historical analysis of the "revolution from above" in Japan in Barrington Moore, *Social Origins of Dictatorship and Democracy: Lord and Peasant in the Making of the Modern World* (Boston: Beacon Press, 1996), chapter 5.

31. *Understanding the Value of the British Monarchy as a Brand*, special jubilee issue, *BrandFinance Journal*, June 2012, https://brandfinance.com/images/up load/bf_jr_2012_web_sp.pdf; Stephen Greyser, John Balmer, and Mats Urde, "The Monarchy as a Corporate Brand: Some Corporate Communications Dimensions," *European Journal of Marketing* 40, nos. 7–8 (2006): 902–8; John Balmer, "Scrutinising the British Monarchy: The Corporate Brand That Was Shaken, Stirred, and Survived," *Management Decision* 47, no. 4 (2009): 639–75.

32. Kenneth Ruoff, *The People's Emperor: Democracy and the Japanese Monarchy, 1945–1995* (Cambridge, MA: Harvard University Asia Center, 2001), chapter 6; Judd, *Eclipse of Kings*, chapters 6 and 7.

33. Samuel Huntington, *Political Order in Changing Societies* (New Haven, CT: Yale University Press, 1968), 177–80.

34. Among the Arab monarchies, only that of Bahrain faced any significant challenge from popular uprisings. With the military and financial support of the neighboring kingdoms, however, this monarchy was able to restore order eventually. See Sean L. Yom and F. Gregory Gause III, "Resilient Royals: How Arab Monarchies Hang On," *Journal of Democracy* 23, no. 4 (October 2012): 83–84.

35. Joseph Kostiner, "Introduction," in *Middle East Monarchies: The Challenge of Modernity*, ed. Joseph Kostiner (Boulder, CO: Lynne Rienner Publishers, 2000), 9–10; Michael Ross, "Does Oil Hinder Democracy?" *World Politics* 53, no.3 (April 2001): 325–61.

36. Mohammed El-Katiri, *The Future of the Arab Gulf Monarchies in the Age of Uncertainties* (Carlisle, PA: Strategic Studies Institute, 2013), 1–2.

37. Yom and Gause, "Resilient Royals," 83–84.

38. Lisa Anderson, "Absolutism and the Resilience of Monarchy in the Middle East," *Political Science Quarterly* 106, no. 1 (Spring 1991): 1–15.

39. For a comparison between the Thai bourgeoisie and others in Southeast Asia, see Takashi Shiraishi, "The Rise of New Urban Middle Classes in Southeast Asia: What Is Its National and Regional Significance?," Research Institute of Economy, Trade, and Industry Discussion Papers, February 2004, http://www.rieti.go.jp/jp/publications/dp/04e011.pdf.

40. The Four Asian Tigers at that time were Hong Kong, Singapore, South Korea, and Taiwan.

41. See Suehiro Akira, *Capital Accumulation in Thailand, 1855–1985* (Chiang Mai: Silkworm Books, 1989); Porphant Ouyyanont, "The Crown Property Bureau in Thailand and the Crisis of 1997," *Journal of Contemporary Asia* 38, no. 1 (February 2008): 166–89.

42. Tatiana Serafin, "The World's Richest Royals," *Forbes*, August 20, 2008. Since 2008 Forbes has published lists of the world's richest royals three times, in 2009, 2010, and 2011, and Rama IX took the top spot in all of them. See the latest ranking in "The World's Richest Royals," *Forbes*, April 29, 2011.

43. Porphant, "Crown Property Bureau."

44. Tatiana Serafin, "Thailand's 40 Richest," *Forbes*, August 30, 2011; "Thailand's Richest: Charoen Sirivadhanabhakdi," *Forbes*, July 9, 2008; "Thailand's Richest: Dhanin Chearavanont," *Forbes*, July 9, 2008.

45. "The World's Billionaires," *Forbes*, March 6, 2018.

46. "Thai King Maha Vajiralongkorn Named Owner of Chakri Dynasty's Billions," *Japan Times*, June 16, 2018; "Thai King Maha Vajiralongkorn Granted Full Ownership of Crown Billions," *Straits Times*, June 16, 2018; "Thai King Signs Crown's $30bn Assets over to Himself," *Al Jazeera*, June 17, 2018.

47. Thongchai McIntyre, "The Picture Every Home Has" [รูปที่มีทุกบ้าน], a song celebrating the king's eightieth birthday by Nitipong Honark, December 5, 2007.

48. A good example of this is the British monarchy, whose three financial sources—the sovereign grant, the Privy Purse, and the queen's personal income—are clearly separated, checked by the parliament, and accountable to the public. See "Royal Finances," accessed September 30, 2015, http://www.royal.gov.uk/TheRoyalHousehold/Royalfinances/Sourcesoffunding/TheSovereignGrant.aspx.

49. Mao Zedong, *The Chinese Revolution and the Chinese Communist Party* (1939), Marxist Internet Archives, accessed February 27, 2015, https://www.marxists.org/reference/archive/mao/selected-works/volume-2/mswv2_23.htm.

50. Bagehot and Nairn, for example, similarly argue that the British monarchy is influential in national politics and culture. Both, however, understand the monarchy in Britain as a passive actor that is used by the bourgeois elite to tame the poor and uneducated masses. See Bagehot, *English Constitution*, 97; Nairn, *Enchanted Glass*, 316–17.

51. See Fred Riggs, *Thailand: The Modernization of a Bureaucratic Polity* (Honolulu: East-West Center Press, 1966); David L. Elliott, *Thailand: Origins of Military Rule* (London: Zed Press, 1978); Anek Laothamatas, *Business Associations and the New Political Economy of Thailand: From Bureaucratic Polity to Liberal Corporatism* (Boulder, CO: Westview, 1992).

52. Irene Stengs, Porphant Ouyyanont, and Serhat Ünaldi admitted that most scholars studying the Thai monarchy have to deal with the problem of self-censorship due to the strict lèse-majesté law in Thailand. See Irene Stengs, *Worshipping the Great Moderniser: King Chulalongkorn, Patron Saint of the Thai Middle Class* (Singapore: National University of Singapore Press, 2009), x; Porphant, "Crown Property Bureau," 167; Serhat Ünaldi, *Working towards the Monarchy: The Politics of Space in Downtown Bangkok* (Honolulu: University of Hawai'i Press, 2016), xi.

53. Benedict Anderson, "Studies of the Thai State: The State of Thai Studies," in *The Study of Thailand: Analyses of Knowledge, Approaches, and Prospects in Anthropology, Art History, Economics, History, and Political Science*, ed. Eliezer B. Ayal (Athens: Ohio University Center for International Studies, Southeast Asia Program, 1978), 193–247; Christine Gray, "Thailand: The Soteriological State in the 1970s" (PhD diss., University of Chicago, 1986); Kevin Hewison, "The Monarchy and Democratisation," in *Political Change in Thailand: Democracy and Participation*, ed. Kevin Hewison (New York: Routledge, 1997), 58–74; Duncan McCargo, "Network Monarchy and Legitimacy Crises in Thailand," *Pacific Review* 18, no. 4 (December 2005): 499–519; Paul Handley, *The King Never Smiles: A Biography of Thailand's King Bhumibol Adulyadej* (New Haven, CT: Yale University Press, 2006); Somsak Jeamteerasakul, *The Invented History* [ประวัติศาสตร์ที่เพิ่งสร้าง] (Bangkok: October 6th Memorial Press, 2001); Thongchai Winichakul, *Democracy That Is the Monarchy above Politics* [ประชาธิปไตยที่มีกษัตริย์อยู่เหนือการเมือง] (Nonthaburi: Fa Diew Kan, 2013).

54. The first case is exemplified in McCargo, "Network Monarchy," and the latter in Porphant, "Crown Property Bureau."

55. Anderson, "Studies of the Thai State"; Gray, "Thailand"; Peter Jackson, "Royal Spirits, Chinese Gods, and Magic Monks: Thailand's Boom-Time Religions of Prosperity," *South East Asia Research* 7, no. 3 (November 1999): 245–320; Ünaldi, *Working towards the Monarchy*; Patrick Jory, *Thailand's Theory of Monarchy: The Vessantara Jataka and the Idea of the Perfect Man* (Albany: State University of New York Press, 2016).

56. Stengs and Maurizio Peleggi attempted to reveal this aspect of the Thai monarchy. Both, however, focus on the figure of King Chulalongkorn, or Rama V (r. 1868–1910), who reigned in the late nineteenth and early twentieth centuries, the era in which the seeds of capitalism had just been planted in Thailand. See Stengs, *Worshipping the Great Moderniser*; Maurizio Peleggi, *Lords of Things: The Fashioning of the Siamese Monarchy's Modern Image* (Honolulu: University of Hawai'i Press, 2002).

57. McCargo, "Network Monarchy"; Thak Chaloemtiarana, *Thailand: The Politics of Despotic Paternalism* (Ithaca, NY: South East Asia Program Publications, Cornell University, 2007); Eugénie Mérieau, "Thailand's Deep State, Royal Power, and the Constitutional Court (1997–2015)," *Journal of Contemporary Asia* 46, no. 3 (2016): 445–66; Paul Chambers and Napisa Waitoolkiat, "The Resilience of Monarchised Military in Thailand," *Journal of Contemporary Asia* 46, no. 3 (2016): 425–44.

58. Ernst Kantorowicz, *The King's Two Bodies: A Study in Medieval Political Theology* (Princeton, NJ: Princeton University Press, 1957).

59. Eric Hobsbawm, "Introduction: Inventing Traditions," in *The Invention of Tradition*, ed. Eric Hobsbawm and Terence Ranger (Cambridge: Cambridge University Press, 2004), 1.

60. Karl Marx, *Capital*, vol. 1, trans. Ben Fowkes (New York: Penguin Books, 1990), 254.

61. Hal Draper, *Karl Marx's Theory of Revolution*, vol. 2, *The Politics of Social Classes* (Seattle: Create Space Independent Publishing Platform, 1978), 169.

Chapter 1.
The Genesis of the Bourgeois Monarchy

1. Kevin Hewison, *Bankers and Bureaucrats: Capital and the Role of the State in Thailand* (New Haven, CT: Council on Southeast Asian Studies, Yale University, 1989), 33. In this chapter, I employ a Marxist analysis of Thai feudalism, which argues that the Thai economy before the mid-nineteenth century was predominantly a precapitalist, subsistence economy. For those who are interested in an alternative analysis arguing that the Thai economy was market oriented, profit driven, and active with international trade long before that time, see Katherine Bowie, "Peasant Perspectives on the Political Economy of the Northern Thai Kingdom of Chiang Mai in the Nineteenth Century: Implications for the Understanding of Peasant Political Expression" (PhD diss., University of Chicago, 1988); Nidhi Eoseewong, *Pen and Sail: Literature and History in Early Bangkok* [ปากไก่และใบเรือ: รวมความเรียงว่าด้วยวรรณกรรมและประวัติศาสตร์ต้นรัตนโกสินทร์] (Nonthaburi: Fa Diew Kan, 2012).

2. Kullada Kesboonchoo Mead, *The Rise and Decline of Thai Absolutism* (London: RoutledgeCurzon, 2004), 12; Chit Phumisak, *The Real Face of Thai Feudalism* [โฉมหน้าศักดินาไทย] (Bangkok: Sri Panya, 2007), 127.

3. Seksan Prasertkul, "The Transformation of the Thai State and Economic Change, 1855–1945" (PhD diss., Cornell University, 1989), 12.

4. James C. Ingram, *Economic Change in Thailand, 1850–1970* (Stanford, CA: Stanford University Press, 1971), 14; Seksan, "Transformation of the Thai State," 3n5; Pasuk Phongpaichit and Chris Baker, *Thailand: Economy and Politics* (New York: Oxford University Press, 1995), 11.

5. Seksan, "Transformation of the Thai State," 5; Tomas Larsson, *Land and*

Loyalty: Security and the Development of Property Rights in Thailand (Ithaca, NY: Cornell University Press, 2012), 31; Chit, *Real Face of Thai Feudalism*, 123.

6. Ingram, *Economic Change in Thailand*, 12; Seksan, "Transformation of the Thai State," 9–10.

7. According to Perry Anderson, the key feature of feudalism in Western Europe was the fragmentation and parcelization of sovereignty. See his *Lineages of the Absolutist State* (New York: Verso, 2013), 19.

8. Seksan, "Transformation of the Thai State," 6n15; Pasuk Phongpaichit and Chris Baker, *A History of Thailand* (Cambridge: Cambridge University Press, 2009), 83; Pasuk and Baker, *Thailand*, 46n5.

9. According to Ellen Wood, what distinguishes the precapitalist modes of production, like feudalism, from capitalism is the application of extraeconomic coercion. While extraeconomic force was primarily employed by surplus extractors in the former modes of production, it was barely used in the latter. See Ellen Wood, "The Separation of the Economic and the Political in Capitalism," *New Left Review* 1, no. 127 (May–June 1981): 80–85; Ellen Wood, *The Origin of Capitalism: A Longer View* (New York: Verso, 2002), 96; Ellen Wood, *Empire of Capital* (New York: Verso, 2003), 10.

10. Chit, *Real Face of Thai Feudalism*, 40.

11. Seksan, "Transformation of the Thai State," 11; Kullada, *Rise and Decline of Thai Absolutism*, 12; Hewison, *Bankers and Bureaucrats*, 34.

12. Seksan, "Transformation of the Thai State," 42.

13. There were four major types of taxes in Thai feudalism. Besides the farm tax, there were taxes collected in kind from the populace (*suai*); transit taxes levied on inland shipments of commodities at various checkpoints and imports brought in by foreign vessels (*chang kop*); and taxes collected on services provided by the state to its subjects (*ruecha*). See Seksan, "Transformation of the Thai State," 8n17; Chit, *The Real Face of Thai Feudalism*, 172.

14. Seksan, "Transformation of the Thai State," 49–50; James C. Scott, *The Art of Not Being Governed: An Anarchist History of Upland Southeast Asia* (New Haven, CT: Yale University Press, 2009), 24, 29–30; Pasuk and Baker, *History of Thailand*, 85; Katherine Bowie, "Slavery in Nineteenth-Century Northern Thailand: Archival Anecdotes and Village Voices," in *State Power and Culture in Thailand*, ed. E. Paul Durrenberger (New Haven, CT: Council on Southeast Asian Studies, Yale University, 1996), 114–26.

15. Seksan, "Transformation of the Thai State," 51; Chit, *Real Face of Thai Feudalism*, 17.

16. Pasuk and Baker, *History of Thailand*, 43; Seksan, "Transformation of the Thai State," 10.

17. Pasuk and Baker, *History of Thailand*, 43.

18. Pasuk and Baker, *Thailand*, 12–13; Seksan, "Transformation of the Thai State," 53–54.

19. Ingram, *Economic Change in Thailand*, 19.

20. Seksan, "Transformation of the Thai State," 13-14.

21. Ingram, *Economic Change in Thailand*, 25.

22. Pasuk and Baker, *History of Thailand*, 8.

23. Kullada, *Rise and Decline of Thai Absolutism*, 16; Seksan, "Transformation of the Thai State," 16.

24. Ingram, *Economic Change in Thailand*, 32.

25. Chollada Wattanasiri, "Investment of the Privy Purse, 1890-1932" [พระ คลังข้างที่กับการลงทุนธุรกิจในประเทศ พ.ศ. 2433-2475] (MA thesis, Silpakorn University, 1986), 1, 26.

26. Ibid., 25; Kullada, *Rise and Decline of Thai Absolutism*, 20; Nicholas Grossman and Dominic Faulder, eds., *King Bhumibol Adulyadej: A Life's Work; Thailand's Monarchy in Perspective* (Singapore: Didier Millet, 2012), 285.

27. Ingram, *Economic Change in Thailand*, 32, 177; Chollada, "Investment of the Privy Purse," 32; Kullada, *Rise and Decline of Thai Absolutism*, 21.

28. Kullada, *The Rise and Decline of Thai Absolutism*, 13; Stanley Tambiah, *World Conqueror and World Renouncer: A Study of Buddhism and Polity in Thailand against a Historical Background* (Cambridge: Cambridge University Press, 1977), 98.

29. Tambiah, *World Conqueror and World Renouncer*, chapter 7.

30. Pasuk and Baker, *History of Thailand*, 19.

31. Rosalind Morris, "Photography and the Power of Images in the History of Power: Notes from Thailand," in *Photographies East: The Camera and Its Histories in East and Southeast Asia*, ed. Rosalind Morris (Durham, NC: Duke University Press, 2009), 124-25; Peleggi, *Lords of Things*, 45; Sing Suwannakij, "King and Eye: Visual Formation and Technology of the Siamese Monarchy" (PhD diss., University of Copenhagen, 2013), chapter 1.

32. Pasuk and Baker, *History of Thailand*, 19.

33. Tambiah, *World Conqueror and World Renouncer*, 522.

34. Pasuk and Baker, *History of Thailand*, 20.

35. Dhani Nivat, "The Old Siamese Conception of the Monarchy," *Journal of the Siam Society* 32, no. 2 (1947): 91-106; Phya Anuman Rajadhon, "Kingship in Siam," *Journal of the Siam Society* 42, no. 1 (1954): 1-10.

36. The term *kasat* (king) in Thai is derived from *kṣatriyaḥ* in Sanskrit. The latter was used to define the ruling and military elites of Vedic society in India.

37. Tambiah, *World Conqueror and World Renouncer*, 96-97; Pasuk and Baker, *History of Thailand*, 11, 41, 46.

38. Tambiah, *World Conqueror and World Renouncer*, 522.

39. Martin Platt, "Culture of Monarchy: A Repertory Theatre through Time," in *Saying the Unsayable: Monarchy and Democracy in Thailand*, ed. Soren Ivarsson and Lotte Isager (Copenhagen: Nordic Institute of Asian Studies Press, 2010), 95.

40. Gray, "Thailand," 41, 45, 47.

41. G. William Skinner, *Chinese Society in Thailand: An Analytical History*

(Ithaca, NY: Cornell University Press, 1957), 41, 83; Pasuk and Baker, *History of Thailand*, 31; Gray, "Thailand," 207–8; Nidhi, *Pen and Sail*, 90–93.

42. Kullada, *Rise and Decline of Thai Absolutism*, 13, 41; Hewison, *Bankers and Bureaucrats*, 35.

43. Kullada, *Rise and Decline of Thai Absolutism*, 16; Skinner, *Chinese Society in Thailand*, 119–20; Chollada, "Investment of the Privy Purse," 50, 58; Pasuk and Baker, *Thailand*, 43.

44. Kullada, *Rise and Decline of Thai Absolutism*, 13, 41.

45. Ibid., 43.

46. Seksan, "Transformation of the Thai State," 23–28.

47. Kullada, *The Rise and Decline of Thai Absolutism*, 18; Seksan, "Transformation of the Thai State," 55–56.

48. Skinner, *Chinese Society in Thailand*, 99–101.

49. Suehiro Akira, *Capital Accumulation in Thailand* (Chiang Mai: Silkworm Books, 1989), 78; Nidhi, *Pen and Sail*, 99–100; Thak Chaloemtiarana, "We Are Not Them? The Portrayal of the Chinese People in Thai Literature in the 20th Century" [เราไม่ใช่เขา? ภาพเสนอของคนจีนในวรรณกรรมไทยศตวรรษที่ 20], *Aan* 5, no. 1 (July–December 2013): 125.

50. Kullada, *Rise and Decline of Thai Absolutism*, 22.

51. Pasuk and Baker, *Thailand*, 99; Gary G. Hamilton and Tony Waters, "Ethnicity and Capitalist Development: The Changing Role of the Chinese in Thailand," in *Essential Outsiders: Chinese and Jews in the Modern Transformation of Southeast Asia and Central Europe*, ed. Daniel Chirot and Anthony Reid (Seattle: University of Washington Press, 1997), 265; Hewison, *Bankers and Bureaucrats*, 48.

52. Ingram, *Economic Change in Thailand*, 20; Pasuk and Baker, *Thailand*, 98; Skinner, *Chinese Society in Thailand*, 119–20.

53. Hamilton and Waters, "Ethnicity and Capitalist Development," 258–59.

54. Chollada, "Investment of the Privy Purse," 11, 15.

55. Skinner, *Chinese Society in Thailand*, 58.

56. Ibid., 82.

57. Hewison, *Bankers and Bureaucrats*, 41, 43.

58. Ibid., 38.

59. Skinner, *Chinese Society in Thailand*, 32, 64, 83; Ingram, *Economic Change in Thailand*, 58–59; Kullada, *Rise and Decline of Thai Absolutism*, 24; Seksan, "Transformation of the Thai State," 56; Gray, "Thailand," 297.

60. Pasuk and Baker, *Thailand*, 25.

61. Ibid., 24.

62. Regarding the impact of the Bowring Treaty, see Ingram, *Economic Change in Thailand*, 33–37; Pasuk and Baker, *History of Thailand*, 44–45; Seksan, "Transformation of the Thai State," chapter 3; Hewison, *Bankers and Bureaucrats*, 40–41; Kullada, *Rise and Decline of Thai Absolutism*, 32–33.

63. Ingram, *Economic Change in Thailand*, 35.

64. Ibid., 37.

65. Craig J. Reynolds and Hong Lysa, "Marxism in Thai Historical Studies," *Journal of Asian Studies* 43, no. 1 (November 1983): 77–104; Chaiyan Rachagool, *The Rise and Fall of the Thai Absolute Monarchy: Foundations of the Modern Thai State from Feudalism to Peripheral Capitalism* (Bangkok: White Lotus, 1994); Songchai Na Yala, "The Problem of the Study of Thailand's Mode of Production regarding the Theory of Semicolonialism, Semifeudalism" [ปัญหาการศึกษาวิถีการผลิตของไทยอันเนื่องมาจากทฤษฎีกึ่งเมืองขึ้น-กึ่งศักดินา], *Warasan Settasatkanmueang* 1, no. 2 (March–April 1981): 3–98; Somsak Jeamteerasakul, "Thai Society: From Feudalism to Capitalism" [สังคมไทย จากศักดินาถึงทุนนิยม], *Warasan Thammasat* 11, no. 2 (June 1982): 128–64.

66. Kullada Kesboonchoo Mead and Kengkij Kitirianglarp, "Transition Debates and the Thai State: An Observation," in *Essays on Thailand's Economy and Society for Professor Chattip Nartsupa at Seventy-Two*, ed. Pasuk Phongpaichit and Chris Baker (Bangkok: Sangsan, 2013), 91–118; Chaithawat Tulathon, "From the Debate of the Transition from Feudalism to Capitalism to the Thesis That 'Democracy under the Monarchy as the Head of State' Is the Form of the Thai Bourgeois State" [จากวิวาทะการเปลี่ยนผ่านจากศักดินาสู่ทุนนิยมสู่บททดลองเสนอว่าด้วยระบอบประชาธิปไตยอันมีพระมหากษัตริย์เป็นประมุขในฐานะรูปแบบรัฐกระฎุมพีของไทย], *Fa Diew Kan* 13, no. 1 (January–April 2015): 203–33.

67. Pasuk and Baker, *Thailand*, 237.

68. Pasuk and Baker, *History of Thailand*, 91.

69. In spite of this promulgation of laws that guaranteed property rights during Rama V's reign, these laws were not seriously or universally applied. In fact Thailand had to wait until the second half of the twentieth century before property rights were effectively guaranteed by the state. See Larsson, *Land and Loyalty*, 33–34.

70. Anderson, "Studies of the Thai State," 193–247; Pasuk and Baker, *History of Thailand*, 59–61.

71. Pasuk and Baker, *Thailand*, 244, 251.

72. Chollada, "Investment of the Privy Purse," 16.

73. Ibid., chapter 2.

74. Thai monarchs before the twentieth century were prolific and polygamous. For example, Rama I had forty-two children by twenty-eight mothers, Rama II had seventy-three children by forty mothers, Rama III had fifty-one children by thirty-seven mothers, Rama IV had eighty-two children by thirty-five mothers, and Rama V had seventy-seven children by thirty-six mothers. Pasuk and Baker, *A History of Thailand*, 31.

75. Chollada, "Investment of the Privy Purse," 35, 38; Thanapol Eawsakul and Chaithawat Tulathon, "Royal Wealth under the Absolutist Regime and during the Transitional Period" [พระราชทรัพย์ในระบอบสมบูรณาญาสิทธิราชย์และในระยะเปลี่ยนผ่าน], in *Brahma Helping Us Prosper: The Political Economy of the Crown*

Property Bureau after 1932 [พระพรหมช่วยอำนวยให้ชื่นฉ่ำ: เศรษฐกิจการเมืองว่าด้วย
ทรัพย์สินส่วนพระมหากษัตริย์หลัง 2475], ed. Chaithawat Tulathon (Nonthaburi: Fa
Diew Kan, 2014), 9–14.

76. Chollada, "Investment of the Privy Purse," 113–14.

77. Ibid., 112.

78. Ibid., 119–20.

79. Ibid., 127–28.

80. The PPB owned three hundred of the initial three thousand shares of
the SCB. When the bank later faced a financial crisis and was revived with 3 million baht of new capital, 1.6 million baht of it came from the PPB. Meanwhile,
the PPB owned nearly three-quarters of the initial capital of the SCC. See
Chollada, "Investment of the Privy Purse," 156, 166; Ian Brown, *The Elite and the
Economy in Siam, c. 1890–1920* (Oxford: Oxford University Press, 1988), 130, 153;
Porphant, "Crown Property Bureau," 168–69.

81. Akira, *Capital Accumulation in Thailand*, 90–93; Chollada, "Investment of
the Privy Purse," 174–92.

82. Chollada, "Investment of the Privy Purse," 152.

83. Thongchai Winichakul, "The Existing Legacy of Absolutism" [มรดก
สมบูรณาญาสิทธิราชย์ในปัจจุบัน], in *Democracy That Is the Monarchy above Politics*
[ประชาธิปไตยที่กษัตริย์อยู่เหนือการเมือง] (Nonthaburi: Fa Diew Kan, 2013), 199–219.

84. Pasuk and Baker, *History of Thailand*, 13.

85. Ibid., 247–48.

86. Thongchai Winichakul, *Siam Mapped: A History of the Geo-body of a Nation* (Honolulu: University of Hawai'i Press, 1994), 101–2.

87. Pasuk and Baker, *Thailand*, 249.

88. Kullada, *Rise and Decline of Thai Absolutism*, 139.

89. Thongchai Winichakul, *Thailand's Hyper-royalism: Its Success and Predicament* (Singapore: Institute of Southeast Asian Studies, 2016), 15.

90. Chollada, "Investment of the Privy Purse," 165; Brown, *The Elite and the
Economy in Siam*, 128.

91. Chollada, "Investment of the Privy Purse," 122; Brown, *The Elite and the
Economy in Siam*, 143.

92. Chollada, "Investment of the Privy Purse," 184, 188.

93. John Bowring, *The Kingdom and People of Siam* (Kuala Lumpur: Oxford
University Press, 1969), 1:410–11, quoted in Peleggi, *Lords of Things*, 23.

94. Ibid.

95. Florence Caddy, *To Siam and Malaya* (Singapore: Oxford University
Press, 1992), 144, quoted in Peleggi, *Lords of Things*, 19.

96. Ibid.

97. Pasuk and Baker, *History of Thailand*, 69.

98. Office of Educational Affairs, "A History of the Royal Scholarship and
the Government Scholarship" [ประวัติความเป็นมาของทุนเล่าเรียนหลวงและทุนรัฐบาล],
accessed March 7, 2016, http://www.oeadc.org/ContactOEA/ScholarHistory.

99. Kullada, *Rise and Decline of Thai Absolutism*, 128.

100. Paradee Tungtang, "Shakespeare in Thailand" (PhD diss., University of Warwick, 2011).

101. Morris, "Photography and the Power of Images," 124–25; Peleggi, *Lords of Things*, 45.

102. Morris, "Photography and the Power of Images," 126.

103. Peleggi, *Lords of Things*, 14.

104. Morris, "Photography and the Power of Images," 137.

105. Peleggi, *Lords of Things*, 70.

106. Matthew Copeland, "Contested Nationalism and the 1932 Overthrow of the Absolute Monarchy in Siam" (PhD diss., Australian National University, 1993), chapter 5; Scot Barmé, *Woman, Man, Bangkok: Love, Sex, and Popular Culture in Thailand* (New York: Rowman & Littlefield, 2002), chapter 4.

107. Kullada, *Rise and Decline of Thai Absolutism*, 67.

108. Ibid., 117.

109. According to Kullada (ibid., 74), many students from royal or noble families who went to study abroad did not perform well and were sent home. The reasons for their failure were that they "were sent abroad thanks to their family background" and that "personal qualifications were not taken into consideration whatsoever."

110. Chaiyan, *Rise and Fall of the Thai Absolute Monarchy*, 156.

111. Pasuk and Baker, *Thailand*, 237; Skinner, *Chinese Society in Thailand*, 166.

112. Pasuk and Baker, *Thailand*, 114.

113. Ibid., 110.

114. G. William Skinner, *Leadership and Power in the Chinese Community of Thailand* (Ithaca, NY: Cornell University Press, 1958), 14.

115. Skinner, *Chinese Society in Thailand*, 61, 63.

116. Hewison, *Bankers and Bureaucrats*, 39, 52; Skinner, *Chinese Society in Thailand*, 32, 67.

117. Pasuk and Baker, *Thailand*, 95, 114; Hamilton and Waters, "Ethnicity and Capitalist Development," 268; Hewison, *Bankers and Bureaucrats*, 76.

118. Skinner, *Chinese Society in Thailand*, 91.

119. Ibid.

120. Ibid., 92–96.

121. Ibid., 8, 11.

122. Asavabahu (King Vajiravudh), *The Jews of the Orient and Wake Up, Siam* [พวกยิวแห่งบูรพาทิศ และเมืองไทยจงตื่นเถิด] (Bangkok: Foundation in Memory of King Rama VI, 1985), 80–84, quoted in Kasian Tejapira, "Imagined Uncommunity: The Lookjin Middle Class and Thai Official Nationalism," in *Essential Outsiders: Chinese and Jews in the Modern Transformation of Southeast Asia and Central Europe*, ed. Daniel Chirot and Anthony Reid (Seattle: University of Washington Press, 1997), 77.

123. Ibid.

124. The irony of Thai history is that Thai royals have long been ethnically mixed with Chinese. As Skinner genealogically revealed, King Taksin was the son of a Chinese father who worked for the palace as a tax collector, and the king himself could speak both Thai and Chinese. Similarly, all the monarchs of the Chakri dynasty were partially Chinese; Rama I was one-half Chinese by ancestry, Rama II one-quarter, Rama III one-eighth, Rama IV one-half, Rama V one-quarter, Rama VI one-half, and Rama VII one-half. See Skinner, *Chinese Society in Thailand*, 20, 26. Rama VIII and Rama IX, as Handley pointed out, were sons of a part Chinese commoner, Sangwan Talapat. See Handley, *The King Never Smiles*, 3, 13.

125. Brown, *The Elite and the Economy in Siam*, chapter 1.

126. Chula Chakrabongse, *Lords of Life* (London: Alvin Redman, 1960), 307, quoted in Handley, *The King Never Smiles*, 42.

127. Benjamin A. Batson, *The End of the Absolute Monarchy in Siam* (Singapore: Oxford University Press, 1986), 205.

128. Handley, *The King Never Smiles*, 42.

129. Max Weber, *Economy and Society*, ed. Guenther Roth and Claus Wittich (Oakland: University of California Press, 1978), 2:1147.

130. Nakarin Mektrairat, *The 1932 Siamese Revolution* [*การปฏิวัติสยาม พ.ศ. 2475*] (Bangkok: Foundation for the Promotion of Social Science and Humanities Textbooks Project, 1992), 40, 174.

131. Ibid., 64, 78.

132. Pasuk and Baker, *History of Thailand*, 118; Nakarin, *1932 Siamese Revolution*, 15.

133. Pasuk and Baker, *History of Thailand*, 88.

134. Hewison, *Bankers and Bureaucrats*, 60; Chollada, "Investment of the Privy Purse," 170; Brown, *The Elite and the Economy in Siam*, 136, 141.

135. Chollada, "Investment of the Privy Purse," 186, 203; Brown, *The Elite and the Economy in Siam*, 156–57.

136. Nakarin, *1932 Siamese Revolution*, 29–32.

137. Chollada, "Investment of the Privy Purse," 200.

138. Ibid., 204–5.

139. Ibid., 212–18.

140. Batson, *End of Absolute Monarchy in Siam*, 249.

141. Chollada, "Investment of the Privy Purse," 219–20.

142. Peleggi, *Lords of Things*, 14–15, 40.

143. Thak Chaloemtiarana, "Through Racing Goggles: Modernity, the West, Ambiguous Siamese Alterities, and the Construction of Thai Nationalism" [*ล้อหมุนเร็ว: การแข่งรถ วรรณกรรมการแข่งรถ ชาตินิยมไทย*], *Aan* 7, no. 1 (August 2015): 141.

144. Chanan Yodhong, *Male Courtiers under the Reign of Rama VI* [*นายในสมัย รัชกาลที่ 6*] (Bangkok: Matichon Press, 2013), 30–31.

145. Walter F. Vella, *Chaiyo! King Vajiravudh and the Development of Thai Nationalism* (Honolulu: University of Hawai'i Press, 1978), 170. Siam was the official name of the country before it was changed to Thailand in 1939. Thailand was renamed Siam from 1945 to 1949. After that it reverted to Thailand again.

146. As Benedict Anderson remarked, "The policies, style, mistakes, and problems of Rama VI's reign cannot be understood without acknowledging the ruler's homosexuality." While the other monarchs' female sexual partners were barred from holding public office and thus offered no political competition to princes, nobles, and the military, Rama VI's male sexual partners were eligible for public office and this royal favoritism thus aroused frustration and enmity among the male elites. See Anderson, "Studies of the Thai State," 208n24.

147. *Bangkok Kanmuang*, December 31, 1924, reprinted in Copeland, "Contested Nationalism," 226.

148. *Bangkok Kanmuang*, August 21, 1923, reprinted in Copeland, "Contested Nationalism," 102.

149. *Kro Lek*, April 18, 1926, reprinted in Copeland, "Contested Nationalism," 141.

150. Pasuk and Baker, *Thailand*, 46; Nakarin, *1932 Siamese Revolution*, 60.

151. Benjamin A. Batson, *Siam's Political Future: Documents from the End of the Absolute Monarchy* (Ithaca, NY: Cornell University Press, 1974), 97.

152. Nakarin, *1932 Siamese Revolution*, 77; Pasuk and Baker, *History of Thailand*, 111.

153. Nakarin, *1932 Siamese Revolution*, 80.

154. Batson, *Siam's Political Future*, 97.

155. Ibid.

156. *Sri Krung*, August 4, 1931, reprinted in Copeland, "Contested Nationalism," 185; Nakarin, *1932 Siamese Revolution*, 133.

157. Hewison, *Bankers and Bureaucrats*, 58.

158. Pasuk and Baker, *History of Thailand*, 111.

159. Seksan, "Transformation of the Thai State," 276–77.

160. Batson, *End of Absolute Monarchy in Siam*, 303–4.

161. Skinner, *Chinese Society in Thailand*, 220.

162. The irony of Thai history unfolded again here. Like Thai royalty, many leaders of the People's Party themselves were partly of Chinese ancestry. The crucial figures in the party, such as Pridi Banomyong, Phraya Phahonphonphayuhasena, and Luang Wichitwathakan, were all sons of Chinese fathers. See ibid., 244.

163. Ibid., 262–69; Akira, *Capital Accumulation in Thailand*, 108–9; Hewison, *Bankers and Bureaucrats*, 69; Daniel Unger, *Building Social Capital in Thailand: Fibers, Finance, and Infrastructure* (Cambridge: Cambridge University Press, 1998), 52.

164. Skinner, *Chinese Society in Thailand*, 360.

165. Sungsidh Piriyarangsan, *Thai Bureaucratic Capitalism, 1932–1960* (Bangkok: Social Research Institute, Chulalongkorn University, 1983); Akira, *Capital Accumulation in Thailand*, 5, 10, 137–38; Unger, *Building Social Capital in Thailand*, 53.

166. Suphot Chaengreo, "The Case of Seizing Rama VII's Property" [คดียึด ทรัพย์พระบาทสมเด็จพระปกเกล้า], *Sinlapa Watthanatham* 23, no. 8 (June 2005): 62–80; Thanapol and Chaithawat, "Royal Wealth under the Absolutist Regime," 62–66.

167. Thanapol and Chaithawat, "Royal Wealth under the Absolutist Regime," 58.

168. Suphot, "Case of Seizing Rama VII's Property," 62–66. Eventually, however, the government did not sell the royal properties that belonged to Rama VII. Instead most were returned to the crown thanks to the revival of the Thai monarchy early in Rama IX's reign.

169. This figure was calculated from data in Ingram, *Economic Change in Thailand*, 192, table XVI.

170. Royal Thai Government Gazette, *Crown Property Act of 1936* [พระราช บัญญัติจัดระเบียบทรัพย์สินฝ่ายพระมหากษัตริย์ พ.ศ. 2479], June 15, 1937; Grossman and Faulder, *King Bhumibol Adulyadej*, 288.

171. Porphant, "Crown Property Bureau," 170.

172. Akira, *Capital Accumulation in Thailand*, 126–27, 132; Porphant, "Crown Property Bureau," 170; Pharut Phenphayup, "What Is the Crown Property Bureau?" [ทรัพย์สินส่วนพระมหากษัตริย์คืออะไร?], in *Brahma Helping Us Prosper: The Political Economy of the Crown Property Bureau after 1932* [พระพรหมช่วยอำนวยให้ชื่นฉ่ำ: เศรษฐกิจการเมืองว่าด้วยทรัพย์สินส่วนพระมหากษัตริย์หลัง 2475], ed. Chaithawat Tulathon, 161–203 (Nonthaburi: Fa Diew Kan, 2014), 180–82.

173. Handley, *The King Never Smiles*, 76–79; Somsak Jeamteerasakul, "The Mystery of the King's Death" [ปริศนากรณีสวรรคต], *Fa Diew Kan* 6, no. 2 (April–June 2008): 116–35.

Chapter 2.
The Rise and Triumph of the Bourgeois Crown

1. Denis D. Gray, "Thailand's Working Royals," in *The King of Thailand in World Focus*, ed. Denis D. Gray (Singapore: Didier Millet, 2008), 123; Nattapoll Chaiching, *To Dream the Impossible Dream: The Counterrevolution against the Siamese Revolution, 1932–1957* [ขอฝันใฝ่ในฝันอันเหลือเชื่อ: ความเคลื่อนไหวของขบวนการ ปฏิวัติสยาม พ.ศ. 2475–2500] (Nonthaburi: Fa Diew Kan, 2013), 41.

2. Thak, *Thailand*, 29–32; Nattapoll, *To Dream the Impossible Dream*, 39–40; David Streckfuss, "Freedom and Silence under the Neo-absolutist Monarchy Regime in Thailand, 2006–2011," in *"Good Coup" Gone Bad: Thailand's Political Development since Thaksin's Downfall*, ed. Pavin Chachavalpongpun (Singapore: Institute of Southeast Asian Studies, 2014), 114–15.

3. The Royal Thai Government Gazette, *Crown Property Act of 1948* [พระราช
บัญญัติจัดระเบียบทรัพย์สินฝ่ายพระมหากษัตริย์ พ.ศ. 2491], February 3, 1948.

4. Thak, *Thailand*, 210–14.

5. Royal Thai Government Gazette, *The Announcement from the Office of the
Prime Minister regarding the King's Birthday as the National Day* [ประกาศสำนักนายก
รัฐมนตรีเรื่องให้ถือวันพระราชสมภพเป็นวันเฉลิมฉลองของชาติไทย], May 24, 1960.

6. Handley, *The King Never Smiles*, 212–13.

7. Chit, *Real Face of Thai Feudalism*, 127; Craig J. Reynolds, *Thai Radical Discourse: The Real Face of Thai Feudalism Today* (Ithaca, NY: Cornell University
Press, 1987), chapter 1.

8. Katherine Bowie, *Rituals of National Loyalty: An Anthropology of the State
and the Village Scout Movement in Thailand* (New York: Columbia University
Press, 1997); Benedict Anderson, "Withdrawal Symptoms: Social and Cultural
Aspects of the October 6 Coup," in *Exploration and Irony in Studies of Siam over
Forty Years* (Ithaca, NY: Cornell University Press, 2014), 47–76.

9. Bowie, *Rituals of National Loyalty*, 3.

10. Handley, *The King Never Smiles*, chapter 12.

11. As Tyrell Haberkorn points out, unofficial estimates of the number of
people killed, injured, and arrested were much higher than what the government claimed. Above all, "More than forty years later," she notes, "the perpe-
trators of the violence still enjoy complete impunity; there has never been a
public state investigation of the violence, let alone anyone held to account for
it." Tyrell Haberkorn, *In Plain Sight: Impunity and Human Rights in Thailand*
(Madison: University of Wisconsin Press, 2018), 110.

12. Handley, *The King Never Smiles*, 238.

13. Pasuk and Baker, *History of Thailand*, 194–95.

14. Streckfuss, "Freedom and Silence under the Neo-absolutist Monarchy,"
114–15.

15. Ibid., 116.

16. Pasuk and Baker, *History of Thailand*, 144–50; Anderson, "Withdrawal
Symptoms," 53; Nattapoll, *To Dream the Impossible Dream*, chapter 8; Jim Glassman, *Thailand at the Margins: Internationalization of the State and the Transformation of Labour* (New York: Oxford University Press, 2004), 37; "Thailand's
Involvement in Vietnam War," March 29, 2015, http://thevietnamwar.info
/thailand-involvement-vietnam-war/.

17. Benedict Anderson, "Introduction to *In the Mirror*," in *Exploration and
Irony in Studies of Siam over Forty Years* (Ithaca, NY: Cornell University Press,
2014), 77–99.

18. Handley, *The King Never Smiles*, 149; Charles Keyes, *Finding Their Voices:
Northeastern Villagers and the Thai State* (Chiang Mai: Silkworm Books, 2014), 95;
Bowie, *Rituals of National Loyalty*, 91; Jim Glassman, "Thailand in the Era of the
Cold War and Rama IX," *Human Geography* 2, no. 1 (2009): 33.

19. Quoted in Grossman and Faulder, *King Bhumibol Adulyadej*, 109.

20. Quoted in Handley, *The King Never Smiles*, 147.

21. Thak, *Thailand*, 221.

22. Handley, *The King Never Smiles*, 155; Thak, *Thailand*, 210n76.

23. Office of His Majesty's Principal Private Secretary (hereafter OHM), *Yearbook of Royal Activities 1970* [หนังสือประมวลพระราชกรณียกิจปี พ.ศ. 2513], May 12, 1970 (Bangkok: Thai Wattana Panich, 1970).

24. Bowie, *Rituals of National Loyalty*, 108-9; Handley, *The King Never Smiles*, 237.

25. National Statistical Office of Thailand (TNSO), *Statistical Yearbook of Thailand 1947* [รายงานสถิติรายปี ประจำปี พ.ศ. 2490] (Bangkok: Statistical Data Bank and Information Dissemination Division, National Statistical Office, 1947).

26. Ingram, *Economic Change in Thailand*, 175.

27. Ibid., 216.

28. Glassman, *Thailand at the Margins*, 39.

29. Unger, *Building Social Capital in Thailand*, 62.

30. Hewison, *Bankers and Bureaucrats*, 103-5.

31. Ibid., 117, 125.

32. Akira, *Capital Accumulation in Thailand*, 187-88; Hewison, *Bankers and Bureaucrats*, 100.

33. Pasuk and Baker, *History of Thailand*, 158.

34. Grossman and Faulder, *King Bhumibol Adulyadej*, 232-35; Royal Chitralada Projects, "His Majesty's Personal Projects," accessed September 23, 2016, http://kanchanapisek.or.th/kp1/notbusi_th.html.

35. Bhumibol Adulyadej, "The King's Commencement Address at Kasetsart University on July 18, 1974," OHM, July 18, 1974.

36. The Department of International Trade Promotion, Ministry of Commerce, the Royal Thai Government, "Get to Know the SUPPORT Foundation of Her Majesty Queen Sirikit of Thailand," accessed September 23, 2016, https://www.thaitradeusa.com/home/?p=8391.

37. Denis D. Gray, "Queen Sirikit: An Interview," in *The King of Thailand in World Focus*, ed. Denis D. Gray (Singapore: Didier Millet, 2008), 139.

38. Frank Prochaska, *Royal Bounty: The Making of a Welfare Monarchy* (New Haven, CT: Yale University Press, 1995).

39. Porphant, "Crown Property Bureau," 170.

40. In 1972 the SCC revamped its corporate structure and rebranded itself as the SCG. The company, however, still uses its former abbreviation (SCC) when it comes to its investments in the stock market of Thailand. Siam Cement Group, "SCG's Corporate Profile: Milestones in 1972," accessed June 10, 2018, https://www.scg.com/en/01corporate_profile/03_milstone.html.

41. Akira, *Capital Accumulation in Thailand*, 240, table 7.7. Calculation of the historical exchange rate from Thai baht to US dollars that appears throughout this book is based on the information in Fxtop.com, "Converter in the Past," accessed March 13, 2017, http://fxtop.com/en/currency-converter-past.php.

42. Akira, *Capital Accumulation in Thailand*, 248, table 7.9.

43. Ibid., 187.

44. TNSO, *Statistical Yearbook of Thailand 1950* [รายงานสถิติรายปี ประจำปี พ.ศ. 2493]; TNSO, *Statistical Yearbook of Thailand 1960* [รายงานสถิติรายปี ประจำปี พ.ศ. 2503]; TNSO, *Statistical Yearbook of Thailand 1970* [รายงานสถิติรายปี ประจำปี พ.ศ. 2513].

45. Among these three countries, only the monarchy of Cambodia was restored, in 1993.

46. Chanida Chitbundid, *The Royally Initiated Projects: The Making of King Bhumibol's Hegemony* [โครงการอันเนื่องมาจากพระราชดำริ: การสถาปนาอำนาจนำใน พระบาทสมเด็จพระเจ้าอยู่หัว] (Bangkok: Foundation for the Promotion of Social Science and Humanities Textbooks Project, 2013), chapter 3.

47. Rama IX cut down on his trips to the hinterland once communism was no longer considered a threat to the throne. In 1994 and 1995, for example, he spent only nine and four days a year in rural provinces, respectively. See Prakan Klinfung, "King Bhumibol's Visits to Provincial Areas, 1950–1987" [การเสด็จพระราชดำเนินท้องที่ต่างจังหวัดของพระบาทสมเด็จพระเจ้าอยู่หัวภูมิพลอดุลยเดช พ.ศ. 2493–2530] (MA thesis, Chulalongkorn University, 2008), 4, table 1.1.

48. Keyes, *Finding Their Voices*, 11, 95.

49. Handley, *The King Never Smiles*, 265–67; Grossman and Faulder, *King Bhumibol Adulyadej*, 137.

50. Handley, *The King Never Smiles*, 290.

51. Thak, *Thailand*, 214.

52. Gray, "Thailand," 816–17; Christine Gray, "Hegemonic Images: Language and Silence in the Royal Thai Polity," *Man* 26, no. 1 (March 1991): 57–59.

53. Anderson, "Withdrawal Symptoms," 55.

54. Ibid., 73–74.

55. Benedict Anderson, "Radicalism after Communism in Thailand and Indonesia," in *Exploration and Irony in Studies of Siam over Forty Years* (Ithaca, NY: Cornell University Press, 2014), 120; Thikan Srinara, *After October 6: The Ideological Conflict between Student Activists and the Communist Party of Thailand* [หลัง 6 ตุลาฯ: ว่าด้วยความขัดแย้งทางความคิดระหว่างขบวนการนักศึกษากับพรรคคอมมิวนิสต์แห่ง ประเทศไทย] (Bangkok: October 6 Memorial Press, 2009), 56–69.

56. Roger Kershaw, *Monarchy in South-East Asia: The Faces of Tradition in Transition* (New York: Routledge, 2001), 85.

57. Thikan, *After October 6*, 35, 51, 128.

58. Anderson, "Radicalism after Communism," 121.

59. Ibid.

60. Reynolds and Lysa, "Marxism in Thai Historical Studies"; Songchai, "Problem of the Study of Thailand's Mode of Production"; Somsak, "Thai Society."

61. Anderson, "Radicalism after Communism," 121.

62. Nicholas Grossman, ed., *Chronicle of Thailand: Headline News since 1946* (Singapore: Didier Millet, 2009), 247.

63. Ibid., 252.

64. Anderson, "Radicalism after Communism," 122, 125.

65. Bowie, *Rituals of National Loyalty*, 289, table A.4.

66. William A. Callahan, *Imagining Democracy: Reading "The Events of May" in Thailand* (Singapore: Institute of Southeast Asian Studies, 1998), 45.

67. Somsak Jeamteerasakul, "Post–October 14" [หลัง 14 ตุลา], *Fa Diew Kan* 3, no. 4 (October–December 2005): 169.

68. Robert Dayley and Clark D. Neher, *Southeast Asia in the New International Era* (Boulder, CO: Westview, 2013), 22.

69. Handley, *The King Never Smiles*, 290.

70. Pasuk and Baker, *History of Thailand*, 236.

71. Handley, *The King Never Smiles*, 357–60.

72. Pasuk and Baker, *History of Thailand*, 240–41; Thongchai, *Democracy That Is the Monarchy above Politics*, 12.

73. Kittisak Sujittarom, "Thai Newspapers' and Public Intellectuals' Views on the Status and Role of the Monarchy between 1992 and 1997" [ทัศนะของสื่อหนังสือพิมพ์และปัญญาชนสาธารณะที่มีต่อสถานะและบทบาทของสถาบันกษัตริย์ ระหว่าง พ.ศ. 2535–2540] (MA thesis, Thammasat University, 2014), 49, table 2.5.

74. In addition to Rama IX's speech, the OHM annually publishes the public addresses of Queen Sirikit and Princess Sirindhorn.

75. McCargo, "Network Monarchy," 516.

76. Ibid., 506.

77. Mérieau, "Thailand's Deep State"; Chambers and Napisa, "Resilience of Monarchised Military in Thailand."

78. "Thaksin Tells All (Almost)," WikiLeaks, April 7, 2006; "Thaksin Sees Self as Thailand's Aung San Suu Kyy," WikiLeaks, May 18, 2006; "Thaksin Predicts National Unity Government," WikiLeaks, July 23, 2008; "Thailand: Senior Statesmen Seeking the King's Approval to Push Aside PM Samak," WikiLeaks, September 3, 2008.

79. Unger, *Building Social Capital in Thailand*, 1.

80. TNSO, *Statistical Yearbook of Thailand, 1960–2010* [รายงานสถิติรายปี ประจำปี พ.ศ. 2503–2553].

81. Paweł Bożyk, "Newly Industrialized Countries," in *Globalization and the Transformation of Foreign Economic Policy* (Burlington, VT: Ashgate Publishing, 2006), 164; Mauro F. Guillén, "Multinationals, Ideology, and Organized Labor," in *The Limits of Convergence: Globalization and Organizational Change in Argentina, South Korea, and Spain* (Princeton, NJ: Princeton University Press, 2001), 126, table 5.1; David Waugh, *Geography: An Integrated Approach* (Oxford: Oxford University Press, 2000), 578; David McNally, "Globalization on Trial: Crisis and Class Struggle in East Asia," in *Rising from the Ashes? Labor in the Age of "Global" Capitalism*, ed. Ellen Meiksins Wood, Peter Meiksins, and Michael Yates (New York: Monthly Review Press, 1998), 143.

82. Hewison, *Bankers and Bureaucrats*, 121.

83. Pasuk Phongpaichit and Chris Baker, *Thailand's Boom and Bust* (Chiang Mai: Silkworm Books, 1998), 4.

84. Ibid., 36.

85. Ibid., 98.

86. Pasuk and Baker, *History of Thailand*, 259.

87. Pasuk and Baker, *Thailand's Boom and Bust*, 124–25.

88. Pasuk Phongpaichit and Chris Baker, eds., *Thai Capital after the 1997 Crisis* (Chiang Mai: Silkworm Books, 2008), 14.

89. Ibid., 12–13.

90. Ibid., 6.

91. Natenapha Wailerdsak, "Companies in Crisis," in *Thai Capital after the 1997 Crisis*, ed. Pasuk Phongpaichit and Chris Baker (Chiang Mai: Silkworm Books, 2008), 54, figure 1.5.

92. Marx, *Capital*, vol. 1, chapter 25.

93. Akira, *Capital Accumulation in Thailand*, 239.

94. Porphant, "Crown Property Bureau," 174.

95. Natenapha, "Companies in Crisis," 39, table 1.4; Porphant, "Crown Property Bureau," 175.

96. Porphant, "Crown Property Bureau," 175–76.

97. Natenapha, "Companies in Crisis," 44–47; Porphant, "Crown Property Bureau," 176–80.

98. Porphant, "Crown Property Bureau," 179.

99. Siam Cement Group, "SCG's Corporate Profile: Milestones in 2001," accessed September 23, 2016, http://www.scg.co.th/en/01corporate_profile /03_milstone.html.

100. Porphant, "Crown Property Bureau," 182; Wikipedia, "List of Largest Shopping Malls," accessed September 23, 2016, https://en.wikipedia.org /wiki/List_of_largest_shopping_malls#cite_note-Fich-1.

101. Sucheera Pinijparakarn, "SCB Leads Profit Growth," *The Nation*, January 22, 2014.

102. Grossman and Faulder, *King Bhumibol Adulyadej*, 148–52; Pasuk and Baker, *History of Thailand*, 238–39.

103. Bhumibol Adulyadej, "The King's Speech Given to the Audience of Well-Wishers on the Occasion of the King's Birthday at the Dusidalai Hall, Chitralada Royal Villa, on December 4, 1991," OHM, December 4, 1991.

104. Ibid.

105. David Harvey, *A Brief History of Neoliberalism* (New York: Oxford University Press, 2011), 2.

106. Bhumibol Adulyadej, "The King's Speech Given to the Audience of Well-Wishers on the Occasion of the King's Birthday at the Dusidalai Hall, Chitralada Royal Villa on December 4, 1997," OHM, December 4, 1997.

107. Ibid.

108. Quoted in Handley, *The King Never Smiles*, 415.

109. Bhumibol, "King's Speech," December 4, 1997.

110. Bhumibol Adulyadej, "The King's Speech Given to the Audience of Well-Wishers on the Occasion of the King's Birthday at the Dusidalai Hall, Chitralada Royal Villa, on December 4, 1998," OHM, December 4, 1998.

111. Bhumibol, "King's Speech," December 4, 1997.

112. Handley, *The King Never Smiles*, 415.

113. TNSO, *Statistical Yearbook of Thailand*, various years.

114. Ibid.

115. Jim Glassman, "The Provinces Elect Governments, Bangkok Overthrows Them: Urbanity, Class, and Post-democracy in Thailand," *Urban Studies* 47, no. 6 (May 2010): 1304.

116. Endo Gen, *Diversifying Retail and Distribution in Thailand* (Chiang Mai: Silkworm Books, 2013), 39, table 2.4.

117. Ibid., 66, table 3.2.

118. Ibid., 100, table 4.1.

119. Seven-Eleven Japan, "7-11 Around the World," accessed September 24, 2016, http://www.sej.co.jp/company/en/g_stores.html; FamilyMart, "Investor Relations: Number of Stores," accessed September 24, 2016, http://www.family.co.jp/english/investor_relations/stores.html.

120. Japan is the world's largest location for convenient stores for both franchises. In 2016 it had 18,785 and 11,656 7-Eleven and FamilyMart stores, respectively.

121. TNSO, *Statistical Yearbook of Thailand*, various years.

122. TNSO, *Statistical Yearbook of Thailand, 1990*.

123. TNSO, *Statistical Yearbook of Thailand*, various years.

124. Ibid.

125. In 2016, 76 and 171 of higher education institutions were located in Bangkok and the rest of the country respectively. Thailand Office of Higher Education Commission, "Statistics of Higher Education in Thailand" [สถิติการศึกษาในระดับอุดมศึกษาในประเทศไทย], accessed September 24, 2016, http://www.info.mua.go.th/information/.

126. Anderson, "Radicalism after Communism," 122.

127. Somsak, "Post–October 14," 171; For more on the contemporary lives of former leftists in Thailand, see Kanokrat Lertchoosakul, *The Rise of the Octobrists in Contemporary Thailand: Power and Conflict Among Former Left-Wing Student Activists in Thai Politics* (New Haven, CT: Council on Southeast Asian Studies, Yale University, 2016).

128. Thongchai Winichakul, "Nationalism and the Radical Intelligentsia in Thailand," *Third World Quarterly* 29, no. 3 (2008): 575-91.

129. Ibid., 587.

130. Jean-Jacques Rousseau, "Discourse on the Origin and Foundations of Inequality among Men," in *Rousseau: The Basic Political Writings*, ed. and trans. Donald A. Cress (Indianapolis: Hackett Publishing, 2012), 93-120; Marx,

Pre-Capitalist Economic Formations; Friedrich Engels, *The Origin of the Family, Private Property, and the State* (New York: Penguin, 2010).

131. Somsak, "Post–October 14," 170.

132. Karl Marx, *Grundrisse: Foundations of the Critique of Political Economy*, trans. Martin Nicolaus (New York: Penguin, 1993), 246.

133. I collected the information about corporate donation in this section from OHM, *Yearbook of Royal Activities*, a book produced annually and released by the OHM during Rama IX's reign. It provides the formal and daily schedules of the king, queen, and members of the royal family as they performed their royal duties throughout the year. These activities normally began in the early morning and ended in the late evening. Besides representatives of the business sectors, the court frequently welcomed guests of the state, civil servants, high-ranking generals, prominent professors, senior judges, award-winning artists, media moguls, professional athletes, celebrities, and NGO leaders.

134. Thak, *Thailand*, 216, table 16.

135. OHM, *Yearbook of Royal Activities*, various dates, 2008–9.

136. Royal Thai Government Gazette, *An Announcement regarding the National Broadcasting of Radio, Television, and Telecommunications* [ประกาศคณะกรรมการกิจการกระจายเสียง กิจการ โทรทัศน์ และกิจการ โทรคมนาคมแห่งชาติ], February 27, 2013.

137. See, for example, OHM, "Court News," accessed September 24, 2016, http://www.ohm.go.th/th/court-news; Apptividia Co., Ltd., "OHM Book Shelf" (mobile app), accessed August 22, 2018, https://itunes.apple.com/us/app/ohm-books-shelf/id830154941?mt=8.

138. OHM, *Yearbook of Royal Activities*, various dates, 2008–2010.

139. Thak, *Thailand*, 218.

140. OHM, *Yearbook of Royal Activities*, January 22, 2007; June 1, 2007; December 5, 2007.

141. Prem, the President of the Privy Council, for example, was an honorary chairman of CP and the Bangkok Bank. See Handley, *The King Never Smiles*, 376–77. For an example of a case in which a Privy Council member introduced capitalists to the crown, see OHM, *Yearbook of Royal Activities*, February 12, 2010.

142. OHM, *Yearbook of Royal Activities*, October 3, 1996; October 13, 1994.

143. OHM, *Yearbook of Royal Activities*, April 25, 1997; September 21, 1997; October 21, 1990.

144. Bureau of the National Budget, *Annual Budget*, various years [งบประมาณประจำปี] (Bangkok: Bureau of the National Budget, various years).

145. Ibid.

146. Stock Market Exchange of Thailand, "Sammakorn Public Company Limited (SAMCO) Factsheet," "Thai Insurance Public Company Limited (TIC) Factsheet," "Minor International Public Company Limited (MINT) Factsheet," and "Amarin Printing and Publishing Public Company Limited (AMARIN) Factsheet," accessed September 24, 2016, http://www.set.or.th.

147. Ibid.

148. Siam Piwat, "Real Estate Development," accessed September 24, 2016, http://www.siampiwat.com/index.php?m=2.

149. Adam Pasick, "Bangkok's Lavish, Air-Conditioned Malls Consume as Much Power as Entire Provinces," *Quartz*, April 6, 2015, http://qz.com/376125 /bangkoks-lavish-malls-consume-as-much-power-as-entire-provinces/.

150. Ünaldi, *Working towards the Monarchy*, 157.

151. Karl Marx, *Capital*, vol. 3, trans. David Fernbach (London: Penguin Books, 1991), chapter 25; David Harvey, *The Limits to Capital* (London: Verso, 1999), 95.

152. William Mellor, "Thai King Strengthens Grip on Stocks as Nation's No. 1 Investor," *Bloomberg*, August 4, 2007; "Thai King Strengthens Grip on Stocks as Nation's No. 1 Investor," *CNN*, June 25, 2010.

153. Porphant, "Crown Property Bureau," 184.

154. Serafin, "World's Richest Royals."

155. "The World's Richest Royals," *Forbes*, April 29, 2011.

156. "The World's Billionaires, 2011," *Forbes*, March 9, 2011.

157. Serafin, "Thailand's 40 Richest."

158. Tom Wright, "Thai Monarch Is a Factor in Dispute," *Wall Street Journal*, May 23, 2014.

159. Royal Thai Government Gazette, *Crown Property Act of 1948*.

160. Somsak Jeamteerasakul, "What Is the Crown Property Bureau?" [สำนักงานทรัพย์สินส่วนพระมหากษัตริย์คืออะไร?], *Fa Diew Kan* 1, no. 1 (January–March 2006): 67–91.

161. For the case of the British monarchy, see "Head of State Expenditure" and "Annual Financial Report," June 29, 2009, http://www.royal.gov.uk/Latest NewsandDiary/AnnualFinancialReports/Annualfinancialreports.aspx.

162. Somsak, "What Is the Crown Property Bureau?," 85.

Chapter 3.
The King and (Bourgeois) Eyes

1. See the information about this event on its official website, Bike for Dad, especially "About the Activities" and "Programme of Activities," accessed March 5, 2016, https://www.bikefordad2015.com/home.php. Beyond Bangkok, this event was replicated in miniature in many urban areas throughout the kingdom.

2. Rama IX was born on Monday, December 5, 1927. According to Thailand's astrological tradition, Monday is assigned the yellow color. Since the monarch was born on a Monday, yellow is perceived as the symbolic color of him and his reign.

3. According to the official website of this event, the registered number of bikers was 99,999 in Bangkok alone, 498,105 throughout Thailand, and 9,805 people in other countries.

4. See the information about this event in its official website, Bike for Mom, especially "About the Activities" and "Programme of Activities," accessed March 5, 2016, http://www.bikeformom2015.com/home.php.

5. Pasuk and Baker, *History of Thailand*, 14.

6. Bhumibol Adulyadej, *The Story of Thongdaeng* [เรื่องทองแดง] (Bangkok: Amarin Printing and Publishing, 2002); "Thongdaeng Is A National Sensation," in *Chronicle of Thailand: Headline News since 1946*, ed. Nicholas Grossman (Singapore: Didier Millet, 2009), 369.

7. Bhumibol Adulyadej, *The Story of Thongdaeng: A Cartoon Version* [เรื่อง ทองแดง ฉบับการ์ตูน] (Bangkok: Amarin Printing and Publishing, 2004); *Khun Thong Daeng: The Inspirations*, Saha Mongkol Film International, 2015.

8. "Demand for Pink Polo Shirts Soars," in *Chronicle of Thailand: Headline News since 1946*, ed. Nicholas Grossman (Singapore: Didier Millet, 2009), 403; Jocelyn Gecker, "Dressing Like the King: Pink and Pastel," in *The King of Thailand in World Focus*, ed. Denis D. Gray (Singapore: Didier Millet, 2008), 207.

9. Morris, "Photography and the Power of Images"; Jackson, "Royal Spirits, Chinese Gods," 245–320; Peter Jackson, "Virtual Divinity: A 21st-Century Discourse of Thai Royal Influence," in *Saying the Unsayable: Monarchy and Democracy in Thailand*, ed. Soren Ivarsson and Lotte Isager (Copenhagen: Nordic Institute of Asian Studies Press, 2010), 29–60; Peleggi, *Lords of Things*; Irene Stengs, "A Kingly Cult: Thailand's Guiding Lights in a Dark Era," *Etnofoor* 12, no. 2 (1999): 41–75; Stengs, *Worshipping the Great Moderniser*; Ünaldi, *Working towards the Monarchy*; Jory, *Thailand's Theory of Monarchy*.

10. Ooi Keat Gin, ed., *Southeast Asia: A Historical Encyclopedia, from Angkor Wat to East Timor* (Santa Barbara, CA: ABC-CLIO, 2004), 1484.

11. Handley, *The King Never Smiles*, 4, 65.

12. The Golden Jubilee Network, "Biography of His Majesty King Bhumibol Adulyadej," accessed March 7, 2016, http://kanchanapisek.or.th/biography /hmk.th.html.

13. John Stanton, "Young King with a Horn: After an 18-Year Idyl in Switzerland, Siam's Monarch Is Going Home," in *The King of Thailand in World Focus*, ed. Denis D. Gray (Singapore: Didier Millet, 2008), 32.

14. Gray, "Queen Sirikit," 139–40.

15. Handley, *The King Never Smiles*, 104.

16. Susan Buck-Morss, "Visual Empire," *Diacritics* 37, nos. 2–3 (Summer–Fall 2007): 172.

17. Maurizio Peleggi, "Semiotics of Rama IX" (Asia Research Institute Working Papers Series, no. 114, February 24, 2009), 11.

18. Grossman and Faulder, *King Bhumibol Adulyadej*, 336.

19. In Thai this is "พระบาทสมเด็จพระเจ้าอยู่หัว" and "ขอเดชะฝ่าละอองธุลีพระบาท ปกเกล้าปกกระหม่อม," respectively. Handley, *The King Never Smiles*, 151.

20. Pasuk and Baker, *History of Thailand*, 20.

21. Grossman and Faulder, *King Bhumibol Adulyadej*, 103.

22. Thak, *Thailand*, 211–12.

23. Ibid., 63–64, 99, 155–59, 168–70.

24. Quoted in Grossman and Faulder, *King Bhumibol Adulyadej*, 109.

25. Norman Bowman, "King Who's Real Cool 'Cat' Visits IBM," in *The King of Thailand in World Focus*, ed. Denis D. Gray (Singapore: Didier Millet, 2008), 62; Winzola McLendon, "Legend Bows to Royalty: Queen Goes from Tuesday to Saturday in a Day," in *The King of Thailand in World Focus*, ed. Denis D. Gray (Singapore: Didier Millet, 2008), 63–64.

26. Handley, *The King Never Smiles*, 171.

27. On the role of the United States in the revival of the monarchial power in Thailand, see Nattapoll, *To Dream the Impossible Dream*, chapter 8.

28. Platt, "Culture of Monarchy," 95.

29. Handley, *The King Never Smiles*, 290.

30. Stengs, *Worshipping the Great Moderniser*, 224–26.

31. Grossman and Faulder, *King Bhumibol Adulyadej*, 117.

32. "King Bhumibol the Great: Forty Million Thais Vote on the New Title in Nationwide Poll," in *Chronicle of Thailand: Headline News since 1946*, ed. Nicholas Grossman (Singapore: Didier Millet, 2009), 277.

33. The six monarchs were King Ram Khamhaeng (r. 1279–98), King Naresuan, King Narai (r. 1656–88), King Taksin, King Rama I, and King Rama V.

34. Buck-Morss, "Visual Empire," 183.

35. Suchit Wongthet, "When the Land and Provinces Are Invaded by Enemies" [เมื่อจังหวัดปักษ์ใพรีรุก], a newspaper poem celebrating the king's birthday, *Siam Rath*, December 4, 1970.

36. "O, All Thais Are So Lucky to Have a God" [ชาวไทยเอ๋ยยังเคราะห์ดีมีพระเจ้า], a newspaper poem celebrating the king's birthday, *Siam Rath*, December 5, 1972.

37. Thip Chang Motion Picture, "Long Live the King" [ทรงพระเจริญ], a print advertisement celebrating the king's birthday, *Thai Rath*, December 5, 1975.

38. Toyota Motor Thailand Ltd., "Every Grain of Rice Comes from Dad's Doctrine" [ข้าวทุกคำจากคำสอนพ่อ], a print advertisement celebrating the king's birthday, *Thai Rath*, December 5, 2008; Nestlé Thailand Ltd., "Reviving the National Economy Together By Knowing How to Spend Prudently" [ร่วมใจกันฟื้นฟูเศรษฐกิจของชาติด้วยการรู้จักใช้จ่ายอย่างเหมาะสม], a print advertisement celebrating the king's birthday, *Thai Rath*, December 5, 1998; Charoen Pokphand Group Ltd., "Wish to Do Good Things for Returning a Favor to Dad's Kindness" [ปณิธานทำดีทดแทนพระคุณพ่อแห่งแผ่นดิน], a print advertisement celebrating the king's birthday, *Phuchatkan*, December 5, 2008; Amway Thailand Ltd., "Dad's Home, People's Happiness" [บ้านของพ่อ ความสุขของปวงชน], a print advertisement celebrating the king's birthday, *Thai Rath*, December 5, 2006; Central Group Ltd., "Dad's Home" [บ้านของพ่อ], a print advertisement celebrating the king's birthday, *Thai Rath*, December 5, 1999.

39. Khom Khamthap, "The Royal Sweat That Bathes His Royal Body Feeds All Thais" [พระเสโทอาบองค์ทรงเลี้ยงไทย], a print advertisement celebrating the king's birthday, *Siam Rath*, December 6, 1996.

40. Epson Corporation Thailand Ltd., "A Picture of His Majesty Working Everywhere He Goes" [ภาพพระองค์ทรงกิจทุกทิศท่อง], a print advertisement celebrating the king's birthday, *Thai Rath*, December 5, 2005.

41. See, for example, Natural Park, Plc., "The Lord of Thailand Is the World's Hardest Worker" [พระเจ้าแผ่นดินไทยทรงงานหนักที่สุดในโลก], a print advertisement celebrating the king's birthday, *Phuchatkan*, December 5, 2005; Amway Thailand Ltd., "For All 75 Years, How Many Days His Majesty Has Lived Like Kings in the Fairy Tale?" [ตลอด 75 ปี จะมีสักกี่วันที่ในหลวงของเราดำเนินชีวิตอย่างกษัตริย์ในนิทาน], a print advertisement celebrating the king's birthday, *Thai Rath*, December 5, 2002.

42. According to Prakan, Rama IX's days of visiting to provincial areas of Thailand significantly decreased from 40.14 percent of a calendar year in the 1970s, to 38.03 percent in the 1980s and 14.82 percent in the 1990s. See Prakan, "King Bhumibol's Visits to Provincial Areas," 7.

43. Somsak Jeamteerasakul, "So, for Royalists, How Do You Know or Prove That the King Has 'Done Good Things' And 'Worked Hard'?" [ตกลงว่าบรรดาคนที่จงรักภักดี รู้หรือจะพิสูจน์ได้ยังไงนะครับว่า 'ในหลวงทำดี' 'ในหลวงทำงานหนัก'], Facebook, July 21, 2012, https://th-th.facebook.com/somsakjeam/posts/384031784983440.

44. UCOM Group Plc., "His Majesty Makes Me Realize That I Have Not Lost Yet [ในหลวงทำให้ผมรู้ว่า ผมยังไม่แพ้]," a print advertisement celebrating the king's birthday, *Phuchatkan*, December 5, 1997.

45. Gray, "Thailand," 41, 45, 47.

46. Peleggi, *Lords of Things*, 27.

47. See the details of this story in Faculty of Dentistry, Chulalongkorn University, *Good Teeth, Good Health* [ฟันดี สุขภาพดี] (Bangkok: Chulalongkorn University Press, 2007), iii–v.

48. Ministry of Energy of Thailand. "The Royal Toothpaste Tube" [หลอดยาสีพระทนต์], a television commercial celebrating the king's eightieth birthday on December 5, 2007; "The Royal Toothpaste Given by His Majesty" [หลอดยาสีพระทนต์พระราชทาน], Museum of Dentistry, Chulalongkorn University, Bangkok, Thailand.

49. Thai Rath TV, "Dad's Shoes" [รองเท้าของพ่อ], November 26, 2014, YouTube, https://www.youtube.com/watch?v=FNcJjad3Zt8; Channel 3 TV, "Sonkrai Naensinin: The Repairer of the Royal Shoes" [ศรไกร แน่นศรีนิล: ช่างซ่อมฉลองพระบาท], YouTube video, 14:49, posted by "Krobkruakao 3," November 27, 2014, https://www.youtube.com/watch?v=TPcBL8wuT00.

50. Grey Ray Stationery, "His Majesty's Pencils [ดินสอของในหลวง]," August 18, 2017, https://www.grey-ray.com/single-post/2017/04/18/ดินสอของในหลวง.

51. Mae Fah Luang Foundation, "The Hall of Inspiration" [หอแห่งแรงบันดาลใจ], accessed September 29, 2018, http://www.maefahluang.org/?p=3251&lang=th.

52. Ministry of Energy of Thailand, "Fried Rice" [ข้าวผัด], a television commercial celebrating the king's eighty-fourth birthday, December 5, 2011.

53. Ministry of Energy of Thailand, "A Great Deal of Energy Goes into Making a Dish of Fried Rice" [กว่าจะได้ข้าวผัดหนึ่งจานสิ้นเปลืองพลังงานมากมาย], a print advertisement celebrating the King's birthday, *Thai Rath*, December 5, 2011.

54. Even though many Thais today perceive King Ram Khamhaeng and Rama V as father kings, they call them the "father chief" (*phokhun*) and "royal father" (*sadet pho*), respectively. Rama IX, on the other hand, was casually called "dad" (*pho*).

55. Suramaharaj Ltd., "One Dad Who Unites and Unifies" [พ่อหนึ่งซึ่งอยู่รั้งรวมศูนย์], a print advertisement celebrating the king's birthday, *Siam Rath*, December 5, 1989.

56. ThaiBev Plc., "Dad Is Like Water Pouring over Thais So They Do Not Suffer" [พ่อดั่งน้ำชโลมไทยไร้ทุกข์เข็ญ], a print advertisement celebrating the king's birthday, *Siam Rath*, December 6, 2005.

57. Thai Life Insurance Ltd., "Nothing Can Stop the Loyalty That All Thais Have for the King" [ไม่มีอะไรปิดกั้นความจงรักภักดีของคนไทยทุกคน], a print advertisement celebrating the king's birthday, *Thai Rath*, December 5, 2010.

58. Central Group Ltd., "Dad's Home" [บ้านของพ่อ], a print advertisement celebrating the king's birthday, *Thai Rath*, December 5, 1999.

59. Amway Thailand Ltd., "Dad's Home, People's Happiness" [บ้านของพ่อความสุขของปวงชน], a print advertisement celebrating the king's birthday, *Thai Rath*, December 5, 2006.

60. UCOM Group Plc., "Unite and Come Together and Be Good Citizens in Order to Keep His Majesty's Smile with Us Forever" [ร่วมด้วยช่วยกันเป็นคนดีของสังคม เพื่อเก็บรักษารอยยิ้มของพระองค์ท่านให้คงอยู่ตลอดไป], a print advertisement celebrating the king's birthday, *Siam Rath*, December 6, 2004.

61. Dream Team Thailand Plc., "Wish to See Dad Able to Smile" [อยากเห็นพ่อยิ้มได้], a print advertisement celebrating the king's birthday, *Siam Rath*, December 5, 2010.

62. ThaiBev Plc., "Thais' Smile Is Dad's Smile" [รอยยิ้มของคนไทยคือรอยยิ้มของพ่อ], a print advertisement celebrating the king's birthday, *Phuchatkan*, December 5, 2009.

63. John Hoskin, "The King as Artist," in *King of Thailand in World Focus*, ed. Denis D. Gray (Singapore: Didier Millet, 2008), 166–67.

64. William Stephenson, *A Man Called Intrepid* [นายอินทร์ผู้ปิดทองหลังพระ], trans. Bhumibol Adulyadej (Bangkok: Amarin Printing and Publishing, 1994); Phyllis Auty, *Tito* [ติโต], trans. Bhumibol Adulyadej (Bangkok: Amarin Printing and Publishing 1995); Bhumibol Adulyadej, trans., *The Story of Mahajanaka* [พระมหาชนก] (Bangkok: Amarin Printing and Publishing, 1996); Bhumibol, *Story of Thongdaeng*.

65. Of these forty-eight songs, only two—"Love" [รัก] and "Egg Menu" [เมนูไข่]—were composed after 1980. The former was composed in 1994, the latter in 1995. Rama IX never composed any songs subsequently. See Kasetsart

University, "Royal Songs" [เพลงพระราชนิพนธ์], accessed March 12, 2016, https://web.ku.ac.th/king72/2530/music.htm.

66. H.M. Blues Album Artists, *H.M. Blues Sing and Play Dad's Songs* [*H.M. Blues ร้อง บรรเลง เพลงของพ่อ*], Butterfly Records, 2006. Compact disc.

67. Boon Rawd Brewery Co. Ltd., *Music Composed by His Majesty: Songs in the Hearts of Subjects* [*คีตราชนิพนธ์: บทเพลงในดวงใจราษฎร์*], directed by Nonzee Nimibutr, Wanlop Prasopphon, Phakphum Wongphum, and Yongyut Thong-kongthun, 2015.

68. UCOM Group Plc., "His Majesty Makes Me Realize That I Have Not Lost Yet" [ในหลวงทำให้ผมรู้ว่า ผมยัง ไม่แพ้], a print advertisement celebrating the king's birthday, *Phuchatkan*, December 5, 1997.

69. Shin Corporation Plc., "His Majesty, the Genius" [พระผู้เป็นอัจฉริยะ], a print advertisement celebrating the king's birthday, *Thai Rath*, December 5, 1991, 18; PTT Plc., "To Follow His Majesty, the Thinker" [ขอเดินตามพระองค์ผู้ทรงเป็นนักคิด], a print advertisement celebrating the king's birthday, *Thai Rath*, December 5, 2013.

70. Central Group Ltd., "No Word on Earth Can Elaborate the Meaningful Word 'Dad'" [มิอาจหาคำใดในหล้า ร้อยเรียงเทียบค่าคำว่า 'พ่อ'], a print advertisement celebrating the king's birthday, *Siam Rath*, December 5, 1994; Nestlé Thailand Ltd., "Wish His Majesty a Long and Healthy Life" [ขอจงทรงพระเจริญ มีพระพลานามัย สมบูรณ์], a print advertisement celebrating the king's birthday, *Thai Rath*, December 5, 2000.

71. For the notion of the "two souls" of the paradoxical ideologies of the European bourgeoisie, see Franco Moretti, *The Bourgeois: Between History and Literature* (New York: Verso, 2013), 35; Margaret Hunt, *The Middling Sort: Commerce, Gender, and the Family in England, 1680–1780* (Oakland: University of California Press, 1996); Deirdre McCloskey, *The Bourgeois Virtues: Ethics for an Age of Commerce* (Chicago: University of Chicago Press, 2006). For the American bourgeoisie, see Steve Fraser, *Wall Street: America's Dream Palace* (New Haven, CT: Yale University Press, 2009); Daniel Bell, *The Cultural Contradictions of Capitalism* (New York: Basic Books, 1996); David Brooks, *Bobos in Paradise: The New Upper Class and How They Got There* (New York: Simon & Schuster, 2001).

72. Takashi Fujitani, *Splendid Monarchy: Power and Pageantry in Modern Japan* (Oakland: University of California Press, 1998).

73. Pierre Bourdieu, *Distinction: A Social Critique of the Judgement of Taste*, trans. Richard Nice (Cambridge, MA: Harvard University Press, 1984), 253.

74. Thongchai, *Democracy That Is the Monarch above Politics*, chapter 12.

75. Nop Ponchamni, "Dad's Song" [เพลงของพ่อ], written by Boyd Kosiya-bong, a song celebrating the king's birthday, *Love Is Music*, December 5, 2008.

76. Thai banknotes are designed and produced by the staff of the Note Printing Works, an institution under the jurisdiction of the Bank of Thailand (BOT), and approved by the governor of the BOT and the minister of finance. See Bank of Thailand, "The Banknote Printing Process," accessed January 27,

2017, https://www.bot.or.th/English/Banknotes/production_and_security/Pages/Banknote_production.aspx; "Before Becoming Banknotes" [กว่าจะเป็นธนบัตร], *Phuchatkan*, August 9, 2005.

77. Chatri Prakitnontakan, "Images, Design, and Symbols of Thai Banknotes: Political Reflection" [รูปภาพ ลวดลาย และสัญลักษณ์ธนบัตรไทย: ภาพสะท้อนการเมือง], in *Thai Architecture after the September 19, 2006, Coup* [สถาปัตยกรรมไทยหลังรัฐประหาร 19 กันยา 49] (Nonthaburi: Aan, 2015), 131.

78. The images of Thai banknotes from various series that appear in this section come from the Bank of Thailand, *Banknotes in the Reign of King Rama IX* [ธนบัตรรัชกาลที่ 9] (Bangkok: Bank of Thailand, 2017).

79. Ibid., 140.

80. Satang is a currency unit equivalent to one-hundredth of a Thai baht.

81. Bank of Thailand, "Histories and Series of Banknotes," accessed October 20, 2016, https://www.bot.or.th/English/Banknotes/HistoryAndSeriesOfBanknotes/Pages/evolution_and_series.aspx.

82. Chatri, "Images, Design, and Symbols of Thai Banknotes," 157–58.

83. Bank of Thailand, "Histories and Series of Banknotes."

84. Ibid.

85. Even though the portrait of the British monarchs was occasionally depicted on the pound sterling bills before the twentieth century, it was not regularly practiced by the Bank of England until 1960. See V. H. Hewitt and J. M. Keyworth, *As Good as Gold: 300 Years of British Bank Note Design* (London: British Museum Publications, 1987).

Chapter 4.
The Crown versus the Crowd

1. "Diamond Jubilee Celebration," in *The King of Thailand in World Focus*, ed. Denis D. Gray (Singapore: Didier Millet, 2008), 208.

2. Handley, *The King Never Smiles*, 448.

3. Central Intelligence Agency, "The World Factbook: Distribution of Family Income, Gini Index," accessed December 21, 2016, https://www.cia.gov/library/publications/theworldfactbook/rankorder/2172rank.html.

4. Pasuk Phongpaichit, ed., *Towards an Equal Society in Thailand* [สู่สังคมไทยเสมอหน้า] (Bangkok: Matichon, 2012), 15.

5. Data adapted from NESDB (National Economic and Social Development Board), *Yearbook of the National Economic and Social Development Board* [รายงานประจำปีสำนักงานคณะกรรมการพัฒนาเศรษฐกิจและสังคมแห่งชาติ] (Bangkok: National Economic and Social Development Board, various years).

6. Ibid.

7. Duangmanee Laovakul, "The Concentration of Wealth in Thai Society" [การกระจุกตัวของความมั่งคั่งในสังคมไทย], in *Towards an Equal Society in Thailand*, ed. Pasuk Phongpaichit (Bangkok: Matichon, 2012), 37–59.

8. Glassman, "Provinces Elect Governments," 1304.

9. NESDB, "Poverty and Income Distribution" [ความยากจนและการกระจายราย ได้], September 9, 2016, http://social.nesdb.go.th/SocialStat/StatSubDefault_Final.aspx?catid=13.

10. Pasuk Phongpaichit, "Inequality, Wealth and Thailand's Politics," *Journal of Contemporary Asia* 46, no. 3 (2016): 409.

11. Ibid., 411.

12. The MPI is an average of the top fifty oligarchs in a nation divided by the average wealth per capita. See T. F. Rhoden, "Oligarchy in Thailand?," *Journal of Current Southeast Asian Affairs* 34, no. 1 (2015): 6, 12.

13. Ibid., 17.

14. Pasuk Phongpaichit and Chris Baker, *Thaksin: The Business of Politics in Thailand* (Copenhagen: Nordic Institute of Asian Studies, 2004), 80.

15. Wanya Phuphinyo, *Eyes on the Stars, Feet on the Ground* [ตาดูดาวเท้าติดดิน] (Bangkok: Matichon, 1999).

16. Natenapha, "Companies in Crisis," 48; Ukrist Pathamanand and Chris Baker, "Hello and Goodbye to the Mobile Phone," in *Thai Capital after the 1997 Crisis*, ed. Pasuk Phongpaichit and Chris Baker (Chiang Mai: Silkworm Books, 2008), 110.

17. Pasuk and Baker, *Thaksin*, 101.

18. Ibid., 89.

19. Handley, *The King Never Smiles*, 424.

20. McCargo, "Network Monarchy," 513.

21. Bhumibol Adulyadej, "The King's Speech Given to the Audience of Well-Wishers on the Occasion of the Royal Birthday Anniversary at the Dusidalai Hall, Chitralada Royal Villa, on December 4, 2002," OHM, December 4, 2002.

22. Kevin Hewison, "A Book, the King, and the 2006 Coup," *Journal of Contemporary Asia* 38, no. 1 (2008): 201.

23. Pasuk and Baker, *Thaksin*, 129; Hewison, "A Book, the King, and the 2006 Coup," 203; Handley, *The King Never Smiles*, 425.

24. Glassman, "Provinces Elect Governments," 1318.

25. Pasuk and Baker, *Thaksin*, 107.

26. Pran Phisitsetthakan, ed., *Thaksinomics and Thailand's CEO* [ทักษิโณมิคส์และ CEO ประเทศไทย] (Bangkok: Matichon, 2004), 93, quoted in Pasuk and Baker, *Thaksin*, 103.

27. Pasuk and Baker, *Thaksin*, 97.

28. Kevin Hewison, "Thailand's Capitalism: The Impact of the Economic Crisis," *University of New England Asia Centre Asia Papers*, no. 1 (1999): 36, http://pandora.nla.gov.au/nph-wb/19990829130000/http://www.une.edu.au/asiacenter/Hewison.pdf.

29. Jim Glassman, "Recovering from Crisis: The Case of Thailand's Spatial Fix," *Economic Geography* 83, no. 4 (2007): 349-70.

30. David Harvey, *Seventeen Contradictions and the End of Capitalism* (New York: Oxford University Press, 2015), 151–54.

31. Glassman, "Recovering from Crisis," 358.

32. Pasuk and Baker, *Thaksin*, 71.

33. Chumphon Pratraphon, *How Rich Is Thaksin Really!* [ทักษิณรวยเท่าไหร่แน่!] (Bangkok: Thawatchai Pitchphon, 2002), 105, quoted in Pasuk and Baker, *Thaksin*, 101.

34. Pasuk and Baker, *Thaksin*, 240.

35. Pran, *Thaksinomics*, 68, quoted in Pasuk and Baker, *Thaksin*, 116.

36. Pran, *Thaksinomics*, 375–76, quoted in Pasuk and Baker, *Thaksin*, 187.

37. Pasuk and Baker, *Thaksin*, 187.

38. Election Commission of Thailand, "The Result of February 6, 2005, General Election" [การเลือกตั้งสมาชิกสภาผู้แทนราษฎรเป็นการทั่วไป เมื่อวันที่ 6 กุมภาพันธ์ 2548], accessed December 19, 2016, http://www.ect.go.th/th/wp-content/uploads/2013/10/mp48.pdf.

39. Pasuk and Baker, *Thaksin*, 142.

40. Pasuk and Baker, *Thai Capital after the 1997 Crisis*, 10.

41. Pasuk and Baker, *Thaksin*, 206.

42. Kasian Tejapira, "Toppling Thaksin," *New Left Review* 39 (May–June 2006): 5–37; Oliver Pye and Wolfram Schaffar, "The 2006 Anti-Thaksin Movement in Thailand: An Analysis," *Journal of Contemporary Asia* 38, no. 1 (2008): 38–61; Elliot Norton, "Illiberal Democrats versus Undemocratic Liberals: The Struggle over the Future of Thailand's Fragile Democracy," *Asian Journal of Political Science* 20, no. 1 (April 2012): 46–69; Aim Sinpeng, "Corruption, Morality, and the Politics of Reform in Thailand," *Asian Politics and Policy* 6, no. 4 (2013): 421–40.

43. Duncan McCargo, "Thai Politics as Reality TV," *Journal of Asian Studies* 68, no. 1 (February 2009): 12.

44. Handley, *The King Never Smiles*, 432.

45. Hewison, "A Book, the King, and the 2006 Coup," 207.

46. Daniel Unger and Chandra Mahakanjana, *Thai Politics: Between Democracy and Its Discontents* (Boulder, CO: Lynne Rienner, 2016), 9.

47. Marx and Engels, "Communist Manifesto," 242.

48. Kevin Hewison, "Crafting Thailand's New Social Contract," *Pacific Review* 17, no. 4 (2004): 503–22.

49. Glassman, "Provinces Elect Governments," 1313.

50. Bhumibol Adulyadej, "The King's Speech Given to the Audience of Well-Wishers on the Occasion of the Royal Birthday Anniversary at the Dusidalai Hall, Chitralada Royal Villa, on December 4, 2005," OHM, December 4, 2005.

51. McCargo, "Network Monarchy," 513.

52. Ibid., 515.

53. Thanapol Eawsakul and Chaithawat Tulathon, "Who's Who in the Privy Council under Democracy with the King as Head of the State?" [ใครเป็นใคร

ในองคมนตรีแห่งประชาธิปไตยอันมีพระมหากษัตริย์เป็นประมุข], *Fa Diew Kan* 12, no. 2 (May–August 2015): 68.

54. Thongchai Winichakul, "Toppling Democracy," *Journal of Contemporary Asia* 38, no. 1 (February 2008): 30.

55. Hewison, "A Book, the King, and the 2006 Coup," 206.

56. Ibid.

57. "The Lost Sheep" [ลูกแกะหลงทาง], *Phuchatkan*, September 9, 2005.

58. Khamnun Sitthisaman, *The Sondhi Phenomenon: From Yellow Shirts to Blue Scarves* [*ปรากฏการณ์สนธิ: จากเสื้อเหลืองถึงผ้าพันคอสีฟ้า*] (Bangkok: Ban Phra Athit, 2006); "Sondhi Expands on 'Finland Plan,'" *Bangkok Post*, May 21, 2006; "Thaksin Clearly Wanted Republic, Critics Charge," *The Nation*, May 25, 2006.

59. Michael Connors, "Article of Faith: The Failure of Royal Liberalism in Thailand," *Journal of Contemporary Asia* 38, no. 1 (February 2008): 143–65.

60. Kasian, "Toppling Thaksin," 36.

61. Ibid., 9.

62. Bhumibol Adulyadej, "The King's Speech Given to the Judges of the Supreme Administrative Court at Klai Kangwon Palace, Hua Hin, on April 25, 2006," OHM, April 25, 2006.

63. Streckfuss, "Freedom and Silence," 121.

64. Pavin, *"Good Coup" Gone Bad*, 292–93.

65. Giles Ji Ungpakorn, *A Coup for the Rich: Thailand's Political Crisis* (Bangkok: Workers Democracy Publishing, 2007).

66. Federico Ferrara, "Unfinished Business: The Contagion of Conflict over a Century of Thai Political Development," in *"Good Coup" Gone Bad: Thailand's Political Development since Thaksin's Downfall*, ed. Pavin Chachavalpongpun (Singapore: Institute of Southeast Asian Studies, 2014), 38.

67. Of 480 seats in the House of Parliament, the PPP took 233 while the Democrat Party took 165. Election Commission of Thailand, "The Result of December 23, 2007, General Election" [การเลือกตั้งสมาชิกสภาผู้แทนราษฎรเป็นการทั่วไปเมื่อวันที่ 23 ธันวาคม 2550], accessed December 19, 2016, http://www.ect.go.th/th/?page_id=494.

68. Truth for Reconciliation Committee of Thailand, *The Final Report of Truth for Reconciliation Committee of Thailand* [*รายงานฉบับสมบูรณ์คณะกรรมการอิสระเพื่อตรวจสอบหาข้อเท็จจริงเพื่อการปรองดองแห่งชาติ*] (Bangkok: Truth for Reconciliation Committee of Thailand, 2012).

69. According to these scholars, the Red Shirts (and the Yellow Shirts) were too diverse to be categorized and were not driven by class-based issues. Ammar Siamwalla and Somchai Jitsuchon, for example, asserted, "There is no substantial difference in the social backgrounds of people who support the Red and Yellow points of views." Likewise, Shawn Crispin claimed, "For all the romantic portrayals of a rich-versus-poor class struggle, Thailand's political battle boils down to a fight between competing elites who, for all their pretensions of fighting for democracy and social justice, are in actuality illiberal mirror images

of one another." Ammar Siamwalla and Somchai Jitsuchon, "The Socio-economic Bases of the Red/Yellow Divide: A Statistical Analysis," in *Bangkok, May 2010: Perspectives on a Divided Thailand*, ed. Michael Montesano, Pavin Chachaval- pongpun, and Aekapol Chongvilaivan (Singapore: Institute of Southeast Asian Studies, 2012), 65; Shawn Crispin, "Thailand's Classless Conflict," in *Bangkok, May 2010: Perspectives on a Divided Thailand*, ed. Michael Montesano, Pavin Cha- chavalpongpun, and Aekapol Chongvilaivan (Singapore: Institute of Southeast Asian Studies, 2012), 118.

70. To be precise, 68 percent of the Red Shirt protesters came from outside Bangkok; among these, 48 percent lived in the North and Northeast. As Thai- land's average monthly wage during 1999–2006 was 13,803.15 baht, 42 percent of the Red Shirt protesters earned less than this average. In terms of education, 74 percent did not hold bachelor or advanced degrees. See Asia Foundation, *Profile of the Protestors: A Survey of Pro- and Anti-government Demonstrators in Bangkok on November 30, 2013* (Bangkok: Asia Foundation, 2013), 4–7.

71. Even though this survey was not a survey of the PAD per se, as it was based on an examination of hundreds of thousands of demonstrators who gathered in late 2013 under the banner of the People's Democratic Reform Committee (PDRC), I consider the PDRC to be a mass movement that continued to espouse PAD's political ideas and shared many of the same participants. Therefore, they can be generally categorized as Yellow Shirts. According to the survey, 57 percent of the Yellow Shirt protesters lived in Bangkok, 63 percent earned more than the monthly national average wage, and 32 percent even earned five times more than the national average. Furthermore, 68 percent had degrees from institutions of higher education. Asia Foundation, *Profile of the Protestors*, 4–7.

72. Naruemon Thabchumpon and Duncan McCargo, "Urbanized Villagers in the 2010 Thai Redshirt Protest: Not Just Poor Farmers?," *Asian Survey* 51, no. 6 (2011): 993–1018.

73. Charles Keyes, "Cosmopolitan Villagers and Populist Democracy in Thailand," *South East Asia Research* 20, no. 3 (2012): 343–60.

74. Andrew Walker, "The Rural Constitution and the Everyday Politics of Elections in Northern Thailand," *Journal of Contemporary Asia* 38, no. 1 (2008): 84–105.

75. Claudio Sopranzetti, "Burning Red Desires: Isan Migrants and the Poli- tics of Desire in Contemporary Thailand," *South East Asia Research* 20, no. 3 (2012): 361–79.

76. Ibid., 373.

77. Jim Glassman, "From Reds to Red Shirts: Political Evolution and Devo- lution in Thailand," *Environment and Planning* 42, no.4 (2010): 769.

78. Jim Glassman, "Cracking Hegemony in Thailand: Gramsci, Bourdieu, and the Dialectics of Rebellion," *Journal of Contemporary Asia* 41, no. 1 (2010): 38.

79. Ibid., 40.

80. Glassman, "From Reds to Red Shirts," 770.

81. Brown, *The Elite and the Economy in Siam*, 81–86.

82. Glassman, "Cracking Hegemony in Thailand," 40–41.

83. Ian Storey and Lee Poh Onn, eds., *Regional Outlook: Southeast Asia, 2009–2010* (Singapore: Institute of Southeast Asian Studies, 2009), 49.

84. Sopranzetti, "Burning Red Desires," 373.

85. Karl Marx, *Grundrisse: Foundations of the Critique of Political Economy*, trans. Martin Nicolaus (New York: Penguin Books, 1993), 612.

86. Ibid., 613.

87. Ibid., 288.

88. Ibid., 286.

89. Marx, *Capital*, vol. 1, 873.

90. Ibid.

91. Ibid., 874, 876.

92. Daniel Unger, "Sufficiency Economy and the Bourgeois Virtues," *Asian Affairs: An American Review* 36, no. 3 (2009): 148.

93. Keyes, "Cosmopolitan Villagers," 345, 353.

94. Pattana Kitiarsa, "From Red to Red: An Auto-ethnography of Economic and Political Transitions in a Northeastern Thai Village," in *Bangkok, May 2010: Perspectives on a Divided Thailand*, ed. Michael Montesano, Pavin Chachavalpongpun, and Aekapol Chongvilaivan (Singapore: Institute of Southeast Asian Studies, 2012), 232, 246.

95. Ibid., 243.

96. Phruek Thaothawin, "The Practice of the Sufficiency Economy in a Village: The Elite's Control of the Countryside" [ปฏิบัติการพอเพียงในหมู่บ้าน: การควบคุม ชนบทของชนชั้นนำ], *Fa Diew Kan* 6, no. 2 (April–June 2008): 70–86.

97. Andrew Walker, "Royal Sufficiency and Elite Misrepresentation of Rural Livelihoods," in *Saying the Unsayable: Monarchy and Democracy in Thailand*, edited by Soren Ivarsson and Lotte Isager (Copenhagen: Nordic Institute of Asian Studies Press, 2010), 243–44.

98. Nick Nostitz, "The Red Shirts: From Anti-coup Protesters to Social Mass Movement," in *"Good Coup" Gone Bad: Thailand's Political Development since Thaksin's Downfall*, ed. Pavin Chachavalpongpun (Singapore: Institute of Southeast Asian Studies, 2014), 181.

99. Thongchai Winichakul, "The Monarchy and Anti-monarchy: Two Elephants in the Room of Thai Politics and the State of Denial," in *"Good Coup" Gone Bad: Thailand's Political Development since Thaksin's Downfall*, ed. Pavin Chachavalpongpun (Singapore: Institute of Southeast Asian Studies, 2014), 97.

100. In Thai culture, *water buffalo* (*khwai*) is a contemptuous term referring to a stupid person.

101. Pongpat Wachirabunjong, "Speech Accepting the Best Supporting Actor Award at the Natarat Ceremony, 2010" [คำกล่าวสุนทรพจน์ในฐานะผู้ชนะรางวัลนักแสดง สมทบชายยอดเยี่ยมรางวัลนาฏราช ปี 2553], quoted in "Stars Wept in the Natarat

Ceremony and Saluted the King" [ดาราหลั่งน้ำตาในงานนาฏราช น้อมเกล้าเทิศทูน ในหลวง], *Thai Rath*, May 16, 2010.

102. "Queen Attends Slain Protester's Cremation," *The Nation*, October 14, 2008.

103. Pavin, *"Good Coup" Gone Bad*, 6.

104. Khorapin Phuaphansawat, "My Eyes Are Open but My Lips Are Whispering: Linguistic and Symbolic Forms of Resistance in Thailand during 2006–2016" (PhD diss., University of Massachusetts Amherst, 2017), chapters 3 and 4.

105. David Streckfuss, "Kings in the Age of Nations: The Paradox of Lèse-Majesté as Political Crime in Thailand," *Comparative Studies in Society and History* 37, no. 3 (July 1995): 446, 472.

106. "Weapons of the weak" is the term Scott used to describe "everyday arts of resistance" in which forms of opposition remain characteristically and deliberately subtle, nonconfrontational, and anonymous. Those forms of resistance include rumor, gossip, jokes, disguises, linguistic tricks, metaphors, euphemisms, folktales, ritual gestures, anonymity, and name-calling. See James C. Scott, *Weapons of the Weak: Everyday Forms of Peasant Resistance* (New Haven, CT: Yale University Press, 1985), xvii; James C. Scott, *Domination and the Arts of Resistance: Hidden Transcripts* (New Haven, CT: Yale University Press, 1990), 156.

107. Faiyen, "One Drop of Sweat" [เหงื่อหยดเดียว], on *Songs for a Democratic Revolution* [บทเพลงปฏิวัติประชาธิปไตย], produced by Yonok, mixed by Khoontong, 2013, compact disc.

108. Phiangkham Pradapkhwam, "The Ones Who Work Industriously Are the People" [ผู้ตรากตรำทำงานหนักคือประชาชน], in *All Beloved Citizens* [รามฎรที่รักทั้ง หลาย] (Bangkok: Aan, 2011), 56–57.

109. Ünaldi, *Working towards the Monarchy*, 216.

110. Faiyen, "Advertising Gone Wrong" [โฆษณาพาจน], on *Songs for a Democratic Revolution* [บทเพลงปฏิวัติประชาธิปไตย], produced by Yonok, mixed by Khoontong, 2013, compact disc.

111. Ünaldi, *Working towards the Monarchy*, 216.

112. Ibid.

113. Ibid.

114. Mainueng Ko Kunthi, "Constituting the People's Constitution" [สถาปนาสถาบันประชาชน], in *The People's Poet* [กวีรามฎร] (Bangkok: Klum Patinya Na San, 2014), 138–44.

115. Faiyen, "Dad" [พ่อ], on *Decay* [เสื่อม], written by Port, mixed by Khoontong, 2016, music download.

116. Ünaldi, *Working towards the Monarchy*, 217.

117. Ibid., 216.

118. James Buchanan, "Translating Thailand's Protests: An Analysis of Red Shirt Rhetoric," *ASEAS: Austrian Journal of South-East Asian Studies* 6, no. 1 (2013): 77.

119. Nostitz, "Red Shirts," 185.

120. Phiangkham Pradapkhwam, "God Gave Birth to Me, the Free; This God's Name Is the People" [พระเจ้ากำเนิดข้ามาเสรี-พระเจ้าองค์นี้ชื่อประชาชน], in *All Beloved Citizens* (Bangkok: Aan, 2011), 66–68.

121. Rangsan Haruehanroengra, "Full Democracy . . . Not!" [ประชาธิปไตยที่สมบูรณ์ . . . เหรอ], in *40 Years of October 14: Protect a Will to a Full Democracy of the October 14 Heroes* [40 ปี 14 ตุลา: จงพิทักษ์เจตนารมณ์ประชาธิปไตยสมบูรณ์ของวีรชน 14 ตุลาคม] (Bangkok: Committee of the October 14 Memorial, 2013), 47–48.

122. Anon Nampa, "Big Boss" [นายใหญ่], in *40 Years of October 14: Protect a Will to a Full Democracy of the October 14 Heroes* (Bangkok: Committee of the October 14 Memorial), 115–18.

123. Faiyen, "Black Shirts" [คนเสื้อดำ], on *Decay* [เสื่อม], written by Au, Jom, Khoontong, and Glauy, mixed by Khoontong, 2016, music download.

124. Vincent Boudreau, *Resisting Dictatorship: Repression and Protest in Southeast Asia* (Cambridge: Cambridge University Press, 2001), 3.

125. Corey Robin, *The Reactionary Mind: Conservatism from Edmund Burke to Sarah Palin* (New York: Oxford University Press, 2011), 5.

126. Corey Robin, *Fear: The History of a Political Idea* (New York: Oxford University Press, 2004), 6.

127. Thongchai, "Monarchy and Anti-Monarchy," 97.

128. Sarun Krittikarn, "Entertainment Nationalism: The Royal Gaze and the Gaze at the Royals," in *Saying the Unsayable: Monarchy and Democracy in Thailand*, edited by Soren Ivarsson and Lotte Isager (Copenhagen: Nordic Institute of Asian Studies Press, 2010), 68.

129. Ibid., 69.

130. Thongchai McIntyre, "The Picture Every Home Has" [รูปที่มีทุกบ้าน], written by Nitipong Honark, a song celebrating the king's eightieth birthday, December 5, 2007.

131. Asanee and Wasan Chotikul, "To Be a Servant under His Feet in Every Afterlife" [ขอเป็นข้ารองบาททุกชาติไป], written by Nitipong Honark, a song celebrating the king's eighty-fourth birthday, December 5, 2011.

132. Sala Nakbamrung, *The Comics for Celebrating King Rama IX* [การ์ตูนเทิดให้องค์ราชันย์รัชกาลที่ 9] (Bangkok: Amarin Printing and Publishing, 2011).

133. Campaign of Thinking Sufficiently according to the Sufficiency Economy Philosophy, *The Celestial Couple: The Two Charismatic Royals* [คู่ฟ้า สองพระบารมี] (Bangkok: Internal Security Operations Command, 2010).

134. Chatri, "Images, Design, and Symbols of Thai Banknotes," 160–61.

135. Ernest Mandel, "Introduction," in Karl Marx, *Capital*, vol. 1, trans. Ben Fowkes (London: Penguin Books, 1990), 49.

136. Louis Althusser, *On the Reproduction of Capitalism: Ideology and Ideological State Apparatuses*, trans. G. M. Goshgarian (New York: Verso, 2014).

137. Election Commission of Thailand, "The Result of July 3, 2011, General Election" [การเลือกตั้งสมาชิกสภาผู้แทนราษฎรเป็นการทั่วไป เมื่อวันที่ 3 กรกฎาคม 2554],

accessed December 19, 2016, http://www.ect.go.th/th/wp-content/uploads /2013/10/mp_54.pdf.

138. Keyes, "Cosmopolitan Villagers," 357; Glassman, "Provinces Elect Governments," 1317.

139. *Asian Correspondent*, "Constitution Court Judge: High Speed Rail Not Necessary for Thailand," January 9, 2014, https://asiancorrespondent. com/2014/01/constitution-court-judge-high-speed-rail-not-necessary-for -thailand/.

140. Chris Baker, "The 2014 Thai Coup and Some Roots of Authoritarianism," *Journal of Contemporary Asia* 46, no. 3 (2016): 391–93; Kasian Tejapira, "The Irony of Democratization and the Decline of Royal Hegemony in Thailand," *Southeast Asian Studies* 5, no. 2 (August 2006): 229–31.

141. Prayut Chan-o-cha, quoted in Veerayooth Kanchoochat and Kevin Hewison, "Introduction: Understanding Thailand's Politics," *Journal of Contemporary Asia* 46, no. 3 (2016): 375.

142. Baker, "2014 Thai Coup," 389–90.

143. Ibid., 390.

144. Claudio Sopranzetti, "Thailand's Relapse: The Implications of the May 2014 Coup," *Journal of Asian Studies*, 75 no. 2 (May 2016): 299–316.

145. Chambers and Napisa, "Resilience of Monarchised Military," 440.

146. Baker, "2014 Thai Coup," 390.

147. Ibid.

148. "Government Defends Lese Majeste Sentences," *Bangkok Post*, August 9, 2015.

149. FIDH (International Federation of Human Rights), "Thirty-Six and Counting: Lèse-Majesté Imprisonment under Thailand's Military Junta," February 26, 2016, https://www.fidh.org/IMG/pdf/fidh_thailand_report_lese_ majeste.pdf.

150. These are the cases of Thanakorn Siriphaiboon, Sulak Sivaraksa, Aree Klapsatien, Pornthip Munkong and Patiwat Saraiyeam, Glyn Davies, Chaowanat Musikabhumi, and Thaweeporn Kummetha respectively. See each case in detail in ibid.

151. Khorapin, "My Eyes Are Open," chapter 1.

152. Karl Marx, *Critique of Hegel's "Philosophy of Right,"* ed. Joseph O'Malley, trans. Annette Jolin and Joseph O'Malley (Cambridge: Cambridge University Press, 1977), 33.

153. Bagehot, *English Constitution*, 118.

154. Ibid., 119.

155. Ibid., 119–20.

156. "Profile: Thailand's New King Vajiralongkorn," BBC, December 1, 2006.

157. David Jolly and Thomas Fuller, "Thai Prince's Plane Is Impounded in Germany," *New York Times*, July 31, 2011; "Thailand's Crown Prince Has Plane Impounded in Germany," *The Telegraph*, July 14, 2001.

158. James Hookway, "Thailand's Royal Fortune Looms over Crown Prince's Ascension to the Throne," *Wall Street Journal*, November 17, 2016; Thomas Fuller, "Thai Princess, Queen-to-Be, Gives Up Title," *New York Times*, December 12, 2014; "The Minister of Finance, on Behalf of the Head of the Crown Property Bureau, Clarifies the Issue of Royal Grants Given to Miss Srirasmi Suwadee" [การชี้แจงของรัฐมนตรีว่าการกระทรวงการคลัง ในฐานะประธานสำนักงานทรัพย์สินส่วนพระมหากษัตริย์ กรณีการพระราชทานเงินให้ท่านผู้หญิงศรีรัศมิ์ สุวะดี], *Ministry of Finance News*, December 15, 2014.

159. For the history of Thailand's royal succession, see "The Crown: Succession," in *King Bhumibol Adulyadej: A Life's Work; Thailand's Monarchy in Perspective*, ed. Nicholas Grossman and Dominic Faulder (Singapore: Didier Millet, 2012), 325–33.

160. "Thai Fortune Teller Held under Royal Defamation Law Found Dead," *The Guardian*, November 9, 2015; "Never Saw It Coming: A Purge of Prominent People Is Causing Alarm in Thailand," *Economist*, November 24, 2015; Alison Smale and Thomas Fuller, "Thailand Looks to Likely Future King with Apprehension," *New York Times*, October 14, 2016.

161. "PM: Nation Is in Its Greatest Sorrow, Expects New King by Tradition," *Bangkok Post*, October 13, 2016.

162. "Thailand's Crown Prince to Delay Ascension to Throne after Father's Death," *The Guardian*, October 16, 2016; Annie Gowen, "Thailand Delays Elevating a New King," *Washington Post*, October 15, 2006.

Chapter 5.
All Hail the King

1. "Thailand Stocks, Currency Slump amid Concern over King's Health," *Bloomberg*, October 12, 2016.

2. Richard Paddock, "'The Greatest Loss and Despair': Thais Mourn Their King," *New York Times*, October 13, 2016.

3. "Kingdom Grieves," *The Nation*, October 14, 2016.

4. Sarah Dean, "Thousands Line the Streets of Bangkok as a Convoy Returns Thailand's King to His Grand Palace and the Crown Prince Presides over the Bathing of His Body in a Traditional Buddhist Funeral Rite," *Daily Mail*, October 14, 2016.

5. "Rush for the King's Memorabilia," *Bangkok Post*, October 25, 2016.

6. David Li, "Thailand's New Playboy King, Crown Prince Maha Vajiralongkorn," *New York Post*, October 13, 2016; Benjamin Kentish, "Crop-Tops, Mistresses, and Flying Poodles: Meet the Next King of Thailand," *The Independent*, October 15, 2016.

7. David Streckfuss, "In Thailand, a King's Coup?," *New York Times*, April 9, 2017.

8. Royal Thai Government Gazette, *Royal Service Administration Act, 2017*

[*พระราชบัญญัติระเบียบราชการ ในพระองค์ พ.ศ. 2560*], May 1, 2017; Royal Thai Government Gazette, *Royal Decree Organizing Governmental Affairs and Personnel Administration for Royal Service, 2017* [*พระราชกฤษฎีกาจัดระเบียบและการบริหารงานบุคคลของ ราชการ ในพระองค์ พ.ศ. 2560*], May 10, 2017.

9. Royal Thai Government Gazette, *Crown Property Act of 2017* [*พระราช บัญญัติจัดระเบียบทรัพย์สินฝ่ายพระมหากษัตริย์ พ.ศ. 2560*], July 16, 2017; Royal Thai Government Gazette, *Crown Property Act of 2018* [*พระราชบัญญัติจัดระเบียบทรัพย์สินพระมหา กษัตริย์ พ.ศ. 2561*], November 3, 2018.

10. "Thai King Maha Vajiralongkorn Named Owner of Chakri Dynasty's Billions," *Japan Times*, June 16, 2018; "Thai King Maha Vajiralongkorn Granted Full Ownership of Crown Billions," *Straits Times*, June 16, 2018; "Thai King Signs Crown's $30bn Assets Over to Himself," *Al Jazeera*, June 17, 2018.

11. Suprani Khongnirandonsuk, "Unveiling the Twilight Zone, the Crown Property Bureau" [*เปิดแดนสนธยาสำนักงานทรัพย์สินฯ*], *Phuchatkan Rai Sapda*, November 1992.

12. Royal Thai Government Gazette, *An Announcement regarding an Appointment of the Crown Property Bureau's Board of Directors* [*ประกาศแต่งตั้งคณะ กรรมการทรัพย์สินส่วนพระมหากษัตริย์*], July 17, 2017.

13. Amy Lefevre, "Thai Royal Agencies Brought under Control of New King," *Reuters*, April 21, 2017; Michael Peel, "Thailand's Monarchy: Where Does Love End and Dread Begin?," *Financial Times*, October 12, 2017.

14. Royal Thai Government Gazette, *An Announcement regarding an Appointment of Privy Counselors* [*ประกาศแต่งตั้งองคมนตรี*], December 6, 2016.

15. Royal Thai Government Gazette, *An Announcement regarding an Appointment of Privy Counselors* [*ประกาศแต่งตั้งองคมนตรี*], March 12, 2017.

16. Pracharath Rak Samakkhi Social Enterprise Co. Ltd., "About Our Company," PRS Thailand, accessed July 22, 2018, http://prsthailand.com/en/aboutus.

17. Committee for Developing a Grassroots Economy and a Civil State, *United Forces for a Civil State* [*สานพลังประชารัฐ*] (Bangkok: Amarin Printing and Publishing, 2016), 80.

18. Thatma Prathumwan, "Pasuk Phongpaichit: 'Deep Capital,' an Analysis of the Civil State as a Consequence of State-Capital Relationships" [*ผาสุก พงษ์ ไพจิตร: 'ทุนพันลึก' บทวิเคราะห์ประชารัฐ ผลพวงจากความสัมพันธ์ รัฐ-ทุน*], *Prachatai*, June 18, 2018, https://prachatai.com/journal/2018/06/77470.

19. "Bangkok Observation Tower to Be Built with No Bidding," *Bangkok Post*, June 27, 2017.

20. Wichit Chantanusornsiri, "Treasury: Observation Tower Will Generate B47 Billion," *Bangkok Post*, June 30, 2017.

21. Grand Canal Land Public Company Limited, "The Super Tower: The ASEAN's Tallest Building," accessed July 22, 2018, http://www.grandcanalland.com/en/contact.php.

22. Peter Jackson, "A Grateful Son, A Military King: Thai Media Accounts of the Accession of Rama X to the Throne," *ISEAS Perspective*, no. 26 (April 2017): 1–7.

23. "Pictures of Happiness, His Majesty and the Royal Family" [เปิดภาพอบอุ่นในหลวงกับพระบรมวงศานุวงศ์], *Khaosod*, October 14, 2016; "Picture Perfect, His Majesty Prostrated Himself before King Rama IX and the Queen" [ภาพประทับใจสมเด็จพระเจ้าอยู่หัวทรงกราบพระบาทในหลวงร.9-พระราชินี], *Matichon*, July 25, 2017.

24. "Appreciating Pictures of a Warm Relationship among King Rama X, His Daughters, and His Son" [ชมภาพความอบอุ่นสายสัมพันธ์ในหลวง ร.10 และพระราชธิดาพระราชโอรส], *Matichon*, December 5, 2016.

25. "King Rama X Granted His Drawings for Making a New Year Card and Fund-Raising for the Flood Alleviation Scheme in the South" [ร.10 พระราชทานภาพวาดฝีพระหัตถ์ทำบัตรอวยพร ระดมทุนช่วยน้ำท่วมใต้], *Thai Rath*, January 21, 2017.

26. Nick Pritchard, "Monarch Madness," *The Sun*, May 17, 2017; Natalie O'Neill, "Thailand's New King Used His Poodle to Spite His Father," *New York Post*, October 14, 2016; "Thai-Protz-Prinz Maha Vajiralongkorn: Warum die Thailänder diese Fotos nicht sehen dürfen," *Bild*, October 14, 2016.

27. "Thai King to Pardon up to 150,000 Inmates, Including Royal Insult Convicts," *Reuters*, December 13, 2016.

28. Freedom of Expression Documentation Center, "Nunhayati: A Blind Woman Sharing a Leftist Article" [นูรฮายาตี: หญิงตาบอดแชร์บทความเอียงซ้าย], accessed July 23, 2018, https://freedom.ilaw.or.th/case/813.

29. Freedom of Expression Documentation Center, "Wichai: Faking a Facebook Account That Insults Royalty" [วิชัย: ปลอมเฟซบุ๊กหมิ่น], accessed July 23, 2018, https://freedom.ilaw.or.th/th/case/722.

30. Thai Lawyers for Human Rights, "A Verdict of 6 Teenagers Who Set Fire to the Royal Arches: A Consequence of Political Conflicts That Have Been Repressed" [ชี้ชะตา 6 วัยรุ่นเผาซุ้มฯ ผลพวงความขัดแย้งทางการเมืองที่ถูกกด], January 31, 2018, http://www.tlhr2014.com/th/?p=6162.

31. "Number of Mourners at Palace Tops 12 Million," *The Nation*, October 3, 2017.

32. "Thailand Kicks Off Sumptuous Funeral of King Bhumibol Adulyadej," *Reuters*, October 25, 2017.

33. Rom Bunnak, *The Royal Cremation Complex: The Royal Crematorium and Royal Chariots in the Bangkok Era* [พระเมรุมาศ: พระโกศและราชรถสมัยกรุงรัตนโกสินทร์] (Bangkok: Sayam Banthuek, 2008), 67. If inflation is taken into account, the cost of Rama VIII's funeral would be equivalent to US$1,414,094 in 2017.

34. "Nineteen Million People Laid Funeral Flowers for Rama IX," *Bangkok Post*, October 27, 2017.

35. "Bangkok Pauses for Final Farewell," *Bangkok Post*, October 11, 2017.

36. Smith, *Theory of Moral Sentiments*, 52–58.

37. Draper, *Karl Marx's Theory of Revolution*, 2:171, 232.

38. Max Weber, *From Max Weber: Essays in Sociology*, trans. and ed. H. H. Gerth and C. Wright Mills (New York: Oxford University Press, 1946), 347.

39. "Donald Trump Profile," *Forbes*, July 23, 2018.

40. Hayley Richardson, "Comb Sweet Comb," *The Sun*, November 15, 2016.

41. "Putin Says Will Step Down as President after Term Expires in 2024," *Reuters*, May 25, 2018.

42. "China's Xi Allowed to Remain 'President for Life' as Term Limits Removed," BBC, March 11, 2018.

43. Peter Kenyon, "Turkey's President and His 1,100-Room 'White Palace,'" National Public Radio, December 24, 2014.

44. Thomas Piketty, *Capital in the Twenty-First Century* (London: Belknap Press, 2014), chapter 11.

45. Karl Marx, "Preface to the First Edition," in *Capital*, vol. 1, trans. Ben Fowkes (London: Penguin Books, 1990), 91.

Bibliography

English-Language Sources

Aim Sinpeng. "Corruption, Morality, and the Politics of Reform in Thailand." *Asian Politics and Policy* 6, no. 4 (2013): 421–40.

Akira, Suehiro. *Capital Accumulation in Thailand, 1855–1985*. Chiang Mai: Silkworm Books, 1989.

Althusser, Louis. *On the Reproduction of Capitalism: Ideology and Ideological State Apparatuses*. Translated by G. M. Goshgarian. New York: Verso, 2014.

Ammar Siamwalla and Somchai Jitsuchon. "The Socio-economic Bases of the Red/Yellow Divide: A Statistical Analysis." In *Bangkok, May 2010: Perspectives on a Divided Thailand*, edited by Michael Montesano, Pavin Chachavalpongpun, and Aekapol Chongvilaivan, 64–71. Singapore: Institute of Southeast Asian Studies, 2012.

Anderson, Benedict. "Introduction to *In the Mirror*." In *Exploration and Irony in Studies of Siam over Forty Years*, 77–99. Ithaca, NY: Cornell University Press, 2014.

———. "Radicalism after Communism in Thailand and Indonesia." In *Exploration and Irony in Studies of Siam over Forty Years*, 117–27. Ithaca, NY: Cornell University Press, 2014.

———. "Studies of the Thai State: The State of Thai Studies." In *The Study of Thailand: Analyses of Knowledge, Approaches, and Prospects in Anthropology, Art*

History, Economics, History, and Political Science, edited by Eliezer B. Ayal, 193–247. Athens: Ohio University Center for International Studies, Southeast Asia Program, 1978.

———. "Withdrawal Symptoms: Social and Cultural Aspects of the October 6 Coup." In *Exploration and Irony in Studies of Siam over Forty Years*, 47–76. Ithaca, NY: Cornell University Press, 2014.

Anderson, Lisa. "Absolutism and the Resilience of Monarchy in the Middle East." *Political Science Quarterly* 106, no. 1 (Spring 1991): 1–15.

Anderson, Perry. "Components of the National Culture." *New Left Review* 50 (July–August 1968): 3–57.

———. *Lineages of the Absolutist State*. New York: Verso, 2013.

———. "Origins of the Present Crisis." *New Left Review* 23 (January–February 1964): 26–52.

———. "Socialism and Pseudo-Empiricism." *New Left Review* 35 (January–February 1966): 2–42.

Anek Laothamatas. *Business Associations and the New Political Economy of Thailand: From Bureaucratic Polity to Liberal Corporatism*. Boulder, CO: Westview Press, 1992.

Aristotle. *Politics*. Translated by Ernest Barker. Oxford: Oxford University Press, 1995.

Asia Foundation. *Profile of the Protestors: A Survey of Pro- and Anti-government Demonstrators in Bangkok on November 30, 2013*. Bangkok: Asia Foundation, 2013.

Bagehot, Walter. *The English Constitution*. Ithaca, NY: Cornell University Press, 1966.

Baker, Chris. "The 2014 Thai Coup and Some Roots of Authoritarianism." *Journal of Contemporary Asia* 46, no. 3 (2016): 388–404.

Balmer, John. "Scrutinising the British Monarchy: The Corporate Brand That Was Shaken, Stirred, and Survived." *Management Decision* 47, no. 4 (2009): 639–75.

Barmé, Scot. *Woman, Man, Bangkok: Love, Sex, and Popular Culture in Thailand*. New York: Rowman & Littlefield, 2002.

Batson, Benjamin A. *The End of the Absolute Monarchy in Siam*. Singapore: Oxford University Press, 1986.

———. *Siam's Political Future: Documents from the End of the Absolute Monarchy*. Ithaca, NY: Cornell University Press, 1974.

Bell, Daniel. *The Cultural Contradictions of Capitalism*. New York: Basic Books, 1996.

Bendix, Reinhard. *Kings or People: Power and the Mandate to Rule*. Oakland: University of California Press, 1980.

Bhumibol Adulyadej. "The King's Commencement Address at Kasetsart University on July 18, 1974." OHM, July 18, 1974.

———. "The King's Speech Given to the Audience of Well-Wishers on the

Occasion of the King's Birthday at the Dusidalai Hall, Chitralada Royal Villa." OHM, various years.

———. "The King's Speech Given to the Judges of the Supreme Administrative Court at Klai Kangwon Palace, Hua Hin, on April 25, 2006." OHM, April 25, 2006.

Boudreau, Vincent. *Resisting Dictatorship: Repression and Protest in Southeast Asia*. Cambridge: Cambridge University Press, 2001.

Bourdieu, Pierre. *Distinction: A Social Critique of the Judgement of Taste*. Translated by Richard Nice. Cambridge, MA: Harvard University Press, 1984.

Bowie, Katherine. "Peasant Perspectives on the Political Economy of the Northern Thai Kingdom of Chiang Mai in the Nineteenth Century: Implications for the Understanding of Peasant Political Expression." PhD diss., University of Chicago, 1988.

———. *Rituals of National Loyalty: An Anthropology of the State and the Village Scout Movement in Thailand*. New York: Columbia University Press, 1997.

———. "Slavery in Nineteenth-Century Northern Thailand: Archival Anecdotes and Village Voices." In *State Power and Culture in Thailand*, edited by E. Paul Durrenberger, 114–26. New Haven, CT: Yale Southeast Asia Studies, 1996.

Bowman, Norman. "King Who's Real Cool 'Cat' Visits IBM." In *The King of Thailand in World Focus*, edited by Denis D. Gray, 62. Singapore: Didier Millet, 2008.

Bowring, John. *The Kingdom and People of Siam*. 2 vols. Kuala Lumpur: Oxford University Press, 1969.

Bożyk, Paweł. "Newly Industrialized Countries." In *Globalization and the Transformation of Foreign Economic Policy*, 164–72. Burlington, VT: Ashgate Publishing, 2006.

Brooks, David. *Bobos in Paradise: The New Upper Class and How They Got There*. New York: Simon & Schuster, 2001.

Brown, Ian. *The Elite and the Economy in Siam, c. 1890–1920*. Oxford: Oxford University Press, 1988.

Buchanan, James. "Translating Thailand's Protests: An Analysis of Red Shirt Rhetoric." *ASEAS: Austrian Journal of South-East Asian Studies* 6, no. 1 (2013): 60–80.

Buck-Morss, Susan. "Visual Empire." *Diacritics* 37, nos. 2–3 (Summer–Fall 2007): 171–98.

Caddy, Florence. *To Siam and Malaya*. Singapore: Oxford University Press, 1992.

Callahan, William A. *Imagining Democracy: Reading "The Events of May" in Thailand*. Singapore: Institute of Southeast Asian Studies, 1998.

Chaiyan Rachagool. *The Rise and Fall of the Thai Absolute Monarchy: Foundations of the Modern Thai State from Feudalism to Peripheral Capitalism*. Bangkok: White Lotus, 1994.

Chambers, Paul, and Napisa Waitoolkiat. "The Resilience of Monarchised Military in Thailand." *Journal of Contemporary Asia* 46, no. 3 (2016): 425–44.

Chibber, Vivek. *Postcolonial Theory and the Specter of Capital*. New York: Verso, 2013.

Chula Chakrabongse. *Lords of Life*. London: Alvin Redman, 1960.

Connors, Michael. "Article of Faith: The Failure of Royal Liberalism in Thailand." *Journal of Contemporary Asia* 38, no. 1 (February 2008): 143–65.

Copeland, Matthew. "Contested Nationalism and the 1932 Overthrow of the Absolute Monarchy in Siam." PhD diss., Australian National University, 1993.

Crispin, Shawn. "Thailand's Classless Conflict." In *Bangkok, May 2010: Perspectives on a Divided Thailand*, edited by Michael Montesano, Pavin Chachavalpongpun, and Aekapol Chongvilaivan, 108–19. Singapore: Institute of Southeast Asian Studies, 2012.

"The Crown: Succession." In *King Bhumibol Adulyadej: A Life's Work; Thailand's Monarchy in Perspective*, edited by Nicholas Grossman and Dominic Faulder, 325–33. Singapore: Didier Millet, 2012.

Dayley, Robert, and Clark D. Neher. *Southeast Asia in the New International Era*. Boulder, CO: Westview Press, 2013.

"Demand for Pink Polo Shirts Soars." In *Chronicle of Thailand: Headline News since 1946*, edited by Nicholas Grossman, 403. Singapore: Didier Millet, 2009.

Dhani Nivat. "The Old Siamese Conception of the Monarchy." *Journal of the Siam Society* 32, no. 2 (1947): 91–106.

"Diamond Jubilee Celebration." In *The King of Thailand in World Focus*, edited by Denis D. Gray, 208. Singapore: Didier Millet, 2008.

Draper, Hal. *Karl Marx's Theory of Revolution*. Vol. 2, *The Politics of Social Classes*. Seattle: Create Space Independent Publishing Platform, 1978.

El-Katiri, Mohammed. *The Future of the Arab Gulf Monarchies in the Age of Uncertainties*. Carlisle, PA: Strategic Studies Institute, 2013.

Elliott, David L. *Thailand: Origins of Military Rule*. London: Zed Press, 1978.

Engels, Friedrich. *The Origin of the Family, Private Property, and the State*. New York: Penguin, 2010.

———. *Socialism: Utopian and Scientific*. New York: International Publishers, 2015.

Ferrara, Federico. "Unfinished Business: The Contagion of Conflict over a Century of Thai Political Development." In *"Good Coup" Gone Bad: Thailand's Political Development since Thaksin's Downfall*, edited by Pavin Chachavalpongpun, 17–48. Singapore: Institute of Southeast Asian Studies, 2014.

Fraser, Steve. *Wall Street: America's Dream Palace*. New Haven, CT: Yale University Press, 2009.

Fujitani, Takashi. *Splendid Monarchy: Power and Pageantry in Modern Japan*. Oakland: University of California Press, 1998.

Gecker, Jocelyn. "Dressing Like the King: Pink and Pastel." In *The King of Thailand in World Focus*, edited by Denis D. Gray, 207. Singapore: Didier Millet, 2008.

Gen, Endo. *Diversifying Retail and Distribution in Thailand*. Chiang Mai: Silkworm Books, 2013.

Giles Ji Ungpakorn. *A Coup for the Rich: Thailand's Political Crisis*. Bangkok: Workers Democracy Publishing, 2007.

Gin, Ooi Keat, ed. *Southeast Asia: A Historical Encyclopedia, from Angkor Wat to East Timor*. Santa Barbara, CA: ABC-CLIO, 2004.

Glassman, Jim. "Cracking Hegemony in Thailand: Gramsci, Bourdieu, and the Dialectics of Rebellion." *Journal of Contemporary Asia* 41, no. 1 (2010): 25–46.

———. "From Reds to Red Shirts: Political Evolution and Devolution in Thailand." *Environment and Planning* 42, no.4 (2010): 765–70.

———. "The Provinces Elect Governments, Bangkok Overthrows Them: Urbanity, Class, and Post-democracy in Thailand." *Urban Studies* 47, no. 6 (May 2010): 1301–23.

———. "Recovering from Crisis: The Case of Thailand's Spatial Fix." *Economic Geography* 83, no. 4 (2007): 349–70.

———. *Thailand at the Margins: Internationalization of the State and the Transformation of Labour*. New York: Oxford University Press, 2004.

———. "Thailand in the Era of the Cold War and Rama IX." *Human Geography* 2, no. 1 (2009): 29–44.

Gray, Christine. "Hegemonic Images: Language and Silence in the Royal Thai Polity." *Man* 26, no. 1 (March 1991): 43–65.

———. "Thailand: The Soteriological State in the 1970s." PhD diss., University of Chicago, 1986.

Gray, Denis D. "Queen Sirikit: An Interview." In *The King of Thailand in World Focus*, edited by Denis D. Gray, 139–40. Singapore: Didier Millet, 2008.

———. "Thailand's Working Royals." In *The King of Thailand in World Focus*, edited by Denis D. Gray, 123. Singapore: Didier Millet, 2008.

Greyser, Stephen, John Balmer, and Mats Urde. "The Monarchy as a Corporate Brand: Some Corporate Communications Dimensions." *European Journal of Marketing* 40, nos. 7–8 (2006): 902–8.

Grossman, Nicholas, ed. *Chronicle of Thailand: Headline News since 1946*. Singapore: Didier Millet, 2009.

Grossman, Nicholas, and Dominic Faulder, eds. *King Bhumibol Adulyadej: A Life's Work; Thailand's Monarchy in Perspective*. Singapore: Didier Millet, 2012.

Guillén, Mauro F. "Multinationals, Ideology, and Organized Labor." In *The Limits of Convergence: Globalization and Organizational Change in Argentina, South Korea, and Spain*, 123–56. Princeton, NJ: Princeton University Press, 2001.

Haberkorn, Tyrell. *In Plain Sight: Impunity and Human Rights in Thailand*. Madison: University of Wisconsin Press, 2018.

Hamilton, Gary G., and Tony Waters. "Ethnicity and Capitalist Development: The Changing Role of the Chinese in Thailand." In *Essential Outsiders: Chinese and Jews in the Modern Transformation of Southeast Asia and Central Europe*, edited by Daniel Chirot and Anthony Reid, 258–84. Seattle: University of Washington Press, 1997.

Handley, Paul. *The King Never Smiles: A Biography of Thailand's King Bhumibol Adulyadej*. New Haven, CT: Yale University Press, 2006.

Harvey, David. *A Brief History of Neoliberalism*. New York: Oxford University Press, 2011.

———. *The Limits to Capital*. London: Verso, 1999.

———. *Seventeen Contradictions and the End of Capitalism*. New York: Oxford University Press, 2015.

Hegel, G. W. F. *Elements of the Philosophy of Right*. Edited by Allen W. Wood. Translated by H. B. Nisbet. Cambridge: Cambridge University Press, 1991.

———. *Introduction to the Philosophy of History*. Translated by Leo Rauch. Indianapolis: Hackett Publishing, 1988.

Hewison, Kevin. *Bankers and Bureaucrats: Capital and the Role of the State in Thailand*. New Haven, CT: Council on Southeast Asia Studies, Yale University, 1989.

———. "A Book, the King, and the 2006 Coup." *Journal of Contemporary Asia* 38, no. 1 (2008): 190–211.

———. "Crafting Thailand's New Social Contract." *Pacific Review* 17, no. 4 (2004): 503–22.

———. "The Monarchy and Democratisation." In *Political Change in Thailand: Democracy and Participation*, edited by Kevin Hewison, 58–74. New York: Routledge, 1997.

———. "Thailand's Capitalism: The Impact of the Economic Crisis." *University of New England Asia Centre Asia Papers*, no. 1 (1999): 21–49. http://pandora.nla.gov.au/nph-wb/19990829130000/http://www.une.edu.au/asiacenter/Hewison.pdf.

Hewitt, V. H., and J. M. Keyworth. *As Good as Gold: 300 Years of British Bank Note Design*. London: British Museum Publications, 1987.

Hill, Christopher. "The English Revolution." In *The English Revolution, 1640: Three Essays*, 9–82. London: Lawrence & Wishart, 1940.

Hobbes, Thomas. *Leviathan*. Edited by C. B. Macpherson. New York: Penguin Books, 1985.

Hobsbawm, Eric. "Introduction: Inventing Traditions." In *The Invention of Tradition*, edited by Eric Hobsbawm and Terence Ranger, 1–14. Cambridge: Cambridge University Press, 2004.

Hoskin, John. "The King as Artist." In *The King of Thailand in World Focus*, edited by Denis D. Gray, 166–67. Singapore: Didier Millet, 2008.

Hunt, Margaret. *The Middling Sort: Commerce, Gender, and the Family in England, 1680–1780*. Oakland: University of California Press, 1996.

Huntington, Samuel. *Political Order in Changing Societies*. New Haven, CT: Yale University Press, 1968.

Ingram, James C. *Economic Change in Thailand, 1850–1970*. Stanford, CA: Stanford University Press, 1971.

Jackson, Peter. "A Grateful Son, A Military King: Thai Media Accounts of the Accession of Rama X to the Throne." *Institute of Southeast Asian Studies Perspective* 26 (April 2017): 1–7.

———. "Royal Spirits, Chinese Gods, and Magic Monks: Thailand's Boom-Time Religions of Prosperity." *South East Asia Research* 7, no. 3 (November 1999): 245–320.

———. "Virtual Divinity: A 21st-Century Discourse of Thai Royal Influence." In *Saying the Unsayable: Monarchy and Democracy in Thailand*, edited by Soren Ivarsson and Lotte Isager, 22–69. Copenhagen: Nordic Institute of Asian Studies Press, 2010.

Jory, Patrick. *Thailand's Theory of Monarchy: The Vessantara Jataka and the Idea of the Perfect Man*. Albany: State University of New York Press, 2016.

Judd, Denis. *Eclipse of Kings: European Monarchies in the Twentieth Century*. New York: Stein and Day, 1976.

Kanokrat Lertchoosakul. *The Rise of the Octobrists in Contemporary Thailand: Power and Conflict among Former Left-Wing Student Activists in Thai Politics*. New Haven, CT: Council on Southeast Asian Studies, Yale University, 2016.

Kantorowicz, Ernst. *The King's Two Bodies: A Study in Medieval Political Theology*. Princeton, NJ: Princeton University Press, 1957.

Kasian Tejapira. "Imagined Uncommunity: The Lookjin Middle Class and Thai Official Nationalism." In *Essential Outsiders: Chinese and Jews in the Modern Transformation of Southeast Asia and Central Europe*, edited by Daniel Chirot and Anthony Reid, 75–98. Seattle: University of Washington Press, 1997.

———. "The Irony of Democratization and the Decline of Royal Hegemony in Thailand." *Southeast Asian Studies* 5, no. 2 (August 2016): 219–37.

———. "Toppling Thaksin." *New Left Review* 39 (May-June 2006): 5–37.

Kershaw, Roger. *Monarchy in South-East Asia: The Faces of Tradition in Transition*. New York: Routledge, 2001.

Keyes, Charles. "Cosmopolitan Villagers and Populist Democracy in Thailand." *South East Asia Research* 20, no. 3 (2012): 343–60.

———. *Finding Their Voices: Northeastern Villagers and the Thai State*. Chiang Mai: Silkworm Books, 2014.

Khorapin Phuaphansawat. "My Eyes Are Open but My Lips Are Whispering: Linguistic and Symbolic Forms of Resistance in Thailand during 2006–2016." PhD diss., University of Massachusetts Amherst, 2017.

"King Bhumibol the Great: Forty Million Thais Vote on the New Title in Nationwide Poll." In *Chronicle of Thailand: Headline News since 1946*, edited by Nicholas Grossman, 177. Singapore: Didier Millet, 2009.

Kostiner, Joseph. "Introduction." In *Middle East Monarchies: The Challenge of Modernity*. Boulder, CO: Lynne Rienner Publishers, 2000.

Kullada Kesboonchoo Mead. *The Rise and Decline of Thai Absolutism*. London: RoutledgeCurzon, 2004.

Kullada Kesboonchoo Mead and Kengkij Kitirianglarp. "Transition Debates and the Thai State: An Observation." In *Essays on Thailand's Economy and Society for Professor Chattip Nartsupa at Seventy-Two*, edited by Pasuk Phongpaichit and Chris Baker, 91–118. Bangkok: Sangsan, 2013.

Larsson, Tomas. *Land and Loyalty: Security and the Development of Property Rights in Thailand*. Ithaca, NY: Cornell University Press, 2012.

Lewis, Bernard. "Monarchy in the Middle East." In *Middle East Monarchies: The Challenge of Modernity*, edited by Joseph Kostiner, 15–22. Boulder, CO: Lynne Rienner Publishers, 2000.

Machiavelli, Niccolò. *The Prince*. Translated by Harvey C. Mansfield. Chicago: University of Chicago Press, 1998.

Mandel, Ernest. "Introduction." In Karl Marx, *Capital*. Vol. 1. Translated by Ben Fowkes, 11–86. London: Penguin Books, 1990.

Marx, Karl. *Capital*. Vol. 1. Translated by Ben Fowkes. London: Penguin Books, 1990.

———. *Capital*. Vol. 3. Translated by David Fernbach. London: Penguin Books, 1991.

———. "The Class Struggle in France." In *Karl Marx: Selected Writings*, edited by David McLellan, 286–97. Oxford: Oxford University Press, 1977.

———. *Critique of Hegel's "Philosophy of Right."* Edited by Joseph O'Malley. Translated by Annette Jolin and Joseph O'Malley. Cambridge: Cambridge University Press, 1977.

———. "The Eighteenth Brumaire of Louis Bonaparte." In *Karl Marx: Selected Writings*, edited by David McLellan, 300–325. Oxford: Oxford University Press, 1977.

———. *Grundrisse: Foundations of the Critique of Political Economy*. Translated by Martin Nicolaus. New York: Penguin Books, 1993.

———. *Pre-capitalist Economic Formations*. Edited by Eric Hobsbawm. Translated by Jack Cohen. New York: International Publishing, 1965.

———. "Preface to the First Edition." In *Capital*, vol. 1, translated by Ben Fowkes, 89–93. London: Penguin Books, 1990.

Marx, Karl, and Friedrich Engels. "The Communist Manifesto." In *Karl Marx: Selected Writings*, edited by David McLellan, 221–47. Oxford: Oxford University Press, 1977.

Mayer, Arno J. *The Persistence of the Old Regime: Europe to the Great War*. New York: Verso, 2010.

McCargo, Duncan. "Network Monarchy and Legitimacy Crises in Thailand." *Pacific Review* 18, no. 4 (December 2005): 499–519.

———. "Thai Politics as Reality TV." *Journal of Asian Studies* 68, no. 1 (February 2009): 7–19.

McCloskey, Deirdre. *The Bourgeois Virtues: Ethics for an Age of Commerce.* Chicago: University of Chicago Press, 2006.

McLendon, Winzola. "Legend Bows to Royalty: Queen Goes from Tuesday to Saturday in a Day." In *The King of Thailand in World Focus,* edited by Denis D. Gray, 63–64. Singapore: Didier Millet, 2008.

McNally, David. "Globalization on Trial: Crisis and Class Struggle in East Asia." In *Rising from the Ashes? Labor in the Age of "Global" Capitalism,* edited by Ellen Meiksins Wood, Peter Meiksins, and Michael Yates, 142–52. New York: Monthly Review Press, 1998.

Mérieau, Eugénie. "Thailand's Deep State, Royal Power, and the Constitutional Court (1997–2015)." *Journal of Contemporary Asia* 46, no. 3 (2016): 445–66.

Mooers, Colin. *The Making of Bourgeois Europe: Absolutism, Revolution, and the Rise of Capitalism in England, France, and Germany.* New York: Verso, 1991.

Moore, Barrington. *Social Origins of Dictatorship and Democracy: Lord and Peasant in the Making of the Modern World.* Boston: Beacon Press, 1996.

Moretti, Franco. *The Bourgeois: Between History and Literature.* New York: Verso, 2013.

Morris, Rosalind. "Photography and the Power of Images in the History of Power: Notes from Thailand." In *Photographies East: The Camera and Its Histories in East and Southeast Asia,* edited by Rosalind Morris, 121–60. Durham, NC: Duke University Press, 2009.

Nairn, Tom. "The British Political Elite." *New Left Review* 23 (January–February 1964): 19–25.

———. *The Enchanted Glass: Britain and Its Monarchy.* New York: Verso, 2011.

———. "The English Working Class." *New Left Review* 24 (March–April 1964): 43–57.

———. "The Fateful Meridian." *New Left Review* 60 (March–April 1970): 3–35.

———. "The Nature of the Labor Party, part 1." *New Left Review* 27 (September–October 1964): 38–65.

———. "The Nature of the Labor Party, part 2." *New Left Review* 28 (November–December 1964): 33–62.

———. "Twilight of the British State." *New Left Review* 101 (February–April 1976): 11–91.

Naruemon Thabchumpon and Duncan McCargo. "Urbanized Villagers in the 2010 Thai Redshirt Protest: Not Just Poor Farmers?" *Asian Survey* 51, no. 6 (2011): 993–1018.

Natenapha Wailerdsak. "Companies in Crisis." In *Thai Capital after the 1997 Crisis,* edited by Pasuk Phongpaichit and Chris Baker, 17–57. Chiang Mai: Silkworm Books, 2008.

Nietzsche, Friedrich. "The Greek State." In *The Nietzsche Reader,* edited by Keith Ansell Pearson and Duncan Large, 88–100. Oxford: Blackwell, 2006.

Norton, Elliot. "Illiberal Democrats versus Undemocratic Liberals: The Struggle over the Future of Thailand's Fragile Democracy." *Asian Journal of Political Science* 20, no. 1 (April 2012): 46–69.

Nostitz, Nick. "The Red Shirts: From Anti-coup Protesters to Social Mass Movement." In *"Good Coup" Gone Bad: Thailand's Political Development since Thaksin's Downfall*, edited by Pavin Chachavalpongpun, 170–98. Singapore: Institute of Southeast Asian Studies, 2014.

Paradee Tungtang. "Shakespeare in Thailand." PhD diss., University of Warwick, 2011.

Pasuk Phongpaichit. "Inequality, Wealth, and Thailand's Politics." *Journal of Contemporary Asia* 46, no. 3 (2016): 405–24.

Pasuk Phongpaichit and Chris Baker. *A History of Thailand*. Cambridge: Cambridge University Press, 2009.

———. *Thai Capital after the 1997 Crisis*. Chiang Mai: Silkworm Books, 2008.

———. *Thailand: Economy and Politics*. New York: Oxford University Press, 1995.

———. *Thailand's Boom and Bust*. Chiang Mai: Silkworm Books, 1998.

———. *Thaksin: The Business of Politics in Thailand*. Copenhagen: Nordic Institute of Asian Studies, 2004.

Pattana Kitiarsa. "From Red to Red: An Auto-ethnography of Economic and Political Transitions in a Northeastern Thai Village." In *Bangkok, May 2010: Perspectives on a Divided Thailand*, edited by Michael Montesano, Pavin Chachavalpongpun, and Aekapol Chongvilaivan, 230–47. Singapore: Institute of Southeast Asian Studies, 2012.

Pavin Chachavalpongpun, ed. *"Good Coup" Gone Bad: Thailand's Political Development Since Thaksin's Downfall*. Singapore: Institute of Southeast Asian Studies, 2014.

Peleggi, Maurizio. *Lords of Things: The Fashioning of the Siamese Monarchy's Modern Image*. Honolulu: University of Hawai'i Press, 2002.

———. "Semiotics of Rama IX." Asia Research Institute Working Papers Series, no. 114. February 24, 2009.

Phya Anuman Rajadhon. "Kingship in Siam." *Journal of the Siam Society* 42, no. 1 (1954): 1–10.

Piketty, Thomas. *Capital in the Twenty-First Century*. London: Belknap Press, 2014.

Plato. *The Republic*. Translated by Desmond Lee. New York: Penguin Books, 2007.

Platt, Martin. "Culture of Monarchy: A Repertory Theatre through Time." In *Saying the Unsayable: Monarchy and Democracy in Thailand*, edited by Soren Ivarsson and Lotte Isager, 89–101. Copenhagen: Nordic Institute of Asian Studies Press, 2010.

Polanyi, Karl. *The Great Transformation: The Political and Economic Origins of Our Time*. Boston: Beacon Press, 2001.

Porphant Ouyyanont. "The Crown Property Bureau in Thailand and the Crisis of 1997." *Journal of Contemporary Asia* 38, no. 1 (February 2008): 166–89.

Prochaska, Frank. *Royal Bounty: The Making of a Welfare Monarchy*. New Haven, CT: Yale University Press, 1995.

Pye, Oliver, and Wolfram Schaffar. "The 2006 Anti-Thaksin Movement in Thailand: An Analysis." *Journal of Contemporary Asia* 38, no. 1 (2008): 38–61.

Reynolds, Craig J. *Thai Radical Discourse: The Real Face of Thai Feudalism Today.* Ithaca, NY: Cornell University Press, 1987.

Reynolds, Craig J., and Hong Lysa. "Marxism in Thai Historical Studies." *Journal of Asian Studies* 43, no. 1 (November 1983): 77–104.

Rhoden, T. F. "Oligarchy in Thailand?" *Journal of Current Southeast Asian Affairs* 34, no. 1 (2015): 3–25.

Riggs, Fred. *Thailand: The Modernization of a Bureaucratic Polity.* Honolulu: East-West Center Press, 1966.

Robin, Corey. *Fear: The History of a Political Idea.* New York: Oxford University Press, 2004.

———. *The Reactionary Mind: Conservatism from Edmund Burke to Sarah Palin.* New York: Oxford University Press, 2011.

Ross, Michael. "Does Oil Hinder Democracy?" *World Politics* 53, no.3 (April 2001): 325–61.

Rousseau, Jean-Jacques. "Discourse on the Origin and Foundations of Inequality among Men." In *Rousseau: The Basic Political Writings,* edited and translated by Donald A. Cress, 93–120. Indianapolis: Hackett, 2012.

Ruoff, Kenneth. *The People's Emperor: Democracy and the Japanese Monarchy, 1945–1995.* Cambridge, MA: Harvard University Asia Center, 2001.

Sarun Krittikarn. "Entertainment Nationalism: The Royal Gaze and the Gaze at the Royals." In *Saying the Unsayable: Monarchy and Democracy in Thailand,* edited by Soren Ivarsson and Lotte Isager, 29–60. Copenhagen: Nordic Institute of Asian Studies Press, 2010.

Schumpeter, Joseph. *Capitalism, Socialism, and Democracy.* New York: Harper & Brothers, 1975.

Scott, James C. *The Art of Not Being Governed: An Anarchist History of Upland Southeast Asia.* New Haven, CT: Yale University Press, 2009.

———. *Domination and the Arts of Resistance: Hidden Transcripts.* New Haven, CT: Yale University Press, 1990.

———. *Weapons of the Weak: Everyday Forms of Peasant Resistance.* New Haven, CT: Yale University Press, 1985.

Seigel, Jerrold. *Modernity and Bourgeois Life: Society, Politics, and Culture in England, France, and Germany since 1750.* Cambridge: Cambridge University Press, 2012.

Seksan Prasertkul. "The Transformation of the Thai State and Economic Change, 1855–1945." PhD diss., Cornell University, 1989.

Shiraishi, Takashi. "The Rise of New Urban Middle Classes in Southeast Asia: What Is Its National and Regional Significance?" Research Institute of Economy, Trade, and Industry Discussion Papers, February 2004. http://www.rieti.go.jp/jp/publications/dp/04e011.pdf.

Sing Suwannakij. "King and Eye: Visual Formation and Technology of the Siamese Monarchy." PhD diss., University of Copenhagen, 2013.

Skinner, G. William. *Chinese Society in Thailand: An Analytical History.* Ithaca, NY: Cornell University Press, 1957.

————. *Leadership and Power in the Chinese Community of Thailand*. Ithaca, NY: Cornell University Press, 1958.

Skocpol, Theda. *States and Social Revolutions: A Comparative Analysis of France, Russia, and China*. Cambridge: Cambridge University Press, 1979.

Smith, Adam. *An Inquiry into the Nature and Causes of the Wealth of Nations*. Edited by R. H. Campbell and A. S. Skinner. Indianapolis: Liberty Fund, 1981.

————. *The Theory of Moral Sentiments*. Edited by D. D. Raphael and A. L. Macfie. Indianapolis: Liberty Fund, 1982.

Sopranzetti, Claudio. "Burning Red Desires: Isan Migrants and the Politics of Desire in Contemporary Thailand." *South East Asia Research* 20, no. 3 (2012): 361–79.

————. "Thailand's Relapse: The Implications of the May 2014 Coup." *Journal of Asian Studies* 75, no. 2 (May 2016): 299–316.

Spellman, William. *Monarchies, 1000–2000*. London: Reaktion Books, 2006.

Stanton, John. "Young King with a Horn: After an 18-Year Idyl in Switzerland, Siam's Monarch Is Going Home." In *The King of Thailand in World Focus*, edited by Denis D. Gray, 32. Singapore: Didier Millet, 2008.

Stengs, Irene. "A Kingly Cult: Thailand's Guiding Lights in a Dark Era." *Etnofoor* 12, no. 2 (1999): 41–75.

————. *Worshipping the Great Moderniser: King Chulalongkorn, Patron Saint of the Thai Middle Class*. Singapore: National University of Singapore Press, 2009.

Storey, Ian, and Lee Poh Onn, eds. *Regional Outlook: Southeast Asia, 2009–2010*. Singapore: Institute of Southeast Asian Studies, 2009.

Streckfuss, David. "Freedom and Silence under the Neo-absolutist Monarchy Regime in Thailand, 2006–2011." In *"Good Coup" Gone Bad: Thailand's Political Development since Thaksin's Downfall*, edited by Pavin Chachavalpongpun, 109–40. Singapore: Institute of Southeast Asian Studies, 2014.

————. "Kings in the Age of Nations: The Paradox of Lèse-Majesté as Political Crime in Thailand." *Comparative Studies in Society and History* 37, no. 3 (July 1995): 445–75.

Sungsidh Piriyarangsan. *Thai Bureaucratic Capitalism, 1932–1960*. Bangkok: Social Research Institute, Chulalongkorn University, 1983.

Tambiah, Stanley. *World Conqueror and World Renouncer: A Study of Buddhism and Polity in Thailand against a Historical Background*. Cambridge: Cambridge University Press, 1977.

Thak Chaloemtiarana. *Thailand: The Politics of Despotic Paternalism*. Ithaca, NY: South East Asia Program Publications, Cornell University, 2007.

Thongchai Winichakul. "Nationalism and the Radical Intelligentsia in Thailand." *Third World Quarterly* 29, no. 3 (2008): 575–91.

————. "The Monarchy and Anti-monarchy: Two Elephants in the Room of Thai Politics and the State of Denial." In *"Good Coup" Gone Bad: Thailand's Political Development since Thaksin's Downfall*, edited by Pavin Chachavalpongpun, 79–108. Singapore: Institute of Southeast Asian Studies, 2014.

———. *Siam Mapped: A History of the Geo-body of a Nation*. Honolulu: University of Hawai'i Press, 1994.

———. *Thailand's Hyper-royalism: Its Success and Predicament*. Singapore: Institute of Southeast Asian Studies, 2016.

———. "Toppling Democracy." *Journal of Contemporary Asia* 38, no. 1 (February 2008): 11–37.

"Thongdaeng Is A National Sensation." In *Chronicle of Thailand: Headline News since 1946*, edited by Nicholas Grossman, 369. Singapore: Didier Millet, 2009.

Ukrist Pathamanand and Chris Baker. "Hello and Goodbye to the Mobile Phone." In *Thai Capital after the 1997 Crisis*, edited by Pasuk Phongpaichit and Chris Baker, 105–25. Chiang Mai: Silkworm Books, 2008.

Ünaldi, Serhat. *Working towards the Monarchy: The Politics of Space in Downtown Bangkok*. Honolulu: University of Hawai'i Press, 2016.

Unger, Daniel. *Building Social Capital in Thailand: Fibers, Finance, and Infrastructure*. Cambridge: Cambridge University Press, 1998.

———. "Sufficiency Economy and the Bourgeois Virtues." *Asian Affairs: An American Review* 36, no. 3 (2009): 139–56.

Unger, Daniel, and Chandra Mahakanjana. *Thai Politics: Between Democracy and Its Discontents*. Boulder, CO: Lynne Rienner, 2016.

Veerayooth Kanchoochat and Kevin Hewison. "Introduction: Understanding Thailand's Politics." *Journal of Contemporary Asia* 46, no. 3 (2016): 371–87.

Vella, Walter F. *Chaiyo! King Vajiravudh and the Development of Thai Nationalism*. Honolulu: University of Hawai'i Press, 1978.

Walker, Andrew. "Royal Sufficiency and Elite Misrepresentation of Rural Livelihoods." In *Saying the Unsayable: Monarchy and Democracy in Thailand*, edited by Soren Ivarsson and Lotte Isager, 241–65. Copenhagen: Nordic Institute of Asian Studies Press, 2010.

———. "The Rural Constitution and the Everyday Politics of Elections in Northern Thailand." *Journal of Contemporary Asia* 38, no. 1 (2008): 84–105.

Waugh, David. *Geography: An Integrated Approach*. Oxford: Oxford University Press, 2000.

Weber, Max. *Economy and Society*. Edited by Guenther Roth and Claus Wittich. 2 vols. Oakland: University of California Press, 1978.

Weber, Max. *From Max Weber: Essays in Sociology*. Translated and edited by H. H. Gerth and C. Wright Mills. New York: Oxford University Press, 1946.

Wood, Ellen Meiksins. *Empire of Capital*. New York: Verso, 2003.

———. *The Origin of Capitalism: A Longer View*. New York: Verso, 2002.

———. *The Pristine Culture of Capitalism: A Historical Essay on Old Regimes and Modern States*. New York: Verso, 1991.

———. "The Separation of the Economic and the Political in Capitalism." *New Left Review* 1, no. 127 (May–June 1981): 66–95.

Yom, Sean L., and F. Gregory Gause III. "Resilient Royals: How Arab Monarchies Hang On." *Journal of Democracy* 23, no. 4 (October 2012): 7–88.

Zedong, Mao. *The Chinese Revolution and the Chinese Communist Party* (1939). Marxist Internet Archives. Accessed February 27, 2015. https://www.marxists .org /reference/archive/mao/selected-works/volume-2/mswv2_23.htm.

Thai-Language Sources

Anderson, Benedict. "Modern Monarchies in a Global Comparative Perspective" [ราชาสมัยใหม่ในมุมมองเปรียบเทียบระดับโลก]. *Fa Diew Kan* 10, no. 1 (January–June 2012): 59–78.

Anon Nampa. "Big Boss" [นายใหญ่]. In *40 Years of October 14: Protect a Will to a Full Democracy of the October 14 Heroes* [40 ปี 14 ตุลา: จงพิทักษ์เจตนารมณ์ประชาธิปไตยสมบูรณ์ของวีรชน 14 ตุลาคม], 115–18. Bangkok: Committee of the October 14 Memorial, 2013.

Asavabahu (King Vajiravudh). *The Jews of the Orient and Wake Up, Siam* [พวกยิวแห่งบูรพาทิศ และเมืองไทยจงตื่นเถิด]. Bangkok: Foundation in Memory of King Rama VI, 1985.

Auty, Phyllis. *Tito* [ติโต]. Translated by Bhumibol Adulyadej. Bangkok: Amarin Printing and Publishing, 1995.

Bank of Thailand. *Banknotes in the Reign of King Rama IX* [ธนบัตรรัชกาลที่ 9]. Bangkok: Bank of Thailand, 2017.

Bhumibol Adulyadej, trans. *The Story of Mahajanaka* [พระมหาชนก]. Bangkok: Amarin Printing and Publishing, 1996.

———. *The Story of Thongdaeng* [เรื่องทองแดง]. Bangkok: Amarin Printing and Publishing, 2002.

———. *The Story of Thongdaeng: A Cartoon Version* [เรื่องทองแดง ฉบับการ์ตูน]. Bangkok: Amarin Printing and Publishing, 2004.

Bureau of the National Budget. *Annual Budget* [งบประมาณประจำปี]. Bangkok: Bureau of the National Budget, various years.

Campaign of Thinking Sufficiently according to the Sufficiency Economy Philosophy. *The Celestial Couple: The Two Charismatic Royals* [คู่ฟ้า สองพระบารมี]. Bangkok: Internal Security Operations Command, 2010.

Chaithawat Tulathon. "From the Debate of the Transition from Feudalism to Capitalism to the Thesis That 'Democracy under the Monarchy as the Head of State' Is the Form of the Thai Bourgeois State" [จากวิวาทะการเปลี่ยนผ่านจากศักดินาสู่ทุนนิยมสู่บททดลองเสนอว่าด้วยระบอบประชาธิปไตยอันมีพระมหากษัตริย์เป็นประมุขในฐานะรูปแบบรัฐกระฎุมพีของไทย]. *Fa Diew Kan* 13, no. 1 (January–April 2015): 203–33.

Chanan Yodhong. *Male Courtiers under the Reign of Rama VI* [นายในสมัยรัชกาลที่ 6]. Bangkok: Matichon Press, 2013.

Chanida Chitbundid. *The Royally Initiated Projects: The Making of King Bhumibol's Hegemony* [โครงการอันเนื่องมาจากพระราชดำริ: การสถาปนาอำนาจนำในพระบาทสมเด็จพระเจ้าอยู่หัว]. Bangkok: Foundation for the Promotion of Social Science and Humanities Textbooks Project, 2013.

Chatri Prakitnonthakan. "Images, Design, and Symbols of Thai Banknotes: Political Reflection" [รูปภาพ ลวดลาย และสัญลักษณ์ธนบัตรไทย: ภาพสะท้อนทางการเมือง]. In *Thai Architecture after the September 19, 2006, Coup* [สถาปัตยกรรมไทยหลังรัฐประหาร 19 กันยา 49], 129–61. Nonthaburi: Aan, 2015.

Chit Phumisak. *The Real Face of Thai Feudalism* [โฉมหน้าศักดินาไทย]. Bangkok: Sri Panya, 2007.

Chollada Wattanasiri. "Investment of the Privy Purse, 1890–1932" [พระคลังข้างที่กับการลงทุนทางธุรกิจในประเทศ พ.ศ. 2433–2475]. Master's thesis, Silpakorn University, 1986.

Chumphon Pratraphon. *How Rich Is Thaksin Really!* [ทักษิณรวยเท่าไหร่แน่!]. Bangkok: Thawatchai Pitchphon, 2002.

Committee for Developing a Grassroots Economy and a Civil State. *United Forces for a Civil State* [สานพลังประชารัฐ]. Bangkok: Amarin Printing and Publishing, 2016.

Duangmanee Laovakul, "The Concentration of Wealth in Thai Society" [การกระจุกตัวของความมั่งคั่งในสังคมไทย]. In *Towards an Equal Society in Thailand* [สู่สังคมไทยเสมอหน้า], edited by Pasuk Phongpaichit, 37–59. Bangkok: Matichon, 2012.

Election Commission of Thailand. "The Result of February 6, 2005, General Election" [การเลือกตั้งสมาชิกสภาผู้แทนราษฎรเป็นการทั่วไป เมื่อวันที่ 6 กุมภาพันธ์ 2548]. Accessed December 19, 2016. http://www.ect.go.th/th/wp-content/uploads/2013/10/mp48.pdf.

———. "The Result of December 23, 2007, General Election" [การเลือกตั้งสมาชิกสภาผู้แทนราษฎรเป็นการทั่วไป เมื่อวันที่ 23 ธันวาคม 2550]. Accessed December 19, 2016. http://www.ect.go.th/th/?page_id=494.

———. "The Result of July 3, 2011, General Election" [การเลือกตั้งสมาชิกสภาผู้แทนราษฎรเป็นการทั่วไป เมื่อวันที่ 3 กรกฎาคม 2554]. Accessed December 19, 2016. http://www.ect.go.th/th/wp-content/uploads/2013/10/mp_54.pdf.

Faculty of Dentistry, Chulalongkorn University. *Good Teeth, Good Health* [ฟันดีสุขภาพดี]. Bangkok: Chulalongkorn University Press, 2007.

Khamnun Sitthisaman. *The Sondhi Phenomenon: From Yellow Shirts to Blue Scarves* [ปรากฏการณ์สนธิ: จากเสื้อเหลืองถึงผ้าพันคอสีฟ้า]. Bangkok: Ban Phra Athit, 2006.

Kittisak Sujittarom. "Thai Newspapers' and Public Intellectuals' Views on the Status and Role of the Monarchy between 1992 and 1997" [ทัศนะของสื่อหนังสือพิมพ์และปัญญาชนสาธารณะที่มีต่อสถานะและบทบาทของสถาบันกษัตริย์ ระหว่าง พ.ศ. 2535–2540]. MA thesis, Thammasat University, 2014.

Mainueng Ko Kunthi. "Constituting the People's Constitution" [สถาปนาสถาบันประชาชน]. In *The People's Poet* [กวีราษฎร], 138–44. Bangkok: Klum Patinya Na San, 2014.

Nakarin Mektrairat. *The 1932 Siamese Revolution* [การปฏิวัติสยาม พ.ศ. 2475]. Bangkok: Foundation for the Promotion of Social Science and Humanities Textbooks Project, 1992.

Nattapoll Chaiching. *To Dream the Impossible Dream: The Counterrevolution against the Siamese Revolution, 1932–1957* [ขอฝันใฝ่ในฝันอันเหลือเชื่อ: ความ

เคลื่อนไหวของขบวนการปฏิวัติสยาม พ.ศ. 2475–2500]. Nonthaburi: Fa Diew Kan, 2013.

NESDB (National Economic and Social Development Board). *Yearbook of the National Economic and Social Development Board* [รายงานประจำปีสำนักงานคณะกรรมการพัฒนาเศรษฐกิจและสังคมแห่งชาติ]. Bangkok: National Economic and Social Development Board, various years.

Nidhi Eoseewong. *Pen and Sail: Literature and History in Early Bangkok* [ปากไก่และใบเรือ: รวมความเรียงว่าด้วยวรรณกรรมและประวัติศาสตร์ต้นรัตนโกสินทร์]. Nonthaburi: Fa Diew Kan, 2012.

OHM (Office of His Majesty's Principal Private Secretary). *Yearbook of Royal Activities* [หนังสือประมวลพระราชกรณียกิจ]. Bangkok: Thai Wattana Panich, various years.

Pasuk Phongpaichit, ed. *Towards an Equal Society in Thailand* [สู่สังคมไทยเสมอหน้า]. Bangkok: Matichon, 2012.

Pharut Phenphayup. "What Is the Crown Property Bureau?" [ทรัพย์สินส่วนพระมหากษัตริย์คืออะไร?]. In *Brahma Helping Us Prosper: The Political Economy of the Crown Property Bureau after 1932* [พระพรหมช่วยอำนวยให้ชื่นฉ่ำ: เศรษฐกิจการเมืองว่าด้วยทรัพย์สินส่วนพระมหากษัตริย์หลัง 2475], edited by Chaithawat Tulathon, 161–203. Nonthaburi: Fa Diew Kan, 2014.

Phiangkham Pradapkhwam. "God Gave Birth to Me, the Free; This God's Name Is the People" [พระเจ้ากำเนิดข้ามาเสรี–พระเจ้าองค์นี้ชื่อประชาชน]. In *All Beloved Citizens* [ราษฎรที่รักทั้งหลาย], 66–68. Bangkok: Aan, 2011.

———. "The Ones Who Work Industriously Are the People" [ผู้รากตรำทำงานหนักคือประชาชน]. In *All Beloved Citizens* [ราษฎรที่รักทั้งหลาย], 56–57. Bangkok: Aan, 2011.

Phruek Thaothawin. "The Practice of the Sufficiency Economy in a Village: The Elite's Control of the Countryside" [ปฏิบัติการพอเพียงในหมู่บ้าน: การควบคุมชนบทของชนชั้นนำ]. *Fa Diew Kan* 6, no. 2 (April–June 2008): 70–86.

Prakan Klinfung. "King Bhumibol's Visits to Provincial Areas, 1950–1987" [การเสด็จพระราชดำเนินท้องที่ต่างจังหวัดของพระบาทสมเด็จพระเจ้าอยู่หัวภูมิพลอดุลยเดช พ.ศ. 2493–2530]. MA thesis, Chulalongkorn University, 2008.

Pran Phisitsetthakan, ed. *Thaksinomics and Thailand's CEO* [ทักษิโณมิคส์และ CEO ประเทศไทย]. Bangkok: Matichon, 2004.

Rangsan Haruehanroengra. "Full Democracy . . . Not!" [ประชาธิปไตยที่สมบูรณ์ . . . เหรอ]. In *40 Years of October 14: Protect a Will to a Full Democracy of the October 14 Heroes* [40 ปี 14 ตุลา: จงพิทักษ์เจตนารมณ์ประชาธิปไตยสมบูรณ์ของวีรชน 14 ตุลาคม], 47–48. Bangkok: Committee of the October 14 Memorial, 2013.

Rom Bunnak. *The Royal Cremation Complex: The Royal Crematorium and Royal Chariots in the Bangkok Era* [พระเมรุมาศ: พระโกศและราชรถสมัยกรุงรัตนโกสินทร์]. Bangkok: Sayam Banthuek, 2008.

Royal Thai Government Gazette. *An Announcement regarding an Appointment of the Crown Property Bureau's Board of Directors* [ประกาศแต่งตั้งคณะกรรมการทรัพย์สินส่วนพระมหากษัตริย์], July 17, 2017.

————. *An Announcement regarding an Appointment of Privy Counselors* [*ประกาศ แต่งตั้งองคมนตรี*], December 6, 2016.

————. *An Announcement regarding an Appointment of Privy Counselors* [*ประกาศ แต่งตั้งองคมนตรี*], March 12, 2017.

————. *An Announcement regarding the National Broadcasting of Radio, Television, and Telecommunications* [*ประกาศคณะกรรมการกิจการกระจายเสียง กิจการ โทรทัศน์ และ กิจการ โทรคมนาคมแห่งชาติ*], February 27, 2013.

————. *The Announcement from the Office of the Prime Minister regarding the King's Birthday as the National Day* [*ประกาศสำนักนายกรัฐมนตรีเรื่อง ให้ถือวันพระราชสมภพเป็น วันเฉลิมฉลองของชาติไทย*], May 24, 1960.

————. *Crown Property Act of 1936* [*พระราชบัญญัติจัดระเบียบทรัพย์สินฝ่ายพระมหากษัตริย์ พ.ศ. 2479*], June 15, 1937.

————. *Crown Property Act of 1948* [*พระราชบัญญัติจัดระเบียบทรัพย์สินฝ่ายพระมหากษัตริย์ พ.ศ. 2491*], February 3, 1948.

————. *Crown Property Act of 2017* [*พระราชบัญญัติจัดระเบียบทรัพย์สินฝ่ายพระมหากษัตริย์ พ.ศ. 2560*], July 16, 2017.

————. *Crown Property Act of 2018* [*พระราชบัญญัติจัดระเบียบทรัพย์สินพระมหากษัตริย์ พ.ศ. 2561*], November 3, 2018.

————. *Royal Decree Organizing Governmental Affairs and Personnel Administration for Royal Service, 2017* [*พระราชกฤษฎีกาจัดระเบียบและการบริหารงานบุคคลของราชการ ในพระองค์ พ.ศ. 2560*], May 10, 2017.

————. *Royal Service Administration Act, 2017* [*พระราชบัญญัติระเบียบราชการในพระองค์ พ.ศ. 2560*], May 1, 2017.

Sala Nakbamrung. *The Comics for Celebrating King Rama IX* [*การ์ตูนเทิด ไท้องค์ราชันย์ รัชกาลที่ 9*]. Bangkok: Amarin Printing and Publishing, 2011.

Somsak Jeamteerasakul. *The Invented History* [*ประวัติศาสตร์ที่เพิ่งสร้าง*]. Bangkok: October 6th Memorial Press, 2001.

————. "The Mystery of the King's Death" [ปริศนากรณีสวรรคต]. *Fa Diew Kan* 6, no. 2 (April–June 2008): 116–35.

————. "Post–October 14" [หลัง 14 ตุลา]. *Fa Diew Kan* 3, no. 4 (October–December 2005): 168–71.

————. "Thai Society: From Feudalism to Capitalism" [สังคมไทย จากศักดินาถึง ทุนนิยม]. *Warasan Thammasat* 11, no. 2 (June 1982): 128–64.

————. "What Is the Crown Property Bureau?" [สำนักงานทรัพย์สินส่วนพระมหา กษัตริย์คืออะไร?]. *Fa Diew Kan* 1, no. 1 (January–March 2006): 67–91.

Songchai Na Yala. "The Problem of the Study of Thailand's Mode of Production regarding the Theory of Semicolonialism, Semifeudalism" [ปัญหาการ ศึกษาวิถีการผลิตของไทยอันเนื่องมาจากทฤษฎีกึ่งเมืองขึ้น-กึ่งศักดินา]. *Warasan Settasat-kanmueang* 1, no. 2 (March–April 1981): 3–98.

Stephenson, William. *A Man Called Intrepid* [*นายอินทร์ผู้ปิดทองหลังพระ*]. Translated by Bhumibol Adulyadej. Bangkok: Amarin Printing and Publishing, 1994.

Suphot Chaengreo. "The Case of Seizing Rama VII's Property" [คดียึดทรัพย์พระบาท สมเด็จพระปกเกล้า]. *Sinlapa Watthanatham* 23, no. 8 (June 2005): 62–80.

Thailand Office of Higher Education Commission. "Statistics of Higher Education in Thailand" [สถิติการศึกษาในระดับอุดมศึกษาในประเทศไทย]. Accessed September 24, 2016. http://www.info.mua.go.th/information/.

Thak Chaloemtiarana. "Through Racing Goggles: Modernity, the West, Ambiguous Siamese Alterities, and the Construction of Thai Nationalism" [ล้อหมุนเร็ว: การแข่งรถ วรรณกรรมการแข่งรถ ชาตินิยมไทย]. *Aan* 7, no. 1 (August 2015), 134–55.

———. "We Are Not Them? The Portrayal of the Chinese People in Thai Literature in the 20th Century" [เราไม่ใช่เขา? ภาพเสนอคนจีนในวรรณกรรมไทยในศตวรรษที่ 20]. *Aan* 5, no. 1 (July–December 2013): 122–53.

Thanapol Eawsakul and Chaithawat Tulathon. "Royal Wealth under the Absolutist Regime and during the Transitional Period" [พระราชทรัพย์ในระบอบสมบูรณาญาสิทธิราชย์และในระยะเปลี่ยนผ่าน]. In *Brahma Helping Us Prosper: The Political Economy of the Crown Property Bureau after 1932* [*พระพรหมช่วยอำนวยให้ชื่นฉ่ำ: เศรษฐกิจการเมืองว่าด้วยทรัพย์สินส่วนพระมหากษัตริย์หลัง 2475*], edited by Chaithawat Tulathon, 3–72. Nonthaburi: Fa Diew Kan, 2014.

———. "Who's Who in the Privy Council under Democracy with the King as Head of the State?" [ใครเป็นใครในองคมนตรีแห่งประชาธิปไตยอันมีพระมหากษัตริย์เป็นประมุข?]. *Fa Diew Kan* 12, no. 2 (May–August 2015): 51–76.

Thatma Prathumwan. "Pasuk Phongpaichit: 'Deep Capital,' an Analysis of the Civil State as a Consequence of State-Capital Relationships" [ผาสุก พงษ์ไพจิตร: 'ทุนพันลึก' บทวิเคราะห์ประชารัฐ ผลพวงจากความสัมพันธ์ รัฐ-ทุน]. *Prachatai*, June 18, 2018. https://prachatai.com/journal/2018/06/77470.

Thikan Srinara. *After October 6: The Ideological Conflict between Student Activists and the Communist Party of Thailand* [*หลัง 6 ตุลาฯ: ว่าด้วยความขัดแย้งทางความคิดระหว่างขบวนการนักศึกษากับพรรคคอมมิวนิสต์แห่งประเทศไทย*]. Bangkok: October 6 Memorial Press, 2009.

Thongchai Winichakul. *Democracy That Is the Monarchy above Politics* [*ประชาธิปไตยที่มีกษัตริย์อยู่เหนือการเมือง*]. Nonthaburi: Fa Diew Kan, 2013.

———. "The Existing Legacy of Absolutism" [มรดกสมบูรณาญาสิทธิราชย์ในปัจจุบัน]. In *Democracy That Is the Monarchy above Politics* [*ประชาธิปไตยที่มีกษัตริย์อยู่เหนือการเมือง*], 199–219. Nonthaburi: Fa Diew Kan, 2013.

TNSO (National Statistical Office of Thailand). *Statistical Yearbook of Thailand* [*รายงานสถิติรายปี*]. Bangkok: Statistical Data Bank and Information Dissemination Division, National Statistical Office, various years.

Truth for Reconciliation Committee of Thailand. *The Final Report of Truth for Reconciliation Committee of Thailand* [*รายงานฉบับสมบูรณ์คณะกรรมการอิสระเพื่อตรวจสอบข้อเท็จจริงเพื่อการปรองดองแห่งชาติ*]. Bangkok: Truth for Reconciliation Committee of Thailand, 2012.

Wanya Phuphinyo. *Eyes on the Stars, Feet on the Ground* [*ตาดูดาวเท้าติดดิน*]. Bangkok: Matichon, 1999.

Index

Note: page numbers in italics refer to illustrations or tables.

New Perspectives

in Southeast Asian Studies

Hamka's Great Story: A Master Writer's Vision of Islam
    for Modern Indonesia
James R. Rush

Dead in the Water: Global Lessons from the World Bank's
    Hydropower Project in Laos
Edited by Bruce Shoemaker and William Robichaud

The Social World of Batavia: Europeans and Eurasians
    in Colonial Indonesia, second edition
Jean Gelman Taylor

Everyday Economic Survival in Myanmar
Ardeth Maung Thawnghmung

Việt Nam: Borderless Histories
Edited by Nhung Tuyet Tran and Anthony Reid

Royal Capitalism: Wealth, Class, and Monarchy in Thailand
Puangchon Unchanam

Thailand's Political Peasants: Power in the Modern Rural Economy
Andrew Walker

Modern Noise, Fluid Genres: Popular Music in Indonesia, 1997–2001
Jeremy Wallach